# The Face of Mammon

# THE FACE OF MAMMON

## *The Matter of Money in English Renaissance Literature*

David Landreth

OXFORD
UNIVERSITY PRESS

**OXFORD**
UNIVERSITY PRESS

Oxford University Press is a department of the University of Oxford.
It furthers the University's objective of excellence in research, scholarship,
and education by publishing worldwide.

Oxford New York
Auckland Cape Town Dar es Salaam Hong Kong Karachi
Kuala Lumpur Madrid Melbourne Mexico City Nairobi
New Delhi Shanghai Taipei Toronto

With offices in
Argentina Austria Brazil Chile Czech Republic France Greece
Guatemala Hungary Italy Japan Poland Portugal Singapore
South Korea Switzerland Thailand Turkey Ukraine Vietnam



Published in the United States of America by
Oxford University Press
198 Madison Avenue, New York, NY 10016



First issued as an Oxford University Press paperback, 2017



Library of Congress Cataloging-in-Publication Data
Landreth, David, 1973–
The face of mammon : the matter of money in English Renaissance literature / David Landreth.
p. cm.
Includes bibliographical references and index.
ISBN 978-0-19-977329-9 (hardcover : alk. paper); 978-0-19-062822-2 (paperback : alk. paper)
1. English literature—Early modern, 1500–1700—History and criticism. 2. Money in literature.
3. Coinage in literature. 4. Wealth in literature. 5. Material culture in literature.
6. Money—Great Britain—History—16th century. 7. Money—Great Britain—History—17th century.
I. Title.
PR428.M66L36 2011
820.9'3553—dc22
2011002596

*For my parents*

# CONTENTS

# LIST OF ILLUSTRATIONS

# ACKNOWLEDGMENTS

Leonard Barkan has been guiding this project into being since before it knew it was a project. I am excited to present him with this realization of his work in mine. Ernest Gilman, John Guillory, Mary Poovey, and Edward Tayler have shaped me as a thinker and a critic, and my debt to their scholarship and conversation is manifest on each of the pages that follow.

My colleagues at Berkeley have been unstinting in their support. For their counsel and guidance, their lightly worn and freely shared expertise, and their tireless work on my behalf, I have particularly to thank Joel Altman, Oliver Arnold, Ian Duncan, Catherine Gallagher, Kevis Goodman, Steven Justice, Jeffrey Knapp, Jennifer Miller, Maura Nolan, Samuel Otter, and Joanna Picciotto. On the campus and off, I thank Elizabeth Bearden, Vikram and Melanie Chandra, Kathleen Donegan, Nadia Ellis, Eric Falci, Tom Jacobs, Michael Harrison, Will Kenton, Dan Lorge, Steven Lee, Gerard Passannante, John Philip, Noah Pollack, Kent Puckett, Asad Raza, Michael Rubenstein, Scott Saul, Julia Schleck, Namwali Serpell, Kelly Stage, and Emily Thornbury for their fellowship and their attentive reading.

Berkeley has offered me many wondrous experiences and opportunities. But what I'm most grateful for is the chance to have known Janet Adelman. Janet was this project's fiercest supporter and its most shrewd and powerful critic, constantly working to clear my path toward clarity and good faith. Her solicitude and care toward a young colleague, newly arrived in a strange place, is a single instance of the active generosity she expected of herself, and which her example drew forth from everyone she encountered. We treasure her memory.

The book owes its final shape to the generous and penetrating critiques of David Hawkes and a second, anonymous reader at OUP. I thank Brendan O'Neill and Shannon McLachlan for guiding the project through the publication process expertly and with brio. My work on the book has been supported by grants from Berkeley's Humanities Research Fund and from the

Folger Shakespeare Library in Washington, D.C. I thank the staff at the Folger for their support. I am likewise grateful to Ben Alsop at the British Museum for his help in finding such superb examples of the coin types illustrated in the book.

A portion of chapter 1 appeared in an earlier state as "At Home with Mammon: Matter, Money, and Memory in Book Two of *The Faerie Queene*," in *ELH* 73.1 (Spring 2006), pages 245–74. I thank the Johns Hopkins University Press for the right to reprint this material. Other aspects of my argument have been aired at meetings of the Group for Early Modern Cultural Studies, the Shakespeare Association of America, and the Modern Language Association, and in lectures at Stanford, Berkeley, and U. C. Davis. I am grateful to each of these audiences for their engagement, and for their patience when it was tested.

My parents, Elizabeth and Sam White, have cherished and nourished me as a reader, as a writer, and more importantly as a person who hopes to be as loving and resourceful as they are themselves. This is their book. For their love, curiosity, wisdom, and lunacy in each of their seasons, I thank my sister, Sarah Landreth, and all the Joneses and Whites, most of all my grandmothers, Anne K. Jones and Jehanne P. White. I am saddened not to be able to share the book with three of its—and my—biggest fans, Edward Powis Jones, F. L. Peter White, and Frances H. Jones. I thank Carol and Micheal Hillier, for welcoming me into their wonderful family. Last on this list and first in my thoughts comes Melissa. Our love is all of God's money.

# The Face of Mammon

# Introduction

## *Mammon in the Tudor Common Wealth*

And I say unto you, Make to yourselves friends of the mammon of unrighteousness; that, when ye fail, they may receive you into everlasting habitations.

—Luke 16:9

This is a book about the Mammon of Renaissance England, as he appeared to English writers and thinkers from the declining years of Henry VIII up to the accession of James I. "Mammon" is an Aramaic word meaning "riches" that appears in two of Christ's sayings in the Gospels; it is the name of a demon who personifies those riches, who in Spenser's *Faerie Queene* calls himself "God of the world and worldlings"; and we might define the relation of object to personification in Mammon as the principle that "money talks."[1] That money talks is not, of course, an insight peculiar to the Renaissance. Money is the chattiest and most persuasive of human inventions, bar discourse itself, and the comparison of money to discourse is as old as money is.[2] Nevertheless, I want to claim that there is something meaningfully specific about Mammon as he is confronted by sixteenth-century Englishmen: something at once historically unique and, in that uniqueness, significant to our understandings both of the English Renaissance and of the material history of money in its relation to discourse.

I will argue that this historical specificity inheres in both faces of the Renaissance English Mammon: in his aspect as material thing, the accumulation of silver and gold coins, and in his aspect as discursive personification. The sixteenth century was a moment of unprecedented and in some ways still unmatched pressure upon its monetary objects, a pan-European inflation so rapid and so sustained as to be known to modern historians as "the price revolution." This crisis was compounded in England by the wholesale debasement of the coinage under Henry VIII and Edward VI, from sterling silver to brazen dross, which contemporary observers perceived as the proximate cause of the inflation in England. The reformation of the material purity of the coinage became a central plank of Crown policy throughout the reign of Elizabeth, in parallel to the pursuit of domestic peace and the religious settlement, making the coins that bore her image into material manifestations of the regime's ideology.

The idea that the calibration of monetary instruments could be cited in the same sentence as the juridical keeping of the peace and the theological establishment of the Thirty-Nine Articles of the Elizabethan church as convergent instances of a continuous policy—which they are, on Elizabeth's tomb in Westminster Abbey—suggests how the material particularities of Renaissance money shade into what I'm pointing to as a discursive particularity, one which distinguishes the Mammon of the Renaissance from that of modernity as firmly as the crisis of inflation and debasement distinguished him from that of the English past. Our money is the object proper to a discourse, economics, formulated over the past four centuries to account for a particular subset of social behaviors mediated by money—such as saving and exchange—as a domain unto themselves. In the sixteenth century those behaviors of course existed, but the idea that a particular disciplinary discourse needed to fraction them off from other behaviors in order to comprehend them did not.[3] Rather, questions of individuals' savings and exchanges, profits and losses, were integral to debates over the shape of the domestic polity—an integrity neatly expressed by the name of domestic polity in English, "commonwealth." For advocates of the political unity of "commonwealth," fiscal, juridical, and religious considerations were continuous in the country's pursuit of a godly and harmonious prosperity. That pursuit was, in the tumults of the sixteenth century, more visible in the breach than in the observance; it is well emblematized by Hugh Latimer's royal sermons of Lent, 1549, in which England's foremost preacher stood before the King and Court to denounce the corruption of the coinage and, through it, of English morals and policies, in the invective of an Old Testament prophet.

The debased and reformed coins of sixteenth-century England present a conflation of material and discursive problems that is unfamiliar and provocative both to the historical understanding of contemporaries and to our historical understanding. The strange provocations of this Renaissance Mammon are heard not only in the endorsement of "commonwealth" within political circles but in texts that do not limit themselves to advocating particular policies to the politically active elite—texts that address broader audiences through the media of theater and print, and that are as concerned with the pleasures that make those media effective as they are with any specific aspect of policy; that is, the kinds of texts we now call literary. As I'll argue in the chapters that follow, Mammon elbows his way into a dizzying array of literary contexts that seem to have little to do in themselves with monetary exchange. When Spenser's Sir Guyon descends into the underworld in Book 2, canto 7 of *The Faerie Queene*, he is enacting an epic topos that he shares with Odysseus and Aeneas, but Guyon does so to speak not with the dead but with Mammon—with money. To take a contrary example, everyone knows that *The Merchant of Venice* is all about money, but if the characters of that play know it too, they do their best to hide it. Each of the characters insists that he or she is really motivated by something that isn't money and that cannot be expressed in the terms of monetary exchange, on which the three thousand ducats of Antonio's bond just happen to be intruding.

The argument of this book focuses on instances of money's intrusion into literary contexts that otherwise—in the claims of the characters, in the previous establishment of the scene, in the intertextual relations of genre and trope to precedent conventions—don't seem directly motivated by the concerns we'd call economic, those of getting, saving, and spending. I hope that the range of texts, genres, and media that I treat here, which includes Spenser's epic, the drama of Shakespeare and Marlowe, the manuscript elegies of Donne, and the popular prose of Nashe, will indicate the pervasiveness of that intrusion. I have had to be selective rather than inclusive in defining that range; once I began to look for Mammon in the literature of the English Renaissance, I found his face almost everywhere. I argue that there are three reasons for this discursive ubiquity. One, which almost goes without saying, is that it is money's particular job to be ubiquitous: that's what it means to be currency, to be current, that money flows across otherwise uncrossable distances, and over such otherwise insuperable divides as those that characterized Elizabethan social theory.[4] The second, as I've sketched in above, is that the flexible political category of "commonwealth" means that the appropriate discursive context of money is much broader in Renaissance writing than it is today, and that the mutual implication of fiscal, juridical, and religious contexts is not intellectually scandalous, as it would be today (as a failure of disciplined, properly economic analysis), however morally and politically scandalous may be the behaviors expressed as transgressing the concatenated interest of the commonwealth.

The third reason I propose for this discursive ubiquity of money proceeds from the first two, and is the central claim of this book. A Renaissance coin is at once unitary and disparate, a single thing that is different kinds of things, as the diffuse continuities of the concept of "commonwealth" suggest. The coin's value arises from two apparently opposite sources: the precious metal that provides its matter and the stamp of the prince that authorizes its currency. The importance of its material composition makes a coin an object for the discourse of ontology, which analyzes the conditions of materiality; its role as "the common drudge 'tween man and man," a means of horizontal social relations that construe their participants as peers, makes it an object for the discourse of ethics; and its status as a sovereign production delegated to the good of individual users and of the commonwealth makes it an instance of vertically hierarchical social relations, an object for the discourse of politics.[5] The writers whom I study use the coin to demonstrate the inseparability of these competing discourses as they converge upon a single, ubiquitous object. I argue that the interaction of material qualities and socially determined values in gold and silver coins propels these objects beyond the circuits of exchange they are minted to serve into literary texts that seek to define the contested relations among poetics, human institutions, and material substance. English Renaissance writers use coined money to present matter itself as a basis of social meaning.[6] For these authors, an understanding of the world that humans make for themselves relies upon understanding how the material world is made.

The production of money to arbitrate and store values is a paradigmatic instance of the conventionality of the social world—of relations among humans motivated not by divine injunction or example but by material conveniences that manifest themselves as at once arbitrary, contingent, and binding. The chthonic character of Mammon is that of human institutions writ small; he is the demon we have made in our own image. Nevertheless, the authors I study do not propose merely to repudiate Mammon, through ascetic retreat from the material and social world. Instead, they seek to understand why we have made him: what contingent but necessary relations coins exist to facilitate and have come also to embody. These include not only the horizontal social relations among individuals that are the scope of ethics, but also the vertical relations that join those individuals to the body politic whose lifeblood proverbially circulates in the form of silver and gold and to the prince whose face the coinage bears. Situated between the material and the social worlds, the coin bears a strange, even parodic likeness to the human bodies among whom it changes hands. For moralists, that apparent similarity can become the ground of an absolute differentiation between the stuff of money and the stuff of life, but it can also make it hard to tell where a person stops and where a coin starts. The coin's utter dependence on market demand and state power for its form in turn offers a model for the ways in which personhood depends upon an individual's integration into social institutions. And in order to understand why we've made Mammon as our likeness, these authors strive to understand *how* we have made Mammon: how, through the process of a coin's crafting, this material object comes to generate value.

In examining the work of a coin in terms of its making, my argument construes that coin to be at once a thing and a relation. Physically it is unitary and discrete, easily encompassed by a hand, while conceptually it is a specific combination of two different things—it is the coordination of extrinsic and intrinsic value, through the material imprinting of stamp upon bullion. The coin, itself an interior relation, imposes specific relations between itself and other things wherever it goes: it's that exterior relationality that is its motion. Through the exchange value that is the yoking of its disparate interior values, the coin adequates other objects to itself, and shuttles thereby from hand to hand through the circuits of exchange. Adequation is the relation through which Mammon himself might define the world, according to his own place in it. For Mammon, all meaning is price. But adequation is not definitive of the place of money in the worlds of the texts I study here, which specifically engage Mammon within relations that are not those of exchange. Instead, these texts use coined money to define a variety of larger relations that integrate embodied human selves into the material world. The coin's adequation appears as a common medium and means for these material relations that enfold it, neither as a self-contained relationship nor as an end in itself. I organize the chapters that follow around the diversity of these larger material relations, which, my writers insist, encompass and reinscribe the circuits of exchange within their own meanings.[7] The material relations between body and world which their coins mediate include those of consumption and instrumentality, which (in chapter 1) I argue Spenser and Marlowe each present as dialectically opposite; that of reproduction (in chapter 2), which Shakespeare assesses in terms not only of the sexual reproduction of bodies but of the imposition of the will to shape events and of authority to shape the commonwealth, in the political plays *King John* and *Measure for Measure*; that of disavowal (in chapter 3), the fetishistic repudiation of money's material centrality, as it manifests itself in *The Merchant of Venice*; and that of waste (in chapter 4), in which the squandered coin becomes the means of materialization for the witty textualities of Donne's elegies and Nashe's prose.

In the following pages of this introduction, I will explicate the terms in which "mammon" arises in the diction of the Gospels, and how those terms open onto the status of coins as privileged objects for the metaphysical discourse of ontology, the analysis of being. I will discuss the place of my coins in their historical setting, that of the disastrous inflation and debasement of the sixteenth century, and in the analysis of "commonwealth," through which contemporaries strove to understand and to critique inflationary phenomena. And I will conclude the introduction by referring that sixteenth-century discourse to two strains of current criticism: the "new economic criticism," which focuses on the relation of discursive and rhetorical categories to the analyses of value and of price, and the criticism of "material culture," which analyzes what Arjun Appadurai called "the social life of things."

## I. FRIENDS OF MAMMON

Although the history of money reaches back to the preclassical Aegean, the history of Mammon begins with Christianity. In the Sermon on the Mount, according to Matthew, Christ tells his followers, "No man can serve two masters: for either he will hate the one, and love the other; or else he will hold to the one, and despise the other. Ye cannot serve God and mammon" (Mat. 6:24; all biblical citations KJV unless otherwise noted). In retaining the Aramaic word for "riches" while rendering the rest of Christ's saying in Greek, the author of Matthew suggested that wealth should be read in the passage as a proper name, demonically personified. "Mammon" was retained by Jerome in the Vulgate and by Tyndale and most of his sixteenth-century followers in English, though the Geneva translators opted against it.[8] Luke's gospel also includes this verse (16:13), but prefaces it with the ironic parable of the unjust steward who, learning that he would be fired by his master once his accounts were settled, conspired with his master's debtors to cheat the master in hopes of finding a new place with one of them. Jesus concludes:

> And the lord commended the unjust steward, because he had done wisely: for the children of this world are in their generation wiser than the children of light. And I say unto you, Make to yourselves friends of the mammon of unrighteousness; that, when ye fail, they may receive you into everlasting habitations. He that is faithful in that which is least is faithful also in much: and he that is unjust in the least is unjust also in much. If therefore ye have not been faithful in the unrighteous mammon, who will commit to your trust the true riches? (Luke 16:8–11)[9]

For Matthew, "Ye cannot serve God and mammon" is one of several parallel gnomic sayings that define faith in Christ as the rejection of worldly cares in the Sermon, such as the example of "the lilies of the field, how they grow; they toil not, neither do they spin: And yet I say unto you, That even Solomon in all his glory was not arrayed like one of these" (6:28–9). Luke removes the phrase from the contexts of those sayings (which mostly appear instead in Luke 12) and situates it more complexly: the ironic praise of the unjust steward makes the opposition of God to mammon ambiguous rather than straightforward, demanding some coordination of the wisdom of the "children of light" to the contrary and ironic wisdom of the "children of this world" while "their generation" holds present sway. Further, Luke inserts this aspect of the sermon into Christ's theo-political rivalry with the Pharisees: "And the Pharisees also, who were covetous, heard all these things: and they derided him" (16:14). Having successfully provoked the Pharisees through the parable and its interpretation, Christ takes the occasion to rebuke their hypocrisy for the rest of the chapter. Rather than using "mammon" to spurn the world and demonstrate the faith that God will provide, as Matthew suggests, Luke makes mammon the controvertible means of engaging the world, using the world's own means and "wisdom" against it.

Throughout the New Testament, the threshold between the community of believers who follow Christ and the world that each of them has left behind is the communal purse. The discipular community was itinerant and communist: entry to it was achieved by severing the claims of family, place, and property, as Christ frequently insists. That severance, as we see in chapters 4 and 5 of Acts, was a cashing out—the devotee had to liquidate his or her property and hand the proceeds over to the communal purse:

> Neither was there any among them that lacked: for as many as were possessors of lands or houses sold them, and brought the prices of the things that were sold, And laid them down at the apostles' feet: and distribution was made unto every man according as he had need. (Acts 4:34–5)

It's for attempting to hold a bit of their own back while contributing to the community, trying to serve both God and Mammon, that Ananias and his wife are struck dead. A disciple who, unlike Ananias, makes that choice successfully has left behind his need for money in joining the community. But the community itself still requires money—not only to demonstrate the completeness of its exaction upon the individual disciple but to use in the community's dealings with the unredeemed world outside itself, to buy food and to give to the poor. The episodes of the tribute money and of the riddle of the penny (which I'll discuss below) represent the claims of the unredeemed world upon the insular community of believers in terms of money; money denotes the ways in which the community is not self-contained but in the world and subject to demands at once fiscal and political. And the purse is the means by which the Pharisees at last seize the body of Christ. The communal treasurer who "had the bag" is Judas Iscariot (John 13:29): the apostle given the most trust, from a worldly point of view, is the least trustworthy, the one who betrays Christ for thirty (more) pieces of silver.[10] Judas's role in handling the money that the rest of the community has given up singles him out as the weak link among the twelve, the one who remains corruptible—despite the practical necessity of that role to the life of the community, which converges in Judas with the ironic, eschatological necessity that Christ be betrayed. Alone among the disciples, Judas served Christ by serving Mammon, and in that double service he, like Ananias, is destroyed.

In opposing the service of God to that of Mammon, Christ defined money as a paradigmatic instance of the claims of the merely human upon the community of believers. In citing Caesar's image on the penny, he asserted an elusive but inescapable relation between the arbitrary forms of human authority and the divine will, to which those human institutions are ephemeral and indifferent:

> And [the chief priests and scribes] watched him, and sent forth spies, which should feign themselves just men, that they might take hold of his words, that so they might deliver him unto the power and authority of the governor.
>
> And they asked him, saying, Master, we know that thou sayest and teachest rightly, neither acceptest thou the person of any, but teachest the way of God truly: Is it lawful for us to give tribute unto Caesar, or no?
>
> But he perceived their craftiness, and said unto them, Why tempt ye me? Shew me a penny. Whose image and superscription hath it?
>
> They answered and said, Caesar's.
>
> And he said unto them, Render therefore unto Caesar the things which be Caesar's, and unto God the things which be God's.
>
> And they could not take hold of his words before the people: and they marvelled at his answer, and held their peace. (Luke 20:21–6)

The riddling formula "Render therefore unto Caesar the things which be Caesar's, and unto God the things which be God's" affirms the claim of Caesar to the penny, and so baffles the Pharisees.[11] But the opposition of Caesar's image to "the things which be God's" proceeds to make the affirmation of the image a nullity. The riddle of the penny articulates the tension between divine and human authorities as a feature of the coin's makeup. It is a penny by virtue of the image impressed upon it to give it form, which is that of human authority, Caesar. But "the things which be God's," read ironically, relegates the imprint of Caesar to the status of epiphenomenon, or surface effect. Given that everything is God's, "the things which be Caesar's" becomes a merely notional category, an empty set, constituted by insubstantial images. Substance, then, is God's claim on the coin. Insofar as the penny bears Caesar's "image and superscription," it is Caesar's. Insofar as it exists in the universe, it is God's.

The penny bifurcates itself between these two kinds of authority in order to be what it is. If it were not made from some part of the substance of creation, it would not exist; but if it did not bear Caesar's "image and circumscription," it would not *work*—that is, it would not arbitrate other values through its own as currency. The riddle of the penny implies that the insubstantial and formal claim of Caesar upon the penny is also unreal: that what is real in the penny is matter, the silver that God has made and that man has merely manipulated into a particular and impermanent shape. The paradoxical inversion of idealism (the reality of a transcendent God) and materialism (the reality of matter) in Christ's riddle recalls the mystery of the Incarnation and anticipates that of the Eucharist. It works here by analogizing the material to the ideal in their mutual opposition to the category of images, those merely formal differentiations that are offered as reliably and definitively unreal. Effective as this maneuver is in confounding the Pharisees by simultaneously acknowledging and trivializing state power, the riddle of the penny also provides a formula for Christian obedience to a power that may or may not itself be godly. Political rule is a thing indifferent from this perspective, an epiphenomenon with no meaningful relation to what matters in the calculus of personal salvation; the Christian should follow the divine injunction to obedience in his own person without presuming, or bothering, to judge the magistrates whom he is bound, "in their generation," to obey.

The rationale for temporal obedience I'm tracing here is a Pauline one; the canonical books composed by Paul or in his orbit—Luke, Acts, and the epistles attributed to him—emphasize the ways in which a revolutionary church may accommodate itself to a vast and indifferent empire.[12] The penny in Jesus' riddle becomes the microscopic instance of such an accommodation, one which works by taking a small, petty, and apparently unitary object and proceeding to elevate it into the discourse of ontology—the philosophical analysis of being—which bifurcates the penny into two aspects, material and formal, of which only the former is real. The maneuver of articulating the material unreality of an image in order to affirm the reality of a transcendent ideal reflects the influence of Platonic ontology on Paul; it converges with the Judaic repudiation of idols, in his thought and in the iconoclastic controversies to come, including those of sixteenth-century England.[13] But it is by no means the only authoritative account of the meaning of matter for the Renaissance. In the ontology derived by scholasticism from Aristotle, matter is only hypothetically divisible from form, as a prior potentiality: form is the realization of matter, through which any material thing comes to exist.[14] Nor does the denigration of the penny's currency through this ontological riddle constitute the Gospels' own last word on monetary value. In Jesus' parabolic descriptions of the kingdom of Heaven, not only quanta of wealth but individual coins—the talent at usury, the widow's mite, the lost piece of silver—serve to express transcendental values in terms of worldly ones, by articulating value as a category continuous across these two opposite contexts.[15] Christ's uses of value adumbrate a claim made explicit by Georg Simmel, that value is not simply an intramaterial measurement but a metaphysical category comparable to that of being, and that monetary objects therefore demand a privileged and complex relation to the discourse of ontology.[16] What the riddle of the penny exemplifies is how this ontological complexity within this everyday object, a small silver coin, opens out into the social relations of ethics and politics, arbitrating them in its own ontological terms. Large practical questions, such as the right relation of the faithful individual to the state, turn out to depend upon minute theoretical distinctions within an apparently petty and pedestrian object.

In monetary exchange, the categorical distinction of practice and theory tends to map onto the relative distinction between the phenomenal—the immediate, the noteworthy, the obvious—and the trivial and esoteric. Money did much the same practical work in Roman Galilee, and in the English sixteenth century, that it does today: it offered itself as the medium of exchange among goods and services and as a repository of value. But the ways in which a coin made of precious metal accomplished that monetary work were significantly different from the ways in which a paper and electronic currency accomplishes its corresponding work. Renaissance coins measured their own value as a quantum of precious metal, but the ideal relation of the mineral ("intrinsic") value to the face value of the coin in exchange could never be fixed: not only might different coin series vary greatly in their purity, but the intrinsic value of an individual coin was itself subject to the daily fluctuations of price in the international market for precious metals. To compensate for this variability, the coin was understood to manifest a second, "extrinsic," value, which made up the difference between its metal price and its face value and kept the face value stable by fluctuating inversely to the price of metal.

While the intrinsic value was defined by the dynamics of the market, the extrinsic value was produced by the authority of the state. The royal stamp of the coin's face yoked together three kinds of value—intrinsic, extrinsic, and exchange value—in order to enable even the simplest everyday cash transactions. A Renaissance coin relied upon its precious materiality for both its being and its primary value, yet that materiality was itself necessarily incomplete.

But all of these factors of value, and the complex balancing act a precious coin sustains among them, are elided in the practice of exchange. It's not necessary to consider the ways in which the coin produces its value in using that value to buy something; such a consideration could even be counterproductive, postponing and probably confusing the successful completion of an ordinary and, in practical terms, straightforward transaction. While that transaction is proceeding, the material differences between one form of current money and another—for example, between silver and paper—are trivial and practically invisible, no matter how physically obvious they may be.

Like other instruments, money submerges itself into the relation between actors that it serves to effect. As long as it works in practice—as long as the actors know how to use it and succeed in that use—the question of *how* an instrument does its work is an esoteric one. Had I world enough and time, I am sure I would be interested in finding out how the software by which I'm composing this sentence operates, but as long as I can keep producing the sentence by means of the software, the software is for all my practical purposes transparent. As mediating instruments go, the precious coin is more like this software than it is like, say, a hammer. The means by which a hammer mediates the motion of my hand to drive a nail are intuitively legible, in the leverage of the shaft and the hardness of the head. The software and the coin both need to keep the details of their operation submerged in order that their interface, the experience of their use, may seem easy and intuitive.

At the point that the instrument fails to work as its users expect it to work, however, the theoretical question of *how* it was supposed to work imposes itself urgently upon practice; how the instrument ought to be functioning has to be articulated in order to begin addressing the question of how it is that the instrument is failing to do what it's supposed to in this instance. Julian Yates discusses a range of early modern instruments and prostheses (from the printed page to the priest-hole) as exemplifying the theoretical urgency of practical failure:

> Each of these objects straddles the line between nature and culture, organizing streams of matter and people. . . . Each works by aspiring to forget its origins, its

status as a construction, and so to make of itself a foundation or black box. The success of these objects may be gauged by their relative invisibility. If they work well, no one notices them. The problem is that none of these devices works quite so well as its makers claim.[17]

The circumstances under which sixteenth-century coins might emerge to such a defective visibility, however, were not only those of their immediate use—the individual failed transaction—but those of a large-scale disaster, inflation, which overtook the normative systems of value, savings, and exchange which those coins synecdochically represented.

In sixteenth-century England, money veered off from its expected functions in a disastrous, spectacular, and, to the understanding of contemporaries, unprecedented fashion. By the middle of the century, England was swept up in the pan-European inflation that historians have come to call "the price revolution."[18] Inflation was not a novel phenomenon, but its pace had in the medieval period been slow enough that its effects were perceptible only across the scope of generations.[19] A visible rise in prices between one year and the next was understood to be caused by a poor harvest, a costly war, or similarly circumscribed and specific events, which is why the Renaissance term for a state of high prices, "dearth" (i.e., "dearness"), has the continuous meaning of "a scarcity"; when the situation returned to normalcy, so too should prices (even if such a putative normalcy was in practice more the exception than the rule). But the inflation of the sixteenth century was a "marvelous dearth[,] that in such plenty comes, contrary to his kind," as Sir Thomas Smith wrote in 1549.[20] Smith did not mean "marvelous" as praise: he meant that this "dearth" was unprecedented, dire, and freakish. It was not dependent on scarcity, but persisted in the midst of "plenty." It was not isolated chronologically according to the yearly cycles of an agricultural economy, but sustained its growth over decades and showed no signs of abating. The periodic crisis of "dearth" had, "contrary to his kind," established itself as a permanent crisis.

The commonwealth of sixteenth-century England was much less capable of absorbing the effects of prolonged inflation than a modern economy might be. Only some of the prices according to which wealth circulated were free to rise and fall in the market; others were subject to very long-term contractual obligations, as were many agricultural rents, or to regulation by statutes that had likewise been set at the turn of the century, as were many laborers' wages. The price revolution was a national trauma, but it was one that made its greatest exactions upon those least able to bear them: the laboring poor. "Poore wee bare the losse," says the country laborer called "People" in the midcentury political allegory *Respublica*, as he weighs the changes that have recently overtaken the commonwealth and its money supply.[21] The urge to find individuals and groups to blame for a systemic crisis was, then as ever, directed toward those who seemed to be profiting from the hardships endured by the rest of the commonwealth—the merchants and craftsmen who were able to charge prices commensurate to their expenses, unlike actors in the highly regulated agricultural sector; those landlords who escaped the now ruinous terms of old leases by rack-renting or enclosure. But the disastrous problem of inflation was not only thought of as a problem of individual misbehavior. It was also, very visibly, a problem with money. The complex interaction of kinds of value integrated and stabilized by the coin's stamp was evidently decaying: the same silver penny could buy only half as much bread.

The responsiveness of prices to cycles of agricultural scarcity, as "dearth," was understood as an aspect of how money worked. The fact that "dearth" had now effectively institutionalized itself in England, independent of the fluctuations of harvests, suggested to analysts such as Sir Thomas Smith that English money had stopped working as it should and had embarked upon a perverse and apparently self-sustaining malfunction.[22] And the character of that perversion, argued Smith and his fellows, was plain for all to see. English silver currency, once fine sterling, had been debased by the Crown in the 1540s to the point of being literally, as well as figuratively, brazen: "they blushe for shame," wrote John Heywood of these red-faced coins.[23] The way in which English money had gone wrong—in failing to calibrate prices, in failing to store value—was induced by something materially wrong within the object of money, the silver coin itself. And that material wrongness was in turn induced by an exploitative governmental policy, which was using these objects to extort profits from the political relation that the coins embodied between the subject commonwealth and the Crown. As both the substance and the value of England's coinage deteriorated, the incompletely material character of coins presented itself as a shockingly immediate ontological and political problem.

## II. THE RED FACES OF DEBASEMENT

For William Harrison, introducing his account of English coins in the 1586 *Description of England*, the history of mint production is only barely a story. It contains only two events. After an indefinite period of medieval purity—in which the mint price of an ounce of silver came at some point to be set at twenty coined pence, "and so continued"—the English coinage falls into narrative by the mismanagement of Henry VIII, "who first brought [the price of the ounce of silver at the mint] to three shillings and foure pence, & afterward our siluer coine vnto brasse & copper monies, by reason of those inestimable charges, which diuerse waies oppressed him."[24] That is—to draw out certain implications of the narrative—Henry's profligate foreign policies led him on to an entirely novel debasement in the domestic sphere: he first cut the silver value of his coins by more than a third, and then continued incrementally to debase the coinage until it was utterly evacuated of silver—i.e., worthless, save for the stamp of their maker's image. Attempts at reform of the coinage followed, with "good purpose" but little effect, according to Harrison, under both Edward VI and Mary, but only

> [a]fter hir decease the ladie Elizabeth hir sister, and now our most gratious queene, souereigne and princesse, did finish the matter wholie, vtterly abolishing the vse of copper and brazen coine, and conuerting the same into guns and great ordinance, she restored sundrie coines of fine siluer, as peeces of halfepenie farding, of a penie, . . . of six pence vsuallie named the testone, and shilling of twelue pence, whereon she hath imprinted hir owne image, and emphaticall superscription.[25]

Harrison's tone in setting forth the events of what historians have come to call the Great Debasement of 1541–1562 is less judgmental than that of most writers; one modern historian of English money denounces the Debasement as "the single greatest fraud deliberately carried out by any English government on its own people," and a second surrenders to the same judgment in admitting that "It is difficult to avoid the impression of a deliberate and gigantic fraud."[26] But even Harrison's attempt at flat impartiality casts the history of Henrician debasement and Elizabethan restoration of purity into a familiar and apparently inevitable shape. It is, like so many other stories that emerge from the mid-sixteenth century in England, a conversion narrative: a descent into the gutter and a calling back to grace.

The Henrician debasement already presented itself to contemporary Englishmen as a "fraud," as these historians put it, but one that deceived nobody for long. It did not even need to fool anyone in order to succeed, for the mint price was among the king's prerogatives, and what choice did anyone have?[27] Instead, the debasement was legible as an abuse of the means whereby sovereign power interacted with the market, and thereby invited a new definition of those means—both of the coinage, and of the extent of the Crown's power stamped upon it—among the midcentury writers who responded to the multidimensional crises of policy during the upheavals of Edward and Mary's reigns by writing sermons, epigrams, royal pageants, and didactic treatises, all concerning the state of the "commonwealth." Even in 1606, forty years after these events, this moralized account of the Debasement was fresh in memory and vital to policy. The epitaph on the tomb James built for Elizabeth in Westminster Abbey begins by listing the reformation of the coinage as third among her supreme achievements: "*Memoriae Sacrum: Religione ad primaevam sinceritatem restaurata, Pace fundata, Moneta ad iustum valorem reducta...*" [Sacred to memory: Religion to its primitive Purity restored, Peace settled, Money restored to its just value... ].[28] The chiastic juxtaposition and syntactical correspondence with the religious settlement, likewise formulated as a reform stripping away the dross of the Catholic centuries to reclaim an ancient purity, present the reformation of sterling as a turning away from past decadence and as a continuous moral imperative in the present. The inextricability of political and moral choices is a precondition of these attempts to harmonize the material interests of the Crown and of the kingdom; the material purity of the sterling standard manifests itself as a moral standard once it is controverted, in Henry's sinning against his own responsibility.

The coinage proclaimed itself as the monarch's instrument and responsibility simply and definitively, by representing the monarch in words and image. The coin's face and the ruler's face were the same, through representation and even by law, for the coinage shared with the royal seal the legal privileges of the monarch's person. To violate either image, by destroying, clipping, or counterfeiting it, was lèse-majesté and punishable as high treason. But, although this law was of medieval origin and derived from classical precedent, the use of mimetic portraiture on coins was a novel and specifically Tudor phenomenon.[29] The image of kingship that had been stamped on Plantagenet coins was a beardless, boyish crowned head that had no mimetic ambitions; the Lancastrian Henry VI and the Yorkist Edward IV both allowed this same image to represent their power over the circulating medium (fig. 1). Dispensing with the show of continuity that this permanent figure of the crown offered, Henry VII began around 1504 to replace it with his own beaky profile (fig. 2).[30] In this gesture he followed the latest numismatic fashions of the Continent: Francesco Sforza had placed his portrait on Milanese coins in the early 1450s, in imitation of ancient coinage, and most of the princely states of Europe came to follow suit within the next hundred years.[31] Henry VIII was not prompt, however, to replace his father's image with his own, and continued to mint coins bearing the old king's profile for seventeen years before replacing it with a type of his; nor, in their turn, did the noblemen whose charge was Edward VI immediately strike coins representing the new king. Some English coins never acquired a royal portrait, notably the denominations in "old" or "angel" gold, which adhered to ancient standards of purity and advertised them by retaining the medieval iconography of the Archangel Michael smiting the dragon Satan.[32]

Figure 1: Earlier Henry VII groat: face and reverse © Trustees of the British Museum

Figure 2: Late Henry VII groat, featuring a life portrait: face © Trustees of the British Museum

The use of portraiture on the coinage was a purposeful innovation, making available particular opportunities for the self-representation of the Tudor monarchs. However, it also opened a venue for the critique of the sovereign through his monetary manifestations.[33] Writing around 1547, John Heywood rebukes royal policy in an epigram, "of redde Testons":

> These Testons looke redde: how like you the same?
> Tis a tooken of grace: they blushe for shame.[34]

The term "teston" specifies the portrait coinage: the first Italian portrait coins were dubbed *testone,* meaning "big head," and the name accompanied the new coin type across Europe.[35] These coins are those that bear the young king's face, and that face has turned red from debasement, as the silver that now comprises less than a third of their mass can no longer effectively color the dross of its alloy (fig. 3). The blushing testons have more "grace" than those who have made them, for at least they are ashamed of their own base composition—unlike, we are to infer, the brazen-faced masters of monetary policy. Edward's stampéd face supplies here the "shame" that the boy-king ought to wear on his own.

The Mint was a revenue-generating business of the Crown. The extrinsic value of each coin—the discrepancy between its value as bullion and its greater face value—entirely coincided with the prince's profit in minting that coin, a royal privilege called "seigniorage." The temptation to dilute these standards of value to enhance the profit of the state had proven irresistible to nearly all the

Figure 3: 1549 debased shilling of Edward VI: face and reverse © Trustees of the British Museum

princes of Europe; at the turn of the sixteenth century, no Continental silver currency approached the purity of sterling. In 1541 Henry VIII, too, decided to employ his coined image more lucratively. He and his ministers began experimenting with debasement of the coinage, decreasing the proportion of precious metal to base in the alloy from which coin blanks were made while continuing to stamp the same type upon them.[36] Thus the same exchange value as before was assigned to a coin containing less silver; indeed, to coins containing less and less silver, since debasement proceeded incrementally over the next ten years. After Henry's death in 1547 Edward's protectors, Somerset and then Northumberland, continued to further debase the coinage. By the time the practice was ended by Northumberland in 1551, the fineness of the coins had declined from the sterling standard of 11.1 ounces silver (out of twelve) to three ounces. The goal of each debasement was to maximize direct revenue for the Crown. Inflating the value of the coinage relative to silver meant that everyone who owned silver, either as coin or as plate (i.e., household implements made of silver), would profit by bringing that silver to the Mint to be melted down and recoined in the new standard, and—while the value returned to the customer as coin was more and more entirely extrinsic—for each use of the services of the Mint the Crown kept its own, grossly inflated seigniorage in pure silver. During the debasements, Mint activity was so brisk that satellite mints were established at Canterbury, York, Southwark, and Bristol to supplement the central facilities at the Tower.

Debasement thus relied not only on forcing the country to accept the diminished coins as current but on providing price incentives that would continue to attract fine silver into the Mint to be returned in that coin. At this time the English mint's procedures remained nearly identical to those developed in the ancient Mediterranean. Raw material—silver bullion—entered the mint as a purchase: individuals sold old or foreign coins or plate to the mint, and it was melted down and purified (or debased) to the current standard of fineness and returned to the seller as coin at the price established by the Crown for bullion. Sellers did not necessarily get back as coin the same batch of silver that they had sold as bullion, but the continuity between the money form and the bullion form of wealth in the fluidity of silver across this single transaction, iterated not invisibly at the state-bank level but by a multiplicity of single economic actors, is striking and strange enough to modern expectations to be worth emphasizing. Indeed, that fluidity had two directions, not one, for coin became bullion again whenever a particular series was called back from circulation for recoining—or whenever the international price of bullion might rise higher than the domestic value of silver money, despite the legal facts that exporting coin was felonious and melting it down outside the Mint was treason.

England had no silver mines of its own; it was a given that the stuff of these commonplace objects had some far-fetched origin, and that during its tenure in the country the silver had moved back and forth through multiple manufactured forms, of which the coin was only one. The small-scale fluidity of the mint transaction itself suggested that each quantum of silver matter had both a future and a past as form, as well as a history of circulation and of exchange; as the principal speaker declares in Smith's 1549 *Discourse of the Commonweal*:

> For you know all the treasure [i.e., precious metal] of this realm must once in few years come to the King's Highness hands, by one means or other, and from him it should go abroad again to his subjects, as all springs run to the ocean sea and out of it they are spread abroad again. Then as they came in of late in good metal, they came forth in such as you now see. (85)

Another of the prolific John Heywood's epigrams on the debasement, "Of Brasse and Silver," is as much about the prior fate of church furnishings as it is about the present coinage:

> Brasse hath beene a loft, with silver set up.
> Come down Brasse and drinke on an ashen cup.[37]

The recusant Heywood densely and circumspectly negotiates the destruction of the old, elaborate silver chalices on the pretext of their idolatry, which mandated their replacement by the chastened form of the Protestant communion "cup" and left the silver in the hands of the Crown's purifying commissioners; the debasement of the silver into "ash" to serve that same greed of the powers that be; and the hauling down of church bells from the "loft" to be melted down in turn, that their brass might fuel the debasement.[38] The recent, and outrageous, incorporation of the bells into the silver money itself evokes and implicates the means by which the silver had first been gathered off the altar. In the 1540s Heywood and Smith are by no means alone in their scorn both for the present objects of the debased coinage and for the means and motives by which those objects have come to be. These texts emerge from, and find an audience within, a larger circle of private and public men dismayed by the inequities of Tudor society and the misjudgments of the Tudor state, who voiced their hopes for redress under the idealistic rubric of "commonwealth."

The perceived fracturing of the English people into rival private interests, in which the strong chose constantly to exploit their position for short-term profit to the ultimate detriment of all, was the constant concern of "commonwealth" advocates throughout the Tudor period, an analysis that had its roots in the medieval idealization of societal integrity as the "body politic."[39] Thomas Starkey insists in the *Dialogue between Pole and Lupset* (c. 1530) that the political bond depends on the sharing of material interest:

> to this all men are born and of nature brought forth: to commune such gifts as be to them given, each one to the profit of other, in perfit civility, and not to live to their own pleasure and profit, without regard of the weal of their country, forgetting all justice and equity.[40]

Writers during the Debasement themselves looked back to the examples of the previous generation, from the anti-enclosure satire of More's *Utopia* to the idealized education in statecraft of Elyot's *Booke Called the Governour*.[41] All shared an anxiety that English society was passing through unheard-of disruptions—the dissolution of the monasteries, rampant inflation, the rejection of the mass, the reshaping of agriculture and of trade, the imposition of the Prayer Book—that, separately or together, might provoke massive unrest throughout the kingdom, of which each local uprising seemed the immediate harbinger. Appealing to fear sometimes as much as to charity, the diverse proponents of the commonwealth ideal urged that the scope of private action be curbed in order that a proper balance of interests among trades and between classes be reasserted, and that the public weal—the mutual interest and profit of all—be nurtured. What we would call an economic policy was inextricable from a social and indeed a religious policy in the articulation of "commonwealth." Together they represented the interaction of a very old ideal with the evaluation of current crises that had no precedent in the pre-Reformation past. Lawrence Manley characterizes this discursive crux as a moment

> when the mass disruptions attendant on socio-economic change, coinciding with the advent of a centralizing state, registered verbally in Tudor complaint as a decomposition and realignment of social myths and taxonomic structures and a recomposition of the effects of voice and address. . . . [T]his traditional vocabulary was transformed by the circumstance of its application.[42]

The discourse of commonwealth employed and reshaped the "traditional vocabulary" of complaint to posit a productive relation among the forces of social transformation such that the expanding power of the Crown might harmonize the changing material relations among its subjects.[43]

"Commonwealth matters" thus referred generally to domestic politics, but the phrase tended to define domestic politics as the interdependent relation of individuals' goods to a common good. Every Englishman had a stake in the common weal in this sense. Even the poorest subject derived a good from the maintenance of the common good, no matter how minimal his individual wealth, while a rich man exploiting his advantage over his poorer dependents would be accused of aggrandizing his own interests at the expense of the common weal. The articulation of "common weal" instantiated and exploited a semantic continuum between material and social goods (between properties and benefits) and one between individual and common goods. According to the doctrine of the production of wealth in modern, capitalist economics, the common good (the gross domestic product) is the sum of individual goods, such that the unfettered pursuit of self-interest will enlarge the economic totality regardless of that behavior's ethical content. The ethos of commonwealth instead expected that the maximization of individual interests in the short term would lead in the medium term to the ruin of the common interests through decay or insurrection, including those of the selfish and inevitably shortsighted exploiter. The unlocking of the formula that would link "private vices" in a productive relation to "publick benefits," as Mandeville would come to put it, awaited the development of the discourse of political economy in the seventeenth century.[44]

The insistence with which these midcentury writers tended in particular to define the Crown's interest with that of the prosperity of the commonwealth betrays an uncomfortable consciousness that in practice it might seem quite otherwise. Although voluntary self-restraint on the part of landowners, wool traders, and other such who held the livelihoods of the poorer sort in the balance, was ideal, the "commonwealths-men" were quick to look to the Crown as the power that might impose limits on the behavior of self-interest—especially under Edward, to whom these reformists turned hopefully as a "young Josias."[45] But if the Crown was the lever whereby the public good might be elevated above the preponderant and mutually competing weights of private interests, on what side did the Crown's own finances press? Was it simply true that royal profit was the fruit of public profit—that, as Clement Armstrong put it in 1536, "the king and his lords hath need to minister right order of common weal, or else they must needs destroy their own weal by the very ordinance of God, for they are upholden and borne upon the body [politic]"?[46] Or were the Crown's interests only the greatest and most potentially exploitative among that welter of private interests? The questions of to what extent the Crown might harmonize its own interests to those of the commonwealth, and of how and by what means the Crown's interaction with the market might need to be limited for the public good, became entirely visible in the events of the Great Debasement, as the face of the king on the silver coinage began to turn a brazen red.

The recursive relation between debased coin and the image of the Crown expressed for the commonwealths-men an analysis of "This . . . marvelous dearth that in such plenty comes, contrary to his kind" that was rooted, not simply in the aggregate misbehavior of individual enclosers, middlemen, and such other "caterpillars of the commonwealth," but in a critique of national policy.[47] The most shrewd and thoroughgoing such analysis is the set of dialogues titled *A Discourse of the Commonweal of This Realm of England*, which circulated widely in manuscript in 1549 and was printed, with significant revisions, in 1581. Its authorship is most frequently assigned to Sir Thomas Smith, a protegé of Somerset's and principal secretary to Edward VI.[48] The dialogues portray the fictive encounter of five social types in the inn of a county town: a Knight, a Capper, a Merchantman, a Husbandman, and a learned Doctor or cleric. All complain of the crushing and unprecedented nature of the present "dearth" or inflation, and each, save the Doctor, blames the price rise upon the exploitativeness of his proximate partners in trade; as the Husbandman tells the Knight, "I say you and your sort, men of lands, are the first cause thereof by reason you raise your lands [i.e., rent]," to which the Knight replies, "Undertake that you and your sort will sell us all things at the price you did twenty years ago, and I doubt not to bring all gentlemen to let unto you their lands at the rent they went at twenty years past" (39). By gentle persuasion, the Doctor soothes the barely suppressed hostility that these rival interests bring to the colloquy, and demonstrates the circularity of their complaints against one another.[49] The true cause of dearth, he argues, is not the malfeasance of any one group of citizens against the interests of the commonwealth, but the Crown's misguided policy of debasement.

The Knight objects to this analysis—not, indeed, as an officer of Crown policy (though the character is one, a justice of the peace), but as an advocate of the primacy of extrinsic value in the coinage:

> Forsooth, such a dullard am I indeed that cannot perceive what hindrance it should be to the realm to have this metal more than that for our coin, seeing the coin is but a token to go from man to man. And since it is stricken with the King's seal to be current, what makes it the matter what metal it be of, yea, though it were but leather or paper? (69–70)

Although this view—that it is the will of the prince, as realized in the stamp, that can make any substance money—may seem prescient to us, the Doctor demonstrates it to be reactionary.[50] Leather tokens are acceptable in certain constrained and temporary circumstances, but money needs to be universally current beyond the reach of any individual prince's credit.[51] Gold and silver are the only substances that may claim such a cosmopolitan currency, by virtue of their scarcity—their intrinsic value (73–75). Domestic value cannot be insulated from foreign exchange. The prince's will in valuing the coinage is inevitably subject to the international market; any attempt of the prince to pretend otherwise will be exploited by foreigners through that market, to the ruin of the commonwealth.[52] Domestic dearth is the result, "for we must buy dear all things brought from beyond the seas and therefore we must sell again as dear our things or else we should make ill bargains for ourselves" (79).

Money is, as the Knight contends, an arbitrary institution, "a token." But its arbiter is not the prince, but rather the international market. The Knight asks, therefore, whether the prince has any real responsibility for the coinage at all:

> Why do kings and princes strike these metals and other with a coin but because they would have that coin, of what value soever it be, to bear the state that the coin pretends; which they did in vain if they could make the metal that bears that to be neither better nor worse in estimation? (75)

The Doctor answers, citing Roman history, that the task of weighing and assaying precious metals for market exchange had originally been the province of officers of the commonwealth, "But because . . . it was tedious to tarry for the weighing of these metals and trying, it was thought good that the prince should strike these metals with several marks . . . to assure the receiver the same to be no less than the weight it pretended" (76). The minting power is thus one ceded to the prince by the commonwealth for its own convenience, not an aspect of sovereign prerogative. The prince who attempts to abuse it inconveniences not only the commonwealth as a whole, but himself in particular, for debasement destroys his own credit, and devalues the rents, taxes, and levies which the commonwealth rightfully owes him. By the end of the dialogue, each participant is more or less swayed by the Doctor's arguments that the coinage is an arbitrary but necessary convention of the commonwealth, administered by the prince but not given value by him; that the prince is as subject to the force of the market as the commonwealth is, rather than being able to impose his will on the market through the commonwealth; that the dearth is the result of the Crown's misjudgment of that relationship, not of the exploitative behavior of divided, competing interests; and that therefore the redress of dearth is a matter not of individual restraint but of national policy.

It is the voice of the Doctor, a clergyman, in the *Discourse* that guides the competing voices of the Capper, the Merchant, the Husbandman, and the Knight into harmony. In practice, the prestige, the authority, and the direct economic influence of the clergy had been dealt a staggering blow by the expropriations of the past twenty years. If the Edwardian commonwealths-men were, as they wished, to assign to Reformed religion the economic and social conscience they hoped to inculcate into the state, they would have to invent a position from which the clergy could address such matters. The most prominent clerical voice calling for such a harmony of religious, political, and material interests was Hugh Latimer's. In his first sermon before Edward VI and his court, delivered in Lent of 1549, Latimer took as one of his texts the motto engraved on the king's new shilling (fig. 3):

> We have now a pretty little shilling indeed, a very pretty one; I have but one, I think, in my purse; and the last day I had put it away almost for an old groat; and so I trust some will take them. The fineness of the silver I cannot see: but therein is printed a fine sentence, that is, TIMOR DOMINI FONS VITAE VEL SAPIENTIAE; "The fear of the lord is the fountain of life or wisdom."[53]

Clearly, Latimer's true text is the whole of the shilling, and the motto serves only to ironize the object that bears it. The coin which he ridicules was the result of the most recent and ham-fisted attempt to redress the color of the debased silver, in which the Mint doubled the fineness of the coinage (from 4 ounces back to 8 ounces out of twelve) and instead halved its weight. Thus a new shilling was exactly the same size as an old sixpence, or "almost... an old groat." Contrasting the fineness of the silver to that of the sentiment expressed in the motto, Latimer rebukes the king's "officers" as colluding with the forces of private greed that threaten to destroy the commonwealth. He proceeds to rail against this complicity with enclosers and engrossers by quantifying and redoubling the Deuteronomic injunction against an excess of profit taken by the king, "neither shall he too much multiply to himself silver and gold" (17:17), as he had moralized on the halving of the coinage: "Thus all the enhancing and rearing goeth to your private commodity and wealth. So that where ye had a single too much, you have that; and since the same, ye have enhanced the rent, and so have increased another too much; so now ye have double too much, which is too too much."[54] Two weeks later Latimer returned to the royal pulpit, declaring that certain persons had attempted to intimidate him for his prior "meddling" with the affairs of state at the mint, and proceeded to lade them with scorn.

> I chanced in my last sermon to speak a merry word of the new shilling, to refresh my auditory, how I was like to put away my new shilling for an old groat. I was herein noted to speak seditiously. . . . I have now gotten one fellow more, a companion of sedition; and wot ye who is my fellow? Esay the prophet. I spake but of a pretty little shilling, but he speaketh to Jerusalem after another sort, and was so bold to meddle with their coin. "Thou proud, thou covetous, thou haughty city of Hierusalem": *Argentum tuum versum est in scoriam* [Isa. 1:22]. "Thy silver is turned into," what? into testions? *scoriam*: "into dross."
>
> Ah, seditious wretch! what had he to do with the mint? Why should he not have left that matter to some master of policy to reprove? "Thy silver is dross; it is not fine, it is counterfeit; thy silver is turned; thou hadst good silver." What pertained that to Esay? Marry, he espied a piece of divinity in that policy; he threateneth them God's vengeance for it. He went to the root of the matter, which is covetousness. He espied two points in it, that either it came of covetousness, which became him to reprove; or else that it tended to the hurt of the poor people: for the naughtiness of the silver was the occasion of dearth of all things in the realm. He imputeth it to them as a great crime. He may be called a master of sedition indeed. Was not this a seditious varlet, to tell them this to their beards, to their face?[55]

In Latimer's analysis, the debasement of the silver is not only despicable in its cause, the greed of the masters of policy, but also in its effect; like Smith and others of the commonwealth party, he identifies the unprecedented inflation in prices of the midcentury as the direct consequence of the manipulation of the standard of exchange value. Reading backwards and forwards from the "pretty little shilling"—as the point of material contact between its origin and its consequences, between Biblical Jerusalem and Reformation London—Latimer is able to "espy a piece of divinity in that policy." If, as Whitney R. D. Jones has argued, it is the Henrician subsumption by the Crown of the Church—which had historically served the functions of redistributing wealth (directly, through charitable institutions, and indirectly, through its position as employer and landowner) and of coordinating the diversity of private interests—that prompts commonwealth writers to enjoin a new prerogative and obligation of social policy upon the king, Latimer here employs the object of the coin to reassert a Reformed position for the clergy to intervene in that policy: not from within, as a prince of the Church now fully coopted in the administration of the Crown (for Latimer cites his removal from the diocese of Worcester before embarking on this rebuke), but from without, as a prophetic voice crying out against abuse from the wilderness.

Like any sin, debasement was as damaging to the practitioner as to those around him. Although each single iteration of debasement yielded a massive windfall, debasement could not be a continuous source of revenue to the Crown. Inflating the coinage meant devaluing pure silver; devaluing the domestic silver price made it more lucrative to sell silver on the international market. Thus the Crown's policy, which depended on the continual reconsumption of precious metal by the Mint, was effectively driving that metal entirely out of the Mint's reach, as the Doctor in the *Discourse* details and as Thomas Gresham would recognize.[56] Meanwhile, coined English silver and even gold were no longer acceptable in international transactions: the public credit of Edward's stamp had collapsed abroad, even as it was being challenged at home.[57] Latimer's warnings proved accurate. The end of the Crown's long debauchery of the coinage left England with a substantial hangover, one borne most by the poorest citizens. A new, finer silver coinage was introduced by Northumberland in the summer of 1551, and the old coins were summarily called down, first to nine pence on the shilling and shortly thereafter to six, leaving anyone holding wealth in silver coin with half as much money in October as in April. Despite the devaluation of the base coinage, domestic prices continued rapidly to rise; the citizenry, many of whom lived on wages that had been fixed by statute sometime before the turn of the century, was now simply twice as vulnerable to the effects of inflation.

As Harrison notes, although fine coinage was issued both in the last years of Edward's reign and throughout Mary's, no substantive efforts were made to reform the circulating medium as a whole until the first years of the Elizabethan regime, when redressing the coinage became a central plank of policy.[58] The new coinage began production in 1561. Silver was drawn into the Mint by new laws on the domestic front that declared that all old silver coins were shortly to be no longer current, so that they must be returned to the Mint for recoinage; and by the efforts of Thomas Gresham, the Queen's factor at Antwerp, who, by misrepresenting the strength of the same English currency he was there to shore up, was able to manipulate £75,000 of silver out of the exchange and smuggle it across the North Sea. "This thing is only kept up by art and God's providence," declared Gresham of his machinations.[59] Even this casual reference to the workings of providence is of a piece with the inflection of mint policy by sacred history: the very unscrupulousness of Gresham's "art" is preserved from detection in its service of divine purpose.

The recoinage was complete by September 1562. It had been a massive undertaking, and a dose of bitter medicine. "People at large had lost nearly two-thirds of the amounts for which the coin had been originally issued," though much of that loss had already been determined in the prior reigns. "Two hundred tons of dross . . . were used to build up the roads in and about the Tower."[60] The new, reformed coin was now nearly ubiquitous, and a principal attribute of Elizabeth's brand of governance. What mattered most about sterling to the formulae of Elizabethan rule was not that the standard was silver per se—as if silver itself had a value that was not only intrinsic but essential, imposed by some supernatural fiat from outside the world of exchange—but that it was pure and that it was old. The consequences of debasement were material ones, hardship and inflation, that proceeded from the most basely material motives of avarice in high places; it is within that material context of cause and effect that Latimer speaks through Isaiah to "espy a piece of divinity in that policy," without claiming to perceive a divinity within the silver. The pernicious innovation of debasement was a falling off from the old standards of Mint practice, which corresponded to the more general falling off from the standards of mutually enriching behavior that "commonwealths-men" imagined to have characterized the recent past. But debasement is useful to Latimer precisely because it demonstrates the importance of standards, of measurement, of tradition, of restraint, and of rule, not the importance of silver itself. To solve present problems by a return to the right, old ways is the perpetual call of the prophets to Israel, and as such the reformation of sterling converges with the Protestant agenda of (to repeat the words of the epitaph) *Religione ad primaevam sinceritatem restaurata*.

The iconography of Elizabeth's coinage works to make manifest the integration of purity and authority in her new regime's policy, as characterizing alike the monarch and her sterling. Let's take as exemplary a sixpence from my collection, minted in 1562, at the end of the great recoinage (fig. 4; I've reproduced a specimen of the same issue from the British Museum, which shows detail that has worn away on my own coin).[61] This coin is comparable in circumference to an American quarter; people handling it often joke that I might get it mixed up in my pocket and put it into a vending machine. But it is much thinner and lighter than modern coins, since it is more than 90% silver by weight, and a sixpence's worth of silver was not very massive. Both its light heft and the narrow sharpness of its edge are surprising to our palms and fingers; its thinness invites a bit of at-first-hesitant pressure between forefinger and thumb, to see if it will flex like a playing card. (It won't.) In its making, the sixpence is a material conjunction, silver and base alloy, themselves joined to

Figure 4: 1562 Elizabeth sixpence, milled issue: face and reverse © Trustees of the British Museum

a signifying pairing of words and portrait. The deficit between its mineral value and its exchange or "face" value is supplied by the stamp that constitutes its face and reverse. The stamp defines its own edge by a serrated ring, thereby preventing clipping; within that ring reads the clockwise legend

ELIZABETH.D.G.ANG.FRA.ET HIB.REGINA*

which we may expand by a knowledge of conventional numismatic abbreviations and of Latin into "Elizabeth, by the grace of God Queen of England, France, and Ireland." Inside that circle of words is the delicately worked profile bust of the crowned Elizabeth, facing left—her right—with her left shoulder open to a degree toward the viewer. The bridge of her nose meets her high forehead with no indentation under the brow. Her hair flows loose from the crown and the pearled headdress that circles her face, down over her shoulders in finely drawn locks; her shoulders and chest are tightly defined by a dress whose dense decoration implies a heavy brocade, although the patterns depicted on it are conventionalized floral motifs. Her neck is shown in its full length by a high, tight collar in a quincunx pattern, topped by a narrow ruff. Elizabeth's personal purity, as unmarried virgin, is celebrated on this newly pure portrait sterling. Where the coins struck during Mary's bachelorhood (1553–1554) delineate the Queen's hair simply, and the coins from her marriage to Philip portray its veil with a converse ostentation (figs. 5 and 6), Elizabeth's new coinage luxuriates in the long maidenly waves of the Queen's hair—and in their conjunction with the closed arches and studded jewels of an imperial crown.[62] The monarch's status as unmarried woman—a liability to Mary, which she succeeded in rectifying as promptly as possible—is already, on this early coin, Elizabeth's most manifest iconographic asset. Elizabeth was twenty-nine years old when this coin was issued and had been Queen for four of those years; her youth and beauty are on display in this image, in its emphasis on her slim and elongated figure and long free hair, and the elaborate state crown at once contrasts compellingly with the equally but oppositely detailed cascade of hair and fits firmly atop it. Elizabeth's femininity and her power converge as a paradox of elegance in this slender piece of sterling, and in thousands more like it.

Figure 5: 1553 Mary groat: face and reverse © Trustees of the British Museum

Figure 6: 1554 Philip and Mary shilling: face © Trustees of the British Museum

Their combination is formulated differently on the reverse: here, a shield shape holds most of the field, charged with the quartered arms of England and France, three lions couchant and three fleurs-de-lis. The date, 1562, rests atop the arms, and out of the lines that quarter the shield emerge four leafy flourishes that divide the rest of the coin's circle, including the inscription, into four arcs; this is how this coin expresses the "cross" that marked all English coin issues, and which appears so frequently as a synecdoche for coinage in Renaissance slang. The motto of the reverse reads

POSUI DEUM A.DIUTOREM.MEUM

"I have placed God as my helper," a paraphrase of Ps. 54:4 that had appeared on English coins since the reign of Edward III. The reverse manifests Elizabeth's person not as a charismatic individual, as does the mimetic portrait of the coin's face, but as the heir of a continuous sequence of English sovereigns reaching back, through their rights to the royal arms, to the Norman conquest.[63]

The recoinage was a great success, ideologically. It accomplished a literally massive intervention of policy upon the commonwealth's behalf, one that the Edwardian and Marian regimes had found impossible even to contemplate achieving. It defined both the ascendancy and the surprising effectiveness of the commonwealth reformers, in the person of such men as Cecil, Gresham, and Smith, while at the same time formulating that policy as an iconographic manifestation of the virginal majesty of Elizabeth throughout the circulating medium. But the recoinage still did not have the economic effect for which its proponents among the commonwealths-men had hoped: it did not succeed in halting inflation, much less in bringing prices back down to the levels of the 1530s before the debasement began.[64] The *Discourse of the Commonweal* was brought into print in 1581, as if to demonstrate that the problems that it was written a generation earlier to address continued to bedevil the commonwealth. The only major revisions in that edition were made to the passages that I have here discussed, concerning the debasement and its consequences.[65] In this version, the Doctor continues to ascribe the initial price rise to the debasement, but argues (following a theory recently advanced in French by Jean Bodin) that the inflation is sustained in the present by

> the great store and plenty of treasure which is walking in these parts of the world, far more in these our days than ever our forefathers have seen in times past. Who does not understand of the infinite sums of gold and silver which are

gathered from the Indies and other countries, and so yearly transported unto these coasts?[66]

"Dearth," only newly recognized as a problem of national policy in the 1549 manuscript, has already by 1581 passed out of the commonwealth's power to control.[67] It is morally and politically incumbent upon the prince to maintain the best money for the commonwealth's use, as the Doctor continues to insist in this revised edition, but even the best money has evidently failed to maintain the integrity of value, as realized in prices. The pain of inflation persists, resisting the material rectitude of sterling. Mammon is himself a far-fetched stranger, perpetually making himself at home upon "these coasts"; the island commonwealth of England cannot so readily domesticate or circumscribe him.

## III. COINS AMONG THINGS

As Lorna Hutson has demonstrated, the analyses of common weal generated in the moment of debasement shaped what she calls "the profitable discourse of the Elizabethans," an ethical and political orthodoxy, for decades to follow.[68] Many of Elizabeth's principal ministers, including Smith and William Cecil, were themselves veterans of the Edwardian commonwealth party. But that discourse was more successful as an ideology, in generating the conditions of its own self-sustaining coherence, than it was in accounting for the material conditions that it had arisen in order to address, as the 1581 revisions to the *Discourse* demonstrate. The epistemological pressure put on sixteenth-century coins by the crisis of inflation had consequences that exceeded the scope of this political discourse, as well as material circumstances that eluded it. In the seventeenth century a new discourse, that of "political economy," would emerge to address those circumstances and consequences in a disciplined way, demarcating them as a particular kind of object that demanded a specialized subset of analytical strategies within the larger rubric of political problems.[69] By the twentieth century "the economy" had become a discursive totality of its own rather than a particular instance of political relations, and the science of "economics" renamed itself accordingly. But before the emergence of political economy from the controversies among the "mercantilist" writers of the early seventeenth century, the kinds of problems that we would be inclined to call economic were as yet undisciplined.[70] When questions of spending, saving, credit, and price were theorized on a large scale, they were articulated as "commonwealth matters," alongside such questions of domestic policy as the religious settlement and the keeping of the King's peace, which we would consider extraneous to the theory and policy of economics, however porous economic choice may still be to such factors in practice.

The term "economy"—or, as Elizabethans usually spelled it, "oeconomie"—instead retained for the Renaissance its Greek meaning, that of the management of a household. Sited in the intimate and human-scaled venue of domestic relations, the Renaissance's discourse of oeconomie was as concerned with the management of subjects—wife, husband, servants, children—as with the management of objects, as such critics as Frances Dolan, Natasha Korda, Lena Cowen Orlin, and Wendy Wall have demonstrated.[71] The people and the things that together constituted the household were mutually implicated in an intimate discipline, one that coordinated the values of ethics and of thrift—and one that tended to single out coins from among the household's effects as instances of failed discipline.[72] Although the nostalgic ideal of a self-sustaining agrarian household that did not depend on the market to meet any of its needs was an impossible one for even the most isolated farmstead to maintain, household manuals such as Thomas Tusser's *Fiue Hundred Pointes of Good Husbandrie* still identified thrift with a self-sufficiency that strove to avoid monetary transactions:

> Wife make thine own candle,
> Spare pennie to handle. . . .
> If pennie for all thing be suffred to trudge,
> trust long, not to pennie, to haue him thy drudge.[73]

Tusser's doggerel elides the articles due to "pennie"—partly for the sake of keeping time, but also with the synechdochic effect of collectivizing and thereby personifying the wife's store of cash as "pennie," which Tusser elaborates in the last quoted line. Pennie presents itself to Tusser's housewife as a labor-saving device that would seem to "make" a candle for her, but that displaced labor does not disappear. Rather, pennie becomes himself a servant laboring in the wife's household, one that "trudges" out to fetch things and bring them back into the house, but who will prove untrustworthy (i.e., run away) if very much is asked of him in this menial vein. Pennie's inability to replenish "his" own capacity for labor makes him ethically (i.e., in his ethos, or personal disposition) inferior to his human fellow-servants—unreliable, heedless of indenture, sullenly resentful of the drudgery from which he is inclined to escape.

That ethical judgment upon the unprofitable servant, "pennie," is directed through the personification onto the housewife who makes too much use of her cash. As Craig Muldrew has demonstrated, there were powerful social imperatives in early modern England for the establishment and continual reinforcement of "credit" among neighbors. The senses of "credit" as fiduciary reliability and as social standing were inextricable in the early modern credit system, which promoted a sense of mutual indebtedness within communities that Muldrew calls "the economy of obligation."[74] The laboriously crafted trustworthiness of an individual householder entailed the expectation that cash could be provided on demand, but the system worked to avoid frequent cash payments in practice; instead, individuals with ongoing business relationships would periodically reckon their mutual debts, and only the difference, if that, would ever change hands as money. The social value of "obligation" generated in the preference of credit transactions to cash ones dovetailed with material constraints; even before the development of monetarized credit instruments, there was far more credit circulating locally in England than there was silver or gold, and the shortage of cash was most acute in the smallest denominations.[75] "Pennie" was for all of these reasons an instrument of last resort in the ethically charged discourses of credit and thrift, to be put to work only when neither credit nor one's own hands could complete the task.

For early modern imaginations as much as for our own, cash represents exchange, synecdochically speaking. But cash transactions are not representative of early modern exchange practices. Instead, they are a limited and, ideally, infrequent subset of exchange practices. Through the credit system, a normative relation between exchange and ethos is made quite explicit, raising the question of whether the somewhat exceptional circumstances of cash transactions are also exceptional in ethical terms.[76] The untrustworthy delinquency of Tusser's penny arises in the moralized tension between spending and saving a resource that cannot renew itself; but the possibility of a penny that could renew itself, by means of monetary interest, was met with an even more implacable hostility on the part of moralists, who cited the combined authorities of Aristotle and Deuteronomy to rebuke the expanding practices of usury. This orthodoxy maintained that, as it was impossible in nature for metal to reproduce itself (as livestock and crops do), it was obscene for the moneylender's artifice to make a coin do so.[77] But the burgeoning demand for monetarized, interest-bearing credit instruments to manage risk wore down the force of these arguments in early modernity. As Lawrence Stone has demonstrated, the relaxation and reformation of strictures against moneylending in the sixteenth and seventeenth centuries would prove central to the foundation of a modern economy in England; as more recent critics have gone on to show, these processes entailed a scandalous and hotly contested transformation of value relations in English culture.[78]

Nevertheless, despite the historical importance of both these questions, neither credit nor usury is directly a subject of this book, which insists on cash up front. I am concerned here with the discursive effects of the presence or absence of coin, in preference to the effects of the deferral of cash into the present absence of debt and interest. The individual manifestations of the problematics of value within coins as they stem from the crisis of inflation and debasement seem to me distinct from those of moneylending, depending as they do on material, centrifugal conundrums within the object rather than on the nominal relation expressed in the usury debates between a transgressively proliferative debt and a materiality there construed as normative, unitary, and self-contained. What my analysis does share with those of many critics who study questions of credit and usury is a close attention to how these different Renaissance debates over the nature of value manifest the category of scandal: the point at which the epistemically alien begins to become thinkable, under the familiar guise of the morally outrageous. I understand the emergence of scandal within normative discourses of value—such as those inhabited by the didactic texts promulgating "commonwealth," which include ontology, ethics, and politics—to represent a venue for the opportunistic discourse of poetics to engage those normative discourses on terms other than their own. This is the opportunity seized by my writers, as they give a scandalous voice to Mammon.

By characterizing the texts I study as opportunistic in their relation to other contemporary discourses, rather than inhabiting a discursive field properly their own, and by characterizing them as together participating in "poetics" rather than in "literature," I imply that, like "economy," "literature" too is a category that emerges from the intellectual moment of the Renaissance, not a category fully articulated within that moment. The discursive differentiation that will give rise to modern disciplinarity is a hallmark of the place of the Renaissance in current accounts of intellectual history.[79] This is the sense in which the humanities have come to describe the spatiotemporal trajectory of humanism and its countercurrents, from the fourteenth century of Petrarch and Boccaccio in the south to the seventeenth century of Descartes, Milton, and Hobbes in the north, as "early modernity": the dialectic between syncretism and specialization developed in the Renaissance study of "letters" provides the foundation for a ramifying model of knowledge production through method that, in the centuries to come, will fit the disciplinary means of producing a knowledge more and more specifically to the object of that knowledge, and define each such object more and more narrowly in relation to its disciplinary means.[80] The sometimes antithetical, sometimes complementary, sometimes mutually parasitic relations of "literature" to the disciplines of material knowledge—history, economics, science—in the development of modern disciplinarity have been richly productive as a subject for recent criticism, and critics of the later sixteenth and seventeenth centuries in England have rightly claimed a privileged position in assessing that development, being in, as they are, at the ground floor with respect to both political economy (from the mercantilists to Petty and Locke) and natural science (from Bacon to the founding of the Royal Society to Newton).[81] The writers whom I study in this book, however, would understand themselves neither as analysts of the economic marketplace nor as producers of "literature" as an aesthetic sphere antagonistic to that of the marketplace. They would know themselves as "poets," in the sense in which Sidney's *Defense* includes imaginative writing in either verse or prose as "poesy"; but, as Sidney makes clear, his poet's role is to mediate particular and otherwise contrary forms of knowledge into a continuous and capacious discourse that, in creating "in effect another Nature," can wholly account for the present world in its own idealist unity.[82] The inability of the analysis of "commonwealth" to account for the phenomena that would eventually come to be known as "economic" demanded the eventual development of a discourse, political economy, that could analyze them exclusively. But before such a specialized solution arose, the failures of "commonwealth" were available to a discourse of holistic solutions: that of sixteenth-century poesy.

The historical theorization of the Renaissance as the point of emergence of the conditions of modernity goes back to Jacob Burckhardt's monumental 1860 study, *The Civilization of the Renaissance in Italy*. In it, Burckhardt presented the ramifying discursive differentiations of modern thought as proceeding from an originary fissure of the newly modern individual from the material and social fabric into which (he asserted) medieval man's self-conception had wholly been woven:

> In the Middle Ages both sides of human consciousness—that which was turned within as that which was turned without—lay dreaming or half awake beneath a common veil. . . . Man was conscious of himself only as a member of a race, people, party, family, or corporation—only through some general category. In Italy this veil first melted into air; an *objective* treatment and consideration of the State and of all the things of this world became possible. The *subjective* side

> at the same time asserted itself with corresponding emphasis; man became a spiritual *individual*, and recognized himself as such.[83]

From this schism, declared Burckhardt, emerged both the subject and the object as mutually constitutive (the object as indeed marginally prior), and from the fundamental dichotomy of subject and object proceeded all of the bifurcated branchings that delineate the family tree of modern, disciplinary thought.[84]

"Object" here encompasses not only material things but abstract totalities such as "the state" imagined, from the perspective of the subject, as if they were material things, discrete, detached from the subject, and self-contained—abstractions that have, in Lukacs's coinage, been reified.[85] The history of reification has sustained Burckhardt's Renaissance subject and his objects as central terms for the materialist analysis of early modernity for the century and a half since their first publication, even as the historicity of his claims about the emergence of subjectivity has been variously qualified or repudiated. Yet, as Richard Halpern demonstrates, even within the rigorous teleology of the Marxist science of history, "early modernity" itself makes for an awkward fit with the material conditions of the English sixteenth century. Although the degeneration of the feudal mode of production and the development of the capitalist mode of production are both open to direct Marxist analysis, the transition between the two has, he argues, remained opaque as an object for the theory:

> The shift to a genealogical mode of analysis in both Marx and Poulantzas [the author of *Political Power and Social Classes*, London 1978] signals the difficulty of fully theorizing a transitional process, if by this one means arguing for its theoretical ineluctability. Yet to have "succeeded" in such a project would have been to impose an iron grid of necessity on history. The determinism for which Marxism can legitimately argue is more modest; it agrees with the etymological sense of the word as a limit on the field of the possible rather than an irresistible compulsion in any one direction. The presence of a genealogical discourse within a narrative of transition is not a mere failure to achieve theoretical closure or completeness, then, but the sign of a certain lack within theory when it confronts the concrete of history.[86]

To redress this unaccountability, Halpern revives the category of "primitive accumulation" from the end of the first volume of *Capital*, as an ephemeral moment that is not exactly part of the history of capital but upon which that history depends. Halpern argues for a negative or retrograde cycle of historical process in the English sixteenth century, one that demolishes the vestiges of feudalism while erecting nothing permanent or progressive—nothing, that is, familiarly protocapitalist—in its place.

Halpern's location of a resistance to "early modernity" in the materialist analysis of sixteenth-century English literature and culture has been replicated by a variety of scholars whose attentions have focused on the status of particular material things. In an influential essay, Margreta de Grazia turns from Burckhardt's account of the subject discovering itself in objectivity to an "anti-early-modern," and finds in *King Lear* a relation of people to things that, she argues, predates but does not prefigure the modern relation of subject to object. Speaking from the perspective of science studies, Bruno Latour announces, exuberantly, that "we have never been modern": that the subject-object distinction is not only a heuristic construction but has always been an evident fiction, one that the West has for some time been using to think but that no one has ever genuinely believed (and that has, Latour goes on to argue, by now outlived its usefulness).[87] Since these complementary positions were staked out, a powerful body of criticism has developed to ascribe a inassimilability to modern objecthood (as well as to objectivity as its corollary) in the thought of the past, in things, and most of all in the things of the past.

This body of scholarship, which draws its methods across the intersections of anthropology, art history, literary history, and the history of science, has mostly been known in literary-critical circles as "material culture" (a phrase originating in anthropology), though Bill Brown has jauntily rechristened it as "thing theory."[88] A benchmark for its propagation across the disciplines was Arjun Appadurai's edited collection *The Social Life of Things* (1986), and its position in Renaissance studies was cemented by de Grazia's *Lear* essay and the essays accompanying it in the collection *Subject and Object in Renaissance Culture* (1996). In rejecting the object-subject divide—and the corollary category of methodological "objectivity" that depends upon that divide—in order to discuss the "thing," this criticism willfully engages the scandal of fetishism, the failure (from modernity's point of view) to distinguish the vacuity of objects from the meaningfulness of subjects. Appadurai cites his techniques as performing a "methodological fetishism," while Ann Rosalind Jones and Peter Stallybrass have explicitly engaged the emergence of "fetish" as a protoanthropological category in early modern trade with Africa.[89]

This criticism of things thus works a great deal of the time by affirming negations and antitheses—by finding sites of resistance to the normative relations subjects expect of their objects and postulating a positive thingliness therein. Heidegger argues that such a positive thingliness manifests itself to us as a truculent perversity on the thing's part, whereby it excepts itself from the "handy" instrumentality through which we arrange our worlds around ourselves: the seeming eruption of the pavement to interrupt my gait as I trip, the hammer that contrives to strike my thumb and not the tack.

> [W]hen something is unusable for some purpose.... [t]he context of equipment [*Zeug*] is lit up, not as something never seen before, but as a totality constantly sighted beforehand in circumspection [i.e., in the wariness of equipment's prospective failure]. With this totality, however, the world announces itself.[90]

The inevitable egotism that would order the phenomenal world into a universal prosthesis is disrupted from moment to moment by the errancy of things-in-themselves, as Julian Yates argues in his aptly titled study, *Error Misuse Failure: Object Lessons from the English Renaissance*. For Peter Schwenger, the disruptions of thingliness within phenomenology are necessarily and foundationally recouped by a kind of sacrificial violence, "the murder of the thing" by language.[91] The adversarial formulae of this criticism do not, however, necessarily assert that the relationship between people and the thing in question is an adversarial one; in *The Botany of Desire*, Michael Pollan speaks, thinks, and understands as a plant in order to give voice to otherwise silent, seductive partners in the symbiotic relationship of domestication.[92] For Latour, the need to give voice to a thing is actually a token of failure. In Latour's novelistic case study of the experimental transit technology called Aramis, Aramis itself speaks in order to chastise the human and institutional actors who have failed to realize it, for the mode of participation in the world that Aramis desires is not that of speech; rather, Aramis wants to be so perfectly realized and integrated into the Parisian transit network as to be entirely taken for granted by its users—to be unremarkable.[93]

Handiness and participation are crucial terms for understanding the thing across these differing perspectives, though Schwenger's "melancholy" and Latour's optimism place inverse values upon them. For Latour, the fact that a thing does not participate in the social world in the way that humans participate—by speech—does not mean that it is not actively participating in a way proper to itself, and the ethical relation that must obtain between human and nonhuman actors is that of "love," not of sacrifice. But neither love nor sacrifice seems like an appropriate ethical relation to the handiest and most participatory of all our things—cash. The readiness of money to participate in our networks (in Latour's vocabulary), its promptness to hand, has seemed like a tactic of seduction on the part of this nonhuman actor. Made by people to serve our purposes, money serves us in order to redefine our purposes as its own, and in so acting achieves a demonic parody of personhood, as Mammon. Latour's unloved Aramis and Schwenger's always-already-sacrificed thing are both importantly innocent in their victimization. But the very handiness of coins defines a disturbing and insidious kind of active compliance on the part of Mammon, and on the part of the object world for which Mammon has appointed himself the representative, mediating actor to our networks. Mammon's gladness to be of use entails the glib rearticulation of all other values and all other things as the same kind of thing, an exchange-value. And yet, as Tusser's contrarian, mutinous penny suggests, a coin's handiness is at the same time its aptness to escape the hand: as using and spending a coin are the same act, "pennie" makes itself indispensable to its user only in order to forsake him, and circulate once more into the networks of exchange. In this way the coin's quality as complaisant "equipment" and its quality as perverse and truculent "thing," in the Heideggerian dichotomy, are uniquely and troublingly continuous.[94]

I do not need—and I don't want—to speak for Mammon in the way that Pollan speaks for the tulip; as I've suggested, Mammon is himself the principle that money talks. One of the challenges of my project is to find a way of speaking about money that is different from what money has to say for itself. The recognition that money talks—that Mammon is a demon of discourse—is not itself subject to historicization, at least not within the scope of the history of money. As Marc Shell has demonstrated in *The Economy of Literature,* money and the philosophy of language have been inextricable since their approximately simultaneous inventions, in the preclassical Aegean. For Shell, the history of that relation is one in which Mammon grows ever chattier over time, as semiotics comes more and more fully to recognize the discursive character of money and the monetary character of discourse, as different facets of a totality of signification-as-exchange. "Between the electrum money of ancient Lydia and the electric money of contemporary America there occurred a historically momentous change," writes Shell in the first sentence of *Money, Language, and Thought.*[95] This change is the progressive divorcing of money's character as sign from its originary materiality, as a lump of metal. Shell differentiates "money itself" from the material objects which are its "tokens."[96] In Shell's account, the deracination of money from the gold standard after the First World War teleologically realizes money's essentially formal, discursive character, which had been working over millennia (like Hegel's *Geist* or Marx's revolutionary "old mole") to burst forth in this moment from its golden cocoon. This chiastic convergence insists that metallic money was always a misrecognition, if an inevitable one, and that the process of history has worked to reveal the real truth of money as the money that we know. Only the material misrecognition is subject to history; the truth of semiosis is transhistorical, and had manifested itself in premodern history through flashing glimpses of transcendence, the episodic instances that make up the body of *Money, Language, and Thought*, spanning the gulf between classical "electrum" and modern "electric" moneys.

Shell's assertion that—to put it crudely—coins are and have always really been signs has attracted renewed attention, even explicit allegiance, in the self-proclaimed "New Economic Criticism" of the past decade.[97] Barbara Correll has recently rebuked both the hermeneutic circularity of Shell's teleology and the political quiescence that it implies in its assertion that the present status of money in the discourse of capitalist ideology is, in one sense, the way things have always really been, and in another sense the way things have always been supposed to become.[98] Correll rejects the ascription of either materialism or historicism to Shell's analyses, which she argues are essentially idealist and structuralist. She suggests that critics interested in the interrelation of coin and sign instead look to the explicitly revolutionary analyses of Jean-Joseph Goux, who points to the formal identity of money with other oppressive signifying structures, such as the Lacanian phallus.

> [W]hen the New Economic Criticism tries to silence hard questions of power and signification and reduces its terrain to one of historicist orthodoxy it fleeces the political and robs us by concealing critique.... [T]he movement that characterizes [Shell's] work, ingenious and brilliant though it can be, is toward delineating a complete anastructure with no residual indeterminacy or social critique. The difference between Shell and Goux is not a matter of historicism [on Shell's part] but rather a difference between Shell's structural functionalism—always, in the end, a kind of restrictive formalism or systematicity—and a more politically invested post-structuralism that does not lose sight of the relations between signifying practices and social relations, or between structures of power and manifestations of resistance.[99]

John Guillory reacts to the debut of the new economic criticism with a similar wariness:

> As the state of social theory now stands, the hypothesis of society as a "unified field" is powerfully attractive in either of the two mutually exclusive forms this

hypothesis takes. On the one hand, the social world can be unified by reducing it to the "material," of which the economic is certain to be the privileged instance. On the other hand, the social world can be unified by reducing it to the "symbolic" or even the "linguistic," of which the cultural is just as surely to be the privileged instance. In the latter case the problem of the "merely metaphoric" instance of capital disappears in the recognition that all capital, economic capital included, is metaphoric, because social being is simply and utterly constituted by language, as an infinitely fungible stock of signifiers. It should be obvious that the temptation to resolve the theoretical problem of social differentiation in favor of the latter proposition is the greatest risk for literary critics who have discovered the economic as a new subject for criticism.[100]

Guillory's prescription to evade the arid tautology of an intrasymbolic structure is to trace the forms imposed upon discourse by its own attempt to incorporate the world of matter: "symbolization is what it is because it is resisted by the material."[101] For both critics, the totalization of a notion of economy as the governing trope of all sixteenth-century texts is immediately tantalizing, but finally circular. What is meaningful is not the hegemonic master-system but chthonic "manifestations of resistance" to such a discursive totality, which deform its political and material registers of abjection and of objectification. As Christopher Pye too has argued, in response to Stephen Greenblatt's *Shakespearean Negotiations,*

> The effectiveness of New Historicism's cultural—or economic—poetics... depends both on the residual empirical aura that clings to such economic language, and, as importantly, on economy's distinctive ability to dissimulate its status as a system.[102]

As I will demonstrate in the chapters that follow, money is not everything in sixteenth-century England. Rather, money is one particular system that presents itself, deceptively, as a universal system. A modern critic who ascribes universality to "economy"—however much he may proceed to condemn that universality—is someone who has been tricked by Mammon into speaking with Mammon's own voice.

I'm offering the material historicity of Renaissance coins as a way of speaking otherwise of Mammon than he would speak for himself. That is, I hope to give the lie to money's universalizing tendencies, its dissemblance of its "status as a system," by pointing to the distinctness of a material form inhabited by money at a particular moment and to the particularities of the social constructions in which that form participates, to the ways in which "the resistance of the material" makes "the symbolic... what it is" in the Renaissance. Historicity, in my argument, offers a boundedness through which we may understand "the economic" not as a transhistorical totality but as a discursive category that came into existence at a particular moment for particular reasons to describe the trajectories of particular objects. Understanding how those objects, and their "social life" (as Appadurai would put it), were discussed before the advent of political economy can help us to imagine the boundedness of Mammon in other historical moments, perhaps including our own.

I draw the means of imposing such a boundedness on Mammon from the rigorous focus upon individual objects that characterizes the "material culture" and "thing theory" of the past decade, as I've discussed above. There are two important ways in which that critical mode may seem to have an ironic or perverse relation to my project, however, rather than a transparently instrumental one. The first is that the special, individuated way of being that critics such as Jones and Stallybrass assert in Renaissance thingliness is frequently expressed as a kind of value that escapes capitalist understandings of exchange. This value arises in a history of making, of use, and of identity formation, and cannot be incorporated in the kind of value imposed by the capitalist commodity form. And the things that express that value express it as an explicit opposition to money:

> [I]n the livery economy of Renaissance Europe, things took on a life of their own. That is to say, one was paid not only in the "neutral" currency of money but also in material that was richly absorbent of symbolic meaning and in which memories and social relations were literally embodied.[103]

Currency, per Jones and Stallybrass, is the thing whose life is not a life of its own: disembodied with respect to "social relations," metallically impermeable to the meanings that textiles soak up as they lie on the surface of the body. Here currency is the same in early modernity as it is in present modernity, "neutral" with respect to historical difference; its life in either moment is that of a familiarly untrammeled instrumentality, with no prospect of the animate autonomy achieved by such things as clothes. In applying the critical tools that aim to differentiate Renaissance "things" from early modern "commodities" and/or "objects" to the very kind of thing from which those other things are being differentiated—coins, which are not handcrafted but mass-produced, not individuated but at least minimally interchangeable, not reservoirs of a value antithetical to exchange but reservoirs of exchange value, not worn on the body but either stored or spent—certainly I risk turning these methods in on themselves, into a merely circular impasse. But my hope instead is to give new directions to those means: to analyze what relations to the human body are proper to a coin (including that of instrumentality), what can in fact be said about a coin's antithetical relation to memorial narrative, and what social relations are "embodied" in its material form.

The second objection is one that has been voiced by critics who note with dismay the chiastic transposition of activist "cultural materialism" into historicist "material culture" as a retrogression into the kind of political quiescence that Correll warns against within the new economic criticism. Alan Sinfield ascribes that chiasmus to the urge emerging in historicist studies toward tangibility in their objects:

> The term "materialism" entered English studies from Marxism. It was invoked in opposition to "idealism," which supposed that literary writing might transcend its conditions of production. However, the abbreviation to an epithet—"material London"—seems to be developing another nuance of the word, focusing on the thinginess of the city. That shift is surely producing valuable results, but some of the Marxian political edge may be slipping away. . . . [in the] attention to clothes, pots and pans, needles and pins, and to books and manuscripts *as objects*. They are, after all, *stuff*, they are *made of* material, let's *touch* them, you can't get more material than that.[104]

The danger that Sinfield suggests is that "material culture" cannot help but endorse, celebrate, and reenact the protocapitalist process of reification as it took place in early modern commodity culture, making good the emerging devotion to "worldly goods," however self-conscious its practitioners may be of their "methodological fetishism" and however dismayed they may be in commemorating the apparent inevitability of that process.[105] For Hugh Grady, the vector of this materialism towards an apparently objective historicism at the expense of the literary object has as its horizon "disciplinary suicide, eventual irrelevance, and a new antiquarianism."[106] On the one hand, Grady's comparison to antiquarianism carries the charge of a merely sterile fussiness, a neglect of ideas in the niggling obsession with things and of the abstract in the obsession with the concrete. On the other, it suggests that the model of comprehensiveness afforded by antiquarian taxonomy offers a delusive totality by which the sum of things may, once reckoned, account for the sum of ideas—the "key to all mythologies" that literature's most notorious antiquary, *Middlemarch*'s Dr. Casaubon, feels tantalizingly to lurk at the very limit of his methods.

It's my hope that making a coin an object within the discourse of material culture, rather than one to which the objects of the discourse are compared (for surely numismatics is the driest, most symptomatic practice of Grady's derided "antiquarianism," just as money is the thing which Stallybrass and Jones's mnemonic object is not), will help to evade or at least to contain the uncritical reproduction of reification that Sinfield and Grady see built into the discourse. A coin is not itself a good, in conventional Renaissance analyses of money, but the means by which goods are to be exchanged; and to the extent that the coin is named as Mammon, it is of course an evil. Writers who give voice to Mammon are enacting a particular kind of devil's advocacy. Particular kinds of good may come of this exercise, which motivate it; I will argue that the position of devil's advocate allows these writers to articulate the complex relations of ethical and social goods to material ones. But the exercise is always and necessarily an ironic one. Irony is the tool by which it works. In confronting Mammon alongside Spenser, Shakespeare, Donne, and Nashe, we are a far cry from the uncritical reification of ethics into materialism in modern capitalism, "the elixir which exchanged the things worth being for the things worth having."[107] Here, instead, the having of coin enables meditation upon the being of its possessor, by contemplating the being of the thing possessed.

In analyzing the *stuff* of coinage, *The Face of Mammon* participates in a turn within material-culture criticism that seeks to evade the reproduction of reification by refounding "the material" in the discourse of ontology. This was a move first suggested in influential essays by Henry S. Turner, Douglas Bruster, and Jonathan Gil Harris, and it has borne fruit in two recent monographs, Jonathan Goldberg's *The Seeds of Things* and Harris's own *Untimely Matter in the Time of Shakespeare.*[108] Goldberg and Harris both consider the legacy of Epicurean atomism to the Renaissance and to modern theory; Goldberg examines the ecstatic influence of the microscopic, universal desire celebrated as Venus in Lucretius's *De rerum natura,* while Harris considers the multitemporal qualities of matters both textual and thingly in the terms of Michel Serres, Epicurus's most prominent contemporary interpreter.[109] I largely follow Turner, however, in considering the normative models of ontology in sixteenth-century England to be those of Aristotelian scholasticism: the binary relations of matter to form, substance to accident, and cause to effect.[110] Epicurean atomism appears in my argument as a particular instance of devil's advocacy, an account of matter as merely contingent and therefore diabolically "resistant," as Guillory would put it, to Aristotelian and providential articulations of causality. What my analyses do share with Goldberg's and Harris's, however, is an attention to how the categories of ontology—the discursive preconditions of worldly existence—recur upon and work to shape the literary articulation of life as it is lived within the everyday human world: how knowledge of the social is mediated by the terms by which the material may be known.

* * *

As *The Face of Mammon* moves back and forth across the registers of material ontology, individual ethics, and hierarchical politics, I trace in each of these registers the diversity of relations into which the coin and the human body implicate each other—from that of consumption, to that of instrumentality, to that of reproduction, to the negative relations of disavowal and of evacuation—each of which, I argue, is shaped by the relation of intrinsic, material value to extrinsic, conventional value as they are yoked within the coin. In the chapters that follow, I examine how some of the major literary figures of the sixteenth century's end continued to confront and to redefine the crisis of material value that emerged in the midcentury moment of debasement. Between the 1560s, when Queen Elizabeth restored the sterling standard to stabilize the coinage, and the emergence in the early seventeenth century of new analyses of money among the theorists of mercantilism, there were few developments in English fiscal theory. The reformist arguments of the commonwealths-men had become a new political and financial orthodoxy. But that orthodoxy, and the proudly reformed sterling that manifested it, proved still unable to check—or even to account for—the persistence of inflation, as value ever more visibly uncoupled itself from standards of material purity. In the last decade of the sixteenth century, it is literary writing that takes up the challenge posed by material conditions to the social ideals of the commonwealth, developing subtle and far-reaching analyses of the relations of coins to human bodies and to the body politic. My argument first considers how coins and bodies may be construed as ethically contrary instances of incorporation, in the first edition of Spenser's *Faerie Queene*, and how the introduction of political considerations in the poem's second edition demonstrates the shortcomings of such an opposition. I move from there to show how, in three plays of Shakespeare, the forces of sovereignty and commonwealth treat bodies *as* coins, with wildly differing results. And I conclude by reading prodigal fictions of Thomas Nashe and John Donne, who define their witty protagonists' bodies through the lack of a single coin.

The texts I study in these chapters appeared within fourteen years of one another, and I construe them as together representing a basically synchronic pattern within a particular historical moment—that of the end of the sixteenth century, when the commonwealth discourse had calcified to articulate not reform, but the status quo, and before the rise of the protodisciplinary analyses of the mercantilists (though I engage individual reactions and revisions where one text responds to another recent publication in the intellectual ferment of the moment). The sequence of my argument is therefore not that of a diachronic progression among the texts but that of a conceptual development on my own part, in which each new rubric is introduced as a complication of concepts established in previous chapters. The argument begins with relations that presuppose the presence of coined money—consumption, instrumentality, reproduction—and moves toward those that articulate negation and abstraction, as disavowal and waste, in which the texts' relation to the materiality of money becomes ever more tenuous and antithetical without being any less ineluctable. My afterword returns to reanimate questions of historical process in the light of these material relations, by considering the epistemic break that separates the commonwealth ideal so troubled by my authors from the concept of economy that, in the seventeenth century, emerges to replace it.

In the first part of my chapter 1, I frame the confrontation in Book Two of *The Faerie Queene* between Spenser's Sir Guyon and the demon Mammon in terms of an ethically correct consumption, in which the boundless and perverse appetite for gold is rejected in favor of a standard of bodily need that would impose itself only minimally upon the will. For Guyon, the composite value forged in the coin becomes delusive and devaluing; materiality itself comes to seem to Guyon a compromising debasement of what he most values. Spenser's Mammon transposes means and ends, "feeding" the knight's eyes with gold rather than using gold to buy bread; in so doing, Mammon reverses the normative relations of time and causality between the knight and the world around him. Through that inversion, Mammon threatens to turn everything's meaning into money. Guyon finds the means of resistance to Mammon's hegemony in the autonomy of his own, ethically temperate body—allegorized as the House of Alma—whose relation to the world is defined not by money's totalized, anachronic circuit of desire and frustration but by his own location in the grand narrative of national history. But, as I go on to demonstrate, Christopher Marlowe doesn't buy this solution. In *The Jew of Malta*, Marlowe moves the bodily site of the confrontation between the individual and the coin from the mouth, the locus of consumption, to the hand, Aristotle's "instrument of instruments." From the point of view of instrumentalized action, it is far more difficult to distinguish the work of bodily hands from the convenient utility—the handiness—of the coin. Neither, upon reflection, does Spenser himself buy Guyon's solution. Book Five of *The Faerie Queene* revisits the differentiation of human and monetary substance with a skepticism that echoes Marlowe's. The adventures of the knight of Justice, Sir Artegall, transpose the ethical problems encountered by Guyon into the register of politics. Here Munera, the embodiment of graft, has both a human body and golden hands; her dismemberment, in the name of differentiating the stuff of money from the stuff of life, is one of the most horrific passages of the poem. In the instrumental realm of politics, the pretense of individual autonomy is as delusive, and indeed as pernicious, as Mammon's claims to material totality.

The bad example set by Mammon makes the coin a good example, in practical terms, to assert the interdependence of materiality and sociability. My second chapter continues to analyze the place of money's ambivalently ironic exemplarity in the political realm of "common wealth." Here I assess both the circulation and the manufacture of coinage in two plays of Shakespeare in terms of the reproduction of the sovereign: in the biological production of heirs, in *King John*, and in the deputizing of officers, in *Measure for Measure*. Each play disturbingly conflates generation, authorization, and minting as the relation that transmits, or fails to transmit, a continuous sovereignty across both national space and national history. *King John* occurs in a strange lapse in the providential history of the English Crown, in which the unitary majesty of the late Richard Coeur de Lion has fragmented among Richard's politic brother John, who has the crown; his helpless nephew Arthur, who has the right to the crown; and Richard's bastard son, the heir only of his heroic body. While Arthur is bought and sold many times by the play's power brokers, the Bastard celebrates his royal lineage irrespective of its illegitimacy, as if in discovering it he had been newly minted. And rather than knowing himself to be autonomously sovereign, John grounds his policy in the pursuit of the monetarized and momentary advantage that the Bastard personifies as "Commodity." John's misplaced allegiance to the Mammon-like Commodity is grounded in a demonic version of Epicurean material philosophy. John's inability to master events, his failure to shape them into a coherent history, is the result of his subjection to an account of the material world as not only atomized but emptied of causality. The world of *King John* is shaped neither by human will nor divine, but by the meaningless and arbitrary perversity according to which Commodity scatters both coins and royal seed about the world. In *Measure for Measure*, conversely, the arbitrariness of the Duke's "pleasure" masquerades as providence, the working out of divine will. But that "pleasure" manifests itself instead as the minting of Angelo as the Duke's instrument, when the Duke reproduces his authority in his deputy in order to himself disappear from the scene. An "angel" might either be God's deputy or the English monarch's coin, and Angelo's humanity is doubly effaced by these contrary impositions of his naming upon his being. Angelo bears the Duke's stamped "figure" at the play's beginning, but bears his own comeuppance in the end; it is the stamp of sovereign pleasure, not the "measure" of justice, that reproduces sovereignty upon the recalcitrant and degraded matter of these two plays in order to shape it into a social order.

In my third chapter, I follow the articulation of coined money into the negative register of disavowal, in which the material centrality of coinage to the commonwealth is acknowledged only by repudiating it. My instance is *The Merchant of Venice*: the characters of this play can't stop talking about "ducats" and "angels," but they insist at the same time that the values they articulate through these objects are themselves immaterial and unquantifiable. Portia's bounty, Antonio and Shylock's bond, and the play's comic resolution are all sustained by the pretense that none of them are about the gold and silver that so dominate the action and vocabulary of *Merchant*. The individuation of ethical and political subjects comes to depend upon this misrecognition of materiality as money's metallic otherness. This perverse work is epitomized, I ague, in the disjunction of a coin's metallic substance from its stamped image, as it is realized among the three metal caskets that together conceal Portia's image. The gold and silver caskets exist not as themselves, but in order that they may be displaced into the lead casket holding "fair Portia's counterfeit." So too does the ubiquitous and complex materiality of the coin underwrite its own disavowal, disingenuously privileging the immaterial values that the Venetians and Belmontese all must profess, if not follow, in order to live together in their common wealth.

The face of a Renaissance coin gathers together values both positive and negative, material and immaterial, into a unitary and putatively stable exchange value. In this coin's tight circle, the atomizing force of individual desire strives against the socializing institutions of the common wealth. My final chapter shows how the prose of Thomas Nashe and the elegies of John Donne work to realize the disruptive possibilities embedded in the coin's matrix of contending values. Both these writers define their anarchic wit in material terms, and each does so by inverting the material relations that join coin to commonwealth into the negative relationship of waste. Nashe is fascinated by the extent to which the substance of coinage may be reduced into a minimal materiality, and thereby produces the physically evacuated and verbally profuse container who speaks as Pierce/Purse Penniless—an ironic counterpart both to the demonic plenitude of Mammon and to the troubled stamping of "angel" Angelo. Donne's metamorphic wit privileges the stuff of gold at the expense of monetary form, and indeed of all forms, up to and including the strictures of the commonwealth and the shape of the human soul. For both writers, the lacking of money asserts a bodily remainder that contests the formulae through which the older generation of the commonwealths-men had balanced the competing claims of materiality and sociability upon coins. Gleefully exhausting these now-tired conventions through the squandering of fictional money, the prodigal wits of the 1590s set the stage for the emergence, in the protoeconomics of the mercantilists, of a Mammon who will heed no discipline but his own.

CHAPTER ONE

# At Home with Mammon

## *Matter, Money, and Memory in* The Faerie Queene *and* The Jew of Malta

Alfred Tiscani, a longtime employee of [Brooklyn scrap yard] A.R.C., said he is constantly amused by the variety of things that people bring in, displaying, for example, an ornate tin lamp that he was saving for his wife. "When I see old cars, I feel bad," he said, recalling the time someone brought in an antique B Model Mack Truck like the one his grandfather drove.

Nobody at the yard knows what happens to any of the scrap metal after it leaves the site. "Metal has no memory," Mr. Monteleone said, looking down at the pen in his hand. "It could be made into this pen tip."

—*The New York Times*, June 27, 2008[1]

Mammon has a twofold character in a Renaissance coin. On the one hand, the immediate question about a coin put to use in exchange is whether or not it will serve that use—whether or not the recipient will accept it as current.[2] But lying behind that binary evaluation of currency are a whole host of factors that have converged to make the coin suitable for this use, which persist in the coin's present embodiment of the history of its making: the relation of its extrinsic value as metal to the exchange value at which it is current, the authority of the prince who has established that currency, and the iconography according to which that authority is manifested as the coin's stamped face. In the material coin, currency coexists uneasily with historicity—with the particular details of how this coin was made at the mint, and with the fact that this coin will not be current indefinitely and the function of currency will at some point in the future move to inhabit a new monetary object and leave this one behind. The abandoned coin will still exist, unless it is melted down, but it won't be money any longer. It will be left as a numismatic object, the matter not of money but of memory.

This dichotomy in a coin's materiality, between its immediate potentiality in exchange and a mnemonic, commemorative potential that seems opposite to the trajectory of exchange, becomes in Spenser's hands a means for analyzing the ethical relation of human bodies to the material world. In confronting his ethically temperate hero, Sir Guyon, with the array of golden forms that surround the demon Mammon, Spenser cites the doctrine of Aristotelian scholasticism that materiality is a temporal phenomenon, in which the imposition of form moves rude and undifferentiated matter into actuality. But the form of currency strangely escapes such an account of proleptic, teleological shaping; Mammon comes to embody a dismally ahistorical sameness that cannot account for the value of memory embodied even in his own coins, "The antique shapes of kings and kesars straunge & rare" (2.7.5).

The method of this chapter is to examine the momentary, constantly elided difference between precious metals and money as a narrative phenomenon that converges with, and contests, the embodiment of memory. My focus is principally on *The Faerie Queene*, but I turn at the midpoint of the chapter to consider an important and sardonic response to the Mammon episode, Christopher Marlowe's *The Jew of Malta*. Through Marlowe, we can recognize that the story that Guyon tries to tell in contesting the way in which Mammon "tells"—that is, counts—his coins is reallly two stories. One is a narrative of right consumption, in which the difference between Guyon and the material worldliness of Mammon is defined in terms of continence, restriction, and nourishment. But Marlowe lays bare a counternarrative about which Guyon himself has disturbingly little to say: that of "right usaunce," in which an actor might effectively participate in the world through the instrumentality of material means (*FQ* 2.7.7).

The question that Guyon chooses to debate with Mammon is how the malleability and the fungibility of silver and gold may be circumscribed within the world of matter and sense. Guyon looks to the most remote reaches of past imagination, the Ovidian Golden Age, to remember a world without Mammon, but finds that he has only brought Mammon back with him. Mammon's currency is a temporal process, but an anachronistic one, which tells itself backwards and makes the past into the terms of Mammon's futurity. Guyon instead learns to posit the limit of money's power to transform through exchange at the human mouth; even within the paradigm of consumption put forth by Mammon, what gold can only fail to be is food, while what currency works to forget, the incommensurable "difference of things," is sustained by the "matter of iust memory."[3] The temperate self embodied in Alma's castle is nourished by memory as it is by supper. The books that Guyon and Arthur read there are objects that sustain the knights' self-definition, the antitheses of coined gold, whose fragile pages defy Mammon's perennial attempt to reduce the matter of history to the indifference of monetary exchange.

Marlowe, conversely, envisions money as both a narrative and a bodily effect, generated in the process of "telling" at the point where silver and gold meet the "fingers' ends" of the individual. Barabas's money is a material account of himself; when his gold is separated from his body, the money form yet lingers upon it, as "bare remembrance, like a soldier's scar." Enacted as narration, the process of minting takes the form of the process of memory, and the latter becomes likewise determined as a material trace upon the body. But such a memory's relation to the body is not that of nutrition but of trauma: the "maim," says Barabas, of an amputated hand, in the severance of an interaction between flesh and gold that is defined in terms not of consumption but of instrumentality. With Barabas's hand in mind, I turn again to the experience of Guyon, focusing now not on the circuit of eating, reading, and speaking between his mouth and his mind, but on the work of the knight's hands. I argue that Guyon's attention to the right kind of consumption in matter allows him to evade the question of "right usaunce," the problem of instrumental agency in matter; his success in refuting the devouring logic of Mammon risks becoming an allegiance to Mammon's prisoner, Pontius Pilate, who spends his eternity trying in vain to wash his hands of filthy matter.

In the final section of the chapter, I address the transposition of Book Two's material ethics into the material politics of Spenser's Book Five, the legend of Justice. There Sir Artegall encounters Mammon's political analogue, Munera, an embodiment of graft whose hands are gold and whose feet are silver. The secure ontological division charted in Book Two, between the nutritive stuff of flesh and the inhuman stuff of metal, has collapsed in Munera's body. The solution found by Artegall's automaton Talus is to reestablish that division as violence: he chops off both hands and feet to display them as guilty instruments. In so doing, Talus too defines the mnemonic role of money as bodily trauma, a brutal lesson we won't soon forget.

## I. ON STUFF

According to the Doctor who guides the dialogue in the 1549 *Discourse of the Commonweal,* precious metals are uniquely suited to take on the form of coinage. Leather, although likewise durable, divisible, and capable of bearing a stamp, cannot be substituted for silver and gold in the circulating medium, for, lacking the rarity that confers universal value upon the precious metals, its currency will extend only so far as the credit of the prince who has stamped it, while precious stones, although even scarcer than gold, cannot easily be divided, much less marked by authority, and their value relative to one another is impossible for anyone but an expert to determine.[4] Conversely, although silver and gold can take on a limitless variety of other forms, only when their circulation is licensed, and their weight and fineness guaranteed, by the authority of the stamp do they assume all the functions of money.

The Aristotelian sense of *materia* as a potentiality, and of change in form as a teleological motion realizing that potentiality, is most readily available to understanding in terms of the metals, which must each be liquefied into undifferentiated matter—*some* iron, silver, or tin—before they take on any of the myriad forms in which solid iron, tin, or silver might find a use, and to which they lose their identity as "stuff": now *an* iron *hoe, a* silver *coin, a* tin *cup.*[5] When in the first scene of *Measure for Measure* Angelo asserts his unevaluated interiority as a potential that may not suffice for the shape the Duke would give it, he does so in terms of this understanding of materiality, in which the stuff is prior to the form but can only be experienced as realized in the form:

> Now, good my lord,
> Let there be some more test made of my mettle
> Before so noble and so great a figure
> Be stamp'd upon it. (1.1.47–50)[6]

It's still no coincidence, however, that Angelo is talking about the stuff of his individuality as bullion to be coined, and not as, say, faulty iron that might not make a good batch of nails. The preciousness of silver and gold keeps the submergence of the identity of those substances into the use-value of the formed object forever incomplete. In his *Historicall Description of the Iland of Britaine,* William Harrison notes the replacement of "treen" utensils by tin or pewter ones in even the lowlier sixteenth-century English households, and of tin and pewter in turn by silver and gold.[7] A silver cup, like a tin cup, is more useful than a wooden one, in being more durable and easier to wash; but the different utilities of the silver cup over the tin one derive entirely from the persistent substance of silver, both directly, as a locus for the storage of value, and indirectly, as a means for the display of status. As Natasha Korda has demonstrated, there was persistent legal controversy as to whether plate was to be included with other utensils in the category of "household stuff" in wills. The jurist Henry Swinburne suggests plate and household stuff should be distinguished according to what use the testator had made of the objects in life, for "ornament" or for "ordinarie service."[8] Reasonable as Swinburne's distinction may seem, it only compounds the problem of defining the relation of precious metals to their particular forms: the referral of the distinction to past practice has to call into being a history of each object, to be articulated either privately, by the testator before setting down the will, or in court, by surviving members of the household. In order to be passed on from owner to owner, the precious object must be categorized in terms of *how* it was possessed, whether its matter or its form determined its use; in order to be categorized, the object must first be narrated.

Silver and gold in their money forms presented no such problem to probate law. Individual coins did not have a story of their use needing to be articulated, or rather they all told the same story. Coinage was the most apparently natural form for these substances, the one that fully realized their potentiality as preciousness, functioning for the circulation of value. At the same time, however, the assumption of the money form, like any realization into form, excludes the potential of the matter to assume any other of its myriad possible forms—plate, jewelry, gilding, silver thread. The stuff of silver and gold passed among a continuum of shapes in the early modern economy, appearing as cash only when it was most convenient for their owners. Coin is merely the most liquid of those possible forms, and the least directly useful. The loss of use-value in sending plate to the mint, not to mention that of the value added to the stuff by the craftsmanship of the goldsmith, kept much precious metal from achieving its apparent telos in the coin.

But this sense of "liquidity" moves my analysis away from these two materialist construals of the money form's interaction with potentiality—where the coin is a solid form and the matter of metal, figured as its molten state, is liquid potential—to the sense of "liquidity" in the market, which refers to how easily any asset may be exchanged as cash. Here wealth, not silver or gold, is the "matter" that has a multitude of forms available for its realization, even if that form is merely a notation of debt. Not even a debt approaches the pure expression of wealth as formless potential, since the contingent circumstances of the debtor limit the scope of its realization. What the potential of wealth wants to be, its oxymoronic telos of liquid form, is cash. It is in this sense that Georg Simmel has defined the money form as sheer potentiality;[9] the solid disks of silver or gold that bear the image of some particular prince constitute wealth at its most liquid, for wherever they make up the circulating medium they can be realized as anything else at all. Silver coins can become a silver cup in this sense of liquid potentiality without ever being melted down. But once the coin becomes the cup, it loses its immediate potential to be everything else, which it maintains so long as the quantum of wealth it constitutes keeps the money form. The coin is a material unit of abstract potentiality.

According to Simmel, the obsession with the physical stuff of gold that marks the conventional behavior of the miser is an attachment not to the materiality that is the formed object but to the persistence of potentiality in money.[10] It is an attempt to experience abstraction as *matter*. Cash is for the miser the stuff of indifference in the sensual world, the only matter that expresses itself without a form.[11] It is this resistance to realization in the money form, its maintenance of potentiality in the face of differentiating objecthood, that constitutes the evil of miserliness to the Renaissance. Avarice is pernicious not only to the sinner but to the world at large, for it keeps money from achieving its material telos in circulation. The hoarding of money was understood as unnatural, a perversion of the destiny inhering in the substance of precious metal for its infinitely reiterated realization in directly useful objects. These are the entirely conventional terms in which Spenser's Sir Guyon first rebukes Mammon upon meeting the demon surrounded by a golden hoard:

> What art thou man, (if man at all thou art)
> That here in desert hast thine habitaunce,
> And these rich heapes of wealth doest hide apart
> From the worldes eye, and from her right vsaunce? (2.7.7)

But, as the canto's narrative unfolds, Guyon's understanding of the "right vsaunce" of money as differentiable from Mammon's behavior shows itself inadequate to the problem of money as material substance, for the terms of Mammon's existence themselves tell what money is.

## II. TELLING COIN

The investigation of *The Faerie Queene* in terms of an object-oriented criticism may seem counterintuitive. Spenser's epic is the text par exellence that refuses to allow a thing to be only itself, as the exteriorized objects that his knights encounter continually resolve themselves into subjective states, the phenomena of interiority. The "material culture" analyses from which this project departs concern themselves principally with the drama, where objects are not only uncoerced into allegory but physically present as properties on the stage.[12] Spenser scholars, conversely, have not often viewed their poet as concerned with the material ontology of objects: Robert M. Schuler has asserted that, "[w]hile Spenser exhibits a general knowledge of cosmogony, he has little interest in theories of matter."[13] As the discussion below will show, I believe Spenser is indeed grappling with theories of matter's temporal existence in his metamorphic depiction of Mammon's gold. Moreover, the incorporating of possessed objects into the interiority of Renaissance subjects has already been a principal concern of critics of the material-culture bent.[14] Spenser's allegorical narrative offers an underexamined venue for such a reading, one whose complexities may enrich our understanding of that interaction of object and subject.

The character of Guyon's experience in Mammon's cave bears an underdetermined, chiastic relation to the readerly experience of Guyon's self-effacing, "shamefast" character, and it has been the subject of wide-ranging debate among scholars (2.9.43).[15] The nightmarish figure of Mammon, despite his availability to readings of "overdetermination" in both its psychological and Althusserian senses, has never enjoyed the same scrutiny, perhaps because he seems so straightforward an allegorical monstrosity; Frank Kermode's remark that the Mammon episode is "without historical dimension," true enough in the old-historical sense (of the figure's not having a referent among the courtiers of Elizabeth), seems to have been accepted with little comment by the New Historicism.[16] I propose to shift the burden of interpretation away from the inscrutable passivity of Guyon for a moment, and to focus first on what Mammon thinks he himself is up to. To begin with Spenser's summary of the canto's argument,

> *Guyon findes Mamon in a delue,*
> *Sunning his threasure hore:*
> *Is by him tempted, & led downe,*
> *To see his secret store* (2.7.arg.),

we may find it easy to infer why Mammon should have a "secret store" underground for his treasure—the trope, ancient in itself, conjoins the material conditions of mining to associations of hidden knowledge and spatial pressure—but why is it important either that Mammon's treasure be ancient (hoary) or that it get some sun from time to time in the course of its long existence? Why does Mammon take his gold out from its hiding place *to play with* in the sun, not only "telling" it ("in his lap a masse of coyne he told," 2.7.4) but then turning it "vpsidowne, to feed his eye" (2.7.4)?

Like other Spenserian enactions of evil, Mammon's counting is absurd in itself. The amount of money that Mammon has is, simply, plenty; it seems impossible to arrive at a numerical value for its sum, which is so vast that its precise assessment would be meaningless. Mammon in any case is taking pleasure not only from the accumulation of number but from the handling and examination of the gold. His turning the hoard "vpsidowne" implies that he is indifferent to the sequencing he is ostensibly enacting, and perhaps even that he starts the enumeration over whenever he finishes. Like Sesame Street's puppet vampire, who is the Count because he loves to count, Mammon finds the process of telling to be its own reward. In an immediate sense, this behavior is the reductio ad absurdum of the miserly type, so often figured in the obsessive and unnecessary act of recounting a hoard that he never allows to diminish.[17] Following the suggestion of Patrick Cheney, however, I'd like to argue that the verb "told" also connects Mammon's activity here to the process of narration[18]—that what is being produced is not merely a number but a story of number. The outcome of Mammon's counting cannot be a quantity, for the total will not be some discrete portion of the gold in the world but, rather, all of it; Mammon's plenty surpasses enumeration. Mammon surrounds himself with wealth as an undifferentiated absolute, and proceeds to enact it through these momentary differentiations; and the name of absolute wealth, of course, is "Mammon."[19] The story he is telling is himself.

The following stanza elaborates the interaction of material difference and indifference into the narration of Mammon:

> And round about him lay on euery side
> Great heapes of gold, that neuer could be spent:
> Of which some were rude owre, not purifide
> Of *Mulcibers* deuouring element;
> Some others were new driuen, and distent
> Into great Ingoes, and to wedges square;
> Some in round plates withouten moniment;
> But most were stampt, and in their metall bare
> The antique shapes of kings and kesars straunge & rare. (2.7.5)

On the one hand, Mammon seems to delight equally, indifferently, in all these forms of gold, without appreciating their rightful and particular purposes. The different utilities of the forms vanish in their agglomeration into "heapes," whose sheer bulk overwhelms quantity to the point that they "neuer could be spent": plenty makes them all equally useless. On the other, as David Read has argued, the different forms are presented in a specific sequence, to represent the accumulation of processes that turns gold from ore into coin; Mammon's "telling" enacts a narrative of mining, smelting, and minting.[20] The potentiality of "rude owre," in becoming more and more defined, moves closer across the stanza to the form that will actuate it. But to realize a potentiality is also to exhaust it. In this sense potentiality is *diminishing* across the stanza, dissipating, as the gold becomes formed, into nothing—for coins bearing "the antique shapes of kings and kesars straunge and rare" are not current money. All the objects Mammon has with him are old, having either failed ever to come into their usefulness or having outlived it; these coins are not everyday money but remote *numismata*, the material traces that the money form has left behind, as evocative in poesy as they are useless in circulation.[21]

This is not to say that there *is* current money available in *The Faerie Queene*. Guyon's colloquy with Mammon is among the only indications of a monetarized market present in the poem, which normatively depicts transactions of exchange and debt in terms of honor or hospitality.[22] The difference between the world of the fiction and the cash-hungry Elizabethan present is understood to be chronological; the legendary time of Gloriana and Arthur is innocent of the gold economy by virtue of predating it. The golden age, the time before what we understand to be history, is present to Guyon. Yet as soon as the knight encounters Mammon, the two of them come together on a story of money in which the golden age is unrecoverably past.

The "antiquitie" of Gloriana's kingdom and the most distant reaches of the European past are alike given substance in Spenser's imagination through the troping of the New World as a prehistory in the present.[23] In Book II's proem, anticipating readerly skepticism toward the matter of his epic, Spenser names *The Faerie Queene* "this famous antique history," which

> Of some th' aboundance of an idle braine
> Will iudged be, and painted forgery,
> Rather then matter of iust memory. (2.pr.1)

The poet does not proceed to claim direct knowledge of these antiquities himself, however. Rather, he cites a precedent for antiquities that have always been true, yet only recently come into the reach of knowledge:

> But let that man with better sence aduize,
> That of the world least part to vs is red:
> And dayly how through hardy enterprize,

Many great Regions are discouered,
Which to late age were neuer mentioned.
Who euer heard of th' Indian *Peru*?...
Yet all these were, when no man did them know. (2–3)

Evidently, the "matter of iust memory" has an existence independent of knowledge, an ontology as substantive as Peru's. The materiality of America recurs as the stuff of memory in canto 10, after Guyon has (barely) survived his three days chez Mammon and gone on with Arthur to the House of Alma, the allegory of the human body as a well-managed household that is the counterpart to Mammon's cave.[24] Visiting the library of Eumnestes, the faculty of memory, each knight "chaunce[s]" upon a text appropriate to his own heritage: Arthur begins reading "An auncient booke, hight *Briton moniments,*" and Guyon one "That hight *Antiquitie* of *Fairie* lond" (2.9.59–60). Fairie lond is already "antique" in its relation to the Elizabethan present, but its age extends back into even more remote "antiquities" of its own. The extent of the Faerie past remains indeterminate, for Guyon "ne yet has ended" reading the book, "that doth far excead/ My leasure, so long leaues here to repeat," as the poet declares (2.10.70). We are told only its present, in the reign of Gloriana, and its very beginning:

The first and eldest, which that scepter swayd,
Was *Elfin*; him all *India* obayd,
And all that now *America* men call. (2.10.72)

Fairie lond shares its antiquity with America, both in the proem and in Eumnestes's book. Spenser insists again on the nondiscovered status of America, for only the name is novel. Spenser uses the name "America" even as he disavows it, and the reader is never told how King Elfin might have called that portion of his empire, forgotten and now recovered by men but claimed throughout by the "iust memory" of Faeries. The equation with India places both Fairie lond and America in the context of the exotic and boundless wealth of the East: Elfin's successor Elfiline enclosed his capital "with a golden wall" (72). Gold here expresses the power and majesty of the past, but, as a material artifact recalled from that past, the wall—like the book that testifies to it—still bears comparison with the "antique shapes of kings and kesars straunge & rare" fondled by Mammon.

As Harrison testifies, Roman coins turned up with great frequency in southern Britain, most often around the old ports of Kent, where "simple fishermen haue had plentie of them, and ... the conies in making profers and holes to breed in, haue scraped them out of the ground in verie great abundance."[25] To the learned antiquaries these objects were themselves "moniments" of Romano-British antiquity, both in that the discovery of coin hoards gave a valuable clue for the location of long-lost Roman settlements and in that the portraits themselves testified to the personae of those "kings and kesars" in an imagined conversation with the past.[26] To the "simple fishermen," as unable as rabbits to recognize the "matter of iust memory," the coins' provenance was inexplicable and probably magical; Harrison records the coins being popularly called "Dwarfs monie, Hegs pence, Feirie groats, ... & by other foolish names not woorthie to be remembred."[27] The difference between a "Feirie groat" and a "moniment" is not, of course, any physical change in the object, which remains a metallic disk with a face on it throughout. It is enacted in the temporal life of the object: through the process of circulation, on the one hand, as the old coin passes from the puzzled fisherman to the eager antiquary, and through that of "telling," on the other, as the already known narratives of kings and kesars replace those of dwarves and fairies improvised upon the mysterious object. Neither of these processes, however, is available to the *numismata* in Mammon's lap. The demon is not interested in the present circulation of these coins, since in the plenitude about his presence they "neuer could be spent," and since he has held them long past the moment of their utility, after their currency has escaped them; no more is he concerned to contemplate and call up their possible pasts. These are objects that generate histories; they are the matter of memory—memory is available as a potential within them—but the "telling" that Mammon extracts from them is not even an erroneous narrative assigned to one or another object (as "Feirie groat"), but a solipsistic and meaningless counting of them all. Mammon obliterates the coins' uniqueness and historicity, and makes them all tell the same story, which is himself.

The books that Guyon and Arthur read in Eumnestes's chamber are objects whose material life interacts with that of their possessors in a similar way. They are not present merely as the momentary vessels of some extramaterial and immortal text; they are unique and vulnerable artifacts, as we may read from Arthur's anguish at finding that his book breaks off at midsentence, "As if the rest some wicked hand did rend" (2.10.68). Jennifer Summit has illuminated the Eumnestes cantos by reference to the breaking up of monastic libraries and to the reconstitution of private, purified, Protestant collections from their materials. She reads the two books as complementary in the crafting of memory: incited by "wonder of antiquitie" where the fragile materials of authority are rent by the "wicked hand" of oblivion, the mind creates new continuities for the past from the stuff of imagination.[28] The incompleteness of the book, like the emblematic exemplarity of the coin, marks the "matter of iust memory" as an underdetermined, imperfected potential in the object, waiting for a subject to realize its final form. This realizing interaction, which generates memory as a form inhering neither in the object nor the subject but in their interdependent relation, is what Mammon acts to suppress—or, rather, to prevent, for Mammon's method is always to come before.

For if Mammon's gold is so old, what, in the fictional, duple chronology of the poem, is it supposed to be older *than*? Is its origin in the far reaches of the classically inspired chronicle of British authority or at the horizon of the "antiquitie of Fairie lond"—or neither, but merely and absolutely older than we can imagine?[29] If, as Summit argues, the distinction in *The Faerie Queene* between historical authority and imagination, *Romanitas* and romance, is a momentary exteriority that has collapsed into the continuum of human memory before the reader can come to know it, the totemic figure for such a unitary historical imagination must be Ovid.[30] The status of the *Metamorphoses* in the humanist canon was of course unshakable, but its self-assured narration of the most preposterous fables as a historical sequence poured into the indefinitely expandable gaps of past knowledge made its author the (oxymoronic) authority of romance. Prior to the cycles of individual metamorphoses, Ovid offers a fable that seeks to account for transformation as the mechanism of all human history: the story of the four ages of gold, silver, brass, and iron. It is with this presentation of the material difference of present and past in terms of a series of ideological ruptures, I argue, that Spenser's thematization of "antiquitie" in Guyon's confrontation with Mammon is wrestling. Guyon marshals a qualitative difference in history in an attempt to come before Mammon, to beat the demon at his own game. He does not yet realize that even to play Mammon's game is to let the demon win.

In their debate over the value of riches, Mammon professes to be confused by the knight's denial of the worth of what the world most wants: "And why, then, . . . / Are mortall men so fond and vndiscreet,/ So euill thing to seek unto their ayd,/ And hauing not complaine, and hauing it vpbraid?" (2.7.14). Guyon replies that, being intemperate, the world does not recognize how little it ought to want, and develops an anecdote to support this thesis:

> The antique world, in his first flowring youth,
> Found no defect in his Creatours grace,
> But with glad thankes, and vnreproued truth,

> The giftes of soueraigne bountie did embrace:
> Like Angels life was then mens happy cace;
> But later ages pride, like corn-fed steed,
> Abusd her plenty, and fat swolne encreace
> To all licentious lust, and gan exceed
> The measure of her meane, and naturall first need. (16)

The utility of this Ovidian topos to Guyon, as to many other moralists, is to define vice as a temporal and contingent phenomenon rather than as one intrinsic to humanity: in the beginning it did not exist, and its present ubiquity has only come about as the fruit of an unfortunate sequence of events. The fable narrates a difference between prehistory and history that is beyond the comprehension of those on either side of the divide. Our ancestors would be as baffled by our interest in silver and gold as we are by their disinterest—or they would come to share our preoccupations, and so we would degrade them into apes of ourselves, as the admirers of the noble savage lamented that Europeans had done to the men of the New World. We are severed from the men of the past, in this telling, by a transformation at once material and ideological; the bettering of material conditions has made men irretrievably and contagiously worse. The fable of the golden age presents past and present as ideologically discontinuous.

This discontinuity is defined, according to Guyon, in a single event, the advent of money, attributed to the overreaching of one "cursed hand":

> Then gan a cursed hand the quiet wombe
> Of his great Grandmother with steele to wound,
> And the hid treasures in her sacred tombe,
> With Sacriledge to dig. Therein he found
> Fountaines of gold and siluer to abound,
> Of which the matter of his huge desire
> And pompous pride eftsoones he did compound;
> Then avarice gan through his veines inspire
> His greedy flames, and kindled life-deuouring fire. (17)

The material progression of gold from earth to ore to processed object, told once in the different forms of gold present around Mammon in stanza 5, is recapitulated here as an etiology. The transition from the golden age to the iron age, as Guyon tells it, is a story in which material and ideological transformation comprise a single phenomenon. Vice is at once the cause and the effect of the discovery of gold, for the "cursed hand" apparently possesses a "huge desire" before even knowing what he will find in the "wombe" and "tombe" of the earth. But only after "gold and siluer" are brought into knowledge can that desire be legible as "avarice," which has somehow predated its object, or reached into the past to call its object—its own condition—into being. This tail-biting solipsism in the origin of sin, between the appearance of an internal readiness to sin and that of an external prompting from temptation, defies the priority of cause to effect.[31] We may recognize it in Althusser's terms as an overdetermination, in which each transformation conditions and is the condition of the other, for I believe that—though Spenser's methods are certainly not proto-Marxian—the poet finds it necessary here to imagine a discontinuity of present conditions from past ones in order to narrate the prehistory of the money form, in which materiality and ideology are inextricable. Sir Guyon is not, then, propounding an allegory of primitive accumulation in this stanza, for who among Spenser and his contemporaries could have guessed that they lived in a moment in which capitalism would later be seen to be marshalling the cars and elephants of its triumphal procession?[32] Rather, I want here to construe "the so-called primitive accumulation" as *itself* likewise an allegory, serving parallel etiological needs for Marxian explications of the capitalist present by means of the indeterminately precapitalist past.[33] It's in this sense that I am comfortable calling the transformations of society and individuals, from prehistory into history, that Spenser postulates here "ideological" ones. Not only is the term most apt for the systemic unity of the change across macro- and microcosm that the poet envisions, but Guyon's explication avoids Christian paradigms in favor of the classical topos, so that although "pride" and "auarice" are inevitably Christian sins, they are placed here in a worldly and material history uninflected by the transcendence of theology.[34]

Indeed, Guyon formulates the action that breaks the new iron age off from the golden age not simply in classical, extra-Christian terms but in exclusively material ones. The stanza's vocabulary figures all aspects of this knotty phenomenon as substantial. The cursed hand's predisposition to sin, "the matter of his huge desire," is a *stuff*, indeterminate in form yet characterized both by "matter" and by extent ("huge"). The matters of gold and silver, though apparently innocent in themselves, immediately upon being found are "compound[ed]" in the act of discovery with "the matter of his huge desire" into the *alloy* "avarice," the finished product of the stanza. Avarice itself is a material phenomenon, the transformation of a formless desire and of an underdetermined metal into gold as we know it—a substance that encompasses both the object of the world's desire and the active, vicious desiring of that world—which is forged continually in the scorching "veines" of every worldling.[35] Metals, societies, individualities, and bodies are alike transformed, and transform each other, in the material rupture, the "wound," that is the advent of the money form.

Fascinating as this rhetorical condensation is to me, Mammon is unimpressed by it. Guyon cannot tell Mammon anything about money that the demon doesn't already know, and that he isn't perfectly willing to admit: the great virtue of monetary exchange is its transparency, its ability to turn the opaque darkness of objects into lucid values, and Mammon wears this secret of his hegemony on his rusty sleeve. Mammon is content for Guyon's fable to be accurate. By defining the discontinuity of the golden age's prehistoric virtues from the vice that marks the iron age of history, the knight has also defined the whole present world, and the reach of its memory to the limit of the past, in terms of that limit, of the rupture constituting the money form.[36] Mammon readily takes that bargain:

> Sonne (said he then) let be thy bitter scorne,
> And leaue the rudenesse of that antique age
> To them, that liu'd therein in state forlorne;
> Thou that doest liue in later times, must wage
> Thy workes for wealth, and life for gold engage. (18)

In celebrating the temperance of the irrecoverable past, Guyon has yielded to Mammon all the present.[37] What he presents as a site of his resistance to the rule of riches becomes in effect the venue of his complicity within it, and the knight leaves himself with nowhere to go but down, into the cave itself.

Guyon's method of argument throughout the debate stanzas (7–20) has been scholastic, in the most unflattering sense of the term: in each strophe of the argument, he peruses his memory to locate a commonplace for the denial of riches and makes his stand upon it. But Mammon, "God of the world and worldlings," is unsurprisingly adept in the *argumentum in utramque partem* of rhetorical place-logic, and rather than resisting Guyon's choices of topos he apparently accedes to them, comes to inhabit them, and transforms them into terms that support his own godhead (2.7.8). Guyon is forced to flee again and again to a new commonplace, and Mammon joins him in each one, making each one a venue of the money form rather than a holdout against it.[38] Mammon's effortless planting of his flag in each of the topoi which Guyon hopes to fortify against him is the general equivalent in action: the money form irresistibly invades and inhabits everything it encounters—every object, every place, every word—turning it into a fungible value, a term for money.

Guyon is certainly aware of this totalizing destiny of money. He knows that things that come into the circuit of Mammon's power of exchange are not simply exchanged as themselves but transformed, reduced to nominal differences within a waste of indifference. To Mammon's offer to "crownes and kingdomes to thee multiply" (11), the knight replies that crown and kingdom are no longer the same things they were, once they have passed through Mammon's hands:

> Ne thine be kingdomes, ne the scepters thine;
> But realmes and rulers thou doest both confound,
> And loyall truth to treason doest incline. (12)

And, as we have seen, Guyon is capable of articulating how such a change might overtake the entire world, by recourse to the trope of the golden age. But saying so is not enough to defy Mammon; instead, it affirms him. Even in Guyon's account of the golden age, the vice of gold is already present, working its way to the surface for its own realization, to become the meaning of the story. There is nothing Mammon wants to hear about more than himself, for Mammon is the general equivalent, and he works to make sure that any account of the world that may be told turns out to have been all about himself.

Mammon is an anomaly in the synchronizing worlds of allegory. He does not stand for any present figure in a typological sense; that is what Kermode means in declaring him "without historical dimension," that the demon is the same figure to the readerly present that he is in the fictive past, in the moment of his confrontation with Guyon. Yet Mammon's ahistorical quality is not simple timelessness, either, a passive endurance in the face of passing epochs, a perserverance of the past, or an exemplum of present antiquity. Rather, Mammon invades the past from the future. At any moment of the imagined past, Mammon is not only present as we, the readers, know him; he is also reshaping that past into a futurity in which gold will have erased all other values. He is always already there, and his work is always already nearly complete. As the unearthing of "The antique shapes of kings and kesars straunge and rare" materially affirmed to Spenser and his contemporaries, money is never simply discovered at some time or place; rather, it discovers itself to have been there—in Ovid's fable, in the mountains of the Andes—all along, so that the golden age recedes indefinitely before the age of gold.

## III. THE LIPS OF TANTALUS

It is disastrous for Guyon to debate Mammon. The terms by which money is spoken of become terms of money, as we have seen, so that even to argue against Mammon is to yield to him. Instead, Guyon must resist Mammon by simply declaring his self-sufficiency, on the one hand, and by refusing to articulate what that sufficiency, or that self, consists of, on the other. For whatever particular phenomenon Guyon declares himself to have enough of already, whether an object such as arms or a concept such as power, Mammon can demonstrate to be equally material and purchasable. He can show that Guyon can buy it, and therefore—in the transumptive material logic that moves to inhabit the fact of the past—that Guyon must already have paid for it. To claim a selfhood untouchable by Mammon, Guyon must make the stuff of himself mystified, unquantifiable, and unspeakable. All he may name is what he is not.

If the fungibility of gold for any other material thing is the controversy of the debate stanzas, its metallic malleability into other shapes seems to be the ocular proof that Mammon invites the knight to "come... and see" (20). Gold is of course present everywhere as Guyon explores Mammon's cave, both as the container ("Both roofe, and floore, and wals were all of gold,/ But ouergrowne with dust and old decay," 29) and as the thing contained. Mammon exhibits the metal to the knight in a multiplicity of forms: I count at least a score in the canto, starting with the demon's gold-lined coat, "Ingoes," and old coins; moving on to the "huge great yron chests and coffers strong" encircled by skulls in stanza 30 (whose desperate strength and sorry surroundings necessarily imply the presence of gold within them), the "exceeding store" guarded by "a couetous Spright" (31–34), and the "molten owre" worked by fiends in Mammon's furnaces (35–39); and proceeding from there to more richly associative forms, such as the gold giant Disdayne (40–42), the chain of Philotime (46–50), and finally the golden apples in the Garden of Proserpina (54–63). The metamorphic potential of gold is evident throughout the variety of these manifestations. Yet the temper of the changes themselves seems to change after Guyon rejects the temptation of the furnace, where "golden metall" is liquefied to be made pure.

The production of gold, rehearsed once in the juxtaposition of forms around Mammon and again in Guyon's etiology of money, is presented for a third time here among the furnaces for the knight to witness as material process:

Therein an hundred raunges weren pight,
And hundred fornaces all burning bright;
By euery fornace many feends did bide,
Deformed creatures, horrible in sight,
And euery feend his busie paines applide,
To melt the golden metall, ready to be tride.
One with great bellowes gathered filling aire,
And with forst wind the fewell did inflame;
Another did the dying bronds repaire
With yron toungs, and sprinckled oft the same
With liquid waues, fiers *Vulcans* rage to tame,
Who maistring them, renewd his former heat;
Some scumd the drosse, that from the metall came;
Some stird the molten owre with ladles great;
And euery one did swincke, and euery one did sweat. (35–36)

The specific process enacted here is smelting, the extraction of pure gold from "molten owre." It is the stage of purification, when the "drosse" is removed and the gold becomes "ready to be tride" against a standard of fineness. There are many more, equally laborious processes in the material life of gold, from the mining of the ore to the production of coin or of plate. But Mammon chooses this stage to show as the heated moment when gold is the most itself, while any impurities are boiling away and before any particular form has been imposed upon its molten matter. Here Mammon's agenda converges with Guyon's own preoccupation with purification and cleansing. The misery of Mammon's slaves surely taints the stuff even as they work to make it pure, but they take much more notice of Guyon than he does of them (save to find their "wonder" at him, couched in such foully guised gazes, intimidating [37]), and Mammon proclaims this scene to show the innocence of his gold of the past crimes by which the knight had suggested it was gotten:

The thing, that thou didst craue so earnestly,
To weet, whence all the wealth late shewd by mee,
Proceeded, lo now is reueald to thee. (38)

This is new-made gold, before a form, before a past. Mammon has refuted the last of Guyon's cavils against gold, that it may have an evil history, by burning history away, as so much dross, to display gold *tout court*. Confronted with the stuff itself, devoid of form or association, Guyon speaks at last with a corresponding simplicity:

> Suffice it then, thou Money God (quoth hee)
> That all thine idle offers I refuse.
> All that I need I haue; what needeth mee
> To couet more, then I haue cause to vse?
> With such vaine shewes thy worldlings vile abuse:
> But giue me leaue to follow mine emprise. (39)[39]

Guyon gives up defining his wants as different from anything Mammon can supply, for Mammon has been able to overwhelm each of those differences. In this stanza, he instead circumscribes himself (using the first person pronoun seven times) in terms of "need." "Need" defines the temperate body's interaction with the world of matter: the body that seeks only to meet its needs will fall into neither the self-destruction of asceticism nor the excesses of spurious desire. Guyon declares that he is entirely self-contained: "All that I need I haue." The stuff of himself suffices; it is incompatible with gold, the stuff of insufficiency, the stuff of desire, the stuff that wants to encompass all other stuffs. At the moment, however, that stuff of Guyon's selfhood remains undefinable, save as a tautology: What does Guyon need? What he has. What does he have? What he needs. This antilogical mystification is enough to resist the devouring logic of Mammon, but it is not enough to define Guyon's actual relation to the material world. As soon as he escapes the cave, he faints, from passing three days underground with nothing to eat.

The cave of Mammon turns out, in the episodes' many correspondences, to have been a parody of the House of Alma, the well-ordered interior of the human body.[40] Yet the parody has managed to anticipate the normative formulation; it would require a very perspicacious reader to guess that the apparently literal depiction of the smelting of gold in 35–37 is also a distortion of an allegorical depiction of digestion two cantos later. As I have argued, this anachronic preemption of systems independent of gold, to transform them into interchangeable terms for gold, is Mammon's particular knack. But here, at last, it avails him nothing. Malleable and ductile, gold can assume any form, and as the general equivalent, the money form, it can replace any other object in the systems of exchange. The narrative of the canto leads gold through dozens of such transformations, in both registers, as Mammon bends his will upon Guyon; indeed, the storied stuff can be shaped into miniature allegories of its own, like the invulnerable Disdayne and the complexly associative chain of Philotime. Yet the culmination of all these changes, of all these re-realizations of the apparently infinite potentiality of gold in the world, displays the metal in a form worse than useless: the golden apples, which require two stanzas' narration of an elaborately ominous pedigree that comes down not to sustenance but to sheer torture. Even before we can recognize that the cave of Mammon aspires to exchange itself for the House of Alma, readers already know that this is the point where Mammon falls short, inches from the lips of Tantalus.

Spenser employs antiquity's greatest sinner here in the service of a dark and deceptively simple joke, a reduction or transumption of the principles of monetary exchange: if gold is an untrammeled potentiality, able to take any form and to occupy the place of any commodity, why can't it become human flesh?—why can't you *eat* it? The joke itself is the one played on Midas in the antique tradition; it is Spenser's innovation to make the fruit that torments Tantalus golden, which allows the poet not only to introduce all the other bad apples of the canon, but to conflate the baffled hunger of Midas with that of Pelops's father, and so to move its register from the comic to the tragic. The golden apples do their tantalizing with a brutally compressed irony, which assimilates a knot of related meanings and misdeeds that converge upon this single sinner. The exemplum of miserliness in one classical tradition, the pryer into divine knowledge in another, and the roaster of his own son in a third, this "greedie *Tantalus*" (60) has overreached the limits of *meum* and *tuum* in every register in attempting to collapse the differentiating structures of exchange, possession, secrecy, and generation into a boundless, all-consuming self.[41] His punishment is to learn for eternity, and so to teach others, what cannot be ingested. Guyon cogently assesses the purpose of the punishment in refusing Tantalus's prayer for his help:

> Nay, nay, thou greedie *Tantalus* (quoth he)
> Abide the fortune of thy present fate,
> And vnto all that liue in high degree,
> Ensample be of mind intemperate,
> To teach them how to vse their present state. (60)

Mammon himself does not understand how the exemplarity of the punishment works, however, and tries to get Guyon to eat the golden apples even after the knight has correctly read their use in torturing the sinner. The demon cannot comprehend his own limit, the limit being enforced upon Tantalus's hunger, the bound of the temperate self in the world. He still thinks that he and his gold are what the world is made of, both inside the self and out.

In his first attempt to refuse Mammon's offer, Guyon scorned the demon's gold as "worldly mucke" (10). This argument, that all earthly things partake of the same contemptible substance and are to be rejected in kind, draws support from the neo-Aristotelian doctrine of *prima materia,* which reads the hylomorphic relation of matter to form back a step: the individual substances, such as silver, wood, or tin, that await their teleological realizations into form (such as a cup) are themselves the result of differentiating motions within the matter of the world, whose primal state is a complete indifference, like the Chaos with which Ovid opens the *Metamorphoses.* All worldly substance is thus reducible to a stuff lacking not only form, not only the characters of individual substances, but qualities themselves, before solid and liquid, before hot and cold—a colorless, lukewarm sludge. Value, being relative in the world, is reducible finally to this undifferentiated, worthless minimality, just as the human body is; it is in this sense that "dust thou art, and to dust thou shalt return."[42] Conversely, the continuity posited among different substances, as themselves only changes effected by motions in the *prima materia,* enables, in minds more ready to embrace value as a relative progression, the concept of a perfection of matter, a teleological destiny of all substances as motion toward a single perfect substance; in alchemy, this is gold.[43] Mammon is not an alchemist—the operations depicted in his furnace are worked on ore, not on dung or lead—but he shares this understanding, so flattering to himself, of gold as a worldly perfection whose substance transcends any form: "Loe here the worldes blis, loe here the end" (32); "Here is the fountaine of the worldes good" (38).[44] The progress of his gold into form belies him, however; there is nothing good about a golden apple.

According to Aristotle's *Politics* and the whole medieval and early modern discourse upon usury that developed from it, metal cannot naturally grow as livestock does, through feeding and breeding, and for art to enjoin money to grow artificially is obscene, a hideously parodic reversal of the order of nature.[45] This constitutes the preeminent difference in Guyon's experience between a house of gold that apes the body and a house made of the *prima materia* that is the body. Alma's house is

> Ne built of bricke, ne yet of stone and lime,
> But of thing like to that *Ægyptian* slime,
> Whereof king *Nine* whilome built *Babell* towre;
> But ô great pitty, that no lenger time

So goodly workemanship should not endure;
Soone it must turne to earth; no earthly thing is sure. (2.9.21)

Though "slime" is no more appealing a word than "mucke"—Guyon's verbal reduction of Mammon's wealth to mere materiality—the stuff that the house is made of is different from that of Mammon's gold; it is as vital and nutritive as the mud of the Nile, from which crocodiles and hippopotami were alleged to be spontaneously generated after the yearly floods.[46] The simile recalls its previous appearance denoting monstrous autochthony in Error's vomit (1.1.21), and will recur again in the immaculate impregnation of Chrysogone (3.6.8). Here, in the context of "no earthly thing is sure," the simile seems to focus our attention on the tight interdependence of corruption and generation: the temporarily stable and beautiful form of the body emerges from, and will return to, incoherent putrescence. The golden stuff of Mammon's house is incommensurate to that of the body in its very incorruptibility, its removal from the circular relation of growth and decay, which qualifies it to be money. The golden apples retreat from Tantalus's hand, while the "cursed hand" who did compound with gold "the matter of his huge desire," a desire spurious to bodily needs, experiences the agonies of avarice "through his veines" as a kind of indigestion. In gold, the boundless potential for nourishment of the *prima materia* is entirely dissipated.

The gold with which Mammon "feed[s] his eye" (2.7.4) is not food for the stomach; neither is it food for thought. In the allegory of the House of Alma, memory is as material a phenomenon as digestion. The knights pass from the stomach to the head and witness both processes being enacted in corresponding terms, of anthropomorphized faculties handling books as they handle chyle.[47] Knowledge of the past defines and sustains the temperate body of Spenser's allegory just as the fortifications of the mouth and the intricate practices of the stomach do: the library of Eumnestes occupies fully half of the description of Alma's castle, and it becomes the seat of resistance to the constant forgetting that is the money form's interaction with history. Not even the torn page that "half seemeth to offend" Arthur in *Briton moniments* is a blank. That rupture in British historiography is the very productive one that has called him into being:

After him *Vther*, which *Pendragon* hight,
Succeding There abruptly did it end,
Without full point, or other Cesure right,
As if the rest some wicked hand did rend. (2.10.68)

Uther, of course, is Arthur's father, unbeknownst to him. Though the prince does not recognize it, the book is torn by the convergence of the past with the present and of the text with its reader. The material of memory gives way perforce to the presence of Arthur, in a complexly ironic and rather Oedipal ripping that alludes to the textual status of the mythical "British history" of Geoffrey of Monmouth as much as it does to the supplanting of fathers by sons. Despite the best debunking efforts of Polydore Vergil, even the most scrupulous sixteenth-century historians remained reluctant to jettison Arthur from the history of the island, for no alternative story had ever been advanced to account for the years after the last Roman authorities fell silent and before the records of the Saxons began. As F. J. Levy has suggested, it was unthinkable that a mere lacuna should appear in such a crucial passage of the narrative of British self-knowledge.[48] If the page weren't already torn by his ignorance of his father, Arthur would have had to do it himself; the prince is sustained by the tear, which marks the whole book as material in its vulnerability and becomes the occasion of his interaction with it. He apostrophizes the Britain he has come to know through its wounded pages:

> . . . Deare countrey, ô how dearely deare
> Ought thy remembraunce, and perpetuall band
> Be to thy foster Childe, that from thy hand
> Did commun breath and nouriture receaue? (2.10.69)

The true value of "countrey" and "remembraunce" alike is asserted in the triplicate "deare," as the book becomes the proof that Guyon had lacked in claiming to Mammon, "Ne thine be kingdomes, ne the scepters thine" (2.7.13). History redeems the country from the consuming terms of exchange and sale. *Briton moniments*, the epitome of the country's "deare" and bountiful greatness, nurtures its "foster Childe" and its princes alike, for Arthur knows himself only as the one and not the other. The "nouriture" that Arthur has drawn from Britain in the past, and draws again through memory into the present, actively opposes and defeats Mammon's sterile futurity in the temperate, temporal body. It is a counternarrative of sustenance to the story of the invasion of the earth, the past, and the "veines" of worldlings by avarice's "life-deuouring fire" (2.7.17). Even study, however, must be pursued with moderation, as Alma reminds the knights in calling them "halfe vnwilling" from their books to their actual supper (2.10.77). There is a time for all things in the everyday maintenance of the temperate self.

## IV. WEARYING HIS FINGERS' ENDS WITH TELLING IT

It remains to be asked what the House of Alma's resistance to the hegemony of Mammon leaves out. The ethical and ontological crux posited here between gold's ability to *buy* food and its inability to *be* food, a nonproblem in classical economic models that posit food as simply one among many commodities (guns versus butter, in the Econ 101 diagram), has marked a limit to the acceptable extent of the self-regulation of the market in many societies besides that of sixteenth-century England.[49] In that immediate context, however, we may recognize it as a "commonwealth" problem of the sort addressed throughout the *Discourse of the Commonweal* and many other civic-minded tracts of the midcentury, a question of when and how the behavior of money should be restricted for the benefit of the people or the advantage of the prince.[50] Guyon's experience posits such a point of restriction upon money at the limit of bodily need, asserting a temperate self-sufficiency that the market cannot touch unless the temptations that besiege our senses are let inside the castle. But it does not occour to the knight to wonder how Alma's staff finds the food the household does need, out there among the riotous superfluities of Maleger, or how the former is distinguished from the latter. Critics, including those not otherwise Marxist, have largely been content to accept this formulation, which declares the commodification of food to be a fiction of the market.[51] But, as Jean Baudrillard has demonstrated, the "anthropological minimum," of the body's need as discrete from superfluous consumption, is only such another fiction:

> In fact, the "vital anthropological minimum" doesn't exist; in all societies, it is determined residually by the fundamental urgency of an excess: the divine or sacrificial share, sumptuous discharge, economic profit. It is this pre-dedication of luxury that negatively determines the level of survival, not the reverse (which is an idealist fiction). Advantages, profits, sacrifice (in the sense of social wealth) and "useless" expenditures are all deducted in advance. And the priority of this claim works everywhere at the expense of the functional side of the balance sheet—at the expense, where necessary, of minimal subsistence.[52]

"O, reason not the need!," Lear implores his daughters; can the body itself sustain so sharp a differentiation of itself and its needs from Mammon? To address this question, we must turn away from Guyon's own perspective in assessing his experience of "need" and evaluate it through other eyes. I will turn first to Christopher Marlowe's ironical engagement of Spenser's Book

Two in *The Jew of Malta*, which manifests a counternarrative of instrumentality in money to complicate Guyon's self-satisfactory account of a consumption bounded by "need." Then, with Marlowe's dark ironies in mind, I will return to Spenser's Book Two to demonstrate how frequently questions of instrumentality do manifest themselves in Guyon's experience, and how rarely those questions are able to claim the knight's attention. In his preoccupation with what goes in and out of his mouth, I argue, Guyon fails to attend to how he should be using his hands. The final turn of the chapter's argument will be to Spenser's returning to the confrontation between a knight and money from the complementary perspective of the 1596 *Faerie Queene*'s Book Five. Where Book Two addresses money as an object within the discourse of ethics, Book Five will address money as an object within the discourse of politics. And just as Book Two's temperate knight, Guyon, engaged money in terms of consumption to the exclusion of questions of instrumentality, so will Book Five's just knight, Artegall, engage money in terms of instrumentality to the exclusion of questions of consumption and "need." The problem of money, then, is adequately addressed neither by ethics nor by politics. The problem with money is also a problem with matter—a problem of ontology.

* * *

In reimagining the cave of Mammon as Barabas's "little room," Marlowe rejects the sure bound of need and instead delineates the points at which money and the body interact—not only at the ends of counting fingers, not only in the slave market where "every one's price is written on his back," but in the persistent trace of memory, where gold and the body have touched to "tell" the money form (1.1.37, 2.3.3, 1.1.11). Spenser's Mammon is as antithetical to memory as he is to food; he replaces bodily sustenance with the agonizing hunger of avarice, he subsitutes his hegemonic futurity for the deeds of the past. But in Barabas's Malta, memory conflates the stuff of money with the stuff of life.

> *Enter Barabas in his counting-house, with heaps of gold before him.*
> *Barabas.* So that of thus much that return was made,
> And, of the third part of the Persian ships,
> There was the venture summed and satisfied.
> As for those Samnites and the men of Uz
> That bought my Spanish oils and wines of Greece,
> Here have I pursed their paltry silverlings.
> Fie, what a trouble 'tis to count this trash!

Well fare the Arabians, who so richly pay
The things they traffic for with wedge of gold,
Whereof a man may easily in a day
Tell that which may maintain him all his life.
The needy groom that never fingered groat
Would make a miracle of thus much coin;
But he whose steel-barred coffers are crammed full,
And all his lifetime hath been tired,
Wearying his fingers' ends with telling it,
Would in his age be loath to labour so,
And for a pound to sweat himself to death.
Give me the merchants of the Indian mines
That trade in metal of the purest mould,
The wealthy Moor that in the eastern rocks
Without control can pick his riches up
And in his house heap pearl like pebble-stones,
Receive them free, and sell them by the weight—
Bags of fiery opals, sapphires, amethysts,
Jacinths, hard topaz, grass-green emeralds,
Beauteous rubies, sparkling diamonds,
And seld-seen costly stones of so great price
As one of them, indifferently rated
And of a carat of this quantity,
May serve in peril of calamity
To ransom great kings from captivity.
This is the ware wherein consists my wealth;
And thus, methinks, should men of judgment frame
Their means of traffic from the vulgar trade,
And, as their wealth increaseth, so enclose
Infinite riches in a little room. (1.1.1–37)

I cite Barabas's first soliloquy nearly in its entirety to make visible the continuity of his rhetorical process, which is one of condensation. Through Barabas's oratory, the discovery space—already packed full with both "heaps of gold" and a floridly dressed actor as the speech begins—comes to be filled with a plenitude of value without ever bulging at its seams, as "infinite riches in a little room." He accomplishes this by transformations of substance, as silver gives way to gold, gold to pearls, pearls to opals, opals to diamonds, diamonds to stones too rare and precious to have a name, defined instead only by their valuable function ("to ransom great kings"). The same volume becomes denser and denser in value; indeed, it extracts value from the rest of the world, for if infinite riches are in the little room, what can be left outside? The silver must be cast off when exchanged for gold to make room for the more precious metal, and likewise the gold in favor of pearls, and so on, but only after the former substance has become meaningless to Barabas. In each transaction the less precious material is sucked clean of value and jettisoned as dross, a mere husk.

Barabas's declaration of scorn for the "trash" with which he is surrounded recalls, with ample irony, the ascetic denial of precious metal as, like all things of this earth, mere pelf. But as he instantly makes clear, his objection is only to silver, as being insufficiently precious. The progress of stuffs through value likewise works upon the continuity of matter across individual substances that I have placed in the context of alchemical theories as well as that of the doctrine of the *prima materia*, but Barabas himself is no more an alchemist than Mammon was. He has no interest in esoterica, whether mystical or magical; rather, his concern throughout the play is that the enormities he achieves be perfectly understood by his audience, for our comprehension is the means by which he extracts our complicity. The transformations of substance he achieves in his soliloquy are accomplished not by the arcane jargon and covert practices of alchemy but by the communal and transparent mechanisms of exchange. Although both the matter and the form of each substance are replaced by a more precious stuff in smaller units in each such exchange, Barabas's speech at the same time implies that the room's volume is a constant form and the matter continually refines itself within it, offering a strange hylomorphic continuity in the destiny of value—or, rather, an antihylomorphic one, for it reverses the temporality of Aristotle's construction: now matter, not form, is the realizing motion.

Patrick Cheney has convincingly documented the extent of Marlowe's intertextual engagement with Spenser's Mammon episode in writing *The Jew of Malta*, from the most evident correspondences of character, scenario, and imagery to specific borrowings of vocabulary and phrasing.[53] Like Mammon, Barabas exerts himself upon his "heapes of gold" by "telling" them (*FQ* 2.7.5 and 4; *Jew* 1.1 s.d. 1, 11, and 16). Unlike Mammon, Barabas will not endure forever in his wealth, counting it over and over until the end of time (or its beginning). "Telling" is a matter of "life" and of "death" in Barabas's soliloquy—"a man may easily in a day/ Tell that which may maintain him all his life" in wedges of gold (10–11)—whereas counting silver may prove lethal:

> . . . he whose steel-barred coffers are crammed full,
> And all his life-time hath been tired,
> Wearying his fingers' ends with telling it,
> Would in his age be loath to labour so,
> And for a pound to sweat himself to death. (14–18)

The decreasing density of relative value across substances passes, between gold and silver, from a fruitful means of "maintaining" life to a counterproductive one. Telling silver is literally not worth the effort, for the telling itself exacts a physical cost that exceeds the price of the silver. Barabas's hyperbole in this comparison would not, of course, be lost on his audience, all of whom, no matter what their personal circumstances, would be better acquainted with "the needy groom that never fingered groat" than with "the merchants of the Indian mines"; but the location of an individual's interaction with money both within the act of narrative ("telling") and upon his body, where the pernicious work of "telling" moves from "his fingers' ends" to some more vital site where "labour" can become "death," defines a double problematic which works throughout the play to make money the remembered measure of the self.

The correlation of the matter of life and death to the precious matter being compressed through the process of the soliloquy into denser and denser value, into "infinite riches in a little room," has been recognized to one degree or another throughout the play's reception history, starting with Shakespeare's glance at Marlowe's own death over "a great reckoning in a little room" (*AYLI* 3.3.15).[54] Marjorie Garber has found the compression motif to operate throughout the registers of the play, from the vocabulary and imagery of this and other scenes, to the many tight interiors enacted on stage (the counting room, the back room where Barabas and Ithamore murder Barnardine, the cauldron in which Barabas is at last trapped), to the suffocating metatheatrical intimacy which Barabas so enjoys with his audience.[55] Cheney refers the motif itself to the prior example of Spenser's many cornucopian interiors, and to the Cave of Mammon in particular.[56] Though Barabas knows himself to be mortal where Mammon does not, the little all that Barabas is "telling" is recognizable, like Mammon's, as himself, the effect which his entire being is bent upon producing: "This is the ware wherein consists my wealth." The relation of "infinite riches" to "a little room," insofar as its own allusive and elusive richness remains mysterious, is likewise recognizable as a formulation of selfhood in paradox that's familiar to Renaissance understandings as that of the soul—the pearl of great price—enclosed within the narrow space of the body (though Barabas himself, as a non-Christian, cannot be referring to his own soul in this way; only the material letter of his speech is within his frame of reference, though the audience must recognize its ironic relation to the spirit).[57] Barabas's "telling" across the soliloquy appears to succeed entirely in accounting for himself as a concatenation of material value. Yet it cannot be entirely accurate; for something persists of Barabas even when all the money is gone.

The soliloquy with which Barabas opens Act 2 recapitulates his proclamation of his selving wealth in a minor mode: dispossessed, homeless, and adrift in space, he now owns the opposite of "infinite riches in a little room." But this opposite is not, interestingly, nothing. In vacating and undoing Barabas's household, wealth has left a remainder behind, in the form of a reminder:

> And of my former riches rests no more
> But bare remembrance, like a soldier's scar,
> That has no further comfort for his maim. (2.1.8–10)

Barabas's wealth, the part of him that ought to be there and isn't, endures as an absence, a ghost limb. It "re-members" itself, asserts its amputated integrity with Barabas, if only as an empty outline; the loss of his wealth itself becomes a trauma marked by a persistent bodily trace, "like a soldier's scar." The place where wealth has been is inscribed upon Barabas's body.

At the same time, Barabas's body is currently pacing around the place where wealth does remain, the gallery where Abigail is searching for his secret hoard, and as he ruminates, it is no longer his wealth but himself that takes on this insubstantial persistence:

> Now I remember those old women's words,
> Who in my wealth would tell me winter's tales,
> And speak of spirits and ghosts that glide by night
> About the place where treasure hath been hid;
> And now methinks that I am one of those.
> For whilst I live, here lives my soul's sole hope,
> And when I die, here shall my spirit walk. (2.1.24–30)

"In my wealth" is a peculiar phrase. It seems to shape itself after "in my youth," when more ordinary characters might recall listening to old wives' tales. "Wealth" is not an amount here, a quantity of money, but a qualitative state of being limited only in time. For Barabas in this soliloquy, "wealth" is a remembered personal completion, a nostalgia for a wholeness of self before his present rupture that has made him so unreal, as a "ghost" haunting the treasure from which his body has been barred and which to his memory is present.

Although the audience has already seen it staged and handled, in a certain sense it is only now that Barabas's wealth becomes real—in that he can't get at it. It is discrete from him even as he posits his own, now ghostly, existence, stalking about under the balcony, to be dependent on it. That small and insuperable distance from the exteriorized object we recognize as fundamental to the constitution of modern subjects; the reification of money in particular, at the expense of what had been real before the advent of money, has been memorably described by Marx:

> Being the external, common medium and faculty for turning an image into reality and reality into a mere image (a faculty not springing from man as man or from human society as society), money transforms the real essential powers of man and nature into what are merely abstract conceits and therefore imperfections—into tormenting chimeras—just as it transforms real imperfections and chimeras—essential powers which are really impotent, which exist only in the mind of the individual—into real powers and faculties.[58]

Nevertheless, I cannot argue that Barabas undergoes some complete transformation here in his moment of spectrality, from (for example) premodern protosubject to a subject-as-we-know-him, since the effect of wealth's loss is so entirely reversible—unlike the decline into the Iron Age, or the fall from Eden—as soon as Abigail tosses the treasure down to him. Awaiting her father above, Abigail asks that sleep may "Give charge to Morpheus that he may dream/ A golden dream, and of the sudden walk,/ Come, and receive the treasure I have found" (36–38). Her prayer neatly transposes spectrality and reality, walker and treasure, from the terms which Barabas has voiced below, and when Barabas is reunited with his daughter and his money he is fully rejuvenated; in the space of two more scenes he will announce that "In spite of these swine-eating Christians/... Am I become as wealthy as I was" (2.3.7–11). Yet a trace of the experience remains, in Barabas's very "spite" for those Christians. Before the expropriation he did not care if the Maltese lived or died. Now he cares very much that they die. He first speaks his new desire for revenge in the very moment of his reunion with his wealth and daughter: "O my girl,/ My gold, my fortune, my felicity,/ Strength to my soul, death to mine enemy!" (2.1.47–49). Just as the memory of wealth maintained him in a spectral existence throughout the moment of its loss, so, in his recompletion when his soul is again strong, the memory of loss persists in the gold that is now at once his soul and his revenge.

The subtle interface between Barabas's body and his wealth marks each as incomplete without the other; the gold is part of him, and to separate him from it is an act of violence, a "maim." That relation is most fully experienced in Barabas's brief separation from the money, in the memory of their now severed integration. This is not a memory that serves for nourishment, however, like the mnemonic sustenance offered by Eumnestes; rather, it sustains itself as trauma in Barabas's present, a mark of incompleteness that lingers. Even when Barabas has fully reassembled his wealth, he does not enjoy the same integrated relation to it that he had. Instead, his projected reincorporation of "gold" and "soul" calls for "death to my enemy" before it can be completed, offering as a delusive prescription for wholeness the proliferating cyclicality of revenge. Gold is still his identity, but the unity of identity is itself deferred into the future, as the anticipated consummation of his revenge. In the present, gold remains to an unstable degree alienated from him as his instrument, at his "fingers' ends," as the means of manipulation through which he will exact revenge.

Unlike most revenge protagonists, Barabas actually attains complete mastery of his enemies and indeed all of Malta by Act 5 of the play; there is no external factor poised to bring him down in the name of dramatic irony. Yet, faced with the prospect of having achieved his projected reintegration, Barabas cracks. Unable to sustain his wished-for consummation, he starts addressing himself by his own name and in the second person, as if that "thou, Barabas" were somebody else:

> Thus hast thou gotten, by thy policy,
> No simple place, no small authority:
> I now am governor of Malta. True,
> But Malta hates me, and, in hating me,
> My life's in danger; and what boots it thee,
> Poor Barabas, to be the governor,
> Whenas thy life shall be at their command?
> No, Barabas, this must be looked into;
> And since by wrong thou got'st authority,
> Maintain it bravely by firm policy,
> At least unprofitably lose it not. (5.2.27–37)

In his dozens of prior asides and soliloquies, Barabas has *never* addressed himself. All those other lines are directed either at unknowing fellow characters or at the uncomfortably complicit audience. Like the hesitantly duple constructions of litotes, "No simple place, no small authority," that here replace the unitary density of "infinite riches in a little room" as Barabas's achievement, the irresistibly forceful persona of Barabas is fragmenting in these lines between an "I" and a "thou," the latter reiterated (in the pronoun, in the imperative, and in the vocative "Barabas") nine times. Once he has finally achieved the revenge that he had expected would redress the trauma of his "maim," Barabas reinflicts that maiming upon himself. It's only after he has done this that he proceeds to recall Ferneze from prison, giving his enemy not death but life and freedom, and the plot unravels for him accordingly.

Memory is working in *The Jew of Malta* as the traumatic compulsion to repeat, not as food for thought, and memory is continuous with the bodily relation to money rather than the positively defined opposite to that relation, for memory emerges in the play when that relation has forcibly been severed, and continues to sustain and re-member the fact of that severance. T. S. Eliot points out that the recitation of horrific and ingenious murders with which Barabas regales Ithamore (2.3.184–201) seems discrepant from the character Barabas establishes for himself in the first act.[59] The passage reads as if the single memory of the "maim" from 2.1 has called into being a whole host of vengefully sociopathic memories to surround and implement its redefinition of who Barabas and his gold now are. The point at which that murderous litany comes closest to the circumstances of Barabas's own trauma is when he recalls (if it even is a recollection) the despair to which he subjected Christian bankrupts, whom his usury had evacuated of their money:

> Then after that was I an usurer, . . .
> And every moon made some or other mad,
> And now and then one hang himself for grief,
> Pinning upon his breast a long great scroll
> How I with interest tormented him. (193–201)

The suicide's "long great scroll" inscribes "upon his breast," like Barabas's "soldier's scar," the place where money has been. Barabas's memories are reorganizing themselves around the trauma that has redefined the character's identification with money. Now he remembers himself not as a merchant, someone who directly handled money as "the ware wherein consists my wealth," but as a usurer whose "ware" was the deferral of coined money into the present absences of debt and interest (1.1.33). Unlike the "matter of iust memory" that sustains Guyon and Arthur in Eumnestes's books, Barabas's memory of his money does not depend upon any concept of exteriorized, historical factuality. Rather, memory is the means of the identity relation between Barabas and his money; as his "telling" of himself is forced to change by the trauma of his severance, his memories reshape themelves to suit his new understanding of himself in the present. In this readiness to serve whatever his present purposes may be, his memory displays itself as fully instrumentalized. Barabas's memory addresses itself only to the purpose of reinscribing Barabas's present relation to money as one that demands the future completion of revenge, and disclaims any reference to an ontologically stable past such as that attributed by Spenser to the materiality of Eumnestes's books.

The comparison of Barabas's disintegrating "thou" soliloquy to the stanza full of "I" and "me" by which Guyon asserts his integrity is a ready one, but the terms by which Guyon is able to make that assertion are themselves undermined in Barabas's experience. Guyon is essentially commending himself in his refusal to mistake gold for food, and in this he distinguishes himself both from the "cursed hand" that invented avarice and experienced it as indigestion and from Tantalus, tormented by his hunger for an apple that would be inedible even if he could reach it. But Barabas's relation to money does not hinge on the question of right consumption at all. Other, Christian characters are hungry for Barabas's gold, and Barabas manipulates them through it (when he isn't directly feeding them poison); their desire to consume Barabas's gold makes the gold his instrument. What makes money a matter of life and death to Barabas himself does not happen at his mouth. It happens between his "fingers' ends" and the stump of his imagined "maim": it's in his hands.

## V. PILATE'S FILTHY HANDS

Guyon's solutions for the problem of defining a temperate interaction between self and material work with reference to the mouth—temperance regulates not only the amount of food entering the mouth but also what qualifies as "food," an appropriate object for appetite (gold, no; bread, knowledge, both yes). Guyon's temperance also shapes what comes out of his mouth, as speech—as we see in his verbal evasions of Mammon and his reproach of Tantalus. And Guyon finds, in his arrival in Eumnestes's library, that the material relation of his body to what it consumes and what it articulates depends upon the "matter of iust memory." As Michael Pollan explicates "the omnivore's dilemma," the question "what is good to eat" depends upon an individuated experience that defines one's self-knowledge as eater: "what has proven good *for me* to eat, and how does that prior experience help me assess the stuff in front of me now?" The right kind of consumption is impossible without the right kind of self-contemplation.[60] Mammon himself is only interested in contemplating what's in his lap, but he rightly understands that Guyon's version of self-satisfaction has pretensions to an interiority, and so takes him on a tour of a constipated, dyspeptic digestive tract that opens out first onto the debased, worldly court of Philotime and then onto Hell. In the House of Alma, the knight's tour follows nutritive matter into the mouth and down to the stomach, but—after the delightful appreciation of the successful expulsion of waste from "Port Esquiline"—they trace the path of that nourishment across the gradations of subtlety through which the body interacts with the soul, from humoral bodily fluid to spirit to passion, in the court of the heart, and from the passions to the conscious mind. As long as the circuit is defined in terms of consumption, what goes in the mouth, Guyon can treat the difference between Alma and Mammon as stable and definitive. But Barabas identifies not the mouth but the "fingers' ends" as the point where the stuff of money and the stuff of life converge. And Munera, Mammon's political counterpart in the 1596 *Faerie Queene*, herself has extremities that demonstrate the indefinability of that bodily limit: golden hands and silver feet. Barabas imagines the loss of the money he has handled as the loss of his hand. In one of the most shocking moments of Spenser's epic, the pitiless "yron man" Talus amputates Munera's metallic hands and feet while she is still alive. Katharine Rowe has demonstrated how the amputation of a hand, Aristotle's "instrument of instruments," problematizes the relation of agency to instrumentality in both the social and material worlds:

> With its close focus on the body part most often associated with intentional, effective action, the trope of manual dismemberment brings to attention the fraught ties between spirit and body, between persons, and between persons and things that constitute agency relations. . . . At the heart of this trope is the perception of the hand as a separate piece of the body, linked to it by metonymy or synechdoche. Whereas philosophers since Aristotle have seen the hand as the special embodiment of the human ability to manufacture and control the material world, dismemberment relocates this part in that material, instrumental world. (3–4)

How does the relation of instrumentality—the remarkable "handiness" of coins, to use Heidegger's vocabulary for the self-effacing compliance of things with people—complicate the firm lines that Guyon seeks to inscribe between himself and his world through the relation of consumption? We have seen how Guyon tries to keep his mind and body nourished but untainted. How should he keep his hands clean?

The short answer would be, he shouldn't. Guyon's obsession with purification and cleansing, his suspicion that all matter is a debasement of his proper self, is legible as at least a potentially positive inclination when it is articulated in terms of consumption. Sooner or later a temperance that defines itself by rejecting consumption will itself be tempered when it crosses the threshold of bodily need, as Guyon does in his faint; this behavior is only an intensification of the scrupulous attention to nutrition urged by orthodox Elizabethan medicine, as Michael Schoenfeldt has demonstrated.[61] The body is a necessary and perforce acceptable accomodation with matter, the fulcrum for the complexly pragmatic balancing act that is temperance; coins are parodic, unfulfilling versions of that accomodation. But if interactions with the material world are instead imagined in terms not of consumption but of agency—of works, accomplishments, heroic deeds—Guyon's urge to prevent or efface the traces of such an interaction on his hands becomes deeply problematic. Pontius Pilate became one of the great villains of Christian history simply by refusing to get his hands dirty. Pilate is the last person Guyon meets in Mammon's cave.

Guyon's "hands" are marked with a suspect ambivalence in the first stanza of the first canto of Book Two, even before the hero himself arrives. Book Two opens with Archimago, but names him only in periphrasis as "That cunning Architect of cancred guile" (2.1.1). In joining "Architect" to "guile," the punning association through the first syllable of Archimago's name introduces a subtler one with the first syllable of Guyon's—a name that is for the first-time reader otherwise empty, having been cited only on the Book's title page and in a single line of the proem. Guyon's guile, through which he strives to beat Mammon at his own game and becomes perhaps too Mammon-like in the process ("So goodly did beguile the Guyler of the pray," 2.7.64), is here associated with the demonic Archimago before we meet the protagonist himself.[62] Left by the Redcrosse knight in custody of Eden's jailors, Archimago has through his "artes" "escaped cleene" "out of caytiues hands" (2.1.1).[63] The failure of human hands has released Archimago back into the world and into a strange association with the hero we have yet to meet, and that failure is itself a malevolent kind of cleansing.

When Guyon does arrive on the scene, Archimago seduces him into confronting Redcrosse by offering a vivid description of rape:

> Or rather would, O would it so had chaunst,
> That you, most noble Sir, had present beene,
> When that lewd ribauld with vile lust aduaunct
> Layd first his *filthy hands* on virgin *cleene*,
> To *spoile* her daintie corse so faire and sheene... (2.1.10, my emphasis)

Archimago's knack for pornographic *enargeia* is familiar from his manipulations of Redcrosse, and here he deftly adapts it to match what most readily stimulates Guyon to action, the sight of women who are victims of violence, in order to make Guyon his instrument.[64] As my emphasis indicates, the axis upon which Archimago manipulates Guyon's wrathful inclination is that between filthiness and cleanliness, and the fulcrum between the two is that of "hands." When the putatively wronged Duessa appears, she is "Wringing her hands...And her fair face with teares was fowly blubbered" (2.1.13). Misled by Duessa's gesture of ineffective despair and her appearance of befouled beauty, Guyon confronts Redcrosse, and only barely shies away from a battle that would shame them both. But Redcrosse gallantly takes blame for the encounter: "me behoueth rather to vpbrayd,/ Whose hasty hand so farre from reason strayd" as to nearly smite the image of Gloriana on Guyon's shield (2.1.28). It's Redcrosse's hand, he says, that should have known better than to take such an action.

The vain and deceptive gesture of Duessa's hand-wringing is contrasted by Redcrosse to a hand that is (or ought to be) so subject to "reason" as itself to be practically reasonable, continuously transmitting the interior judgment of reason into the world as action. This proper work of hands, as the medium of a rightful transmission, is given two registers in the agency of knighthood. Guyon himself "knighthood tooke of good Sir *Huons* hand" (2.1.6); chivalry has been conferred upon him by the hand of another knight, who has passed on the privileges and responsibilities that he, Sir Huon, already embodies to the younger Guyon. And when the Palmer praises Redcrosse's saintly victory over the dragon, Redcrosse modestly refuses the credit for his actions, making himself only the instrument of divine agency:

> Palmer, (him answered the *Redcrosse* knight)
> His be the praise, that this atchieu'ment wrought,
> Who made my hand the organ of his might;
> More then goodwill to me attribute nought;
> For all I did, I did but as I ought. (2.1.33)

"Goodwill," Redcrosse claims, replaces his own control over what his hands accomplish with the agency of God, making the knight's astonishing deeds the proof of God's effectivity in the world. Redcrosse's mental faculties of "reason" and "will" succeed by effacing themselves into a holy instrumentality, ensuring a continuous transmission from supernatural, divine will to material effect through the medium of human hands.

Having been cast down twice into the filthy "mire" surrounding the dragon before his final victory (1.11.45), Redcrosse knows well that implementing God's will can be dirty work. This is not an easy lesson for the fastidious Guyon to appreciate.[65] The horrific sight of Amavia's blood on her baby's hands prompts Guyon to try to clean "His guiltie hands" (2.2.3); as many commentators have noted, the nature of the guilt of the child's hands is frighteningly obscure.[66] The notion that the hands are significantly, rather than simply, dirty emerges from Guyon's surprising inability to clean them at the fountain. But this significance is formulated in anticipation of that failed cleaning as irreducible "guilt" on the hands' part, at the point that Guyon is the agent starting to attempt the cleaning, and retrospectively by the Palmer as the refusal, on the magical fountain's part, to absorb the gore of the hands into its own purity so that the hands may be cleansed. "From thence it comes, that this babes bloudy hand / May not be clensd by water of this well" (2.2.10): the Palmer insists that the failure of the cleansing is at least as much about the fastidious character of "this" fountain as it is about "this" baby. So too, I think, is the frustrated insistence on cleanliness something that Guyon projects onto the baby's hands, which he imagines "guiltie" in their insistence on retaining the material trace of the dead mother's blood. Spenser's paucity of antecedence in stanza 3 suggests that "guiltie" is here arising in such a transference; only sense, and not syntax, suggests that "His guiltie hands" are those of the baby and not of Guyon. Guyon's motive is parenthetically cited by the narrator, whose articulation seems close here to an interior monologue for the knight: "(So loue does loath disdainfull nicitee)" (2.2.3). But "disdainfull nicitee" is exactly why the chaste fountain refuses to wash the baby, and to define "loathing" as an operation of "loue" seems oxymoronic—it's "disdainfull nicitee," not "loue," that loathes things.[67] Guyon's rejection of the baby's stained hand and the fountain's rejection of the baby's stained hand seem more related to each other than either does to any "loue" for the baby himself.

Redcrosse's self-identification as the hand of a God unafraid to get that hand dirty remains forgotten by Guyon as the elf approaches Mammon's cave. Without the Palmer, Guyon finds he enjoys solitude. As Harry Berger has argued, being alone gives Guyon a rather suspect opportunity to think about what a splendid fellow he is: "euermore himself with comfort feedes,/ Of his own vertues, and prayse-worthy deedes" (2.7.2).[68] In ascribing his deeds and their praise-worthiness to "his own vertues"—a praise Redcrosse has explicitly declined for himself—Guyon disregards any self-conception as divine instrument, and imagines his deeds as artifacts of his own agency, produced by him for his own consumption. Solitude becomes self-reinforcing, the occasion of a solipsism that reduces Guyon's world to a vast emptiness populated by one smugly self-sustaining knight: "still he traueild through wide wastfull ground,/ That nought but desert wildernesse shew'd all around" (2.7.2). Indifferent to his surroundings, Guyon imposes that indifference upon his now blank surroundings until, "At last" (2.7.3), he meets the demon who lives on the other side of solitude.

Mammon makes a show of sharing Guyon's inclination to solitude, in residing in the "desert" Guyon has carved out for his own travels and in moving to hide himself and his treasure once Guyon has seen him—though not so quickly as to prevent the knight from stopping him: "*Guyon* lightly to him leaping, stayd/ His hand, that trembled, as one terrifyde" (2.7.6). The paranoid trembling of Mammon's filthy hand, like Duessa's hand-wringing, belies the way in which the demon will proceed to manipulate the knight's expectations. "God of the world and worldlings," Mammon is really the most sociable of demons, if we are willing to accede to the terms by which Mammon defines the sociable—which are the terms, as we have seen, of his own existence. By his own lights Mammon is a generous, even officious, host; by the time Guyon has been in the cave for twenty-nine stanzas, Mammon is offering the knight his daughter's hand in marriage.[69] Philotime is herself the center of "A route of people," a parodic court debased by mercenary "*Ambition*" (2.7.44, 46). What Mammon and Guyon have in common—what draws them together at the beginning of canto 7—is not the condition of solitude but the solipsism that sustains Guyon's solitude and makes it so pernicious.

Mammon's solipsism is the conviction that his own materiality defines the world—that the peculiar terms according to which a coin manifests value in other things are the only truths of the world. Guyon's solipsism is the conviction that his own truth is sufficent, and bears no necessary relation to the world it happens to inhabit. Guyon is optimistic of detaching himself from the world—he is too good for it to make a claim upon him. Within the terms by which Guyon and Mammon confront each other, those of consumption, abstinence, and need, Mammon is more wrong than Guyon is. Guyon is obviously compromised by his contest with Mammon in that he and Mammon use more or less the same tool, "guile," against one another, and in that he faints and needs to be rescued by the combined interventions of the angel, the Palmer, and Arthur. But such a post facto compromise seems from this perspective the point of the exercise: Guyon *ought* to think of his relation to the world as in the first instance rejective, and then qualify that rejection insofar as the standard of need demands compromise, requiring the consumption of particular nutriments that temperance allows to be not unsuitable. Certainly the beseiged House of Alma operates according to this principle, and this is the principle according to which Guyon interprets the exemplum of the intemperate consumer Tantalus. But that principle does not even begin to explain why Tantalus's neighbor in Mammon's torture garden is Pontius Pilate, condemned to stand in the same river that eludes Tantalus's lips, forever washing and failing to clean "both his hands most filthy feculent" (2.7.61). Guyon does not attempt to explain Pilate's presence either. The knight finds a full stanza of reproaches to fling in Tantalus's teeth, but after Pilate identifies himself Guyon has not a single word to say.

There is no obvious reason to associate Pilate with Mammon. Although the four Gospels differ significantly in their accounts of Pilate's motives and his level of complicity in the judicial murder of Christ, none of them accuse him of taking money.[70] If money were at stake in finding a companion for Tantalus from Christian history, Judas would be the more obvious candidate.[71] It seems to me to be more appropriate to consider Tantalus and Pilate as opposite than as parallel, and to locate their opposition not within the specific terms of money—what I've called the terms of Mammon's existence—but at the limit of those terms. The stream, Cocytus, in which the two sinners are plunged defines "the vtmost bound" of Mammon's back garden, which he calls "the *Gardin* of *Proserpina*," and which is apparently separated by the river from Hell proper next door (2.7.56, 53; Hell and "Richesse" are already mentioned as neighbors in stanza 24). Tantalus and Pilate are the two sinners whose intemperance pertains to both Hell and Mammon, and to each other; and it's Tantalus who is the closer to Mammon, for Guyon sees him first, and Guyon seems right to berate him in terms that seem a fitting conclusion to the conversation he has been having with the Money God.

Tantalus and Pilate stand in the same river condemned to contrary, but equally material, punishments. What distinguish their behavior are their perspectives on the matter with which they are damned forever to interact: what's both gold and food to Tantalus is shit to Pilate.[72] Tantalus can't get at it; Pilate can't get it off. The gold-food problem as it dangles before Tantalus is recognizably continuous with Mammon's ambition to anticipate and supplant the House of Alma. But Pilate's "labour vaine and ydle industry" in washing his hands seems much more pertinent to Guyon himself than were any of the putative temptations with which Mammon has tried to tantalize Guyon (2.7.61).

"When Pilate saw that he could prevail nothing, but that rather a tumult was made, he took water, and washed his hands before the multitude, saying, I am innocent of the blood of this just person: see ye to it [i.e., "do it yourselves"]" (Mat. 27:24). As Spenser's Pilate is condemned to forever try, and fail, to replicate his notorious bit of political theater, so too did Guyon's frustrated attempts to wash the bloody babe's hands locate guiltiness in a matter from which a hand might proceed to cleanse itself.[73] For Guyon, the standard of temperate consumption affords a detached position of ethical judgment. Being able to judge what should go into his mouth entitles him to pronounce judgment on other consumers, such as Tantalus, as an indifferent observer. But Pilate calls himself "the falsest Iudge" (2.7.62) in his abdication of agency, his claim that he is merely observing and judging the misjudgment of the Jews without partaking in it.[74] Pilate's judgment in Matthew was "*I* am innocent," despite the prospect of the "just" Christ's being put to death under his authority; the Pilate of Mammon's cave recognizes that his attempt to withdraw from the situation was itself a "wicked doome," the guilt of which cannot be blamed on the world beyond himself and washed away.

Pilate considered himself too good for the situation that he was in, and, finding that he did not have an easy way to shape it to his will, denied that he had any material relation to it at all, and performed the hand-washing to demonstrate that he was not an agent. Washing his hands of "the Lord of life" entails a rejection of the life of which Christ is Lord: the life of the world of matter, which the incarnate Christ did not disdain but which Pilate did, and which Guyon's ambivalently "disdainfull nicitee" risks rejecting in turn. Even Guyon's success in the Bower of Bliss is marked by this propensity to disdain matter, and in so doing to negate his own status as agent:

> But all those pleasant bowres and Pallace braue,
> *Guyon* broke downe, with rigour pitilesse;
> Ne ought their goodly workmanship might saue
> Them from the tempest of his wrathfulnesse,
> But that their blisse he turned to balefulnesse:

Their groues he feld, their gardins did deface,
Their arbers spoyle, their Cabinets suppresse,
Their banket houses burne, their buildings race,
And of the fairest late, now made the fowlest place. (2.12.83)

The "fowlest place" that Guyon "makes" is left at book's end to the hog-man Grill, who is of "The donghill kind" (87): the apparent rite of purification to which Guyon subjects the bower turns it into a pile of shit, displacing Pilate's experience of the circular relation of cleanliness and feculence onto the space of disavowal. But most striking is the effect upon Guyon of finding in that space an appropriate venue for the full scope of his passionate "wrathfulnesse," a situation in which temperance and "tempest" are one. "Passion" and "passive" share a root, and for the Renaissance giving way to passion meant the surrender of reason to a force acting upon it.[75] Guyon's agency disappears across the stanza into the destruction that he wreaks. The last and only moment in the stanza at which either "Guyon" or a pronoun referring to him bears stress in the verse is the beginning of line 2, where it's a countermetrical substitution; "his," "he," and "he" in ll. 4–6 are unstressed between sharply stressed, syntactically inverted objects and verbs. As the formula "Their [object] he [verb]" tightens in repetition in line 6, "he" finally drops out, and stays out (for six iterations of zeugma) until the stanza ends. Clearly nobody other than Guyon is doing these acts of destruction. Yet Guyon's agency has vanished from the stanza, as if the "arbers spoyle" and "banket houses burne" on their own initiative, or as some self-contained realization of what they deserve. Or as if, while the Palmer is busy tying up Acrasia, Guyon performs without thinking or choosing, as an automaton rather than as an agent.

Like Redcrosse (and unlike the Britomart of the 1590 *Faerie Queene*), Guyon has accomplished his quest.[76] But Redcrosse understands how he has come to accomplish it and his own relation to that accomplishment, which, he says, is that of a divine instrument: "His be the praise, that this atchieu'ment wrought,/ Who made my hand the organ of his might" (2.1.33). Guyon, conversely, has in the culmination of his quest vacated any understanding of his own relation to what he's doing. His own agency disperses into the ruination he exacts all around him as a "tempest," a phenomenon of the atmosphere. In this strange moment, Guyon is so fully integrated into the materiality of his environment that he seems to have evaporated entirely, along with all the other forms and structures of the Bower which he "makes" into the feculent "slime" of the *prima materia* (the past horizon of materiality in 2.9.21). It seems consistent with the oscillating pattern of "disdainfull nicitee" toward matter that has characterized both Guyon's triumphs over the temptations to intemperate consumption of adversaries like Mammon and the frustrated horror of uncleanliness in his interactions with matter that he shares with Pilate. If there must be dirt, "slime," and "mucke" to be dealt with in this ultimate instance, let there not be Guyon in dealing with it; he does his job and does it very thoroughly, but without being himself in doing it. Guyon's passionate "wrathfulnesse" is consistent with his character throughout the book, but we've also learned in Alma's court of the passions that his true, governing passion is "*Shamefastnesse*"—shyness, self-effacement, withdrawal (2.9.43, italics *sic*). This dispersal of his agency into an intramaterial and unindividuated force, the "tempest," is preferable to understanding himself as a unitary actor intervening upon the material world through the work of his hands. It's a momentary self-forgetting, one which seems more like the antimnemonic circuit of Mammon, in which exchange value circulates into all the things of the world and erases their difference, than like the lesson of self-sustaining memory taught in Eumnestes's library. In this self-effacing formulation, Guyon cannot hope to understand the significance of his own deeds as Redcrosse has, as themselves the instrumental means of a second, providential intervention upon the world. Guyon's own perverse and impossible aspirations to immaterial transcendence prevent his understanding of how something genuinely transcendent might address the world through the mediating tool of human hands. In this abstracted closedness to understanding he is still like Pilate, who asked Christ "What is truth?" without acknowledging that he was speaking to the concrete, incarnate answer (John 18:38). If we consider Guyon as an insufficiently self-conscious instrument, however—according to the model of sanctified and therefore intermediary agency that Redcrosse has propounded and that Guyon, in his horror of dirty hands, proves unwilling to comprehend—the Spenserian character whom Guyon comes most to resemble in this moment is Book Five's "yron man," the brutal automaton Talus. In the final movement of this chapter, I will turn to Spenser's revaluation in Book Five of the dichotomy between consumption and instrumentality. There the relation between the embodied self and the material world is posited as a political problem, and money recurs there as a defining instance of such a problematic relation. Addressing the problems of materiality from the perspective of politics offers solutions that are different from those propounded by Guyon's ethics-based perspective, but these solutions seem in their own way just as compromised and blinkered as Guyon's—none more so than Talus's bodily mutilation of Munera, the golden-handed embodiment of graft.

## VI. MUNERA'S GOLDEN HANDS

As James Nohrnberg has demonstrated, the system of analogy that shapes the interaction of meanings between the first and second halves of the 1596 *Faerie Queene* is most immediately evident in the symmetries of Books Two and Five. The challenges faced by Justice, like those of Temperance, are worldly ones:

> Spenser conceives temperance as the virtue that secures the private integrity against an unruly physical environment. As a consequence, this virtue is the natural model for personal orderliness and the control of internal power; presumably our allegiance to the institutions of society that maintain law and order is elaborated from the ideal of control established by this early training. This broadening of the virtue seems to be the logic behind Spenser's construction of the legend of justice, where a quest like Guyon's is undertaken on behalf of the social body.[77]

In the matrix of virtues in *The Faerie Queene*, justice proceeds from temperance. Political "order" is the accumulation of individuals who each maintain an "orderly" relation to the world: politics arises as the sum of individual instances of ethics. But—contradictorily—politics is also the singular, macrosopic instance of ethics as performed by "the social body," the commonwealth. Politics is at once aggregate and individuated, at once vertical and horizontal. Nohrnberg is here adopting the interpretation that establishes temperance as the explicit and normative difference between Guyon and Tantalus, which I've argued is undermined by the implicit comparison of Guyon to Pilate. The civic, political structures examined in Book Five are founded on the ethical structures of Book Two; but, as we've seen, those ethical structures are in turn founded in problems of material ontology, of what it is that the "unruly physical environment" is made of, and how an understanding of its making might subject unruly matter to rules of spatial form and temporal sequence. The fissures within Book Two's relation of materiality to ethics—between a model of consumption and a model of instrumentality—ramify in Book Five, as that relation is transumed into the synecdochal relation of ethics to politics.

The difficulties encountered by Artegall in coordinating the theory of Justice to its practice arise in the divide of the ideal from the material, a discrepancy which the ideal herself, Astraea, has given up trying to overcome. In retreating from the material world to the heavens, Astraea has delegated to her changeling Artegall the task of enforcing her justice on earth;

identifying (in an unexceptionable compliment, save for the context) Elizabeth with Astraea in the last lines of the proem, Spenser cites "thy [Elizabeth's] Artegall" as "the instrument" of "thy great iustice praysed ouer all" (5.pr.11). Not only is Elizabeth-Astraea's own relationship to Artegall that of instrumentality, she has also alienated to Artegall's service her own former instrument of enforcement, the implacable "yron man" Talus, who is "Immoueable, resistlesse, without end"—and therefore all means, disturbingly vacant of telos (5.1.12). Talus is Artegall's right-hand man, which in this context means the instrumentality of Artegall's "might":

> Who so vpon him selfe will take the skill
> True Iustice unto people to diuide,
> Had need haue mightie hands...
> For powre is the right hand of Iustice truely hight. (5.4.1)

Single-minded Talus in turn wields a single instrument of his own: "in his hand an yron flale [Talus] did hold,/ With which he threshd out falshood, and did truth unfould" (5.1.12). We rarely see Talus's flail produce these effects in practice, however. "Truth" is not often to be seen in Talus's wake. What's left when he is done using his flail is more likely to be either empty space—"When *Talus* saw they all the field forsooke/ And none appear'd of all that raskall rout,/ To *Artegall* he turn'd" (5.2.54)—or a fine paste of ground-up bone and flesh: "He with his yron flale did thresh [Radegund's followers] so *thin,*/ That he no worke at all left for the leach" (5.7.35, my emphasis). Instrumentality shapes perception. The modern proverb says that to a man holding a hammer, the whole world looks like a nail. To Mammon, constantly fondling his own instrumentality, the whole world looks like a market; to Talus and his flail, the whole world looks like chaff.

I've cited Mammon and Talus as complemetary instances of pure (and metallic) instrumentality, both of whom demonstrate a problematic initiative. As Mammon, money talks, encouraging its possessor to maximize its utility by seeing the world through its eyes as a series of exchange values; eager that his master's "might" exert itself in him, Talus tends to take matters into his own hands.[78] Neither simply lies dormant until the hand of an agent directs them to their "right vsaunce." Instead, they influence, even predetermine, the relationship between their surroundings and their agents that they exist to mediate, effectively arrogating to themselves the directing role of a hand, Aristotle's "instrument of instruments." The problematic handiness of Mammon and that of Talus confront each other unequally in canto 2 of Book Five, in the person of Pollente's daughter Munera, an embodiment of graft. As at Barabas's "fingers' ends," the stuff of life and the stuff of money converge in Munera's extremities: she has golden hands and silver feet. Her "nature is subdu'd to what it works in," as Shakespeare's sonnet 111 puts it, "like the dyer's hand." The trace of the matter that she handles is not only indelible, like the filth of Pilate's guilt; it is not even simply a trace, but the whole hand. There is nothing to the hand but the gold of her criminality. It's impossible to say where the sinner stops—the human body that might be purged and made whole by repentance—and the sin, as the matter of gold, begins. In this way Munera seems like an intensification of the ontological crux of Mammon's cave, between Tantalus's futile desire to ingest the world as gold and Pilate's "labor vaine and idle industry" in washing his hands of it: Munera incorporates gold into an otherwise human body, through the relation of instrumentality located in the hand. But Munera represents a diminution of that Mammonian problem even as she seems to intensify it.[79] As the distaff branch of her father's household, Munera transposes the subordinate relation of political influence to individual wealth that had obtained in Mammon's cave, where Philotime was daughter to Mammon, the political outcome of the corruption of ethics by matter; now the political problem, Pollente, is the big problem, and the problem of graft embodied in Munera is a corollary development from Pollente's "powre extort" (5.2.5). That is, the material convergence of metal and flesh in the person of Munera is a difficulty within the administration of commonwealth, as we have seen that flexible and wide-ranging rubric deployed in the introduction to this book. Once Pollente is dealt with by Artegall, Munera becomes a mere loose end, to be left for the competence of a subordinate to resolve.

In enforcing his private advantage "Through strong oppression of his powre extort," Pollente infringes the privilege of sovereign violence as it has been delegated by Astraea-Elizabeth to her "instrument" Artegall (5.2.5, 5.pr.10). As far as the allegory is here concerned, there isn't any difference between an exploitative landowner and a highwayman; Pollente's beheading realizes in the most forceful way possible the commonwealths-men's ambition to assert the supremacy of the common interest over individual interests by assimilating that supremacy to the sovereign's incontrovertible supremacy of judicial punishments. The centrality of the commonwealths-men's concerns to this episode is underlined intertextually as well. Munera is, as A. C. Hamilton puts it, "the offspring" of Langland's Lady Mede, the problematically complaisant figure at the center of Passus 2–4 of *Piers Plowman*; Mede's fingers "fretted with gold wyre" become Munera's golden hands.[80] The extent of Spenser's technical indebtedness to Langland as allegorist and as stylist has been well studied in recent years.[81] What I am pointing to here, though, is an allusion on Spenser's part to the topical way in which *Piers Plowman* was used across sixteenth-century literate culture as a voice for populist reform.

Langland's great poem was a byword for the advocates of commonwealth in the sixteenth century, as David Norbrook has demonstrated.[82] The poem was printed three times in 1550 by Robert Crowley, a vocal political gadfly who added a pointed preface orienting the poem to the contemporary crises, and reprinted again in 1561.[83] The character Piers Plowman was frequently cited as the embodiment of the commonwealth ethos, and he was revived as a speaker in numerous newly written tracts addressing his reformist perspective to present conditions.[84] The citation of Mede articulates the episode within the discourse of the commonwealths-men, in which social and material "goods" are continuous and the good of the political whole proceeds from the ethical restraint inculcated upon the parts by educative persuasion or force. But the subsumption of the "golden wyre" that had adorned the hands of Mede into the bodily substance of Munera's hands refers the continuity of ethics and politics in "commonwealth" back onto the continuity of ontology and ethics in Mammon's cave, the relation of the individuated material body to the materiality of the world.

The political philosophy of commonwealth does not seem like an optimal solution to the dilemma of consumption and instrumentality faced by Guyon in Book Two, however. At least as Artegall exercises justice in these early cantos of Book Five, the eruption of material interest into political relations is a problem to be dismissed by force and forgotten, not one that is to be resolved in discourse. In Langland, Meed's eroticized availability to any end in her engagement to Fals is a problem that rises up through the courtly structure to be extensively discussed and carefully redressed by the King and his courtiers over the course of three Passus. Mede upends many proposed solutions and comes very close to corrupting the discourse of judgment itself—the King "gan wexe wrothe with Lawe, for Mede almoost hadde shent it"—but the fruit of the conversation becomes a newly intimate relation of counsel among the King, Reason, and Conscience.[85] The scope, the thoughtfulness, and the discursiveness of Langland's episode all work to underline the horror of Talus's efficiently brutal, precipitate truncation of the problem of Munera's golden hands. At the beginning of Passus Four, the King imagines the marriageable hand of "Mede the mayde" as the means of incorporating her power into a reciprocal relation of ethics and politics, by affiancing her to to the poor knight Conscience to grant him power and influence. Conscience spurns Mede, and instead the King establishes the conversational relation of counsel to exclude both Mede and Wrong. But Munera's rich hand is a matter neither for marriage nor for rebuke, but for amputation:

> [Talus] rudely hayld her forth without remorse,
> Still holding vp her suppliant hands on hye,
> And kneeling at his feet submissiuely.
> But he her suppliant hands, those hands of gold,
> And eke her feete, those feete of siluer trye,
> Which sought vnrighteousnesse, and iustice sold,
> Chopt off, and nayld on high, that all might them behold. (5.2.26)

"Hands" and "feet" are first the means of supplication in the stanza. Munera adopts the conventional posture of abjection that demands mercy, her hands in the air, her body at Talus's feet. Her hands are "suppliant" twice, but once their material goldenness is articulated, they become the proof of her ineradicable guilt, at least as far as Talus is concerned, excluding their positional status as "suppliant" that would compel mercy. Her bodily posture kneeling at Talus's feet is correspondingly forgotten, and "feet" becomes about Munera's criminal relation to precious metal and not about her suppliant relation to Talus; no longer are "his feet" cited, only "her feet, those feet of siluer trye." Munera's proferred extremities become the evidence of her crimes and not the means of her claiming mercy. Talus chops them off to demonstrate their new status as evidentia, severing both their felonious continuity with Munera and the merciful relation that Munera had attempted to establish through them between herself and Talus, and he nails them up in public view to serve as an example.

As Jeff Dolven points out, it is difficult to understand what this display of Munera's severed extremities might be an example *of*, other than of the violence inherent in exemplarity itself.[86] Dolven focuses on the opposition of Munera's metallic, bluntly allegorical hands and feet to the tactile detail of her "sclender wast," the center of the fleshly remainder that Talus flushes down the stream in stanza 27—a detail that recalls the erotic appeal of Mede in *Piers Plowman* as well as the way in which she is subjected to the course of masculine, political justice; as Nohrnberg notes, "The clerk who hails Mede into court 'Toke Mede bi the middel.'"[87] What's significant to Talus is Munera's extraordinary and obviously emblematic extremities, and not their integration into an otherwise normal, even shapely, human body.[88] The iron man merely imposes a point of severance upon the continuity in

Munera of metal and flesh, which suffices to make the significance of the metallic members total, to his mind—and meaningless, to ours.

The fleshly core of Munera's body, her "sclender wast," is deliberately wasted by Talus, "drowned in the durty mud:/ But the streame washt away her guilty blood" (5.2.27). Wasted too are her and Pollente's extorted riches, "all that mucky pelfe... The spoile of peoples euill gotten good" (5.2.27). Only the point of convergence between the two, Munera's golden hands and silver feet, are to Talus's mind worth saving; they are exceptional and significant, while the two things they joined are the same anyway, at least once Talus gets done with them. Munera's body (sans hands and feet) and her wealth are both so much "mucke" washed down the stream.

Talus's washing away of the "mucke" that encompasses both flesh and gold achieves what the Pilate of Book Two could only wish for. It is tempting too to see a Pilate-like displacement of the responsibility of judgment in Artegall's pity of Munera: "*Artegall* him selfe her seemeless plight did rew.// Yet for no pitty would he change the course/ Of Iustice, which in *Talus* hand did lye" (5.2.25–26). This is a pity that Artegall indulges to the precise extent that it is ineffectual, unable to move him to intervene against the implacability of his subordinate instrument.[89] Certainly the peculiar, water-borne circulation of "guilt" from blood to pelf seems recognizable in the terms defined by Guyon's hand-washing encounters with Ruddymane and Pilate. All the guilt in these passages seems to be Munera's and Pollente's; there is no indication that the victims of their extortion have been themselves guilty of anything. Yet, once they have passed through Munera's strange hands, these riches are "the spoile of peoples euill gotten good"—and not, say, the evil-gotten spoils of people's good. The evil-getting applies to the good, and thereby to the people that used to have it, as much as to the fact of their spoliation. The commutative transumption of cause and effect here recalls the anti-mnemonic logic according to which Mammon understands himself to have been always already present in any worldly object. It is true that graft enjoins complicity with itself—in a corrupt system, no one can participate without participating in corruption, and Pollente and Munera have forced everyone around them to participate. But making both the "people" and their extorted "good" indifferently guilty of Pollente and Munera's evil-getting is obviously inequitable, even if we accept such a guiltiness to be just. Talus does not consider "that part of Iustice, which is Equity" to be in his job description, and since equity is only articulated in Britomart's arrival at Isis Church, Artegall may not yet think it is his problem either (5.7.3).[90] But this indifference to equitably proportionate degrees of guilt is a positive convenience for Talus and Artegall here. It makes Munera's gold as worthy of destruction as is her flesh. There is no question raised of returning the fruits of exploitation to the exploited; thanks to their being evil-gotten, what were once the people's goods are no longer good.

The question of restitution for the victims of Pollente and Munera's exploitation is not so much begged as obliterated in "the course/ Of Iustice, which in *Talus* hand did lye." Not only the mutilated trunks of Pollente and Munera, not only their "mucky pelfe," but also the castle domineering over the bridge are utterly destroyed by the iron man, "That there mote be no hope of reparation,/ Nor memory thereof to any nation" (5.2.28). The precluded "hope of reparation" is immediately that of any other robber baron who would want to exploit the same position by repairing the castle, but the sense of "amends" or "compensation" is available in early modern English, and that kind of reparation cannot now be hoped for either.[91] "Hope" and "reparation" are both matters for "memory," and in Talus's estimation what the situation calls for is a judicious forgetting of a memory that would prove not sustaining but troublesome for the future—in the possibility of Pollente and Munera's exploitations repeating themselves with new actors, in the possibility of Pollente and Munera's victims demanding present redress of their past losses, and for that matter in the immediate future of the canto's next episode, that of the "egalitarian giant," who uses a language of restitution to argue for redistribution. Yet Talus has already marked the place he is erasing by Pollente's head and Munera's hands and feet, all "nayld on high, that all might them behold" (5.2.26). These extremities serve as a kind of substitute memory to occupy the place of the erasure. In them, the singling out of the hand as agentive instrument condenses and reifies the relation of instrumentality between matter and agent as itself a punishment, a solution to its own problem. The fact of criminality is re-membered in these extremities, now made instruments, but the problematic fruit of their criminal actions—the matter with which they had interacted and, as instrument of instruments, gold hand handling gold, recurred upon—is thereby forgotten together with the bodies of which they had been part.

As Dolven suggests, the lesson taught by the display of Munera's hands and feet is the sheer brutality of teaching someone a lesson she won't soon forget. The productive, nutritive value that "matter of iust memory" had generated for Guyon and Arthur in Eumnestes's library is entirely eclipsed by the instrumental value that Talus places upon a quick and politically expedient solution to a problem that need not, unlike its precedent recalled from Langland, be resolved discursively, when violence will do just as well. Like Barabas's "maim," the power of memory is here not nourishing but traumatic. The dismembered appendages that in the past were joined to Munera's body now join the past to the present, as the material persistence of brutality. Unlike the rotten and weather-beaten limbs of fully human traitors subjected to the same display, the metallically incorruptible tokens of Munera's corruption and punishment will endure.

At the midpoint of this chapter, I turned from the contest over consumption between Mammon and Alma to the problems manifested in Barabas's, Pilate's, and Munera's hands in order to suggest that the normative model of consumption in Guyon's sojourn with Alma and Eumnestes begs the question of instrumentality in defining an ethical relation of agent to matter—that, in focusing so exclusively on what goes in and out of his mouth, Guyon is able to ignore what he is and is not doing with his hands. But Artegall's accession to Talus, in which this robotic "mighty hand" ignores questions of material good in pursuing the social good, and in so doing perpetrates an act of forgetting that at once discounts and monumentalizes its own brutality, suggests that the privileging of instrumentality is a vice of politics just as the privileging of consumption is a vice of ethics. Through Talus's handy initiative, Artegall forgets the material relation of wealth to the mouths left hungry in the present by Pollente and Munera's past extortions; Guyon's verbal fluency in berating Tantalus leaves him, when confronted by Pilate, speechless. Consumption and instrumentality are both true ways of understanding Mammon's relation to human bodies, ways according to which human bodies mediate their own relation to the world of matters and values. They are opposite, in the analysis developed by Spenser and engaged with a productive irony by Marlowe. But they are not, and must not be, exclusive. The material eccentricities of coined value in the Renaissance make Mammon an object both ethical and political, at once commodity and instrument. The fulcrum between these two faces of the coin is memory—the power, in the last instance, to remember that matter need not be either commodity nor instrument, but has a nature that encompasses both consumption and utility. That benignant nature for matter is the providential character of God's creation, in which making and use—first and final cause—are one, a transcendence of temporality that Mammon's oppressive futurity can only ape. Nevertheless—as the example of Talus's handling of Munera suggests, and as I will go on discuss in the next chapter—the oppositional resistance of Mammon's materiality to the purposes of providence can have its own uses.

CHAPTER TWO

# Monetary Policy

## *King John* and *Measure for Measure*

Whereas the previous chapter read out from the conditions of money's materiality to see how problems first ethical and then political could be understood through those conditions, this chapter construes those material conditions as themselves having a political origin. Here, I will consider gold and silver coins in their relation to the state, which not only produces them, but—as I will argue—reproduces itself in them. In what follows, I examine the parts played by coins in two of Shakespeare's political dramas: the offstage role of Commodity, the Mammon-like personification to whose agency is ascribed the ruinous policy of *King John*, and the coin's star turn as Angelo, the strangely monetized villain of *Measure for Measure*. John and Angelo are bad politicians, in both senses of the word "bad." Their incompetence is part and parcel of their viciousness. The badness of their policy, I argue, originates in the way that each defines the material world in terms of coined money. In his allegiance to Commodity, John makes money the thing that makes his world go round (and inevitably astray), while Angelo, minted by the Duke as an "angel," himself thinks as money. Both characters are wrong. But they are wrong in rich and compelling ways; their deviance articulates, Mammon-like, the chthonic pressure of matter upon the top-down theopolitical orthodoxy that each play professes to enforce. In confronting these representatives of Mammon, each play articulates the political world as a contest between the forces of causality—providence, sovereignty, genre, plot—and a truculent, material contingency.

"Commodity" is named by the Bastard in *King John* as a demonic force that privileges contingency over causality to void worldly affairs of their meaning. But in naming that drive toward contingency, the Bastard also gives it a voice, a voice partly his own, but partly, I argue, that of Epicurean atomism. Epicurean natural philosophy was seen in the Renaissance to undermine Aristotelian accounts of material causality, not to mention Stoic doctrines of fate and Christian ones of providence. Coins present a problematic instance for the sequence of cause and effect as it is defined by Aristotelian hylomorphism, as we saw in the previous chapter; and, as the Bastard demonstrates, they make a disturbingly handy example for an Epicurean account of worldly occurrences as being generated in a random, unwilled, and meaningless deviance. But *King John* presents the disastrous subjection of John's illegitimate reign to the contingency of Commodity as an exception proving the rule of causality, a transient deviation within the larger conformity of English history to the providential numen of monarchical sovereignty.[1]

*Measure for Measure*, conversely, uses money to define the enclosure of contingency within the legitimating means of sovereignty. The Duke mints an angel in the play's first scene to serve as his deputy; to become the instrument of the Duke's secondhand governance, the stuff of Angelo's personhood is forcefully "stamp'd" into the form of a large gold coin. In proving tyrannous, Angelo will fail to serve the publicized purposes of his making; in failing to pardon Claudio after having sex with Isabella-Mariana, Angelo will deviate even from the Duke's own shadowy expectations. But Angelo's monetized deviance will nevertheless pay dividends to the Duke. Angelo's eccentric circulation through the diseased market of Vienna cannot but serve the interests of the sovereign who has minted him, no matter how unpredictable his trajectory may be. The strange obscurity of the sovereign interest that Angelo so unpredictably, but so inevitably, serves is called the Duke's "pleasure" throughout the playtext. Joyless as that pleasure is, it marks the unlikable comedy and the debased commonwealth of *Measure for Measure* as alike depending on a sovereign arbitrariness that enfolds material contingency into a social good, even if the only individual who profits from that good is the sovereign.

In grouping providence, sovereignty, genre, and plot together as forces that impose a meaningful relation between cause and effect, I am suggesting that the latter three terms can each be understood, at least in Shakespeare, as modeling their interaction with the particular matters that they shape upon that of providence.[2] As Alexandra Walsham demonstrates, providence had been a principal means of understanding the relation of the immutable divine will to the flux of the material world throughout Christian history, and one that acquired new urgency in the sixteenth century through the Protestant dismissal of miracles and anxiety over predestination.[3] Providence organized the most insignificant events, like Hamlet's "fall of a sparrow," into infinitely subtle and infinitely extensive chains of causes, suffusing each with meaning and purpose (*Hamlet* 5.2.220, citing Mat. 10:29–31).[4] Divines disagreed as to how directly interpretable the relation of any given macroscopic event to its ultimate cause in God's inscrutable will might be, but Hamlet's assertion that the tiniest minutiae were meaningful in God's eyes and integral to God's plan was itself unexceptionable.[5] Political sovereignty, as a phenomenon upon which so many other phenomena themselves depended, was invariably an instance of providence at work. It was possible for Renaissance thinkers to imagine individual forms of government, and individual sovereigns, as indifferent applications by human communities of the divine institution of sovereignty.[6] More often, however, providential reasoning was applied to justify the sovereignty of an individual monarch as specifically willed by God. In the formulae of "sacral kingship" that Debora Kuller Shuger sees mobilized in *Measure for Measure*, a monarch so invested manifests the nature of the divine mind to the world, both as irresistible will and as uncanny knowingness: "I perceive your Grace, like pow'r divine,/ Hath look'd upon my passes," says Angelo when his secret transactions have been brought to light by the Duke (*Measure* 5.1.369–370).[7]

As Jacques Lezra has argued, however, even the word "event," so neutral and factual-seeming to us, has a degraded relation to such a perfect knowledge as the Duke's in Renaissance epistemology.[8] There, "event" connotes an outcome that was neither predicted nor willed, and that in its mere contingency lies below the point of serious consideration. A typical example of this conventionally degraded sense of "event" in its comparison to providence comes in act 2 of Jonson's *Epicoene*, in which, to his friend Clerimont's astonishment, the gallant Truewit claims credit for a positive outcome for his previous actions (making the recluse Morose determined to marry Epicoene), even though those actions had been a misguided attempt to cause the opposite outcome:

> *Clerimont.* Wilt thou ascribe that to merit now, was mere fortune?
> *Truewit.* Fortune? Mere providence! Fortune had not a finger in't. I saw it must necessarily in nature fall out so; my genius is never false to me in these things....
> *Clerimont.* Away, thou strange justifier of thyself, to be wiser than thou wert, by the event!
> *Truewit.* Event! By this light, thou shalt never persuade me but I foresaw it as well as the stars themselves.[9]

Truewit's dismissal of "event" as the belittling antithesis of his professed foreknowledge implicates the word's origin as *eventum*, a term of art in Lucretius's presentation of Epicurean material philosophy. In *De rerum natura*, Lucretius details the mindless, causeless, and microscopic motions of minuscule bodies (atoms or "corpuscles") through void: every so often one atom happens, for no reason, to "swerve" (*declinare*) and bumps into another atom, they careen into other atoms, and once the microscopic swerve has affected enough matter it becomes visible as a macroscopic event. Lucretius explicitly defines this emergence of the phenomenal world from the erratic contingencies of corpuscular matter as a rejection of the teleological claims of fate to order the temporal world into a knowable and inescapable structure. "Event," then, not only connotes a quality of insignificance in the material outcome to which it refers, as opposed to the meaningful principles which can be logically adduced from significant outcomes; it also suggests a kind of recalcitrance towards significance, an almost willful and perverse meaninglessness, on the part of the matter that fails to be elevated in that outcome over the threshold of significance, and that basely retains the quality of the mere event. Contingency and causality confront one another most directly across the perceptual threshold of the trivial and microscopic; to providence, nothing is so small as to be meaningless, but for Epicurean natural philosophy the invisibly tiny arbitrariness of the swerve defines the contingency according to which these minimal events accumulate into perceptible phenomena free of the chains of determinism.

Daniel Tiffany points out that the corpuscular philosophy depends on metaphor to formulate its analyses of the material nature of phenomena.[10] The events it postulates as fundamental are also imperceptible, and must be accommodated to macroscopic phenomena in order to be imagined; they must be translated back across the threshold of minimal perception through metaphor.[11] In *King John*, the phenomenal particles that make atomistic contingency comprehensible are coins. The notoriously erratic movements of coins through the social world, their discrete and atomized smallness, and the everyday triviality of the material exchanges which they traverse—all these factors suit coinage to the task of representing the invisible contingencies making up the nature of things in Epicurean philosophy. But that articulation as coinage also works to deride the philosophical representation that it enacts; it postulates Epicureanism as not only amoral in the way that riches are amoral, but petty as individual material transactions are petty—small-minded, basely mercenary. The natural philosophy is led to deform itself through its own dependence on poetics, its reliance on a means of articulation that is, in this play, essentially hostile to it. *King John* considers the Aristotelian, hylomorphic philosophy of substance to be normative as an account of the world, and normative moreover as an account of its own textuality. The temporal and causal relation of "matter," in both its textual and substantial senses, to form defines the plotting of the play, its generic relation to Shakespeare's previous history plays, and its depiction of sovereign power. All of those forms model themselves on the shaping force of providence upon history, but none of them, in *King John*, actually work. The monetized materialism of *King John* is so degraded as to dissociate itself from the work of providence in guiding England's present into the future, leaving the play's dramaturgy as a sputtering exercise in redundancy. The play uses Epicureanism to present itself as a hiatus or negative cycle in providential history: a merely sublunary moment, corresponding to the reign of John, during which only material advantage propels events, and during which nothing consequently gets anywhere.

In settling on coinage to articulate the Epicurean corpuscle, the play subordinates the bodily satisfactions by which Epicureanism is more usually made notorious to this more historical version of deviance, making hedonism a subset of materialism. Sexual reproduction becomes itself a matter of minting; disavowing both his brother and his dead father, the Bastard cites the inherited resemblance between the two as that of one "half-fac'd groat" to another (1.1.94). In chapter 1, I argued that an individual's relation to the material world could be defined in different ways by prioritizing different bodily interactions with coinage. Spenser articulates the nexus of coins and bodies first in terms of consumption, terms which are normative from the point of view not only of Guyon but also of Alma's bodily castle itself; there, the locus that defines the difference between the stuff of money and the stuff of the body is the mouth. But the presence of Pilate in Mammon's cave adumbrates a more uneasy interaction between bodies and coins, that of instrumentality, which becomes primary in *The Jew of Malta* and in the Munera episode of *The Faerie Queene*'s Book Five. In this interaction, the nature of coins and the nature of bodies are convergent rather than divergent; at the locus of the hand, Aristotle's "tool of tools," it is impossible to tell just where one gives way to the other. *King John* and *Measure for Measure* together offer a third interaction to define what it is that material bodies and material coins have in common, that of reproduction.[12]

In the Vienna of *Measure for Measure*, sexuality is so vividly degraded that the alternative reproduction manifested by the Duke, in "stamping" his authority onto the newly minted Angelo, seems like a valuable corrective. The minting does not permanently supersede sexuality, either in Vienna or in Angelo—rather, it eventually enforces an appropriate, married sexuality on both the deputy and the city as a whole. Its outcome, like other comic inversions of the order of things, is to renew that normative order; the play's action, from the deputization of Angelo to his recall, takes a city divided between prigs and punters, nuns and whores, and reweaves its urban fabric through the institution of marriage and the power of the state to compel it. But during the play's action, while Angelo bears the stamp of authority, that positive resolution seems very far away, and the consensus of audiences and readers who have come to call *Measure for Measure* a generic "problem" has been to find the means by which the play suddenly arrives at that comic horizon to be unsatisfying if not actively unpleasant. One way to begin defining the fascinated distaste with which we respond to the play's comedy might be to say that *Measure for Measure's* comic inversion does not limit itself to the (social) order of things, but dabbles in the nature of things, in the difference between coins and people. Renaissance epistemology does not lend itself to any very positivist distinction between the social and the physical, as the fluid gender of Shakespeare's transvestite heroines attests. But the power of dramatic representation to make a boy into a girl into a boy, as in the case of *Twelfth Night*'s Cesario or *As You Like It*'s Ganymede, still seems of a different order from the Duke's unmimetic but vividly effective minting of Angelo, through which his authority exists in Angelo for most of the play in the form of a stamp upon Angelo's "mettle." Where the interaction between body and coin was contested in Spenser between two points of contact, mouth and hand, in the strange reproductive dynamics of *Measure for Measure* that interaction encompasses Angelo's whole person—and locates itself too upon the mysterious past interaction of other bodies that produced his. "They say this Angelo was not made by man and woman after this downright way of creation.... Some report a sea-maid spawn'd him; some, that he was begot between two stock-fishes [i.e., dried cod]," muses Lucio to the disguised Duke, who has himself made Angelo after another way of creation—one that does encompass both the asexual reproduction of a monad and the production of Angelo's living matter from lifeless matter (3.2.104–109).

Sexual pleasure is evacuated from the minting reproduction that produces angel/Angelo, and that evacuation eventually corrals both the ascetic sterility and the diseased indulgence into which Viennese sexuality had been bifurcated into the normatively productive erotics of marriage. Until the Duke himself volunteers to marry Isabella in the play's last lines, "pleasure" for him has meant not delight but will: his sovereign arbitrariness. The manifestation of that pleasure in Angelo's minting instantiates a relationship between the kind of degraded, material contingency that *King John* identifies with coinage and the successful exercise of sovereignty. The Duke's technique of producing a subordinate to enforce an unpopular policy, upon whom he will capitalize both by retaining the policy and by destroying the subordinate, is a recognizably Machiavellian tactic; as Victoria Kahn has argued, even those readers who decried as amoral Machiavelli's analysis of political technique recognized the value of that analysis in postulating power as the circumscription of contingency.[13] The Duke himself is unable to account for Angelo's erratic behavior once the deputy has been set loose upon the flesh-markets of Vienna. But even that perverse contingency on angel/Angelo's part becomes legible at last as an instrument of the Duke's own, otherwise illegible, sovereign will.

## I. THE BIAS OF THE WORLD

Shakespeare's strange one-off chronicle play *King John* manifests the grand scope of narrative, action, and character that typifies his history plays: it has battles, it has the bombastic passions of princes, it has political intrigue to spare. Yet in each of those registers, the play seems strangely self-defeating. I will argue that this play's perversity toward its own plot and its own means enacts a resistance within materiality toward human purpose that might only be overcome by the divine intent of providence, whose intervention is so vividly deferred throughout the play's five acts. *King John* retreats from the successes of Shakespeare's first tetralogy in shaping chronicle matter, the undifferentiated mass of political events, into a form at once Aristotelian and divine. This play instead presents a world that is deprived of that plotting force, that is shaped instead by the futile, self-canceling collisions of a monetized contingency: a world in which Commodity's "half-fac'd groats" and "fair angels" alike share the ironic deviance attributed to atomic particles by the most perverse of material philosophers, Epicurus. In attempting to tailor his policy to suit the arbitrary and mindless caprice of Commodity, Shakespeare's King John is both a materialist and a failure. But the way in which he again and again fails voices Commodity's ironic claim upon the inscription of political history.

I won't be claiming that *King John* is either a failure as a play or an unjustly neglected masterpiece, although it is true that the play's lapse into relative oblivion is a recent development in its reception history; the nineteenth century had much more use for *King John* than we have had since.[14] I want, rather, to assert that the play makes a strange and deliberate choice to dramatize failure. This is a playtext that (unlike so many other of Shakespeare's plays) dwells in our popular memory in only one half-line aphorism, "gilding the lily," which denotes redundancy. But our phrase itself compresses the playtext's version, "To gild refined gold, to paint the lily" (4.2.11): the playtext's statement of redundancy has itself been found redundant and inefficiently expressed.[15] And that line is itself only one of twenty-five lines asserting through metaphor or anecdote the redundancy of John's second crowning in 4.2, all of which are articulated only after John has done it, but which (according to Salisbury) are exactly what the nobles had also told John before the event, so that what's multiply redundant now is itself a reiteration of what was ineffective then. Foresight and hindsight converge with a scrupulously balanced ineffectuality on the event, neither of sufficient force to shake the conviction of John's terrible idea; their redundancy makes each essentially cancel the other out, while the redundant event of the recrowning itself (following the logic of supplements) serves not to confirm nor to compound John's original crowning but only to call it into question.

The same redundancy recurs throughout the plot, as for example in the sequence of events at the gates of Angiers (2.1–3.1), in which the one-too-many kings of England are told to come back when there's only one of them: they fight; both sides claim victory; neither has victory; they embark on a do-over battle; then they decide instead to destroy the city together before settling their own dispute over the city; then they decide instead on a dynastic marriage; and then, once that's all resolved, the papal legate arrives out of nowhere and gets them to fight again anyway. What we're seeing in the recrowning is not an isolated failure, nor is it a sequence of isolated failures united only by chronological succession. This is a telescoping structure of redundancy, a whole plot made out of the reiteration of self-canceling returns to square one. This structure extends from the details of speech, through the matter of the individual events drawn from the chronicle of the historical John's reign, to the shaping of the playtext into plot. The play's quality of failure is a matter of the most artful deliberation and technical precision. Perversely, the playwright's skill applies itself not to the expectation of the play's own success but to the venturing of failure for its own sake under conditions controlled to make it most evident. *King John* is an experiment in failure.

I will argue that this experiment works through the negation of the forces that, in Shakespeare's first chronicle plays, had assigned form and purpose to history: the providence of God and the genre of tragedy. The weirdly pointless redundancy of *King John*'s plot is determined by this twofold exclusion. *King John* thus offers a version of history temporarily vacated of divine intent, an account of materialism as lack—or, more specifically, of materialism as the bad faith that lurks at all the play's crossed purposes, which is named by the

Bastard as the monetized personification "Commodity." I'll dub this quality of bad faith which the play attributes to the possibility of a materialist, secular history "improvidence," and I will suggest that this quality is formulated in the playtext by means of an antagonistic encounter with the materialist and atheist ontology of Epicureanism and is located by the text in the "groats" and "angels" that reproduce Commodity's mindless deviance.

Although it is not in the play's vocabulary, "improvidence" seems to me the best word for the quality of a world misruled by Commodity, for four reasons. The first is that "improvidence" defines the play's plot as driven by an absence or lack, a negated condition, rather than by a force such as Fortune whom one might otherwise imagine propelling chance. Both Fortune and Heaven are offered as personified agents for history at different points in the play, but their roles are so controverted among the self-interests of the characters as to effectively negate such agency on the part of either. The second reason is that "improvidence" suggests that the lack in question here is that of divine purpose, that the play takes place in a lapse of positive divine intent in history corresponding to the reign of John. Without the active engagement of the divine will to give its material events meaning, the play is subject to an unredeemed contingency operating in place of causality. That subversion of causality is something that we have already seen to accompany the presence of Mammon in Spenser's *Faerie Queene*, where the character's strange atemporality threatened to undo the mnemonic work of history.[16] Shakespeare similarly associates the improvidence of events in the reign of John with the chthonic and perverse influence of "Commodity." Jonathan Lamb argues that the tension between providence and the market as explanatory agents of historical process became more and more evident in the later Renaissance as the market broadened its scope:

> The growth of the market economy was attended with a new sort of ignorance, productive of a keen anxiety about the tendency of events and the constitution of the self. Instead of relying on Providence for a sense of history, people confronted an engine for social development that they had constructed themselves, but that they could neither govern nor understand.[17]

Lamb's analysis is retrospective from the point of departure of his study, in the Restoration, where *King John* seems to me proleptic: the play avoids declaring that providence has lost out to Commodity as an understanding of history, instead pointing to providence as deferring itself to a point just beyond the play's own historical horizon, but the play's consciousness of the tension between providential and mercantile explanations of historical causality contains the germ of Lamb's coming epistemological crisis. My third justification of "improvidence" is that, in its personal sense, the word integrates this history without intention, this succession of mere events, to John's own characteristic misjudgment, the wasteful redundancies of his continually frustrated policy. And the fourth reason to use the word is that by applying the sense of "improvidence" that denotes a failure to address present value to future needs, which makes improvidence the quality of Aesop's grasshopper or Christ's prodigal, we can see the present conditions of the play as the unlooked-to future of a past improvidence, the sexual failure of Richard Cordelion to provide England with a legitimate heir.

In this last sense we might profitably redefine what critics of the Renaissance history play often cite as the "weak-king dilemma," the location of the plots of many history plays in the problem of how to deal with a sovereign who is incompetent or venal, as instead a great-king dilemma: how can a king who is great be succeeded, save by a king who is not so great?[18] The weakness of Henry VI is staged in *Part One*, act 1, scene 1 in the untimely funeral of his great father, Henry V; that of Marlowe's Edward II by the letter announcing the lapse of the iron will of Edward I, "My father is deceased, come, Gaveston,/ And share the kingdom with thy dearest friend"; that of Richard II by the insistent comparisons of the living king not only to his mighty grandfather, Edward III, but to the never realized and therefore putatively infinite potential of his father the Black Prince.[19] Each of these plays addresses the unstaged greatness of the immediate past as a supratheatrical and pretheatrical phenomenon—that is, as the act impossible to follow. The business of these plays is with the impossible but nevertheless necessary following, representing as they do again and again the falling short in the play's staged present of a greatness in the play's memory that surpasses the medium. The elaborate circumspection with which the personification of Shakespeare's theatricality, the prologue of *Henry V*, at last approaches his magnificent subject, and the strangely ostentated inadequacy of theatrical means to the end of representing Henry's greatness throughout that play, give a corroboration of this great-king problem for theater even as Shakespeare's powers approach their height.[20] Here, in what is very much a journeyman piece, the company's sympathies most evidently lie athwart the high points of English history, not to mention athwart the expectant sympathies of an audience—not with the romance-bound magnanimity of Richard the Lionheart but with the not-so-greatness of King John, with the succession of unmitigated and reiterated failure.

The readiest way to verify this claim is to note how consistently and how thoroughly Shakespeare repudiates in this play the technical means of history-playwriting that he had himself developed in this play's immediate predecessors, the Yorkist tetralogy that culminated in *Richard III*.[21] As Jean E. Howard and Phyllis Rackin argue,

> The providential justice that determines the outcome in *Richard III* is nowhere to be seen [in *King John*], and every attempt to resolve the action or make sense of it is immediately frustrated by the moral ambiguities of an episodic plot where success and failure ride on the shifting winds of chance.... *King John* exposes the ideological faultlines that threatened to undermine the genealogical narratives that could make the marriage of Henry Tudor and Elizabeth of York seem a secure resolution to the civil strife which preceded it[.][22]

The first tetralogy as a whole takes the shape of its plotting from classical tragedy as defined by Aristotle and practiced by Seneca. *Richard III* in particular features a sharply defined rising action, a corresponding falling action, an anagnorisis, many lines of stichomythia, and even a chorus; it is more self-consciously classical in its tragic form than *Titus Andronicus*'s otherwise more direct imitation of Seneca. This very self-consciousness about the working out of form suggests that the form has a lot of work to do in *Richard III*, to whip the matter of chronicle history into shape. As Marjorie Garber has argued, the deformity of Richard's body is itself legible as a trace of the force by which the playwright works Richard's story into dramatic form.[23] *Richard III* takes the shape of its plot from (ultimately) Aristotle, but it attributes the force doing the shaping to providence. This providence arranges history into the forms of the *psychomachia*, the confrontation of Virtue and Vice to influence a mortal soul, so that material events may, in concretizing this abstract struggle, make manifest the will of God in the triumph of the good. The play's providential dramaturgy cribs from *The Jew of Malta* in making the soul to be won or lost exterior to the staged action, so that the Vice himself may be the onstage protagonist. In *The Jew*, Barabas, as Vice, is attempting to seduce his audience into complicity with his enormities. In *Richard III*, what the protagonist-Vice seeks to win is not only the allegiance of his present audience but that of his historical England.[24] Here Shakespeare follows, as is well documented, the Tudor historiography of Hall and More, who attribute the fall of Richard and rise of Henry VII to the salvific redemption of England from the prolonged bloodbath of the Wars of the Roses, where the demonic Richard gives way perforce to the saintly Henry Tudor in what becomes Shakespeare's fifth act. The "Tudor myth" defines the accession of Elizabeth's grandfather as an exemplary instance of providential determinism, rather than attributing the outcome, as a materialist historian might, to the last spasm of the dynastic conflict itself, in which the last man standing among the houses of York and Lancaster was handed the crown by the violently reiterated process of elimination—by the mere event.

Providence and genre have a convergent force in *Richard III,* the force of teleological shaping. As we saw in chapter 1, Aristotle analyzes the condition of material existence through the temporal bifurcation of all objects into matter and form, in which matter is passive and inert, while form is active, motive, and purposive, propelling inertia toward telos by giving it shape.[25] The concept of telos integrates Aristotle's material philosophy with his analysis of verbal practice, both in the *Rhetoric* and in the *Poetics,* where the form of tragedy is defined as its plot, and plot is in turn defined in terms of the end of catharsis, the purgative experience of the concatenation of pity and fear. The concept of telos is likewise among the things that make Aristotle's philosophy so congenial to a Christian understanding of history, in which the end of history is determined by its beginning, the originary intent of the Word, and in which the divinity that shapes our ends works itself out through unmiraculous, historical events in time as providence.

Just as Hall and More labored to demonstrate the consistent and inexorable will of God in the events leading to the fall of Richard III and the rise of the house of Tudor, so too did Shakespeare shape that recalcitrant matter into the generic form of providential tragedy. Once that mastery over the matter of chronicle was staged as *Richard III,* however, Shakespeare and his rival Marlowe both seem to me to have become interested in the perverse resistance of the eventful matter of chronicle to such shaping. Marlowe, always alive to the possibilities of perversity, uses the chronicle in *Edward II* to stage the grandeur of sovereignty as the compulsion to repeat: when Edward's barons kill Gaveston to purge the realm of favoritism, the king's obsession with a baseborn man instead replicates itself upon a new favorite, Spencer. And before embarking upon the great teleological arc of the Lancastrian plays, Shakespeare presents a sovereignty so entirely constrained by contingency that it can go nowhere, its purposed ends constantly set at naught by the perversity of the matter it attempts to shape. This is *King John,* the drama not of sovereign compulsion but of sovereign frustration.

*King John* stages its own rejection of Aristotelian dramatic form and telos in its bizarre and abrupt termination, the death of the king by poison. By "termination" I mean to suggest that "end," with its teleological overtones in English, is not even the word for the way in which the play stops happening.[26] How can John offer his audience the catharsis that is the generic promise of tragedy when he can't be purged himself? Waiting for John to die, Salisbury reassures the heir to the throne that Providence will not consign him to follow his father's aimless course, but rather will grant a purpose to him and, through him, to England:

> Be of good comfort, Prince, for you are born
> To set a form upon that indigest
> Which he hath left so shapeless and so rude. (5.7.25–27)

Salisbury refers here to Aristotle's hylomorphism, the distinction within each object between its inert matter and the "form" which gives it both shape and telic purpose. The "indigest" that is the previous five acts' worth of events here, however, is not merely inert, nor is its resistance to the king's shaping will a question of merely neutral inertia; it becomes in Salisbury's account the poisonous matter inside the king's body, which is unable either to digest or to expel it. The resistance of matter to form, of material events to the sovereign will, is perverse and ultimately killing.

In addition to an end, Aristotle tells us a play should have a beginning and a middle. *Doctor Faustus* is famous as the play without a middle, but *King John* is all middle, which is also to say all muddle, "left so shapeless and so rude" without an end to give it anticipatory form, and with only what Elinor calls "a strange beginning":

> *King John.* Now say, Chatillion, what would France with us?
> *Chatillion.* Thus, after greeting, speaks the King of France,
> In my behavior to the majesty,
> The borrowed majesty, of England here.
> *Elinor.* A strange beginning: "borrowed majesty"! (1.1.1–5)

Elinor's repetition of the French ambassador's phrase as a pair of anapests at the end of her line emphasizes the unmetricality of Chatillion's line, imposed by the refusal to contract "borrowed" as "borrow'd," as well as its jarring provocation. But the anapests don't make "borrowed majesty" any less strange as the initiating condition of the play. The majesty that ought to inhere in the monarchical body can by act 3 be "pawn'd" by the French King Philip to Constance (3.1.98), just as Chatillion here asserts it to be "borrowed" by John from Arthur, though John claims to have been left it by his late brother

Richard in a will. But, as Constance later snaps in reply to the reassurances of the French King Philip, an alienated, fungible majesty is no majesty at all:

> *King Philip.* By heaven, lady, you shall have no cause
> To curse the fair proceedings of this day.
> Have I not pawn'd to you my majesty?
> *Constance.* You have beguil'd me with a counterfeit
> Resembling majesty, which being touch'd and tried
> Proves valueless. Forsworn, forsworn! (3.1.96–101)[27]

Coinage appears here as an attribute of majesty, the sovereign's prerogative to reproduce and circulate his own image in authorizing the circulating medium. Sovereignty engages the marketplace by manifesting itself materially in coins, instruments of state policy that proceed to offer themselves to the commonwealth as instruments of everyday exchange. But the king's self-reproduction into a plethora of material objects that circulate his majestic image is, in Constance's outraged rhetoric, the perversion of majesty's own numinous, unitary, inalienable nature—the minting of counterfeits, the instance not of royal prerogative but of royal fraud.

The unitary majesty of Richard Cordelion is alienable from itself in *King John* because it has already been divided upon his death into three parts among three heirs: John, who has the Crown; Arthur, who has the hereditary right; and the Bastard, the heir only of Richard's improvident body.[28] Before the arrival of the Bastard, Elinor is already aware of this trifurcation of majesty as a bifurcation, as she reminds John upon the ambassador's exit:

> *King John.* Our strong possession and our right for us.
> *Elinor.* Your strong possession much more than your right,
> Or else it must go wrong with you and me;
> So much my conscience whispers in my ear,
> Which none but heaven, and you, and I, shall hear. (1.1.39–43)

This naming of heaven in the councils of policy effectively asserts heaven as a passive accomplice in the disjunction of possession from right. As long as John holds the crown in abeyance from right, the providential numen of kingship is likewise in abeyance. John's rule is in effect an interregnum, a middle between two real kings—real because rightful—and heaven will not resume a positive role in guiding England's affairs until John stops; this is the qualitative difference in history that Salisbury asserts to Prince Henry, between their experience of his father's reign and Salisbury's expectation for the Prince's reign to come. Such a negative concept of the working of providence, as a deferral of purposiveness, is not unorthodox. Boethius argues that providence works by allowing the world, or each human life, to go as wrong as it wants to before reeling it back, through its own sinful confounding, into conformity with the divine plan—using an ironic force corresponding perfectly to the extent of each deviance. The continually frustrated action of the five acts worth of middle cancels itself down to waiting for the resumption of divine purpose.

In portraying John's reign as a negative cycle of the movement of providence, Shakespeare himself deviates from contemporary consensus. Jeffrey Knapp has pointed out that King John's attempt to defy the Pope recommended him as a heroic predecessor of nationalistic Protestantism to so many Tudor historiographers (including John Bale in his midcentury interlude *King Johan* and the anonymous rival of Shakespeare who produced *The Troublesome Raigne of King John*) that Shakespeare's avoidance of that normative typology must be seen as a deliberate and provocative omission.[29] As Dorothea Kehler has argued, the hollow mouthing of God's name by realpolitik-ing kings and cardinals throughout the play's action is legible as a secularism, but a secularism that the play posits as a degradation of history from divine intent, a temporary lapse from providence.[30] This is not a lapse into the simply human—not a proto-Enlightened affirmation of the liberatory possibilities of secularism for human institutions. Rather, it is a lapse into materiality, a materiality whose only relation to history is that of a contingency that is poisonously perverse to human intent.

Aristotelian teleology is central to the Christian philosophy of history in its reconciliation of matter to intent; it suggests that nothing in the world can exist without purpose, that substance is unreal except insofar as it is realized through form into a particular telos in the world. I want to suggest now that, in order to imagine a world in which telos is in abeyance, Shakespeare employs as devil's advocate the antiteleological materialism of Epicurus. Epicurean ontology explicitly rejects teleology in the universe in order to celebrate a material basis for the absolute freedom of the human will from the delusional chains of fate.[31] Lucretius's account of Epicurean physical philosophy (the most complete one that survives) postulates an uncreated universe of atoms moving through an infinite void, generally speaking in a straight line—but sometimes, for no particular reason, one atom swerves from its course and bumps into another atom, they careen off together in an eccentric direction, interacting with more atoms, and from such bundles of contingency has accumulated the visible world and everything that has ever taken place in it.[32] In Epicurean cosmogony, this *declinatio* or "aptness to incline," the characteristic deviance of infinitesimal particles, is the reason events come to be. History, as the iteration of events in time, is a material phenomenon induced by a causeless, contingent, and atemporal randomness.

Classical Epicureans had used this elevation of contingency over causality to scandalize the pagan orthodoxy of fate. In the sixteenth century, this account of the universe as the concatenation of unwilled deviance presented itself as not only provocative but literally perverse, in that word's Augustinian sense of "turning away," to anyone with an investment in the divine shaping of human events into a moralized history; the Epicurean defiance of telic causality in the name of the vagaries of individual delight is legible in Christian terms as the repudiation of providence. An interest in atomism was insistently viewed as inseparable from an indulgence in atheism in sixteenth-century England, no matter how assiduously individual thinkers attempted to detach the two and to explore the corpuscular philosophy without controverting providence. But although the condition of atheism shaped the terms by which Shakespeare and his contemporaries might make use of Epicureanism, it did not preclude the use of those terms.[33] To the extent that sixteenth-century writers might attempt to imagine a materialist, mechanistic history uninflected by transcendence, that story is inflected instead by the ironic and often unwelcome presence of Epicureanism, as the ghost in any universal machine.

The Epicurean devil's advocate in *King John* is the voice of the Bastard, and the infiniteness of possibility of a universe unbound by fate becomes the focus of that character's hopes in his ebullient encomium of chance. Upon discovering that he is not the eldest son of a minor knight but the illegitimate son of the late King Richard, the Bastard declares to his brother and rival, "Brother, you take my land, I'll take my chance" (1.1.151), and goes on to celebrate his self-identification with this happy contingency:

> *Elinor.* I am thy grandame, Richard, call me so.
> *Bastard.* Madam, by chance, but not by truth; what though?
> Something about, a little from the right,
> In at the window, or else o'er the hatch.
> Who dares not stir by day must walk by night,
> And have is have, however men do catch.
> Near or far off, well won is still well shot,
> And I am I, howe'er I was begot. (1.1.168–175)

Here "chance" is a deviating quantum that, as it rolls "something about, a little from the right," works to overcome the petty differences among intents such as wretched old Sir Robert's, the Bastard's cuckolded legal father, in their convergence upon the resulting event. The Bastard is only the more Cordelion's natural son in his newfound illegitimacy, as the late king's sanguine magnanimity was one that would brook no bound of patrilinearity, no constraining form of legal and propertied, quantifiable inheritance: Richard would sire no merely legitimate son, his only true heir must be a Bastard.

King Richard's mischievous magnanimity in his life thus becomes legible after his death as prodigality in the spending of his royal seed, as improvidence.[34] The tension between an unpredictable, unbounded plenitude in the lost royalty of Richard and the pinched scarcities of the present regime manifests itself even as Philip Faulconbridge (soon to be "the Bastard") enters this scene, taunting his brother as small change.[35] Philip says Robert's claim is that, because Philip does not resemble the late Sir Robert Faulconbridge, the husband of their mother, as he, Robert, does, Robert and not the elder Philip should be Sir Robert's heir. In fact Robert cites both Sir Robert's will and a time frame that makes it impossible for Philip to be Sir Robert's offspring, but Philip maintains the claim to be only

> Because he hath a half-face like my father!
> With half that face he would have all my land—
> A half-fac'd groat five hundred pound a year! (1.1.92–94)

Philip confirms the mimetic resemblance of the stamped coin to the issuer whose portrait it bears as a transmission from father to son; this is the frame in which the speaker of several of Shakespeare's sonnets also fixates on the production of the Mint. But for Philip that system debases value rather than perpetuating it. His contempt for his father's and brother's physical appearance dovetails with a contempt for the materialization of wealth as money in the antithetical exchange of the "half-fac'd groat," paternal resemblance, for "all my land," his patrimony, which he estimates in terms of income rather than of sale price—as something that generates value, not something that ought to be itself exchanged as a value, for money. The Bastard's notion of patrilinearity is that of the coinage of "half-fac'd groats" like his brother by his equally petty putative father, a perpetuation of adequated value as the very margin of the "valueless"-ness of Constance's "counterfeit resembling majesty." His rather evidently Oedipal fantasy that he was born to indeterminately, unquantifiably better things, and must have been born *from* better things, finds in John and Elinor the recognition that he as much as his brother had been hoping for. The Bastard celebrates the happy contingency that has, he thinks, released him from comparisons that would adequate him, through the real estate quantified at five hundred pounds a year, to his father and his brother, whose already meager price slips from a groat to three farthings even as the Bastard hands over his patrimony to him:

> Madam, and if my brother had my shape,
> And I had his, Sir Robert's his, like him,
> ... my face so thin
> That in mine ear I durst not stick a rose,
> Lest men should say, "Look where three-farthings goes!"
> And to his shape were heir to all this land, ...
> I would give it every foot to have this face. ...
> Brother, take you my land, I'll take my chance.
> Your face hath got five hundred pound a year,
> But sell your face for five pence and 'tis dear. (1.1.138–153)[36]

By "tak[ing] my chance," the Bastard thinks he has claimed the token for entry into a nostalgized world of aristo-chivalric fealty, mutual obligation, and boundless opportunity—the romance world inhabited by his sire, the man whom all the characters in the play believe to have reached one hand into a lion's mouth to rip out the animal's heart.

By the end of act 2, the Bastard has learned that this new world is only a bigger version of the same old world. He has cashiered his brother's risible groats not, he discovers, for something better than money, but only for the prospect of bigger coins, "angels," and those angels have yet to arrive:

> And why rail I on this commodity?
> But for because he hath not woo'd me yet:
> Not that I have the power to clutch my hand
> When his fair angels would salute my palm,
> But for my hand, as unattempted yet,
> Like a poor beggar, raileth on the rich. (2.1.587–592)

The improvident event is doubly perverse, both in the lapse of the Bastard's originary intent—to transcend the world of adequation and exchange whose synecdoche is the stamped circle of the coin—and in the lapse of what the Bastard had posited in act 1 as the opposition to his intent, his own monetary profit. Now that he finds profit the only choice, against which he is powerless to close his open hand, he finds himself unable to profit from it.

But even this perversity of the event would not be so bad if at least it were reliably and predictably bad—or so, at least, the Bastard speculates. What is most horrible about it is its very contingency: to take the grimmest of many examples in the play's plot, that Arthur can not only be fortuitously alive in the moment when the king wants him dead, but can break his own neck just at the point that the king's crossed purposes need to prove him alive. Chance, which the Bastard had taken to be his personal friend, is instead a universal enemy, even to its own self. Recalling the earlier rolling of "chance," "Something about, a little from the right," the Bastard takes as a visible frame of reference the behavior of a bowling ball:

> Commodity, the bias of the world—
> The world, who of itself is peized well,
> Made to run even upon even ground,
> Till this advantage, this vile-drawing bias,
> This sway of motion, this commodity,
> Makes it take head from all indifferency,
> From all direction, purpose, course, intent—(2.1.574–580)[37]

The first thing to note about "this sway of motion" is its macroscopic correspondence to the Epicurean *dilatio* by which the deviation of atoms accrues into historical events, in that it is material, in that it takes place in time as "motion," and in that it is random.[38] The second thing to note is the Bastard's moralization of the phenomenon's contingency as perverse, in that he includes a "purpose" to the particle/world/bowling ball's original "course" from which the ball's characteristic "bias" inevitably, yet unpredictably, deflects it. (In Epicureanism, conversely, we owe all the visible world to this invisible "sway," the life-giving syncopation in the indifference of atoms.) The third thing to note is his naming of the perverse contingency of the material event as a personified function of the market, as "commodity, the bias of the world." The Mammon-like personification of monetary commodity as a force hostile to causality, historicity, and meaning interacts complexly with the Bastard's nullification of his own prior identity by identifying it with small change. Rather than offering a new beginning (which was already paradoxically poised between renewal and nostalgia as the Bastard formulated it in act 1), the Bastard's attempt to fashion himself into a courtly contradiction to monetary value has only made him the more completely subject to the commodity that comes to master John's own sovereignty. Commodity's presumptive function ironizes that of providence; where the divine will suffuses the human world with instrumental, immaterial angels, commodity works by scattering golden angels as its mindless, intentless instruments. And yet it doesn't even do that.

The "chance" that turned Sir Robert's marriage awry, giving the Bastard his fortunate opportunity to go to war by discovering his true parentage, is identical to the "commodity" that now perverts John's advantage in that war into a dynastic marriage. That same apparently opportune contingency also draws King Philip "From a resolv'd and honorable war/ To a most base and vile-concluded peace" (2.1.585–586), it draws John improvidently to surrender his lands in France for Philip's sanction of his "borrowed majesty" and the surrender of Arthur, and it will itself be negated in turn by the fortuitous arrival of the papal legate in the next scene. This exalted chance and this vile commodity are the same phenomenon of random, material motion, reiterated to the temporary profit of some and the continual, aggregate disadvantage of all.[39] The particles which enact this unpredictably perverse motion to bias the rolling of the world at large are as much Sir Robert's own paltry seed as Richard's royal one that debases itself in illegitimacy: not only commodity's "half-fac'd groats" but "his fair angels," the coins whose haphazard circulation the Bastard is as powerless to reject as he is to claim.

"Commodity" crosses John's purposes throughout the play, even though John himself seeks always to act in accordance with it, to make its purposes his own. The king does not recognize that commodity is purposeless, its apparent willfulness not caprice but a thoughtless, meaningless, random perversity inherent in matter, "the bias of the world." In Epicureanism, the microscopic event of *declinatio* is the ground for the absolute freedom of the human will, unconstrained by obeisance to a macroscopic fate. But in his subjection to commodity, John is perhaps the most visibly unfree of any of Shakespeare's protagonists.[40] This depiction of perversity in the matter of history is neither a celebration of Epicurean freedom nor a proto-Enlightened carving out of a space between the transcendental and the material for the perfection of simply human institutions—though the former seems adumbrated with real longing in the Bastard's first ebullience, as surely as does the latter in John's only-almost-heroic rejection of the Pope. Instead, the material is legible here as the negative condition that I have dubbed improvidence, a depiction of the abeyance of meaning in history: the disintegration of shaping purpose into material perversity, which is the disintegration of Cordelion's crown among Arthur's legal claim, the Bastard's paternal resemblance, and John's "strong possession," which the French ambassador calls "borrowed majesty." All three claimants are in this way shadows of King Richard, his substance without form or a form that cannot shape his substance. When Constance loses Arthur to John's prison, she finds that her son too has been swept away by the venal, hollow materialism of "the bias of the world." And she grasps for a substance in which his form might be remolded, be it only the matter of memory:

> *King Philip.* You are as fond of grief as of your child.
> *Constance.* Grief fills the room up of my absent child,
> Lies in his bed, walks up and down with me...
> Stuffs out his vacant garments with his form;
> Then, have I reason to be fond of grief?...
> I will not keep this form upon my head [*tearing her hair*]
> When there is such disorder in my wit. (3.4.92–102)

Descending from the extraordinary poetry that begins this speech to the bathos of its final gesture, Constance in destroying her hairdo to manifest as deformed matter the "disorder in my wit" within her skull anticipates, as something at once inevitable and rather absurd, John's death by the poisonous "indigest." This is the stuff that Commodity leaves behind as it rolls away—the stuff that an improvident, formless, material history is made of.

## II. ABHORR'D OF GOD AND MAN

For the Bastard, the malign influence of Commodity is a perversion enforced in the present upon "the world, who of itself is peized well" in its normal state. In imagining the improvidence of the play's action as only a temporary lapse within the divine intent that will prove to have anticipated and enfolded John's perverse commodity-chasing as soon as his son comes "to set a form upon this indigest," Salisbury offers a return to normative, providential historiography as the horizon of the play, just outside the scope of the play's action, however invisible it may be within that scope. *King John*'s pseudo-Epicurean deviance is a singularity, an exception ultimately enlisted to prove the rule of a providence that exceeds even the most ardent reachings of a uniquely improvident politics for the "fair angels" of Commodity. But the salvific difference of providence looked for by *King John* remains a feature of historical perspective—that is to say, one called for by the dramaturgy of the genre of history play, and one formulated as retrospection. Salisbury looks forward to being able to look back upon events and declare them providential, a thing that for the duration of John's reign he has been unable to do. In turning now from *King John* to *Measure for Measure*, I move away from the historical representation of polity, one which integrates the audience's present with the represented past by means of genealogy, by means of exemplarity, and (most obviously) by means of staged action.

I turn to the comic representation of a polity that's explicitly modern-minded, one where "Novelty only is in request," and where the relation of contingency to causality in monarchical politics seems nearly opposite to that which had obtained in the Plantagenet past of *King John* (*Measure* 3.2.224). In this play too the perverse contingency of matter takes the form of a coin, and here that coin takes the form of a person: Angelo, the Duke's deputy. But rather than simply evading and frustrating the will of the sovereign, as coins do in *King John*, Angelo in his "stamp'd" authority manifests the Duke's will, which is obscure in all other ways save as that minted reproduction. The very unpredictability of Angelo's deviant behavior demonstrates how the Duke's arbitrary "pleasure" anticipates and enfolds contingency, making the truculent resistance of matter to cause itself a means of his governance.

In Lezra's reading of *Measure for Measure*, the contingent event is an *apotropon*, an inassimilable and horrific instance of the failure of explanatory causal systems, an outlier; its macroscopic instance for the play's cramped and involuted urban setting is the offstage figure of the pirate. The Duke expresses the incompatibility of contingent event and providential cause in attempting to articulate them as continuous, upon the arrival of the pirate Ragozine's head to substitute for Claudio's: "Tis an accident that heaven provides" (4.3.77). The bizarre trajectory of Ragozine's head certainly welcomes such a corpuscular reading, but Lezra's emphasis upon the unassimilability and exceptionality of contingent matter seems to me to elide the ways in which the truculence of such matter to authorizing intent is central to the Duke's mode of governance. Rather than focus on the admittedly strange eruption of the pirate's head, I'd like to direct my argument through the most everyday instruments of the Duke's governance, his coins. These familiar objects are themselves estranged, made alienating, by the Duke; he does this in the play's first scene, by strangely minting Angelo into money and so alienating Angelo's personhood. Whatever Angelo may have been as a private individual, he makes bad money. The Duke expects to profit, at a Machiavellian remove, from Angelo's debased deviance. As Victoria Kahn has demonstrated, Machiavelli's political philosophy penetrated England as a system of strategies for accommodating contingency—for maximizing the favors of good fortune and anticipating the disasters of bad fortune.[41] Angelo's behavior proves perverse to the Duke's intent in circulating him, but the Duke's policy is in the end successful in passing off the eccentric movements of the comedy's plot as all subject to the mysterious cause of his "pleasure": as something resembling providence.

In its sophisticated Machiavellianism, its strangely joyless insistence on comic form, and its attention to monetary policy, *Measure for Measure* defines a present relation of sovereignty to the commonwealth. We may contrast the play's modern, comic politics not only in genre but in temporality to the investigation of the money form's relation to the construction of national history in *King John*.[42] In asking how and to what degree the sovereign may impose his will upon the material conditions of the commonwealth—and to what extent he can expect to succeed in doing so—the comedy of *Measure for Measure* recalls the sixteenth-century crisis of "commonwealth" policy in the Great Debasement, a memory that had already shaped policy for a generation. The Duke of *Measure* mints Angelo to serve as his surrogate, intervening through that coinage upon the brothel-driven Viennese market. Angelo proves, as the Duke knew he would, to be debased. As I argued in my introduction, debasement seems readily to be characterized as "a gigantic fraud" practiced by the sovereign upon the commonwealth. Yet what's remarkable about debasement is that the fraud does not need to fool anyone to succeed. Rather, debasement succeeds because it is the prince's pleasure, and the commonwealth's disbelief is a nonissue—public outrage may be able to influence policy, but it does not affect the circulation of the debased coins. Instead, the money market colludes with the will of the prince in driving good money into the Mint, to be replaced by bad money. But in its readiness to absorb bad money, the collusion of the market is also apt to part company with the will of the prince when it comes to the crimes of "coining"—the clipping and counterfeiting practices through which private individuals took upon themselves the royal privilege of making bad money. The law that declared coining to be capital treason was an unbelievable law, "a scarecrow of the law" (*Measure* 2.1.1): it was difficult for crown prosecutions to find twelve jurymen who would buy its rationale for sentencing a man to death, and as a consequence coiners routinely went free. Angelo cites the horrific punishment of counterfeiters in attempting to justify the death penalty for Claudio's illicit sexual reproduction, but what the ill-coined deputy reveals in his diatribe against coining is the defectiveness of his own reproduction—his own transparent insufficiency to the authority impressed upon him.

A relatively familiar example of counterfeiting's place in the official discourse of Renaissance criminality is Richard Baines's testimony to the Privy Council "Containing the opinion of on[e] Christopher Marly/ Concerning his damnable Judgment of Religion, and scorn of Gods word."[43] Among Marlowe's alleged "opinions" cited in this exhilarating document are:

That if he were put to write a new Religion, he would vndertake both a more Exellent and Admirable methode and that all the new testament is filthily written...

That St. John the Evangelist was bedfellow to Christ and leaned alwaies in his bosome, that he vsed him as the sinners of Sodoma...

That he has as good Right to Coine as the Queene of England, and that he was aquainted with one Poole a prisoner in Newgate who hath greate Skill in mixture of mettals and hauing learned some thinges of him he ment through help of a Cunni*n*ge stamp maker to Coin ffrench Crownes pistoletes and English shillinges.

As Jonathan Goldberg has argued, there is a great deal of continuity in the apparently diverse charges leveled by Baines against Marlowe.[44] The counterfeiter, the sodomite, and the heretic are of the Renaissance imagination all compact; traitors alike to God and Crown, they linger at the margins of the self-definitions of early modern community as constitutive Others, closeted enemies within. As another instance of this compression Stephen Orgel and Will Fisher have both cited an emblem by Henry Peacham, titled *"Crimina gravissima"* in the running head (figure 7), the text of which reads,

Vpon a Cock, heere *Ganimede* doth sit,
Who erst rode mounted on *IOVES* Eagles back,
One hand holds *Circes* Wand, and ioind with it,
A cup top-fil'd with poison, deadly black:
  The other Meddals, of base mettals wrought,
  With sundry moneyes, counterfeit and nought.
These be those crimes, abhorr'd of God and man,
Which Iustice should correct, with lawes severe,
In *Ganimed,* the foule Sodomitan;
Within the Cock, vile incest doth appeare:
  Witchcraft, and murder, by that cup and wand,
  And by the rest, false coine you vnderstand.[45]

Peacham does not use the term "treason" directly, though it is easily supplied as context to the cited crimes, especially given the reference to sovereign "*IOVE,*" whom this Ganymede apparently has abandoned or betrayed to live in the gutter. Orgel and Fisher are both interested in Ganymede's relation to the objects he holds—Orgel in "Circe's wand" as the sodomitical version of the royal scepter, the sovereign phallus grasped by a beloved minion, and

VPON a Cock, heere *Ganimede* doth ſit,
Who erſt rode mounted on *IOVES* Eagles back,
One hand holdes *Circes* wand, and ioind with it,
A cup top-fil'd with poiſon, deadly black:
The other Meddals, of baſe mettals wrought,
With ſundry moneyes, counterfeit and nought.

Theſe be thoſe crimes, abhorr'd of God and man,
Which Iuſtice ſhould correct, with lawes ſevere,
In * *Ganimed*, the foule Sodomitan:
Within the Cock, vile inceſt doth appeare:
Witchcraft, and murder, by that cup and wand,
And by the reſt, falſe coine you vnderſtand.

* O fuge te teneræ puerorum credere turbæ, Nam cauſam iniuſti ſemper amoris habent. Tibullus.

Iſta a te puniantur (ô Rex) ne tu pro illis puniaris. Ciprian. de vtilitate Pœnitentiæ.

*Virtutem*

**Figure 7:** Woodcut from Henry Peacham, *Minerva Britanna* (1612): "Crimina gravissima" By permission of the Folger Shakespeare Library

Fisher in the counterfeits as themselves "queer money." For the moment, though, I'd like to consider the way in which the emblem at once articulates and displaces the role played by Jove in Ganymede's activities. It was Jove whose love eroticized Ganymede in the first place, bearing him up to heaven on the "eagle's back"; but the sovereign cannot exactly be a sodomite, since he can't be a criminal, no matter how actively engaged he may be in the sodomitical practices of his minion. If coining was treason, it was a crime against the person of the king, and how could a king be said to transgress his own person?[46] Therefore it is Ganymede alone who may be guilty, and this guilt itself thrusts him from the back of the royal eagle to that of the cock; in the same way, the Gaveston of Marlowe's *Edward II* is routinely named a "traitor" by his baronial rivals, as committing a crime against the person of the king in enjoying the king's favor and doing what the king encourages him to do.[47] This displacement of agency and thus of blame onto the subject minion, generating a safe distance from the body of Jove, recurs onto the "base" counterfeits, in which Ganymede is likewise dabbling feloniously into the person of the sovereign who loves him.

Clearly a royal debasement and a counterfeit are coterminous abuses, but minting and counterfeiting are also continuous practices. In Mary Poovey's analysis, the function of validation is primary in monetary instruments; only once a coin has established its validity can it proceed to announce and authorize a particular value in exchange.[48] Harry G. Frankfurt correspondingly argues that "what is wrong with a counterfeit is not what it is like"—neither what it is made *of*, whether fine or base, nor whether it is made *well*, accurately or inaccurately reproducing the authorized image—"but how it was made": that only the circumstance of whether a coin was produced in a valid or invalid way distinguishes royal and counterfeit production.[49] "That in the captain's but a choleric word,/ Which in the soldier is flat blasphemy," Isabella tells Angelo (2.2.130–131): it is as much the captain's job to utter choleric words in urging his men to action as it is to punish the soldier who blasphemes by saying the same words. In so promiscuously distributing his coined image for the commonwealth's abuse, the monarch necessarily and inevitably colludes in the counterfeiting that he prohibits.

Treason law refused to distinguish between the individual body of the king and his licensing representations. Both to forge the impression of the Great Seal and to counterfeit or even to clip coins were construed alike as a proxy assault upon sovereignty, lèse-majesté against the royal image.[50] Yet the coined image in a certain sense invites the offense, making itself at once the site of public measure and of private profit, placing itself promiscuously into every purse and pocket in the kingdom. Coins are such minuscule and ubiquitous instances of the unique and indivisible sovereign power that almost anyone may appropriate it through them, simply by eliding the hairsplitting distinction between an individual's possession (which coins certainly were) and his property (which they were not, as he was not free to alter or destroy them) in trimming a sliver of metal off the coin's edge. In so doing, according to Blackstone's gloss, the clipper was enacting

> a breach of allegiance, by infringing the king's prerogative, and assuming one of the attributes of the sovereign, to whom alone it belongs to set the value and determinations of coin made at home, or to fix the currency of foreign money: and besides, as all money which bears the stamp of the kingdom is sent into the world upon the public faith, as containing metal of a particular weight and standard, whoever falsifies this is an offender against the state, by contributing to render that public faith suspected.[51]

So much the more heinous, then, for the counterfeiter to insert his own valuation between the royal image, "the public faith," and some base metal. But even the mere clipper was taking what had been legitimate coin and subtracting weight from it, making it a false measure and thus effectively counterfeit.

Throughout the historical record of coining prosecutions, however, a dissonance recurs between the legal definition of coining offenses as high treason and the everyday practices of what amounted to a busy and widespread cottage industry. It was hard to maintain that clipping falsified the true and public measure of value, for example, when all coins that were not underweight were culled out from the circulating medium by knowledgeable merchants as soon as they left the Mint, while nearly every coin that was in circulation was clipped already. The Mint validated coins for use by a flurry of hammer-blows, to force the image and motto of the die's type into the metallic blank. That instantiating violence was followed for these hapless objects by a life of varied indignities and abuses, as the "common drudge" made its way "'tween man and man" (*Merchant* 3.2.103–104). Precious metal could be extracted from legitimate coin in a number of ways: by clipping the edges, by filing the surface, or by a chemical bath such as the one vaunted by Quicksilver in *Eastward Ho!*: "I'll take you off twelvepence from every angel, with a kind of *aqua fortis*, and never deface any part of the image."[52] Those desperate souls who lacked acid, a file, or a pair of shears could shake the coins together in a bag to abrade them, and then pick the scrapings out of the cloth, a process called "sweating." Clipping was the simplest and most effective of these practices; the irregularity of the hammering process meant that a great deal of room for error had to be left between the stamped image and the edge of the coin, and, since a coin was legally current as long as its circular inscription was complete, the tolerance allowed the mint-master in manufacturing was in effect a tolerance extended to the clipper as soon as the coin entered circulation. All these methods extracted some of the precious metal that gave minted coin its intrinsic value, while leaving the coin still current—effectively putting an extra burden of extrinsic value on the shoulders of the stamp, and so inventing a bit of value out of nothing.[53] It was unusual to receive a coin in exchange that bore no such burden; the clipped and abraded bulk of the circulating medium itself proclaimed that its abuse was not an outrageous exception but a rule. If coining was treason, a significant number of otherwise politically quiescent individuals were traitors. The difficulty of securing convictions suggests that an even more significant number of jurymen anticipated Blackstone's later assessment "that this method of reasoning [in the treason law] is a little overstrained: counterfeiting or debasing the coin being usually practiced, rather for the sake of private and unlawful lucre, than out of any disaffection to the sovereign," and that they would rather see their neighbors go free than hang on such reasoning.[54]

It was quite difficult to convince many people that coining was even a sin, much less high treason. As Malcolm Gaskill notes, it required a very ingenious theologian to define counterfeiting as a violation of any of the Ten Commandments.[55] And save for the abused image of the sovereign, the crime was victimless. Nevertheless, jurymen who convicted a counterfeiter faced the possibility of seeing him punished with the most complex brutality available to law: to be hanged, drawn, and quartered, exactly as if he had really attacked the person of the king and not a small metal disk with his picture on the front. In practice, clemency was often extended to those convicted of coining: "As early as the reign of Elizabeth I," writes Gaskill, "[some] coiners were pardoned provided they abjured the realm, and others bailed. In 1580 Edward Kelly, the alchemist, was convicted of coining and merely had his ears cropped; and some offenders—particularly lesser offenders such as receivers of clippings—were let off with a whipping or a fine."[56] But mercy could only arrive after the fact of condemnation if it came at all, and many juries simply refused to convict in the face of what seems to us, and seemed to the prosecution and the national authorities at the time, overwhelming evidence. The Privy Council frequently intervened in high-profile coining cases, anticipating such difficulties by insisting that special care be taken to impanel "indifferent" juries, or by having the trial removed from the local courts to King's Bench in Westminster.[57] In general, then, the excessive harshness of the law that made coining high treason in theory caused the offense to be treated instead with excessive laxity in practice, by which, as sermons frequently complained, both the king's image and the commonwealth's law were derogated.[58]

## III. UNQUESTION'D MATTERS OF NEEDFUL VALUE

The distance traveled by a coin from the mint to the darkness of a private purse places the stampéd face of the king at a far greater remove from the oversight of his ministers and officers than that endured by any other of his images. The coinage was uniquely and massively *exposed*: uniquely relative to the other self-representations of the monarch, but massively in the sheer aggregate bulk of the circulating medium, the many millions of pounds of silver and gold traversing England as small portrait-stamped disks. The exposure of the coined image at the farthest reach from its issuing authority has a double sense in my argument: first, that the circulating coin had only the force of the image it displayed to protect itself, and thus was as *fragile* and vulnerable as the credit extended to the king's money and to his law; second, that the image was *promiscuous*, in that it passed beyond the ability of the Crown to control either its transactions or its reproduction. A handful of legitimately minted coins could engender a debased brood of duplicates from their own clippings, while any coin, whether fresh-minted, clipped, or entirely counterfeit, could find itself in the "clack-dish" of the most beggarly prostitute.

But if the aggressiveness with which the law aimed to treat offenders against the coinage suggests the real fragility of the objects, it also reflects a brittleness within the law itself. The historical reluctance of juries to convict coiners for their necessarily capital offense displays the treason law as itself an overreaching of the Crown, which local societies were both ready and able to reverse in practice. Though the coinage is among the principal instruments of sovereignty, the royal will finds itself fettered in two ways as it manifests itself within each coin. It is constrained by the fragility of its own representation, in the nearly uncontrollable actions of individual possessors of coins who violate the license of the image on a daily basis, and by the very values it works to assess, in the aggregate motion of the market. To an imagination relying on absolute standards either of measure or of power, these constraints might appear to be the incessantly reiterated failures of sovereignty in practice: "Subjected thus," demands Richard II as he contemplates his compromises with the world of matter, "How can you say to me I am a king?" (3.2.167–168). Shakespeare's wilier sovereigns, however, do not despair of these compromises, but find ways to manipulate them to aggrandize their will. In *Measure for Measure*, the coined interaction of sovereign measure with the diseased market of Vienna represents a dispersal of agency that the Duke can exploit; in reproducing his authority through Angelo, he utters a debased "angel" upon the market, and reaps profits upon its recall.[59] Making visible not only the means by which the

Duke imposes his will through Angelo upon his subjects, nor only his failure to control Angelo after he has set him loose, but the way in which Angelo's deviance itself comes to manifest the Duke's unaccountable will, *Measure* displays the enfolding of material contingency by politics as the play's uncomfortably coercive comedy.

As we saw in the introduction to this book, Sir Thomas Smith claimed that the function of minting money was originally an attribute of the Roman commonwealth and that it had been devolved historically to the sovereign out of convenience and as a gesture of trust.[60] The iconography of the royal stamp served to define the precious substance of the coin in both form and purpose; it licensed the coin's currency in the commonwealth by guaranteeing its composition. Following Aristotelian scholasticism, Renaissance theorists of money understood the coin to be, not some essential piece of value in itself, but a public *measure* of value (*mensura publica*), just as weights licensed by the Crown at markets were a public measure of mass.[61] Minting was thus an act of measurement, and of norming the measures in question. The stamp announced both the purity or "fineness" of the coined alloy and the standard mass of the coin type. Multiplying the mass of the coin by the fineness ratio yielded the amount of bullion present in the object. From this fixed amount proceeded the "intrinsic value" of the coin, its worth as bullion; that value itself, however, could not be fixed. Silver and gold were commodities, and their prices varied relative to other commodities, to the money of account, and indeed to each other. Thus the intrinsic value of each coin was a labile sum dependent on the vagaries of the international market in precious metals, though the artifact itself did not change.[62]

The face value in exchange of each coin, conversely, was intended not to be subject to such daily variance. The stamp thus expressed a second measurement, of the coin's exchange value, in addition to its guarantee of a certain mass of pure silver. Even in a relatively fine currency, such as the sterling silver minted by Elizabeth after 1561, the face value needed to be significantly higher than the intrinsic value of the coin; otherwise, a spike in the bullion market would cause all the coin in the kingdom instantly to be melted down. Elizabeth's ministers maintained the bullion price paid at the mint for silver at 92.5% of the face value returned as minted coin throughout most of her reign. The difference remained in the hands of the Crown as seigniorage, which was understood to be a fee paid by the supplier of bullion for the use of the mint, and indeed by the commonwealth generally for the convenience of circulating coin. This discrepancy between the intrinsic value and the exchange value was called, unsurprisingly, the "extrinsic value." It was understood to originate not in the fluctuations of the market but in the fixed will of the prince, as Sir Robert Cotton explained in 1626:

> I must distinguish the Monies of Gold and Silver, as they are Bullion or Commodities, and as they are Measure; One the extrinsick Quality, which is at the King's pleasure, as all other Measures to name; the other the intrinsick Quantity of pure Mettal, which is in the *Merchant* to value. As there the Measure shall be either lessened or inlarged, so is the Quantity of the Commodity that is to be exchanged.[63]

But if the will of the prince imposed stability upon the exchange value of the coin as an entirety, we may deduce that the extrinsic value was as variable within the object over time as the intrinsic value was; indeed, it had to vary inversely with the intrinsic value, diminishing as the price of silver rose and growing as it fell, in order that the exchange value remain constant. Thus, while it was at the prince's "pleasure" to fix the measures both of silver in the coin and of the coin's total exchange value in the money of account, the proportion of extrinsic value that represented the prince's pleasure was itself subject to the bullion market from moment to moment. As we've seen, the extrinsic value—the difference between the value of silver bought by the Mint and the exchange price of the coins produced there—was also the prince's profit. For a fine currency to be maintained, the prince's pleasure and his profit needed to be understood as discontinuous. For Cotton, this discontinuity is a chronological one—the present, momentary appearance of royal profit at the Mint in debasement will shortly be revealed as a universal loss that will not please the prince any more than anyone else—and the agent of that near-term revelation is "the Merchant," whose status as domestic subject is in the moment of royal debasement made secondary to his synecdochic personification of the international market in metals. In the latter capacity, the Merchant cannot choose but bring to light the new standard of his sovereign, valuing commodities according to the new dispensation. An unbridled indulgence of the prince's minting pleasure had, in the events of the period of debasement of 1541–1562, yielded an apparently recursive response from the market, as unbridled "dearth" or price inflation, and the memory of that national trauma lingered as a check both upon Crown policy and upon absolutist theory.[64] It was only in 1626 that a new debasement would be mooted publicly, and Cotton's rebuttal then recalled not only the experience of England in the debasement of the previous century but the commonwealths-men's analyses of the constraints upon the sovereign power at the Mint.

In advancing "the king's pleasure" as integral to the coin's value, Cotton acknowledges the claims of absolutism upon the object; the coin may be whatever the king wills it to be. Measure is a "Quality" emanating from the monarch that cannot itself be assessed or circumscribed, but that imposes "Quantity" upon the material world. When Georg Simmel declared that "the quantity of money is its quality," he was eliding the nexus of sovereignty in producing the means for transforming quality into quantities—or, rather, effectively declaring money to be sovereign.[65] But, as Cotton implies, the units of weight, length, and volume were as recognizably subject in the Renaissance marketplace to "the king's pleasure" as were the coins bearing a royal stamp; Elizabeth had in 1592 required that public weights be licensed by the Crown with such another stamp, and in the same decree had changed the mile from 5,000 feet to 5,280, to make it more easily divisible into furlongs for the purpose of surveying land. English measures of distance were not merely fixed by royal proclamation but, in one well-known account, emanated directly from the sovereign body: Henry I was said to have resolved a welter of conflicts among local systems of measure by inscribing as a national standard the distance from the tip of his nose to the tip of his thumb as the yard.[66]

But once the king releases his measure to the marketplace, its use is resigned to the commonwealth of individual economic actors, and its exchange value not only adequates, but is adequated to, the continuum of already vended values, including its own intrinsic value. Halving the intrinsic value of a shilling by debasing its silver content will simply mean that other commodities will cost twice as much in the new money; the international metal price is not ultimately subject to the sovereign will, and therefore neither are the prices of domestic commodities.[67] In referring to a single *"Merchant"* Cotton personifies the commonwealth at large in the figure of an authority tacitly opposite to the king's, an authority grounded in metallurgic expertise to which even invisible manipulations of the coin's silver will be transparent, and which will make them instantly visible to simpler folk through a rise in prices. Bound as they are in the unitary object as it passes from the Mint to the marketplace, the intrinsic and extrinsic values, sovereign will and common valuation, are not only inextricable but interdependent. Without the sovereign measure, the merchant is helpless to assess the "Commodity" of silver; but without the value of the metallic commodity, as assessed and validated by the public community of merchants, the sovereign's coin is worthless.

Cotton's attachment of "Measure" to "the king's pleasure," conjoined in the coin to a material "Commodity" that is limited by and yet itself constrains that pleasure, invites us to take the title of Shakespeare's comedic interrogation of the means of sovereignty more literally than is often the case.[68] *Measure for Measure* is in this light a play about measuring: considerations of price, purity, weight, and number permeate the speech of its characters.[69] The Duke proclaims comic closure through the closed circle of equivalence by which the Hebrew Bible sets out the *lex talionis,* the adequation of punishments to crimes.[70] But the circuit to which the Duke refers here is only indirectly and invisibly a comic one: "An Angelo for a Claudio, death for death!/ . . . Like doth quit like, and *Measure* still *for Measure*" (5.1.409–411, italics *sic* in F). As far as his onstage audience knows, he is demanding a beheaded Angelo for a beheaded Claudio, and only after Claudio himself is produced and unveiled does it become clear to them that the Duke has a second, living Claudio in stock to exchange for a living Angelo.[71] "Look that you love your wife," the Duke proceeds to admonish Angelo, "her worth worth yours" (5.1.497): the marriage that had seemed the cruelest of jokes in the dead-Claudio circuit is validated as a comic ending in its equation of living subjects. Angelo has learned—or, rather, the Duke is informing Angelo that Angelo has learned—the lesson which Escalus and Isabella alike had sought to enjoin upon him in act 2, to "weigh our brother with ourself" (2.2.126).

In this, however, the Duke is more optimistic than Isabella herself had ever been. She had declared, "We *cannot* weigh our brother with ourself" (my emphasis). Marx would concur: if two unlike things are to be adequated, one must for the moment give up being itself in order to take on the money form, the general equivalence that may assess the other.[72] Despite the Duke's multiply symmetrical formulation, "An Angelo for a Claudio, . . . and *Measure* still *for Measure,*" he cannot honestly pair these circuits as two tautological symmetries, the one related to the other as the specific is to the general. "Measure," rather, is the single point of intervention that enables the exchange by occluding itself in its own recursiveness: "An Angelo for a Measure for a Claudio." To put it more simply, if we are to weigh our brother with ourself, neither he nor we may be holding the scales—so whose invisible hand is?

Although words such as "weigh" and "fit," "try" and "assay," are heard throughout the play, and the *lex talionis* is paraphrased at least twice in the earlier acts (2.1.30 and 3.2.256), the word "measure" goes itself unvoiced until the Duke's homiletic demand for vengeance upon Angelo in act 5 fulfills the expectation with which the play's title has told its audience to listen: "Like doth quit like, and *Measure* still *for Measure.*" In listening for it we instead hear the matching term in Cotton's definition, "pleasure."[73] Angelo is the first to speak it, in his own first line upon entering: "Always obedient to your Grace's will,/ I am come to know your pleasure" (1.1.25–26). "Pleasure" here reproduces "your Grace's will": the "will" is the general principle to which Angelo is always obedient, and the "pleasure" is the particular, present instance of what the Duke may require of him. The replacement of "will" by "pleasure" makes the two indistinguishable in the person of the sovereign. In a private individual, "will" is guided by judgment and "pleasure" by whim, and his peers should distinguish between the two accordingly, but a subject is as answerable to the one as to the other in the sovereign, and—as Cotton emphasizes in using "pleasure" in preference to "will" to describe the king's decision about units of measure—arbitrariness from the sovereign is as important to the commonwealth as his judgment is, since the commonwealth relies on the king to settle questions, such as the proper length of a mile, that need an arbitrary but binding resolution. Thus when Isabella asks Angelo, "When, I beseech you? that in his reprieve,/ Longer or shorter, he may be so fitted/ That his soul sicken not" (2.4.39–41), the measure of the time is not significant, but the act of measurement is—she will "fit" Claudio to any time allotted, and it is only continued uncertainty that would cause his "soul" to "sicken." Likewise, Angelo needs in his first entrance only to know the Duke's "pleasure" so that he may act upon it.

But the Duke does not name his pleasure in reply. Instead he names "Angelo" (1.1.26), completing the pentameter line of Angelo's declarative question, "I am come to know your pleasure." The Duke's chosen instruments to "supply" his sovereign pleasure in his personal absence are interpellated by him—insofar as it is he who first addresses them both by name—as instruments of measure: "Angelo," as most editions of the play note, is an "angel," that large and exceptionally pure gold coin of the English mint, while "Escalus," the name that was the first line of the play, is just as recognizable as "scale."[74] Escalus, however, is placed by the Duke in a vaguely defined subordination to Angelo, the Duke's principal instrument. Just as Escalus is privy to the Duke's decision-making about Angelo but then placed under him, the Duke tells Angelo Escalus is to be "first in question, [yet] thy secondary" (1.1.46). Both Escalus and Angelo find their assigned relationship confusing:

> *Escalus.* [I]t concerns me
> To look into the bottom of my place.
> A pow'r I have, but of what strength and nature
> I am not yet instructed.
> *Angelo.* 'Tis so with me. (1.1.77–81)

By dislocating his authority between Escalus and Angelo, the Duke creates an unmeasured gap between them, projecting the point at which their two powers meet as a unitary sovereignty into a muddy and unsounded depth: Angelo's power is the measure of the Duke's own, but Escalus's subordination as first-yet-second itself measures Angelo's relative priority, so that it is unclear which standard is to obtain between them.

In planning to reproduce his authority in Angelo as his representative, the Duke invokes the language of minting a stamped form upon metal: "What figure of us think you he will bear?" (1.1.16). This is a question that admits that the matter in question may not, in the event, "bear" the sovereign stamp as might be wished. Rather, the matter may deform the "figure" impressed upon it, and Angelo attempts to defer his own representation of the Duke in precisely the same terms: "Let there be some more test made of my mettle/ Before so noble and so great a figure/ Be stamp't upon it" (1.1.48–50), questioning his own unevaluated interiority as perhaps metallurgically inadequate—for the words that we spell "mettle" and "metal" were not firmly differentiated in Renaissance usage or orthography, to which they were largely the same word. But Angelo is already constrained here by the Duke's own choice of vocabulary, so laboriously impressed on all his hearers by the difficulty of following his metaphorics in the paradoxical register of "both thanks and use" through his two convoluted speeches (1.1.3–21, 1.1.26–47), in which "nature, the thrifty goddess" bears some precedent relation to Angelo's own external "kind of character," from whence the Duke proceeds to announce his delegation of authority to Angelo and Escalus, owing to his own hasty departure that "leaves unquestion'd/ Matters of needful value" (1.1.54–55), and slips away, leaving his duple surrogates perplexed. I have the luxury of choosing not to decode these speeches, as I am not the Duke's subject. Instead, I can assess their difficulty as something imposed upon Escalus and Angelo, who are—as something to which they must respond, but by which they remain bewildered after the Duke's exit.[75] In his conversation with Friar Thomas two scenes later, the Duke will make clear what figure of himself he wants and expects Angelo to bear. All that's important here is that that expectation remain uncertain and indecipherable to Angelo, as the Duke invests in the overdetermined name "Angelo" everything he wants him to be; what is transmitted in the Duke's difficult speeches is not meaning but force, the hammer-blows that shape the "mettle" of the golden blank into the angel. This interpellated "Angelo" is himself the Duke's "pleasure," in a successfully mystified form that answers the question by making it unanswerable within the terms Angelo is given to understand it. Angelo is only beginning to grasp at the way he has been defined by the Duke once he has completely debased himself within that definition, in private and at last in public, and he asks for death from his master rather than live to confront his sovereign pleasure.

The word "pleasure" recurs in the same questioning form throughout the play, and the question *never* gets a straight answer. It is always mystified in just this way, most obviously by Angelo in conversing with Isabella, where his attempt to reproduce what he has had impressed upon him makes plain its defect:

> *Isabella.* I am come to know your pleasure.
> *Angelo.* That you might know it, would much better please me
> Than to demand what 'tis. (2.4.31–32)

But the mystification of "pleasure" likewise holds true in the comic business, where the failure of the law's officer, Elbow, to produce information against Pompey compels Escalus to treat incompetence as radical uncertainty:

> *Elbow.* What is't your worship's pleasure I shall do with this wicked caitiff?
> *Escalus.* Truly, officer, because he hath some offenses in him that thou wouldst discover if thou couldst, let him continue in them till thou know'st what they are. (2.1.183–188)

In all but one of these questions, "pleasure" retains Angelo's sense of sovereign decision. The exception is a striking one:

> *Duke.* I pray you, sir, of what disposition was the Duke?
> *Escalus.* One that, above all other strifes, contended especially to know himself.
> *Duke.* What pleasures was he given to?
> *Escalus.* Rather rejoicing to see another merry, than merry at any thing which profess'd to make him rejoice; a gentleman of all temperance. But leave we him to his events.... (3.2.230–238)

In a play so entirely obsessed with sex, this is the only moment that "pleasure" is given its more familiar sense of a taking of delight in some activity. The disguised Duke's question here is apparently motivated by a desire to sound out his unspoken reputation via a less fantastical source than Lucio, who has been torturing him for a hundred lines with news of his (the Duke's) own concupiscence. But even the Duke's indirect enquiry into his own "pleasures" is met with a bizarrely tautological irony—in asking about himself, he is told that he is the kind of person who interrogates himself—and his "pleasure" is displaced, as ever, onto "another" and remains inscrutable to anyone who "professed to make him rejoice" in his own person.

The discursive structures the Duke imposes around the word "pleasure" make it impossible for anyone to articulate what exactly his pleasure might be. Angelo can question the relation of his own matter to the value the Duke professes to "stamp" upon it, but the Duke rejects Angelo's qualm as a temporizing "evasion," saying that "Our haste from hence . . . leaves unquestion'd/ Matters of needful value" (1.1.50–55). This phrase seems to produce "value" in "matters" through the very exclusion from question that the Duke is professing to regret. He ascribes the "unquestion'd" state of these valuable matters to a "haste" that is imposed upon him by remote causes, but which we will shortly learn to be an arbitrary urgency that has not even taken him anywhere "from hence." What the Duke offers in the place of these "unquestion'd matters" is a substitutive discourse—that is, both one that is a substitute and one that refers itself to substitution. This is the register of metallurgical metaphor in which the Duke is coining Angelo to be his proxy. It posits Angelo's interiority as raw material, "mettle"-metal, and proceeds performatively to stamp him in the Duke's "figure" by naming him as deputy. The difficulty of the Duke's speeches yields not the reason but the force for that impression. Angelo's purpose, the Duke soon tells Friar Thomas, is to impress himself upon the unruly commonwealth of Vienna just as the Duke has "on Angelo impos'd the office" (1.3.40). A coin is an instrument whereby sovereignty intervenes upon the market. As we learn from Lucio and his companions in 1.2, the market of Vienna is dominated by a single commodity, female flesh, such that the currency circulating through it is fully exchangeable for venereal disease: "three thousand dolors a year" and "a French crown more" (1.2.50–52). The pimp Pompey warns Escalus that the suppression of his trade will lead to the depopulation of the city and thus to an economic collapse: "If you head and hang all that offend that way but for ten year together, you'll be glad to give out a commission for more heads. If this law hold in Vienna ten year, I'll rent the fairest house in it after threepence a bay" (2.1.238–242).[76] If Angelo is to understand his present authority, the sovereignty reproduced upon him, as a minting, then the ubiquitous exchange of money for sex in Vienna is a perversion. But so too, finally, must sexual reproduction be in itself, unless it can be corralled into the same systems of validation by which a coin is made licit. Angelo stakes his authority not on the punishment of whores and bawds—this is not contested even by Lucio ("If imprisonment be the due of a bawd, why, 'tis his right" [3.2.66–67])—but on the execution of Claudio, who has impregnated Juliet but did not *pay* to do so.[77] Angelo would agree with Poovey that the validity function of a coin is primary, but he doesn't understand how that function, which the Duke has embodied in him, proceeds to pertain to exchange through the value relation. The binary licit/illicit does not serve to explain why Angelo himself would have abandoned his bride Mariana upon the loss of her dowry, nor would it explain why, in her nine marriages, the madam of the brothel is not exemplary but "Overdone by the last" (2.1.202). Minting and intercourse are alternative and insufficiently compatible models for reproduction in the play's discourse. After we have seen the Duke coin Angelo with his words, Lucio instead produces rumors about who or what must have had sex to produce the deputy: "Some report a sea-maid spawn'd him; some, that he was begot between two stock-fishes" (3.2.108–109). Neither model is entirely apt. Lucio's account here is certainly "fantastic," and, as Jonathan Dollimore has pointed out, his georgic praise of sexual increase—"even so her plenteous womb/ Expresseth his full tilth and husbandry" (1.4.43–44)—is essentially self-serving, as it naturalizes Lucio's own role as consumer in the flesh-markets of Vienna.[78] But the highly artificial and complex, even paradoxical, register of the mint seems intended by the Duke more to preclude understanding of reproduction than to further it. It is designed, as Angelo is, to fail.[79]

Naming Angelo after a coin ironizes the character's antimaterial pretensions, calling attention both to his role as a mediator between the Duke's sovereignty and the market and to his role as a matter to be formed by the Duke's shaping will. Naming Angelo after an angel in particular certainly heightens that irony through punning, in that Angelo's aspirations to elevate himself above his fellow men by disavowing his material needs and desires, to be angelic rather than human, themselves cast him into the gutter of demonic hypocrisy.[80] But it also problematizes the Duke's own claim that Angelo's relation to him will be one of representation, of Angelo's "bearing" some more or less accurate mimetic "figure" of the Duke. The angel was distinguished from other English coins not only by its value, nor only by the higher purity of its gold, but as the only coin that did not "bear" a portrait of the monarch on its face at all. The Duke quite evidently intends that Angelo fail to represent him, even within the official frame of mimetic representation: Angelo "may, in th' ambush of my name, strike home,/ And yet my nature never in the fight/ To do me slander," he tells Friar Thomas (1.3.41–43). The difference between the "name" that the Duke allows Angelo to share and the "nature" that he discreetly withholds from his deputy reinscribes, as a deliberate displacement or mystification of agency, the discrepancy between a coin's inscribed exchange value and the intrinsic value of Angelo's "mettle"—the extrinsic value, which represents at once sovereign pleasure and sovereign profit. The Duke expects to make good on Angelo's failure to measure up to the role imposed upon him, even more than he will on Angelo's success.

The Duke's means of producing Angelo and of publicly guaranteeing his worth are those that effectively guarantee his failure. The vocabulary of the mint, in which authority reproduces itself through representation, is impressed upon Angelo by the Duke; it does not recur in scenes where neither of the two is present. It is, moreover, inadequate to the problem of authority's self-reproduction through the practice of regulation, in that reproduction itself is what sovereign authority seeks to regulate throughout *Measure for Measure*. This inadequacy is quite evident when Angelo attempts to defend his judgment of Claudio with it in conversation with Isabella:

> *Isabella.* When, I beseech you? that in his reprieve,
> Longer or shorter, he may be so fitted
> That his soul sicken not.
> *Angelo.* Ha? Fie, these filthy vices! It were as good
> To pardon him that hath from nature stol'n
> A man already made, as to remit
> Their saucy sweetness that do coin heaven's image
> In stamps that are forbid. 'Tis all as easy
> Falsely to take away a life true made
> As to put metal in restrained means
> To make a false one. (2.4.39–49)

Angelo is here adequating the siring of a bastard to murder. The equivalent that mediates between the two is the crime of counterfeiting. Like bastard-making, counterfeiting is an act of unauthorized reproduction; and like murder, counterfeiting is punishable by death. Thus Claudio should die for fathering a child out of wedlock: QED? Readers of this passage have not generally trusted their own judgment enough to acknowledge that Angelo is not making any sense—though Angelo himself recognizes that he is incapable of ordering his faculties in front of Isabella:

> Why does my blood thus muster to my heart,
> Making it both unable for itself,
> And dispossessing all my other parts
> Of necessary fitness? (2.4.20–30)

Angelo never fully differentiates tenor from vehicle in his metaphorizing of bastardy and counterfeiting, nor does he explain how counterfeiting should be compared to murder other than in their effect, the death penalty (the fallacy of the undistributed middle). Moreover, his entire rant here is a non sequitur; Isabella has not asked him "to pardon" Claudio, but simply to tell her how much longer Claudio should expect to be imprisoned before his execution. It is urgent to her that a certain measure of that time be established in order that Claudio "may be so fitted" to it in turn. Angelo's "Ha?" itself indicates that he has been unable to listen to her, and that the speech that follows struggles with his own concerns and fails to address hers.[81]

The vocabulary of the mint is incapable of what Angelo wants it to control here. Angelo's adequation is fallacious within the written scope of law, for counterfeiters had not committed a capital felony, like murder; rather, what they had committed was treason, so the logic behind execution was different in each case. His appeal to the legal status of counterfeiting only calls attention to the defect of that very law, which in early modern England presented a strikingly consistent failure of royal sanction to enforce itself in practice through the jury system. In such a circumstance, sovereignty becomes a recognizably hollow idol, much as Angelo warns Escalus:

> We must not make a scarecrow of the law,
> Setting it up to fear the birds of prey,
> And let it keep one shape, till custom make it
> Their perch and not their terror. (2.1.1–4)

This figuration of the law's lapse in Vienna is significantly different from the Duke's, who instead compared the effectless law to a napping, "o'erfed lion" (1.3.22, echoed by Lucio 1.4.64), and it implies Angelo's own anxieties about his situation. The lion, like the Duke, is recognizably sovereign and need only shake off its passivity (though the Duke's own methods are rather more foxy than that); Angelo's scarecrow is worthless in itself and derives authority by changing its shape to stay threateningly unfamiliar. Its sovereignty is achieved not by an essential royalty, like the lion's, but by its unpredictable mutability that anticipates the mutability of "custom," its subject; its effect is terror and its means caprice. In measuring the law as the unpredictable and unknowable sovereign "pleasure," Angelo is recapitulating the process by which he himself was made. Counterfeiting, likewise, is not the Duke's anxiety—he never mentions it—but Angelo's own, as he attempts to displace upon Claudio his own guilt in wanting to make bastards with Isabella, using the terms that have been enjoined upon him in forming his own authority and that are beginning to seem inadequate to the case. Angelo is afraid not only that he will become a counterfeiter, but that he will prove—

realizing his original self-doubt that asked that "some more test be made of my mettle"—to be a counterfeit.

In this he need not have worried. The Duke continues publicly to back Angelo's value even after he has heard of the deputy's diabolical plot to seduce Isabella. In reassuring Claudio, the disguised Duke reaffirms, lying, the metallurgical appropriateness of Angelo's behavior: "Angelo never had the purpose to corrupt her; only he hath made an assay of her virtue to practice his judgment with the disposition of natures" (3.1.161–164), where not only "assay" but "practice" and "nature" recall the speech by which the Duke first deputized the bewildered Angelo. Angelo cannot be a counterfeit. His maker is not a counterfeiter but the sovereign, who has made him what he is quite deliberately—indeed, by an ostentatious deliberation in front of Escalus, whose purpose as "first in question, [yet] thy secondary" (1.1.46) is as much to vouch for Angelo's legitimacy in public as to mystify the precise extent of Angelo's power.[82] The Duke, again, knows both that Angelo will not bear his own figure and that Angelo's "mettle" is insufficient to the public role imposed upon him. That is what Angelo is for. Angelo stands not as a counterfeit but as a debasement, a deliberate manipulation by the sovereign of the material "measure" of value that represents his own "pleasure" in the transactions of the market. To correct the flesh-markets of Vienna, the Duke issues Angelo as a defectively mimetic version of his, the Duke's, own *mensura publica*, then exposes the defect in the instrument of measure as if the mere instrument were to blame.

In the most obvious sense, that of individual responsibility and of the symmetrical relation between self and neighbor which the Gospel places upon it in declaring "Judge not, lest ye be judged," Angelo is indeed fully to blame for his own actions in power. But the Duke allows the blame to rest upon the fact of Angelo's hypocrisy, as though the execution of Claudio would have been appropriate had Angelo not failed to live up to the standard therein set; it would have been "tyranny" for the Duke to behead Claudio himself after allowing the law to sleep, and it was tyranny for Angelo to attempt to do so after he succumbed to Isabella's inadvertent charms, yet such a beheading remains available to perfect justice in theory, and the newly corrected state of the play's end may yet choose to practice it. The stamp of the mint mystifies what Norman N. Holland first pointed out as a straightforwardly Machiavellian maneuver: as Cesare Borgia used the "cruel and vigorous" Ramirro de Orco to consolidate his authority over the Romagna, then displayed the instrument's decapitated body as a Christmas present to the people of Cesena, so will the Duke profit both from Angelo's behavior during the displacement of sovereign power and from the eventual recall of that power back into the person of the

Duke, as the master exchanges the hatred accrued by the servant's authority for affection toward the Duke's authority, renewed in its reclamation.[83]

Angelo would gladly do the Duke's pleasure if he knew what it was. Instead, he is left to execute private "dark deeds" that are perverse to his own aspirations and to the public role he believes he has been chosen to fulfill. Indeed, the Duke has predicted his perversion before setting him in motion, and expects to profit from that very perversion of his instrument by exposing it as something beyond his control that his sovereign presence will rectify. All that he needs to turn Angelo back around, he proclaims, is the substitution for the object of Angelo's perverse desire, Isabella, of a corrected one, Mariana, via the bed-trick; Isabella is to save Claudio from Angelo, Mariana to save Isabella from him, and the Duke at last to save Vienna from him:

> Twice treble shame on Angelo,
> To weed my vice, and let his grow!
> O, what may man within him hide,
> Though angel on the outward side!....
> Craft against vice I must apply.
> With Angelo tonight shall lie
> His old betrothed (but despised);
> So disguise shall by th' disguised
> Pay with falsehood false exacting,
> And perform an old contracting. (3.2.269–282)

This homiletic passage sets itself off from the dialogue that has come before by rhyming in tetrameter; coming between acts 3 and 4, its ostentatious balancings present the point of balance for the comedy, declaring the bed-trick to be the pivot between the falling and the rising actions. Once a letter arrives from Angelo in the prison, the Duke resumes this chiastic rhyming to indicate how well things are going according to plan, imagining that he has "purchas'd" Claudio's rescue by his discreet dabbling in the unredeemed flesh-market of Vienna:

> This is his pardon, purchas'd by such sin
> For which the pardoner himself is in.
> Hence hath offense his quick celerity,
> When it is borne in high authority.
> When vice makes mercy, mercy's so extended,
> That for the fault's love is th' offender friended.
> Now, sir, what news? (4.2.108–114)

The letter's "news" is that Claudio's execution has not been cancelled but hastened by Angelo's matching Claudio's "fault." The bed-trick, though successfully executed, has failed in its purposed effect. In weighing his newfound brother with himself, Angelo does not conclude that both must live. Rather (as he belatedly explains, in 4.4), the fact that Angelo has found in Claudio not only a brother in vice but a thwarted brother-in-law, whose sister Angelo has, he thinks, debauched, means that Claudio must die to protect Angelo's own life from Claudio's revenge. Coins are ubiquitous instruments of authority, but they achieve that ubiquity by circulating into places where that authority itself does not otherwise extend; they pass beyond the issuer's ability to manipulate them directly, or even to control what happens to them. In minting Angelo, the Duke has sent his debased surrogate beyond his own reach in order to profit, indirectly and discreetly, from Angelo's perversity. In the event, that perversity has unpredictable, unintendable, purposeless ramifications.

These ramifications are in part the result of Angelo's tortured escape from the Duke's interpretive apparatus. He does not act as the Duke expects him to act, because he no longer thinks as the Duke compelled him to think. The metallurgical lexicon whose inadequacy we have been tracing in the first three acts is entirely absent from the fourth; it recurs only when the Duke reinvests himself in his sovereignty to inform Angelo that "your desert... deserves with characters of brass/ A forted residence 'gainst the tooth of time" (5.1.9–12), as a barbed double entendre that implies the brazen debasement of the deputy's prior "kind of character in thy life" (1.1.27). Nor, likewise, does the *lex talionis* mean to Angelo in 4.4 what the Duke expects it to mean. Instead, Angelo concludes that the law of reciprocal punishment means that he must kill Claudio before Claudio can kill him. Meanwhile, the Duke has already been hearing about his progressive loss of control over all his coined instruments, in the many slurs of Lucio. Lucio recognizes the Duke's complicity with both the old license and the new regime, and will not allow Angelo's "ambush" from the Duke's "name" to protect the Duke's own "nature" from "slander." The Duke's licensed image, as circulated by Lucio, is itself promiscuous: "Who? not the Duke? Yes, your beggar of fifty; and his use was to put a ducat in her clack-dish" (3.2.125–127). A "ducat" for Lucio is a liquid measure of ducal semen, distributed without judgment or distinction to the "clack-dish" of the foulest and most desperate whore of the city. But the same may happen to any coin; whether it is the Duke himself who gives it to her or any citizen to whom the coin has passed since its minting, it remains the Duke who has originally licensed it. The minter is to the coin is to the thing bought as the pimp is to the whore to the coin taken: "What, is there none of Pygmalion's images newly made woman to be had now, for putting the hand in the pocket and extracting it clutch'd?" enquires Lucio of Pompey when he sees the bawd led in chains (3.2.44–47). In claiming that the sculptor Pygmalion made his adorable image not for his own love but to profit off others (and equivocating neatly between a hand-job and a pocket-picking as the means of "extracting" the john's money), Lucio transforms the narcissistic closed circuit of that fable of artisanal making into a promiscuously open-ended chain of exploitation through displacement. To Lucio, anything done through the coin of Vienna is done in the Duke's name.

After meeting Lucio, the Duke feels oppressed by the power of slander; not only does he immediately ask Escalus for a second opinion, he continues to brood upon slander whenever he is alone, most surprisingly in the moment when he makes Isabella take Mariana offstage to explain the bed-trick. The ruthlessness with which the play insists on attaching interpretive meanings to names seems to allegorize the pernicious reductiveness of "slander" in attaching such meanings, leaping over the distance between "name" and "nature" whose measure the Duke attempts to inscribe through Angelo (1.3.41–43). Just as Angelo is stuck with being an angel and Escalus a scale, despite their mutually confused inability to exercise the offices of either instrument, so too Isabella is a belle, her name already implying what Angelo cites as "the destined livery" of a *bona roba* that is perverse to her nature (2.4.137), and she is a bell, but one that never gets to ring out her civic alarum against the secret tyranny of the deputy until that signal is corralled into the larger machinations of the Duke. Lucio, suggesting "light" in Italian, heaps with praise "the old fantastical Duke of dark corners," who "yet would have dark deeds darkly answer'd, he would never bring them to light" (4.3.157; 3.2.177–178), comparing the Duke's putative deeds to Claudio's ("clouded"; or "closed," "confined," "secret" [Latin *clausus*]).[84] The Duke hears this praise as slander, and the audience has to hear it as irony; but we can also hear it as the bringing to light of the fact of opacity—both in that Lucio recognizes disguise and substitution as the Duke's preferred means of governance, as Goldberg has shown, and in that Lucio's epithet "Duke of dark corners" is the closest any character comes to giving the Duke a name.[85] Although the list of dramatis personae in the Folio cites the Duke as having the Christian name "Vicentio," that name occurs nowhere in the text of the play—the other characters refer to the Duke exclusively by his title or by the appropriate forms of direct address (for example, "my lord").[86] Not only is the Duke's sovereign pleasure unnamable save through his naming of his subjects, so too is the Duke himself unnamable save through his sovereign title. But the Duke is quite stunned to discover from Lucio that this nominative inscrutability, while part of his mastery of his subjects, is not itself exclusively mastered by him. The Duke's namelessness is as much an instrument of his power as is the nominatively minted Angelo, but like Angelo it is an instrument whose use is in circulating away from him and into the commonwealth, where it proves subject to spectacularly ingenious abuse.

The other character who is addressed by a title and not by a name is the Provost of the prison; his two inmates Barnardine and Ragozine are by the standard of the force of allegorically reductive naming the least interpellated of the characters of the play, in that their names manage to mean not much of anything that I can think of.[87] The different abuses of the discourses imposing sovereign utility enacted by Angelo and Lucio converge in the darkest of all the Duke's corners, the discovery space of Barnardine's "ward" inside the prison. A London audience ought readily to recognize a continuity between the Duke's mint and his prison; the Tower, looming over the City and the Thames, was both.[88] Barnardine, a convicted murderer, is of all the play's characters the most utterly subject to sovereign power. Yet he insists that he may not be executed without his own "consent" (4.3.56), which he withholds, as "I have been drinking hard all night, and I will have more time to prepare me" (4.3.53–54). He cannot refuse to be killed—the jailers can still "beat out my brains with billets" informally and irregularly in the cell (4.3.55)—but he can refuse the forms of legal execution, in which he would be led out to the block and there beheaded.[89] Unfortunately for the Duke, what's needed here is not simply a dead Barnardine but a decapitated one, so that the head may be sent to Angelo in place of Claudio's. One with the brains already clubbed out of it will not serve. Without knowing it, Barnardine simply and utterly denies his use by the Duke; his death, if it comes, must be an end in itself rather than one in a series of sovereign means. As Angelo has done once the Duke loosed him, this instrument most entirely within the Duke's grasp proceeds to slip from his fingers.

The recalcitrance of Barnardine does not exhaust the means of the Duke. Sovereignty has an array of individual means available to it, and one convenience or another—a Ragozine, an Exton or Tyrrel—is always liable to arise to serve its turn. But each individual means has its limit to impose on the sovereign, bounding him in particular ways from moment to moment. Barnardine's refusal to emerge from his ward to be decapitated demonstrates such a particular limit, while the momentary spectacle of the disguised sovereign groping for a substitute substitute exposes the absurd equivocation between contingency and Providence in the readiness of the larger array of sovereign means: "O," exclaims the Duke upon the prospect of Ragozine's head, "'tis an accident that heaven provides!" (4.3.77).[90] Thanks to the prolapsed success of the head-trick, the final scene of *Measure* yields, in its coordination of homiletic piety and Machiavellian policy into comic closure, everything that the Duke could want from his debauched subjects—renewed allegiance and four marriages. Because the different complexities and limits imposed upon the Duke by his variety of instruments have already been staged, however, and because we have seen the principles by which he selects, shapes, and discards them to be, on the one hand, his arbitrary "pleasure," and, on the other, the contingent readiness of each to his hand when the one before has denied its own utility—for these reasons, the comedic resolution of *Measure for Measure* seems as enforced upon the Duke's audiences, onstage and off, as the Duke's "stamp" first was upon Angelo. Comedy itself, the generic shaping of happy endings, is displayed in its end as the last and most irresistible of the Duke's sovereign means.

Opening upon the stage the private spaces of the discreet sovereign "pleasure"—the privy council chamber, the mint, the prison's zone of privation—*Measure for Measure* insists, not upon decoding the opacities of language, substitution, and disguise that protect the *arcana imperii*, but upon identifying them as mystifications. The obscure formulae by which the Duke deputizes Angelo enact not a difficult and meaningful truth but the arbitrary force whereby the sovereign will reproduces itself upon its subjects. In this sense, as the Duke is disconcerted to learn, Lucio knows more about the Duke's "pleasure" than the Duke himself wants to know—for the Duke, surely, wants most of anyone to believe that he does embody the *imitatio Christi* whose mystery he puts on as the close of the play, and that Isabella's silence to his proposal is the voice of modest consent. "The Duke would have dark deeds darkly answer'd; he'd never bring them to light": Lucio is presumably wrong about what the "darkness" around the Duke conceals, but he so accurately locates the Duke's pleasure in the refusal to bring to light that the Duke is unnerved, and asks Escalus about his own "pleasures," receiving as a reply only his own opaque reflection. In this passage Lucio is comparing the Duke's darkness favorably, yet unflatteringly, to Angelo's monetized yen for exposure and transparency. The comparison suggests that Angelo's crime against Isabella is propelled by Angelo's intuition that, to be sovereign like the Duke, he too must have something to hide.

But the Duke does not make Angelo sovereign; he makes him an angel, a monetary instrument of the Duke's own sovereignty, and money is that which has nothing to hide.[91] As I discussed in chapter 1, money works to expose its own character—as exchange value—out of the material opacity of objects, including the coin-object itself; even the fraudulence of debasement is a patent one, an utterly open secret. The inevitability of the commonwealth's coming to know Angelo's debasement is built into "the way [he] is made," through the reciprocity of valuation between merchant and prince. The fact that the character who can articulate that reciprocity in Vienna is Pompey the pimp—"If this law hold in Vienna for ten year, I'll rent the fairest house in it for threepence a bay"—demonstrates that the nastiness of the Duke's behavior is itself measuring a nastiness in the Viennese commonwealth, the exclusivity of Pompey's trade as the market's sole staple, and imposing a new relation between the two in the corrective debasement of Angelo. It is no longer the Duke's pleasure that this state of bawdry persist, and however belated that intervention, however conditioned by the Duke's own prior laxity, the commonwealth depends on the sudden and arbitrary imposition of the Duke's new pleasure to correct its abuses in the present. Incapable of regulating its own desires for self-abuse, the commonwealth relies unhappily on the arbitrary force of sovereign measurement to redefine its pleasures through his.[92]

This pleasure of the Duke's, again, is Angelo, and it is not otherwise articulable. The commonwealth will come inevitably to know what Angelo *is*; that's not the same as its knowing what Angelo is *for*. Angelo's "matter" is preeminent among the "unquestion'd matters of needful value" displaced by the departing Duke onto his subordinates. The value that's needful is that which escapes question; it's the arbitrariness itself by which the Duke uses Angelo to remeasure the relation of commonwealth and sovereign. The Duke's departure is the occasion of the play—but what is the occasion of the Duke's departure? Why choose this moment, after fourteen years of laxity, to impose Angelo between sovereign permissiveness and subject abuse? An arbitrary, Epicurean swerve of the will? A sudden whim to play the friar, perhaps, to be a "ghostly father" rather than the father of the state? The Duke's indulgence in his assumed role, to the extent of hearing confessions and administering extreme unction, certainly suggests that he takes a pleasure in it (one that the Catholic Church would consider outrageous, though the conventional attachment of hypocrisy to Catholic friars and sacraments would defuse much of that scandal among an English audience). But if that's the case, the Duke will not admit it. Instead, he finally articulates Isabella, who has escaped Angelo's pleasure, as the object of his own pleasure. The choice of Isabella is very obviously ex post facto, since the two had never met before the Duke adopted his disguise; this end for the play has nothing to do with its beginning. The telos of Isabella's marriage is a feature of the play's genre to the exclusion of its plot (not to mention her character as novice of a sisterhood); it is, as so many readers of the play have felt, arbitrary, and that arbitrariness is assigned here to the force of comic shaping. I've cited comedy as itself the Duke's pleasure, in that Angelo is most fully subjected to the Duke in being forced to marry rather than burn. But in insisting that he too must be married, the Duke is defining his own pleasure as the pleasure of the audience—the affirmation of comic expectation. Which is not to say that the audience need *enjoy* that affirmation. Instead, the pleasure we're ceded is that of the Duke, that of joy's displacement: "Rather rejoicing to see another merry, than merry at any thing which profess'd to make him rejoice." Through the gap between judgment and desire that is the sovereign "pleasure" manifested in the coining of Angelo, everything that has been done at the Duke's pleasure the Duke finally assigns to our pleasure. But that doesn't mean that we have to like it.

# CHAPTER THREE

# Dismembering the Ducat in *The Merchant of Venice*

In the previous chapters, I have aimed to show how the material and historical peculiarities of Renaissance coins work to shape the articulation of values that go well beyond the context of monetary exchange, so that the discourses of ontology, ethics, and politics all partake of the complexities incorporated and epitomized in angels and groats. In this chapter and the next, I will consider two reactions that engage this ubiquity of the material terms of coined value in striving to negate them: chapter 4 will attend to the poetics of waste in prodigal fictions by Donne and Nashe, and here I will focus on the obsessive ambivalence toward coins expressed throughout *The Merchant of Venice* as a relation I'll call disavowal. Disavowal is a more immediately discursive, and less immediately embodied, performance than are the relations I've discussed in earlier chapters, those of consumption, instrumentality, and reproduction. It's a relation to the material that works by verbally repudiating it. The characters of *Merchant* talk about money all the time, and yet they do so in order to claim that what they are really talking about is something incommensurable to money.

> If every ducat in six thousand ducats
> Were in six parts, and every part a ducat,
> I would not draw them, I would have my bond (4.1.85–87),

declares Shylock when Bassanio offers him twice Antonio's debt in cash, divorcing the "bond" that originated in a monetary transaction from any relation to the heaps of coined gold that now confront him in the courtroom. There is something deeply perverse about this repudiation of the obvious—for

*Merchant* is obviously, even ostentatiously all about money, and it is difficult to imagine what there would be left of *Merchant* to be an object of analysis if we excluded the coin-object and its commensural relations to other objects in the play. The repudiation of coinage is perverse not only to common sense, however, but also to ethical obligation, as the court's bafflement before Shylock's behavior makes clear. The Venetians don't know what to enjoin upon him if he won't even accept being paid back in the currency he lent. And yet, by the time that *Merchant* achieves its resolution, the disavowal of coinage will prove to be not aberrant but foundational to the commonwealth that the play depicts.

*Merchant* construes the object to be disavowed, a coin, as a relationship between metallic matter and the stamped image which defines the metal as form, as quantity, and as value. Disavowing the coin entails dismantling that relationship and rearticulating its terms as disjoined, inverted, or transposed. Shylock verbally dismembers the six thousand ducats in the courtroom to explicate their inadequacy to the dismemberment he aims to enact upon Antonio. Looking for Portia's image within the gold casket, Morocco imagines it as a gold coin turned inside out, while Bassanio succeeds by recognizing that not only must form and matter be so transposed in "fair Portia's counterfeit," so too must be the relative values of the matters in question, gold and lead. The normative place of the coin in these constructions is easy to adduce from the tightly specific and elaborately fantastic circumstances of its disavowal; the riddle of the caskets collaborates with the successful suitor to mystify the prodigious cash value that is preeminent among the attractions of Portia, "a lady richly left" (1.1.161). Portia's virtues and beauty, however excellent they are, are incommensurable to her monetary plenitude, which surpasses even human excellence. Any interaction with Portia cannot but be all about the money, and has to find a way to be about something else.

Both mystification and demystification are monetary operations in *Merchant*; in the riddle-test, money ostentates itself as the thing being mystified, and thereby demands to be acknowledged as the means of demystification. Disavowal does not only work as an indirect affirmation of the conditions of coined existence. It works in a very Mammon-like way to present those particular conditions as universal ones—as the simple, material truth that all these disingenuous idealizations are striving to mystify. Coinage in *Merchant* is accorded a transparency that the characters are trying, and failing, to obfuscate. The operation of disavowal grants coinage the status of, not just *an* explanatory principle, but *the* explanatory principle: the one so obvious as to be exclusive. The ways in which coins are mystified in *Merchant* make their rematerializing, demystificatory powers self-evident.

But self-evidence is not an epistemological solution for the ethical problems presented by *Merchant*. Rather, self-evidence *is* the ethical problem of *Merchant*: "In sooth," says Antonio to open the play, "I know not why I am so sad," and Antonio will insist on the alienated impossibility of his own self-knowledge until Portia at last plucks out the heart of his mystery in the play's last scene, binding him to affirm that "I am th' unhappy subject of these quarrels" (1.1.1; 5.1.238). Self-evidence is the promise of the silver casket, "Who chooseth me shall get as much as he deserves," and the wrongness of the silver casket's tautological self-reflection recurs throughout the mimetic antitheses that proliferate in the playtext (2.7.7). The many dilemmas posed in *Merchant*, as impossible choices within an antithetical dyad (such as that between justice and mercy), refer in this way not only to one another but to the triune problem of the riddle of the caskets and to the unitary problem of the self-evident yet mysterious monad.

In citing the centrality of disavowal to *Merchant*, I borrow freely from the disciplinary vocabulary of psychoanalysis. Freud articulates "disavowal" [*Verleugnung*] most thoroughly in his 1927 essay "Fetishism."[1] In the sexual fetish, he argues, the male child's encounter with the horrific lack of the maternal penis is displaced, and reformulated into some more acceptable venue of knowledge that becomes the object of erotic attachment. But this operation does not work by forgetting or repression:

> In the situation we are considering, on the contrary, we see that the perception [of maternal castration] has persisted, and that a very energetic action has been undertaken to maintain the disavowal. It is not true that, after the child has made his observation of the woman, he has preserved unaltered his belief that women have a phallus. He has retained that belief, but he has also given it up. In the conflict between the weight of the unwelcome perception and the force of his counter-wish, a compromise has been reached. . . . (154)

Although the operation of disavowal, in which a traumatic perception is at once acknowledged and vitiated of its force by what Freud calls a "counter-wish," is for him the occasion of sexual fetishism, Freud argues that fetishism is only one instance of the process (154). Other traumatic perceptions than that of the castration complex may be disavowed, and disavowal may therefore take forms other than that of erotic attachment to extragenital objects; the example that Freud cites is the knowledge of a father's death, which he finds disavowed in two different case studies.

> It was only one current in their mental life that had not recognized their father's death; there was another current which took full account of that fact. The attitude which fitted in with the wish and the attitude which fitted in with reality existed side by side. In one of my two cases. . . . [t]he patient oscillated in every situation in life between two assumptions: the one, that his father was still alive and was hindering his activities; the other, opposite one, that he was entitled to regard himself as his father's successor. (156)

Freud would not call this ghostly father a "fetish," since for him the term directly denotes a specific sexual pathology. Critics working to coordinate the Freudian and Marxian manifestations of "fetish" have expanded his analysis into larger, epistemological registers, but I won't be taking advantage of that work here, since my argument will not be that money is a "fetish" in even the most capacious sense of the term.[2] Rather, I posit the relation of disavowal in order to locate money within it as the thing disavowed—and not, as the fetish would be, as the outcome of disavowal, the manifestation of the "counter-wish." *Merchant* does not deploy a unitary and cohesive object to serve as vessel of the counter-wish, as a successful fetishist would. Instead the counter-wish—the wish that money not be money—projects itself into multiple venues across the moments and the places of the play, venues that each oppose the material object of coined money. These transient, mutually dependent, mutually contradictory manifestations of the counter-wish include the ghostly "will of a dead father"; the "bond" that joins Antonio to Shylock and Shylock to Antonio; the trauma of castration, which in this play is not itself a knowledge to be disavowed but rather a more acceptable knowledge into which the disavowal of money may be formulated; Portia and Nerissa's rings; and, most centrally, the triune identity of the three metal caskets.

What's disavowed in *Merchant*'s money is the centrality of the material relation embodied in a coin—the conjunction of precious metal to validating image—to the social relations that that conjunction in turn facilitates and manifests. Rather than investigating the individuated psychic lives of the characters (or of the text), I will be using the concept of disavowal to evaluate how the characters' claims to individuation profess to differentiate their selves from a material field, and work thereby to integrate those selves into a social field.[3] The hinge between the repudiated materiality and the enacted community is that most basely sociable of objects, the "common drudge 'tween man and man," a coin. In citing dismemberment as the imagined material register of disavowal, I am comparing what's performed discursively upon coins to what Shylock and Antonio aim to achieve upon Antonio's body, and to what Talus achieved upon the golden hands and silver feet of Munera in Book Five of *The Faerie Queene*. I am likewise awakening the pun that would make "dismembering" an antithesis of "remembering," in the way that Munera's severed and monumentalized members are made by Talus to replace the "memory" of her demolished castle (*FQ* 5.2.28). Such a dismembering is not exactly a forgetting, but an antithetical substitute for memory—the counterfeit of knowledge, called into being by a counter-wish. Where the disavowal of coinage works effectively to affirm a coin's demystifying materiality in failing to negate it, the monetarized wrongness of the silver casket substitutes self-deception for the self-knowledge it claims to incorporate, and puts it thereby into circulation. On such a counterfeit self-evidence, the play suggests, the commercial commonwealth of Venice is founded.

## I. PROBLEM SETS

If we are to believe its title character, *The Merchant of Venice* isn't about money. It is about "why" Antonio, the merchant, is "so sad" (1.1.1); and although monetary exchange is preeminent among the social relations that constellate themselves around the mysterious sadness by which Antonio singles himself out as "a tainted wether of the flock,/ Meetest for death" (4.1.114–115), Antonio repudiates the suggestion of Salerio and Solanio that mercantile risk is the condition of his melancholy. Nor is it about the money for Shylock:

> If every ducat in six thousand ducats
> Were in six parts, and every part a ducat,
> I would not draw them, I would have my bond. (4.1.85–87)

The struggle to define the values of profit, loss, and risk in a capitalizing economy, between the figure of the merchant on the one hand and that of the usurer on the other, has yielded a rich vein of critique since landmark analyses of *Merchant* by Marc Shell and Walter Cohen in the early 1980s, and for me to defer money as an immediate critical object within the play may seem as perverse to that established body of literature as to my own project, which is likewise all about money. But Shylock and Antonio both perversely "follow a losing suit," chiastically joined by their mutual loathing and the self-loathing of each to sue together against Antonio's life and Shylock's exponentially growing potential profit for the sake of the pound of flesh (4.1.61). In demanding that the court adjudicate the claim for the pound of flesh as the court would a monetary claim—as if, and *only as if*, the claim were a monetary one—Antonio and Shylock both demand that the monetary form of their claim upon each other be understood not to be the claim's real substance.

This is by no means to assert that commercial self-interest is meaningless in the play. Bassanio is notoriously apt to equivocate between the amorous and auriferous attractions of Portia, nor does Lorenzo seem immune to the charms of Jessica's stolen inheritance. If Antonio and Shylock did not generally act according to their own commercial interests, they would not be rich enough to command their centrality to this play's plot. And Shylock relies on the general self-interest of the Venetian republic to be allowed to "follow... / A losing suit": "Since that the trade and profit of the city/ Consisteth of all nations," the legal rights of alien commerce must not be abrogated in the present case, regardless of its perversity and its malicious intent, as Shylock, Antonio, the Duke, and Portia all agree (4.1.60–61; 3.3.30–31). But, in the exceptional circumstances of this plot, Antonio and Shylock explicitly disdain the conversion of their conflict into monetary quantity, much less into the calculus of mercantile interests.[4] In this extraordinary moment, Shylock and Antonio, and Portia too, will have nothing they care about adequated to money—which would be less problematic if money were not preeminent among the things they care about, as the very terms of their mutual recriminations indicate. Money is contested among them, but they will not have it contested *as* money; rather, at the core of *Merchant's* conflict is a money that isn't money. What might this elusive money that isn't money be? The play entertains a constellation of answers: uncoined precious metal, like the gold and silver caskets; the fetishized, alienable genitals of Shylock or Antonio; a portrait; a counterfeit; death; a common wealth. For Antonio, it's a selfhood that persists by means of his not understanding it.

Antonio's equivocation of "My purse, my person, my extremest means," in offering all three to Bassanio, elevates "means" to the exclusion of ends as the merchant's self, in which Antonio's "person" and the "purse" that is all Bassanio actually asks for disappear into each other by means of an apparently trivializing pun (1.1.138). Antonio wants the money that Bassanio demands of him not to be money, and he accomplishes this by imposing his "person" upon it. The price of this negation of money is that his "person" be enfolded into the negation, as the melancholy mystery of Antonio to himself, "why I am so sad," that can be rightly articulated neither in fiscal nor in affective terms. Once this negation enters the marketplace, to look for three thousand ducats of not-money, Shylock obliges by formulating the bond for the pound of flesh. Antonio embodies the negation of money through a symmetrical relation between the interior and the exterior of his single body: between the melancholy seen by the speculating world in his visible behavior to be weighing on his heart and the pound of flesh on his bodily surface, "Nearest the merchant's heart," through which Shylock aims to lay that heart bare (4.1.233).

As Gail Kern Paster has argued, the interiority defined by the early modern passions is not the post-Cartesian abstraction which we inhabit, but the matrix of organs and fluids pulsing beneath the skin, upon whose passionate tides reason is tossed like a fragile boat.[5] Like Lear's mad desire to "anatomize Regan; see what breeds about her heart. Is there any cause in nature that make these hard hearts?" (*Lear* 3.6.77–79), Shylock's hard-hearted desire to expose Antonio's melancholic heart is not wrong because it is too literal (as critics often have argued), animating a dead metaphor—the bodily heart as emotive center is not only not dead but, Paster demonstrates, not a metaphor. Shylock's desire is vivisection, and as vivisection it is ethically wrong.[6] In this materialist logic, the mysterious relation of Antonio's interior disposition, inside his body, to his behavior visible from outside is not very different from the relation of the inside of any closed container to its outside. The two initial problems of the play, Antonio's mystery of "why I am so sad" and the riddle of Portia's three caskets, postulate themselves in the same terms, as the difficulty of deciphering a content ascribed to an interior through an opaque, but in some way relevant, exterior. Antonio formulates the enclosure of his mystery to interest Bassanio, to whom his purse-and-person "lie all unlock'd" (1.1.139): all he needs Bassanio to do is open him, and he will be solved.[7] But Bassanio is more interested in taking his chances opening the caskets.

In leaving Antonio to venture to Belmont, Bassanio is choosing which of these two problems to solve, the mysterious singularity of Antonio's sadness or the triangulated riddle of "the will of a dead father," each of which is formulated in terms of a material and interdependent dyad of exterior and interior (1.2.25). The problem in two terms, the dyad, is at once recursive upon the problem in one term, Antonio's mystery of himself to himself, and upon that in three terms, the determination of which two caskets are wrong and which one is right.[8] That dyad, moreover, is one of many reflective pairings of concepts and of characters in *The Merchant of Venice*, a play that can seem to be built entirely out of dichotomous oppositions: not only outside and inside, but Jew and Christian, alien and citizen, letter and spirit, flesh and blood, quantity and quality, usury and venture, Laban and Jacob, Antonio and Portia (as competing lovers of Bassanio), Shylock and Antonio (as adversaries at law), friendship and love, justice and mercy, and so on and on. As René Girard argues, the ways in which these superabundant dichotomies tend to blur into one another undermines the possibility of judgment not only among all of them but within each of them:

> In Venice... greed and generosity, pride and humility, compassion and ferocity, money and human flesh, tend to become one and the same. This undifferentiation makes it impossible to define anything with precision, to ascribe one particular cause to one particular event.[9]

So there is one riddle in the play, a problem of three; three mysteries of singular self-knowledge, as I will argue (Antonio, Shylock, and the silver casket), problems of one; and a bewildering plurality of problems of two, the notoriously unstable dilemmas of *The Merchant of Venice*.

By citing Antonio's and Shylock's motivations as instances of mystery, I don't mean to quarrel with readings that deduce specific causes for their behaviors. Auden's recognition that Antonio is in love with Bassanio is one that most post-Stonewall undergraduates are prepared to second, and the institutions of hatred that interpellate Shylock in his quest for revenge have been ably documented by critics since the nineteenth century.[10] I mean that neither Antonio or Shylock is able, when prompted, to explicate his motives himself.[11] Both enfold their respective inarticulacies into the ethos they assert to their interlocutors. Antonio gets to be only the more dejected because he cannot name a cause for sadness, as a named cause would imply the hope of naming and executing a remedy, while Shylock, in declaring "So can I give no reason, nor I will not" for his pursuit of the pound of flesh, makes his inability to answer the question continuous with his defiance of the question (4.1.59). But this perversely self-serving continuity between inarticulacy and ethos itself implies that neither Antonio nor Shylock is able to achieve the position of self-scrutiny, of an exteriorized regard of one's self, that would allow each the insight into his own motives that seems so obvious to us as we regard them. Even if Antonio and Shylock are mysterious only to themselves, that only the more marks mystery as constitutive of their own self-address.

"Mystery" is also constitutive of Christian faith. Not only is the will of God mysterious, so too are the defining features of the Christian creed, including the Incarnation, the Resurrection, and the Last Judgment.[12] Antonio and Shylock both are stuck in degraded relations to the mysteries of faith: Antonio in his lugubriously literal and ultimately thwarted *imitatio Christi* in his passion for Bassanio, and Shylock in the brutal absurdity of Portia's attempt to enforce a behavior on him that she defines as simultaneously ethical and Christian, so that Shylock's failure to be Christian obliges him to be unethical within the scope of civil society:

> Therefore, Jew,
> Though justice be thy plea, consider this,
> That in the course of justice, none of us
> Should see salvation. We do pray for mercy,
> And that same prayer doth teach us all to render
> The deeds of mercy. (4.1.197–202)

The salutary mystery of divine judgment shapes human behavior, says Portia, to imitate the behavior "we" hope God will himself adopt toward "us"; in naming Shylock simultaneously as "Jew" and as "us," she makes his participation in the benignant circulation of mystery as impossible as it is mandatory. The Pauline hardness of "that—than which what's harder?—his Jewish heart" moralizes Shylock's inapprehension of what's incomprehensible (4.1.79–80). Shylock's attempt to make his own mystery part of the ground for his defiance of the Christians' interrogation only defines that individual mysteriousness of himself to himself as parodic of the universal mysteriousness to "us" of God's will.

Questions of individuation, of a person's experience of his self as (often puzzlingly) unique, are in this way suborned into Big Questions—dilemmas that present themselves as transhistorically constitutive of a universal human condition—throughout the text of *The Merchant of Venice*, Big Questions familiar to many a college dorm's bull session the night before the Great Books final.[13] The persistent value of these agonistic topoi to our educational system lies in their undecidability; the fact that neither, say, justice or mercy is simply a correct answer makes the difference between them endlessly productive as an occasion for discourse. In each case, however, the dilemma inside the play proves asymmetrical. One term is always discovered to be privileged over the other as being the other's true and implicit meaning, following the model of subsumption through which Paul argued that the Christian "ministration of the spirit" simultaneously emerged from, superseded, and encompassed the Hebrew law, "the ministration of death" (2 Cor 3:7–8, KJV). And by "always discovered" I mean "always discovered by Portia," whose transvesting of the law seems to embody this interpretive principle.[14] The Christian-cognate half of each dilemma is invisible to Shylock: "I cannot find it, 'tis not in the bond" (4.2.262). For him, the choice between justice and mercy is not an impossible, tragic choice, as it is for the court before Portia's solution, but Hobson's choice: justice or nothing, no choice at all. The comic resolution that Portia produces is to reveal each dilemma as a merely false dichotomy—a cake that can be eaten and still had, no need to choose. Justice as she applies it to Shylock is, from her point of view, itself encompassed within a mercy that proceeds from it.[15] Shylock's forced conversion, and his separation from his usurious monies, might together save his soul in the course of punishing him—albeit while leaving him to starve, so that what Shylock's getting, and need not choose between, is mercy *and* nothing. Dilemma is manifested throughout the play so that Portia can be the solution. Dilemmas are what we can't solve but she can.

The switch that Portia operates in her ministration of dilemma is that between quantity and quality—really, that *behind* quantity and quality: the alternation of scarcity, the condition of quantity, and plenitude, the quality that subsumes all quantities. Georges Bataille distinguishes the "restricted economy," the economy whose condition is scarcity, from the "general economy," the economy whose condition is plenty.[16] The economy of hardship and luxury, inequity and exploitation, that we know is the restricted economy, from whose point of view the general economy is an otherworldly fantasy—the Land of Cockaigne, the Big Rock Candy Mountain, the golden fleece beyond the sea. But, as any few pages of Bataille's cornucopian perversities will make clear, the general economy is not *nicer* than the restricted economy: from the point of view of restriction, the general economy is a condition of unbearable nastiness.[17] The general economy is grotesque, repulsive, abominable, overwhelming, too much; its business is not with thrift and competition but with sacrifice and waste, the constant divestiture of an unstoppable, fecal excess. Nicety is a normative value of the restricted economy, an exclusionary order that puts us in competition with each other for a finite number of nice things while protecting us from desiring the otherwise unrestricted plethora of things that are, by its standard, nasty. In the restricted economy we can have as much of what we don't want as we like, so that Bataille renders the general economy to our restricted understandings as the erotic profusion of shit.[18] The general economy overwhelms the differentiating means of choice—it is everything all at once forever, an ecstatic and horrific universal presence that obviates all the little presences, our selves and the boxes we put them inside, of the restricted economy. Plenty is beyond choosing.

As Shell argues, Portia's cornucopian bounty is defined through repeated references to her as "the golden fleece," the symbol of material plenitude both in ancient myth and in early modern alchemy texts.[19] Yet even in distributing her bounty to Antonio—like her distributing mercy to Shylock, who is given "the grace of God" to the extent that he is deprived of his former "enough" of material means (2.2.150–151)—her generosity is mean, imposing scarcity even as she showers her plenty.[20] Portia's returning of Antonio's material prosperity comes only after Antonio's concession that there is not enough of Bassanio to go round, ceding his claim upon the beloved adventurer to the claim of Bassanio's wife.[21] She extracts that concession through the ring exchange, where she uses her disguise as the "doctor" to demand as a favor for saving Antonio's life the same ring she had given Bassanio, with many heavy oaths, in the previous act. Here Portia imposes a dilemma upon Bassanio that the audience knows to be false, the choice between the wife who is herself and the doctor who is also herself. In doubling herself she makes the ring appear to be scarce. But both horns of this dilemma remain Portia; Bassanio endures the hardship of dilemma, but has neither the power nor the responsibility of an actual choice. Either choice on Bassanio's part would serve to denigrate his relationship to Antonio and elevate his relationship to Portia, whether he were to dismiss the doctor's and Antonio's demand to surrender the ring, or to accede to it (as Bassanio does), which will force Antonio himself to renew in his own voice Bassanio's oaths to keep the ring. In volunteering that "I am th' unhappy subject of these quarrels," Antonio has at once to agree to Portia's conditions and to pretend that they are not her conditions but the free gift of his own generosity, so that Portia's generosity may be seen to make a free gift to him; the terms by which characters accept Portia's making-scarce before they accept her bounty are disavowed even as they are spoken (5.1.238).[22]

Portia has already modeled this disavowal when first she gave herself and the ring to Bassanio, teaching him to locate her extraordinary plenty in what she ostentates as the thoroughly unexceptional singularity, the not-muchness, of her self. "Doubtful whether what I see be true,/ Until confirm'd, sign'd, ratified by you," Bassanio's questioning gaze upon Portia is not answered in the terms of validation for which he enquires (3.2.147–148).

> You see me, Lord Bassanio, where I stand,
> Such as I am. Though for myself alone
> I would not be ambitious in my wish
> To wish myself much better, yet for you,
> I would be trebled twenty times myself,
> A thousand times more fair, ten thousand times more rich,
> That only to stand high in your account,
> I might in virtues, beauties, livings, friends,

Exceed account. But the full sum of me
Is sum of something; which to term in gross
Is an unlesson'd girl, unschool'd, unpractic'd. . . . (3.2.149–159)

As David Bady demonstrates, Portia in citing herself as "sum of something" invokes the conventional formula of the "sum of sums" which the steward of a property periodically yielded up as a total account to its owner, but in rephrasing that formula of validation, she cites it in order to contravene it.[23] Following out the hyperbolic permutations of Portia's math, Bady finds the "sum of something" to be the tautological self-authorization "Portia=Portia." What seems like self-deprecation is a forcefully disingenuous reminder of the incalculable value of Portia's bounty, and the equally disingenuous reminder that Bassanio ought to be able to pretend to ignore that value (which he is not being allowed for one second to forget) in his loving Portia "such as I am." Even as Portia professes that she would like to be able to quantify her qualities as "an unlesson'd girl" such that they would then "exceed account," to arrive at that horizon at which the accumulation of quantity becomes a quality, plenitude, she is disavowing the plenitude that Bassanio has already announced she does embody, as "the golden fleece."[24] She is soon enough ready to turn that plenitude back into any amount of money to save Antonio, at once proclaiming that Antonio's life is important and that the monetary cost of it, "the petty debt" (3.2.307), is trivial; from the point of view of her own plenitude, it's impossible to say which valuation is the pertinent one. Portia's bounty is her way of eradicating Antonio's claim on Bassanio. All that Antonio wants is Bassanio; all that Antonio doesn't want is money, and that latter "all" will, in the final scene, be all he gets.

Dilemma is the impossible choice between two antithetical terms. In her leverage between scarcity and bounty, Portia is able to make such dyadic pairs into either singularities or plenitudes, eliminating the ground of dilemma in oppositional duality. The difference between singularity and plenitude makes for such another antithesis, but it's a disingenuous one, occurring within Portia's arbitrariness rather than in any social or universal necessity, and it shows the dilemmas that cascade from it to be likewise disingenuous: problems of two formulated to unify their answerer, Portia, with their answers. With this understanding of the dilemmas' numerical move from evenness to oddness in mind, I'd like to return to the initial formulations of the play's odd problems, as unitary mystery and as triune riddle, to see what the riddle can tell us about the mysterious relation of individuation to the disavowal of money.

## II. HAZARD PAY

The immediate difference between Antonio's mystery and the casket riddle is that the riddle is wretchedly easy. The point of answering the riddle is to not be one among "many men" (as the gold casket puts it) but to be the one man who will marry Portia. The answer is the one of the three caskets that is both counterintuitive, not what "many men" would choose, and unique. The problem-solving skills that I learned from Sesame Street are sufficient to solve it: which of these things is not like the others, which of these things just doesn't belong? One of the caskets is the answer and two are not. Silver and gold are both desirably precious, which would offer an intuitive relation to the task of claiming Portia as fulfilling one's desire for her, and lead is not. What child is there who would not answer, "lead"?[25]

Yet Morocco and Arragon both get it wrong before Bassanio gets it right. The perversity through which the two failing suitors convince themselves to ignore the obvious makes for a more interesting object to my argument than Bassanio's managing at last to recognize it (though I will be interested in the consequences of that recognition).[26] The most basic way in which Morocco and Arragon mislead themselves is to assume that the test is discursive—that the inscriptions on the caskets are together the substance of the riddle. The riddle is to be found, instead, in the substances of the caskets: gold, silver, or lead. The inscriptions are immaterial. They are not irrelevant or inappropriate, but they have no bearing on the outcome of the trial; they are misleading only to the extent that the suitor thinks that they should lead him at all. Having decided that the caskets refer to something other than themselves, and that they perform that reference by means of discourse, Morocco and Arragon attempt to trace that reference by prolonging that discourse, as if in conversation with the caskets—"What says the silver with her virgin hue?" asks Morocco, quite winningly, in chatting up the putatively interlocutive object to which he addresses himself (2.7.22). Morocco proceeds to infer from this one-sided conversation that what the test is about is Portia; he is wrong. Arragon assumes that the test is about himself, and he is wrong too. The test is about itself; the ideal suitor is the one who can successfully accommodate himself to "the will of a dead father," as it is materialized in the caskets. Bassanio succeeds by addressing himself to the riddle on its own terms, those that perpetuate the father's "will" past his death, for the riddle is itself its own answer. It's a test only of its self-evidence.[27]

That said, I'd like to look further at the way in which the inscribing of the caskets defrauds both Morocco and Arragon of that self-evidence, and lures them into misleading themselves through verbal ratiocination. The inscriptions outside Portia's caskets detail the varieties of desiring subject "Who chooses"; each casket professes itself, "me," to be the object of its particular subject's desire, and implies—without of course asserting—that it is also Portia, that the inscribed metal that is its visible surface has Portia as its interiority. Morocco is wrong when he asserts the lead casket asks him to "give—for what? for lead, hazard for lead?" (2.7.17). Like all the caskets, the lead casket is offering not itself, but Portia, as the object for which it will transume itself once opened, so it is simply reiterating the terms of the riddle as its own terms. These inscriptions together profess a sequence of erotic subjectivities that moves from the desire shared among others (gold, "what many men desire"), where the subject "Who chooses" identifies that community of desire with the desiring self by imitating it, to the self addressing the self (silver, whose reward, "as much as he deserves," is promised in the terms of the Delphic injunction "know thyself"), to the courting of the extinction of the self (lead, to "give and hazard all"). The terms that lead offers are again simply the terms of the contest *tout court*. Everyone who participates in choosing "must give and hazard all he hath," putting his hope of posterity on the chopping block as Abraham did with Isaac for God, and as Antonio, "a tainted wether of the flock," claims to have done with his debt and his bit of flesh for Bassanio (4.1.114).[28]

The continuity among circumcision, castration, and extinction shapes the mutually destructive erotic through which Antonio engages Bassanio, Portia, and Shylock, but the terms of lead are also those with which Lorenzo and Jessica define their weirdly belated courtship in 5.1. Only after their marriage do Lorenzo and Jessica begin to flirt with each other, and they flirt with each other by flirting with disaster. The sequence of doomed and then criminal lovers with whose "nights" they identify their own—from Troilus and Cressida to Thisby, to Dido, to Medea, and finally to each other as thief and as "unthrift" seducer—asserts more and more vehemently the courtship of extinction professed by the lead casket, until whatever unimaginable climax Jessica claims to have in mind—"I would out-night you, did nobody come;/ But hark, I hear the footing of a man"—is headed off by the arrival of Portia's messenger (5.1.22–23).[29] Lorenzo has not needed (in the action of the play) to court Jessica, much less to endure the riddle trial through which Portia's suitors are put. Jessica simply and almost literally drops into his arms. But before she drops into his arms, she drops a single casket. Jessica's casket is full of Shylock's gold and his "two rich and precious stones"; it is full of herself, if we follow Shylock's frenzied equivocation of "my ducats, and my daughter" upon discovering the loss of his posterity; and she herself descends from the balcony inside "the lovely garnish of a boy," a disguise Lorenzo evidently finds erotic, and upon which false-true exterior we may suspect he redirects some of the attraction he feels to the contents of her casket (2.8.20; 2.8.17; 2.6.45). To desire is to choose among the caskets, to engage their erotics of diversely speculating upon a mystified interior, and the choice is no choice. As Jessica and Lorenzo make clear in their belated, mythopoetic enactment of everything that was left unstated and implicit in their balcony scene, all the caskets are the lead casket, Jessica's single stolen casket. What Jessica's casket is finally full of is Lorenzo's necessarily disingenuous "vows of faith" (5.1.19): money as the form of its own disavowal, a not-money that is money.

The interior inscriptions of Portia's caskets profess to reveal the object each suitor has chosen in adopting the desiring subjectivity of the casket's outer inscription—or, rather, to explicate it, as the object is in each case presented emblematically, by means of an image to which a gnomic rubric is subjoined. This is true even in the case of Portia's image, the presence of which, once revealed, might seem sufficiently explained by the terms of the contest itself. Yet the continued puzzlement of Bassanio's interaction with the portrait seems to require not only the note's affirmation that he has won the trial, but even its prompting that now would be a good time to give Portia a kiss. Each of the revealed interiors is, like that of Portia, "the portrait" (as Arragon puts it, 2.9.54) of a head—either a death's-head, a fool's head, or Portia's head.[30] The sequence of insides as objects transposes the sequence propounded by the sequence of outsides as desires: gold, as the desire of others, opens into death; lead, as the courtship of death, opens into the desired other. Portia's late but persistent father may or may not think this smug irony is meaningful in itself. It is, as I've argued, immaterial to Bassanio's success.

Between the inversions of otherness and extinction that lie at either end of the casket continuum, though, is the fulcrum at which Arragon's silver casket exchanges self for self: the erotic of self-knowledge on the outside for the self as erotic object on the inside. Arragon attempts to imagine the silver casket, and the deserving-deserved self with which he identifies it, as embodying a quality, "merit," outside the scope of money—

> O that estates, degrees, and offices
> Were not deriv'd corruptly, and that clear honor
> Were purchas'd by the merit of the wearer! (2.9.41–43)

—where Shylock, Antonio, and Portia tend to desire a money that would be only qualitative and itself inadequated. The Spaniard is not very successful in his rhetorical gymnastics. In the alternate circuit of value he proposes, "honor" remains a commodity to be "purchas'd" by "the stamp of merit" (2.9.39). Here the stuff adopted by the money form would pass from material metal to reified merit, but the money form itself and the adequating form of its transactions persist—Arragon can't outthink them. The sameness of his imagined difference, more perhaps than the arrogance of his "assum[ing] desert," justifies the constellation of solipsism he confronts inside the casket (2.9.51).[31] The emblem inside silver, "the portrait of a blinking idiot," professes at once to be a fool's head, a mirror, Narcissus, Arragon's present self, and Arragon's future self (2.9.54):

> Some there be that shadows kiss,
> Such have but a shadow's bliss.
> There be fools alive, iwis,
> Silver'd o'er, and so was this.
> Take what wife you will to bed,
> I will ever be thy head.
> So be gone, you are sped. (2.9.66–72)

Ovid offers the story of Narcissus, the patron of those "that shadows kiss," as an elaborate joke on the axioms of self-knowledge. "Know thyself" was the universal admonition engraved over the entrance to the oracle at Delphi, but the oracular prophecy given by the androgyne Tiresias for Narcissus was that he, uniquely, would be happy as long as he did not "know himself." The story of Narcissus and Echo is saturated with meaning for the questions of erotic investment, selfhood and otherness, discourse and image, that are central to this chapter, but what's infused with this richness is a gleeful allegory of compulsive masturbation.[32] Early modern English jokes about such an incompetent or misplaced sexuality found a bawdy venue in the fool's brandishing of his phallic "bauble," a stick itself bearing a donkey-eared fool's head in imitation of its holder's—the very head that will mark Arragon, no matter how silver'd o'er with age and no matter to whom he is married, as forever a wanker.[33] The difference between self-evidence as an object lesson in the lead casket and the subject of mystery in Antonio's body (associated as Antonio's mystery of self to self likewise is with castration and with the homoeroticism that, as Alan Sinfield argues, the play is apt to define as an unproductive perversion of sexuality) is the silver casket's Narcissistic wrongness of self-knowledge.[34] As Janet Adelman argues of the play's anxious submergence of the relations of Christian to Jew,

> *Merchant* seems to me everywhere haunted by what it cannot allow itself to know. In its play of glib surfaces, *Merchant* represents self-knowledge as a wound, and one that must be forestalled. In that sense, Antonio is the play's epitome. . . .[35]

But a version of Antonio's otherwise "forestalled," mutilative introspection does come to be enacted when Arragon opens the silver casket and sees what's inside—a version which seems surprisingly inconsequential, if we compare its name-calling ridicule to Morocco's death-bound error, yet which determines the resolution of the riddle.

Within the logic of riddling, it is impossible for silver, the middle term, to be the single, right answer. It is like gold in being precious; it is like lead in being not as precious as gold; it lacks the metaphorical weight of either of the others, just as it lacks their material density.[36] The answer has to be one of the extremes, either gold or lead. Silver is there to be redundant, to be the wrong answer—and to make gold also be the wrong answer, to be like enough to gold to eliminate both from the possibility of being right. Its redundancy is transitive, imposing a decisive asymmetry upon the otherwise impossible choice between gold and lead. As a reflective dyad, the ironic fungibility of gold and lead, desire of the other and desire of death, might be undecidable. The presence of an invalid third term is the means by which one of the possibly valid alternatives can be likewise invalidated.

In Richard Halpern's analysis of *Merchant,* the narcissistic moment of choosing the silver casket is the simplest instance of a dynamic of mirroring that radiates from it across the entire play, generating a reflective series without an originary referent in which each dyad opens onto the next. He argues that this process of mirroring enacts both the ontology of the value-form as described by Marx and the ontology of the Jew as inscribed in both anti-Semitic and philo-Semitic discourses throughout modern history.[37] Sophisticated as Halpern's analysis is, he does seem to me not to acknowledge the simplest of the silver casket's functions, which is to ostentate itself as wrong, and thereby to differentiate the otherwise equivalent caskets of gold and lead. All the caskets articulate themselves in the first person, and in the formula "Who chooseth me shall gain . . ."; the gold and silver caskets both transume their status as grammatical objects into a de facto subject position (here, "I am as much as my chooser deserves"). Analyzing Arragon's interlocution of the silver casket, Halpern declares that "Aragon is, in effect, the Fichtean philosopher who can say 'I am I,' or the twenty yards of linen which tries to express its value in twenty yards of linen."[38] But the silver casket translates the self-evidence of subjecthood, the affirmation "I am I," into "I am wrong."[39] The inside adds, "I am a fool." And both inside and reflective outside proclaim, "I am you, you fool."

According to Mary Poovey, the first function of a coin is to present itself as valid, by means of its stamp, by which the user may see that it is both current, and current at such a rate of correspondence. The coin then proceeds transitively to validate the correspondence between itself and any other object offered in exchange; the value relation is secondary to the validation relation, emerging from it.[40] The silver casket, conversely, ostentates itself as *in*valid, and translates its invalidity onto the correspondingly precious gold casket. The validation of the apparent nullity of the lead casket is a negative one, a process of elimination: the one you want is the one that doesn't belong. The silver casket works as the inverse of money, disestablishing the apparent value of gold. I've already discussed the ways in which money itself appears as an inversion of human ethos, from *The Faerie Queene* to *The Jew of Malta* to *King John* and *Measure for Measure,* in its transposal of the material terms, memory and telos, through which Renaissance individuals imagined their relation to past and future. But there's nothing very affirming about the inversion of that inversion in the silver casket. The silver casket is more like a litotes, a double-negative account of individuation. As far as the caskets are concerned, there is not much difference between being a failure as an individual, as Arragon has chosen to be, and the failure to be an individual—Morocco's choice. Yet the inversion of coined money that Morocco articulates in his choice, "an angel . . . all within," seems quite different from Arragon's.

In his attempt to win over the caskets by making conversation, Morocco finds himself with little to say to lead. "What says this leaden casket?" is a truncated line, the only one in his long speech—he finds it difficult to initiate conversation with it (2.7.15). It is dumb to him. Another man might find the clue to the lead casket's self-evidence in that very dumbness, but Morocco is too focused on finding a discursive solution to pay it much mind.[41] He goes on to articulate his choice instead as a probabilistic progression of relative values from the marketplace:

> One of these three contains her heavenly picture.
> Is't like that lead contains her? 'Twere damnation
> To think so base a thought; it were too gross
> To rib her cerecloth in the obscure grave.
> Or shall I think in silver she's immur'd,
> Being ten times undervalued to tried gold?

O sinful thought! never so rich a gem
Was set in worse than gold. They have in England
A coin that bears the figure of an angel
Stamp'd in gold, but that's insculp'd upon;
But here an angel in a golden bed
Lies all within. (2.7.53–59)

The "thought" of Portia's interiority to the casket, unlikely and "base" in the case of lead, becomes "sinful" in relation to silver. This is consistent with his initial appraisal of the situation: unable to address himself to the lead casket at all, Morocco "stoops not" and is left to define his choice between the two precious caskets, a choice that is no choice (2.7.20). If preciousness is the salient term, the more precious metal must win out; and it must also lead Morocco's rhetoric past the sullen rejection of lead, past the briefly thoughtful self-examination prompted by the silver, to the vast wastes of "Hyrcanian deserts" and "the watery kingdom" excitedly traversed by idolatry (2.7.41, 44). In his refusal to "sin" against an idol by imagining it set only in silver, Morocco is ironically the more sinful; and the homiletic register of "sin" converges with the conventionally ornamented idolatry of the poetic beloved, on the one hand, and the tenuous supersession of the monetary object throughout the play on the other, to prompt the citation of the monetary "angel/ Stamp'd in gold."

Rather than belabor Morocco's idolatry as a moral failure, I'd like to construe it as Bacon would, as an error in method, a fallacy.[42] We may readily chide Morocco for adducing a necessary relationship between exterior and interior, since he had introduced himself to Portia by insisting that she not make such a connection in his own case: "Mislike me not for my complexion" (2.1.1)—though he does go on in that speech to urge Portia to think as well of his complexion as of the redness of his blood. But the process by which he talks himself into choosing the gold casket is more complex, and the strangely articulated crux of the "angel" gives that complexity shape.

Morocco imagines the relation of interior to exterior obtaining in the casket as the inverse of that embodied in the coin, where "the figure of an angel" is "insculp'd upon" golden matter. "Here," conversely, "an angel in a golden bed/ Lies all within": Portia's portrait, to Morocco, is money turned inside out—as is Portia herself, given his inability to distinguish the woman from her picture. The form of the image becomes the interior of an exteriorized matter. As we saw in chapter 1, though, the topological relation of matter to form is also a necessarily chronological one, in which matter is prior to the form that acts upon it, which propels it into the future as its telos, so this is also a temporal inversion, an unmaking of the coin as made. It may not be worthwhile to quibble with Morocco's lack of maker's knowledge, but the transumption of process and confusion of artistic agency here does strike me: in minting, it's the dies that are "insculp'd upon" (OED: carved into) by an artist, and then hammered into the blank so that the coined image emerges in relief. What would such a topochronological inversion of inside and outside, matter and form, look like without the help of sophisticated computer modeling? The awkwardness of the metaphor as image, the difficulty of this verbal artifact to be brought before the eye, seems acknowledged in the incompletion of Morocco's syntax, where the objectless prepositions "upon" and "within" do service as adverbs. What the casket claims it would look like is a skull with a scroll.

On the one hand, the skull inside the casket is Everyman's skull, the universality of death. Morocco immediately allegorizes it as "a carrion Death" without needing to articulate the materiality of the object inside the casket (2.7.63). That this is a three-dimensional skull of bone and not the painting of one is made clear by the fact that the scroll is phallically inserted "within its empty eye" (2.7.65); nevertheless, the emblematic presentation of the object and rubric, like the immediate articulation of "Death," asks us to regard it as a representation as much as an object. Deductively, it is Morocco's skull; his shocking confrontation of it recalls not only the memento mori tradition but the exemplary syllogism "All men are mortal; Socrates is a man; therefore Socrates is mortal." But what Morocco looks to find inside the casket is Portia's portrait, an image of her head. He imagines the interior of the casket to be the icon with which he has already identified "this mortal breathing saint," by means of the contortion of the angel through which he articulates the golden outside of the casket (2.7.40). So what he exposes inside the casket is also *Portia's* skull. In the skull's "empty eye" the adverbial "within" of Morocco's topological inversion has found its prepositional object: this skull is the exteriorized inside of Portia's face.

In identifying his desire with that of "many men," Morocco marks it as what René Girard has defined as a mimetic desire, one that arises in emulous, homosocial rivalry among men rather than in the desiring subject's relation to the object to which it claims to refer.[43] Mimetic desire engages a circuit of aggressive imitation without origin: each desiring man wants to claim as his own that which other desiring men all want to claim. But the gold casket offers nevertheless to name an originary, objective referent as what the community of mimetic desirers want from one another, in opening its secret interior. "What many men desire" is not only "Death"—whether that be the universality of death, their own individual deaths, or the death of the beloved object.

"What many men desire" is what Shylock desires, vivisection. The mimetic desire of the gold casket is the desire *to see* death, to see the momentary interior process of unmaking that transforms a living body into its counterfeit—for "to die is to be a counterfeit," as Falstaff says when he finds himself in at the kill at Shrewsbury (*1H4* 5.4.115–116); it's to appear identical to one's living self while being only its material husk, its outside.[44] This mimetic desire is the desire to be one of many, like all the others, by desiring what they desire, which per the gold casket is to see into another's death—but that vivisected other is necessarily some one to which one has likened oneself, so the death whose sight is desired is one's own in the other's. Morocco expects that the role of "many" rivals in the casket's exterior is to be replaced by Portia when the casket is opened; instead of all the other men, he will get the one woman whom he considers the common object of their desire. His imitative relation to the multiplicity of other men is instead transumed into the unity of the skull, which is at once his and Portia's. Though Portia is not herself the masculine rivals, Morocco's relations to the masculine rivals and to Portia are exposed as continuous in the opening of the casket; in this way, the representation of Portia's face becomes Morocco's Golgotha, the place he has chosen to witness their extinction, his own extinction, and that of his and their desire.

The riddle is a test of self-evidence. Choosing the gold casket defers that self-evidence by the hope to find it in another, through imitating that other in oneself. In that deferral one wants what everyone else wants, which is to disavow the self-evidence of one's own death, through seeing the other's death in one's own stead. The counterwish prompting this complex disavowal is revealed in opening the gold casket as the wish to know oneself to be immortal—like a hunk of metal; like an image; like an angel.

## III. FAIR PORTIA'S COUNTERFEIT

The minted angel is all three of these things by turns, so it's wrong in each of these ways. Since a woman's portrait is what Morocco is supposed to be looking for, the gold angel is recognizably a red herring; the angel was exceptional among English coins in portraying the Queen only emblematically, through her arms and rubric, and not mimetically as a portrait. His assumption that the angel in question is feminine, reclining houri-like on "a golden bed," is likewise belied by the iconography of the church militant that the coin presented, as the archangel Michael in the act of smiting the dragon Satan.[45] But equally important to the representational problem Morocco has lost himself in is the coin's Englishness, which he does cite. The English angel refers Morocco's problem back to the "poor pennyworth in the English" that Portia, only metatheatrically disingenuous, claimed for her conversation with her English suitor, whose handsome speechlessness in any of the languages Portia knows make him "a proper man's picture." The failure of each of these suitors is epitomized in the misunderstanding of English money—Morocco misconceives the angel, while in Portia's account of the Englishman, English money is itself the medium of misunderstanding. As I will argue, Bassanio's success relies on being able to profit from the misconception of money without correcting it. He succeeds by claiming as his own just such another monetary misconception: his "golden fleece" takes the form of "Fair Portia's counterfeit" (1.1.170, 3.2.115).

"What say you then to [i.e., "about"] Falconbridge, the young baron of England?" asks Nerissa of Portia, who punningly replies,

> You know I say nothing to him, for he understands not me, nor I him. He hath neither Latin, French, nor Italian, and you will come into the court and swear that I have a poor pennyworth in the English. He is a proper man's picture, but alas, who can converse with a dumb show? How oddly he is suited! I think he bought his doublet in Italy, his round hose in France, his bonnet in Germany, and his behavior every where. (1.2.66–76)[46]

As with the lead casket, which is inarticulate insofar as Morocco can find nothing to say about what it has to say to him, the nullity of the Englishman's speech is defined as a restriction imposed upon the discursiveness of another, Portia, who says "nothing to him." The lack of a "pennyworth in the English" on Portia's part makes him a picture. Even putting aside the teasing of the audience whom Portia is addressing in garrulous English (while speaking to Nerissa in Italian, within the fiction), this formulation is striking in a number of ways: in the suddenness with which a situational lack of language drops the Englishman out of being a "proper man" and into being his own representation; in the fact that the "pennyworth in the English" is about the only thing that Portia, mistress of the bounty of Belmont, doesn't "have"; and in the way that the making-picture of the Englishman is articulated as a negation (literally an impoverishment) of monetary value. Portia's picture is a precious secret, the interior content implicated in, and waiting to be explicated from, the opaque surfaces of the caskets. The "proper man's picture" is a surface that, however attractive, is deprived of this interiorized value because he leaves nothing to be said.

Portia adds that the Englishman isn't even his own picture. Rather, he is everyone else's picture; his appearance is as promiscuous as his speechlessness is stolid. The indiscriminate and piecemeal affectations of international fashions by English dandies were a commonplace joke, but here they mark the Englishman as a horizon in the mimetic choice of "what many men desire," the risible attempt to ape all kinds of men all at once. His inarticulateness, which relegates him to the status of visual object, likewise serves as a point of reference for the mysterious inability of Antonio to say "why I am so sad," for the dumb self-evidence of the lead casket, and for the extraverbal "fair speechless messages" that Portia's eyes send to Bassanio (1.1.164). As the only other of her suitors that Portia says she finds visually attractive (and, as an Englishman, a shadow of the protagonist's role as audience surrogate), he is Bassanio's counterpart. Bassanio is a proper man's speaking picture, as he demonstrates in ventriloquizing the interior of the lead casket.

"What find I here?" Bassanio asks as he opens the lead casket, and many a critic has been struck by the thoroughness with which he insists on answering this question (or prolonging it):

> Fair Portia's counterfeit! What demigod
> Hath come so near creation? Move these eyes?
> Or whether, riding on the balls of mine,
> Seem they in motion? Here are sever'd lips,
> Parted with sugar breath; so sweet a bar
> Should sunder such sweet friends. Here in her hairs
> The painter plays the spider, and hath woven
> A golden mesh t' entrap the hearts of men
> Faster than gnats in cobwebs. But her eyes—
> How could he see to do them? Having made one,
> Methinks it should have power to steal both his
> And leave itself unfurnish'd. Yet look how far
> The substance of my praise doth wrong this shadow
> In underprizing it, so far this shadow
> Doth limp behind the substance. Here's the scroll,
> The continent and summary of my fortune. *[Reads.]* (3.2.114–130)

The ekphrasis through which Bassanio articulates "fair Portia's counterfeit" is made up more of questions than of answers. He eventually puts those questions aside by citing a chiastically, litotically deferred reality principle (substance ... shadow ... shadow ... substance) that seems to direct him to Portia, although the next thing he actually does is to read the scroll—as if its *logos*, not Portia's presence, were the "substance" of which the visual representation is the "counterfeit." A conventional analysis of the emblem format made its verbal rubric the "soul" of the image to which it was subjoined: the circularity between "the substance" of Bassanio's verbal "praise," the "shadow" that it articulates, and "the substance" of the scroll is a hermeneutic one, upon which Portia herself does not intrude until the scroll tells Bassanio to kiss her.[47] The questions that Bassanio raises within this circuit are not questions about Portia in any immediate way. They are questions about the "counterfeit"; and insofar as they are not questions to which Bassanio expects an answer, they are mysteries of the counterfeit.

Bassanio is not directly finding money in the casket, whether valid or invalid. He uses "counterfeit" in a technical sense, but not that of the legal usage, "false money," which is to modern ears primary; rather, "counterfeit" is praise for the craft (*techne*) of the painter.[48] Within monetary discourse, "counterfeit" and "invalid" are the same thing, but transposed into aesthetic discourse, in which imitation is the goal of craft, "counterfeit" validates a successful achievement. Having followed the disavowal of coinage through the play's discourse to this point, we cannot choose but hear the ironic dissonance between those two senses, but Bassanio is certainly choosing not to hear it; the validation of painterly "counterfeiting" is the ground of his own verbal virtuosity. This praise takes as its occasion the success of the present made object, the counterfeit, and proceeds to unmake it, to reverse its own process of being produced, in the course of wondering how its making had been possible. "What is wrong with a counterfeit is not what it is like but how it was made," argues Harry G. Frankfurt; the same, for Bassanio, is true of what is right with a counterfeit, and Bassanio's unmaking account of "how it was made" reenacts Morocco's inversion of the making of coined angels on the corresponding occasion, the opening of the gold casket.[49] What is wrong with Morocco's angel is the same as what is right with Bassanio's counterfeit: the disavowal of the monetary object, realized here as disassembling its constituent parts, the matter of gold and the form of a picture.

The "fancy" through which this imaginative reversal of the conditions of making takes place "is engend'red in the eyes" (3.2.63–67). The eyes by which Portia had sent him "fair speechless messages" are, Bassanio now imagines, not only communicative but themselves active—only the more so at a representative remove; just one of the portrait's painted eyes "should have power to steal both" of the painter's. The anatomizing convention of the poetic blazon is compared here to the process of composing a portrait, which Bassanio imagines as likewise proceeding feature by feature—the ultimate referent here being the ancient story of the painter Zeuxis's composing a portrait of Helen by choosing a number of models and painting the single most beautiful feature of each.[50] In attributing beauty to a compounding of individually beautiful features rather than to the mutual validation of canonical proportion, the system of relations among those features, Zeuxis risked creating a monster—a pernicious mishmash of ill-fitted parts, like the garb of the Englishman—and Bassanio seems surprised that the painter of Portia's portrait has avoided doing the same. As Halpern points out, had the first eye painted "left itself unfurnish'd" by blinding the painter, the image that Bassanio entertains would be half Portia, half the emphatically eyeless skull of the golden casket.[51] It's not Portia's own *two* eyes that embody this hazard. It's the one eye of the putatively incomplete portrait, in its moment of singularity before it is referred, by the inception of its twin across the nose, to the system of proportion that composes features into a face. At this moment of monstrous incompletion, in which painterly process is envisioned as happening in a representational gap between a blank canvas and a perfect image, the painter's art has the capacity to undo itself, in the dependence of the inscribing hand upon "both" viewing eyes as they view a single inscribed eye.

An "unfurnish'd" Portia is a cyclops with the crippling gaze of the basilisk, or that of the unitary "eye" of heaven, the sun.[52] Yet her painted eye would not just blind the eyes of the painter in his head; "it should have power to steal" them, disassembling the painter's face in the act of his assembling the painting's. Compare the duplicitous splitting that Portia's doubling of herself into the role of the doctor induces upon Bassanio, which she accusingly formulates as his reflection disjoined in the distance between her two eyes:

> *Bas.* I swear to thee, even by thine own fair eyes,
> Wherein I see myself—
> *Por.* Mark you that!
> In both my eyes he doubly sees himself,
> In each eye, one. Swear by your double self,
> And there's an oath of credit. (5.1.244–246)

Here too the unfurnishing of paired eyes into singularities, "each eye," produces both a monster, "your double self" as Siamese twin, and a self-defeating reflection. Monocularity, as in Lorenzo's being "worth a Jewess' eye" (2.5.43), recalls the Deuteronomic *lex talionis* of vengeful reciprocity, "an eye for an eye": what's worth a Jew's eye is another eye. "If thine eye offend thee, pluck it out," advises Christ, but that monocular offense will demand the "unfurnishing" of its opposite eye from the self who "offend[s], himself being offended" (Mat. 18:9, Mark 9:47; 4.1.58). The tricks Launcelot plays on his Oedipally blind father likewise play into this register of the unforgivable, erotic excess of ocularity. The choice among the caskets demands that each of Portia's suitors court castration, putting his "two rich and precious stones" inside the casket in order to see if, in the form of Portia's bountiful counterfeit, he will get them back; so too the ocular courtship of castration—in the continuity of purse, balls, and eyes—is what Bassanio claims it took to complete the portrait and put it inside the casket. A mimetic practice that only barely escapes its own undoing is the revealed object of the erotic shared by all the caskets, the desire to see inside.

As realized in the gold casket, that desire is everybody's and therefore nobody's, the desire to want what everyone else wants. But the lead casket encompasses this X-ray-spective desire in its own self-evidence, in the apparently undirected imperative "Yet look how far/ The substance of my praise doth wrong this shadow."[53] In that comparison, Bassanio places his ekphrastic performance within the dialectical competition between words and images to better represent truth or greatness, a *paragone* for erudite and courtly debate ever since the epigram "painting is a mute poem, poetry a speaking picture" was attributed among the Greeks to Simonides of Ceos.[54] The rivalry of the "sister arts" avoids the apparent urgency with which the tragic choice between justice and mercy is charged, but it shares both the bifurcated form and the symmetrical impossibility of resolution through which that dilemma and its fellows prolong themselves indefinitely into discourse. The self-justification of this irresolvable competition is formulated most cynically by Shakespeare elsewhere, in the race of the Poet and the Painter to flatter the wealthy Timon; here we may certainly refer Bassanio's comparisons to a mercenary motive, but at least as important in this moment is his successful engagement of the open-ended gamesmanship that characterizes *paragoni* as a courtly pastime, practiced in such conduct manuals as Castiglione's. The painter was not courting Portia in producing the portrait, but Bassanio is courting her in claiming that the painter was courting disaster when painting her, and so he instantiates a belated competition between the painter and himself—belated in that the portraitist was done and gone before the portrait ever went into the casket, and belated in that (like Lorenzo in 5.1) Bassanio himself has already won Portia through the riddle, in the moment of recognizing "fair Portia's counterfeit," before he begins this competition. Bassanio's virtuosity here in conducting, and claiming to arbitrate between, both sides of a stylized verbal competition marks him as a gentleman, both in that he can do it and in that he knows it is the appropriate thing to do to make that gentility evident to Portia—unlike both the direct professions of gentility claimed by the snobbish Arragon and the ridiculous brawling among the first batch of Portia's suitors.[55] This is Bassanio's answer to the riddle test—his assertion that he, like Portia's father, is a true gentleman, one who knows what a game is and how best to play it. His remark that the rubric which he finds in the gold casket is "a gentle scroll" affirms the relation of gentility that the test has established between them (3.2.139): gentlemen are like fools in that it takes one to know one.

Among the gentle qualities of the scroll is a certain understatement, an ironic diminution of expectations. The suitor who already has "give[n] and hazard[ed] all he hath" for Portia's sake is now told to "be content" with his "fortune" "and seek no new," as if, like the prodigal ship to which Gratiano compared Lorenzo's courtship, he might reasonably be expected to set sail from this port as soon as he has achieved it (3.2.133–134; 2.6.14–19). The "bliss" of achieving Portia and her plenty through the riddle might seem to leave no desire unachieved, just as the failure to achieve it is supposed to leave the suitor not only desolate but castrated, incapable of achieving any desire. But once the caskets are opened they limit the scope of their claim upon the future: the lead one acknowledges the threat of desire's extinction in its achievement, while the silver one anticipates that Arragon, however indelibly a fool, is not such a fool as never to marry because he once made such a promise to three metal boxes. Like Lorenzo's vows to Jessica, Arragon's oath is necessarily disingenuous, self-invalidating, as much of a travesty to keep as to break. Only in the world of romance would such an oath be keepable—the storybook world from which Morocco has come and to which, disconsolate, he returns.

Morocco imagines the topological inverse of the coined angel to be Portia's portrait. Opening the gold casket makes that inversion instead a death's-head. Morocco is in error, but he has only barely misled himself from the right track. As Bassanio exclaims upon opening the lead casket, the painter's art in producing the portrait narrowly escaped producing such another death's-head. Instead, the painter did produce an inversion of a central term of the monetary angel's character—not of its topology, but of its validity: "Fair Portia's counterfeit." Disjoining the gold "substance" of a coin from the portrait of its face leaves the coined portrait a "counterfeit," and thereby defines any portrait as being immaterial, a "shadow" in its privation of the substance of gold. The portrait's value to this situation is discursive—it is an occasion for Bassanio to articulate his participation in courtly verbal behaviors, what Pierre Bourdieu would define as his symbolic capital: a proper man can talk about pictures.[56] Aesthetic value is in this play defined as the value to be placed on the entrée to the privileged discourse of aesthetics, of *ekphrasis* and *paragone*. And that entry is achieved by the disavowal of what a coin is, a conjunction of precious substance and validating emblem.

As a courtly exercise, Bassanio's performance differentiates his gentility from the crudity and unsophistication of even the most aristocratic of Portia's other suitors: aesthetic distinction works to express social distinction as its implicit ground.[57] More importantly, it allows Bassanio to manifest "the will of [Portia's] dead father" in himself. He makes this identification with the dead father by means of a conversation explicitly about image and appearance and implicitly about class, and which works by articulating a value for "counterfeiting" that inheres in mimesis and not in metal. Neither Morocco nor Arragon had been able to suppress the materiality of Portia's riches in their reflections on the inside-out "angel" or the "stamp of merit"; it's Bassanio's dismantling of the ducat that succeeds in generating a formula by which Portia's money might not be money, in expressing the coin's mutually dependent value relation of stamp to metal as the exclusionary aesthetic value he ascribes to Portia's counterfeit.

By "exclusionary" I mean both that the ascription of value to the "counterfeit" attempts to exclude the role that matter plays in generating coined value and that the counterfeit points to the coin as socially promiscuous, and not (like itself) socially exclusive. What's being disavowed here is not only the integration of matter and form within the coin object. Through that material disavowal, Bassanio and the dead father enact a social disavowal; they are able to locate in the particularities of the ducat the dependence of the glamorous impact of Bassanio and his train at Belmont upon the ducats which "gentle" Bassanio owes the merchant Antonio and which Antonio owes Shylock the Jew—and so to dismiss that dependence.[58] The complex flirtation of making and undoing ascribed to the painter of Portia's counterfeit unmakes the way in which Bassanio's carefully crafted aesthetic self-presentation is made out of Antonio's purse-person, and reinscribes that self-presentation in relation instead to the "gentle scroll" that speaks as Portia's father.[59] In dismantling the materiality of the ducat into lionized image and dismissible material ground, Bassanio and the dead father together detach Bassanio's appearance from its production in Antonio's mercantile class status and in his monetarized materiality, and insert it into an elite and self-perpetuated continuity with the reified "will of a dead father" as it speaks from within his leaden casket.

## IV. A FOOL'S MONEY

Bassanio's performance at Belmont works by disavowing Antonio through the dismembering of a golden ducat into the leaden "counterfeit." The dismemberment is able to sustain itself only momentarily—just long enough for Bassanio, the lead casket, and Portia (and their satellites Gratiano and Nerissa) to complete their transaction under its terms, before a letter arrives in which Antonio demands to be remembered. Once the letter is read and acknowledged, the same force of social distinction which had required Antonio's disavowal for the purposes of the marriage reassembles the ducats for the purpose of protecting him from Shylock. Now it is Shylock's turn to confront and exploit the mystified fissures within the apparently unitary object of the ducat, in order to cut through this golden shield between himself and Antonio's heart. In doing so, he will turn the putative unity of Venice against itself—forcing the Venetian state, its citizens, and its Duke to bow before the Venetian commonwealth and its ducats.

Prompted by the letter to revaluate his friend, Bassanio articulates what he's done to Antonio not as a repudiation, but merely as an omission:

> I freely told you all the wealth I had
> Ran in my veins: I was a gentleman;
> And then I told you true. And yet. . . .
> when I told you
> My state was nothing, I should then have told you
> That I was worse than nothing; for indeed
> I have engag'd myself to a dear friend,
> Engag'd my friend to his mere enemy,
> To feed my means. (3.2.254–263)

As she learns of it, Portia reformulates Bassanio's nearly cannibalistic relation to Antonio's imprisoned body as a merely monetary one, "the petty debt," and gives him enough "gold" to pay it "twenty times over" (3.2.306–307). So reconstituted and multiplied, the ducats would serve to cancel the originary bond, and to reerase it again and again. The expectation of supplementarity, a gilding of gold like that we've seen in *King John,* anticipates the resistance of both Antonio and Shylock to having the ducats that they, like Bassanio, have disavowed be reconstituted on Portia's terms. But it assumes as well that the inexhaustible force of her bounty must sooner or later prove irresistible to Shylock. Without Shylock's help as copartner of the bond, Antonio will find his claim on Bassanio to be bought out by Portia, and redefined to suit her own terms: "Since you are dear bought, I will love you dear" (3.2.313).[60]

Portia underestimates Shylock, of course—and so great theater is born. But it might be more apt, in thinking about the things subject in the play to disavowal, dismemberment, and reconstitution as being as much material relations as unitary objects, to say that Portia underestimates the bond between Antonio and Shylock. Shylock himself reifies the bond, as if it were a thing autonomous from himself and Antonio. But the bond nevertheless articulates for Shylock a sociable commonality among himself, Antonio, and the Venetian citizenry whom Antonio represents—albeit a grimly perverse one:

> You have among you many a purchas'd slave,
> Which like your asses, and your dogs and mules,
> You use in abject and in slavish parts,
> Because you bought them. Shall I say unto you,
> "Let them be free! Marry them to your heirs!
> Why sweat they under burthens? Let their beds
> Be made as soft as yours, and let their palates
> Be season'd with such viands"? You will answer,
> "The slaves are ours." So do I answer you:
> The pound of flesh which I demand of him
> Is dearly bought as mine, and I will have it. (4.1.90–100)

Shylock is immediately refuting any pretense that the court may have that the matter of human life is not a purchasable commodity in Venice. But he articulates a difference as well as a continuity between himself and the slave owners of the court. Antonio is not Shylock's slave, according to the bond; Shylock has not purchased his ongoing labor power to "use in abject and in slavish parts." Shylock has bought the power not to compel Antonio's body but to dismember it. He owns Antonio's death, not his life. Shylock will be a legalized killer, but not a slave owner; Antonio will be a victim, but never a slave.

We hear nothing else of slavery in the play, not even the casual use of "slave" as a scornful epithet that is frequent in Renaissance English. Yet it is urgent to Shylock that slavery be articulated in this moment, as a horizon of commonality between himself and the members of the court from which his case nevertheless differs. The figure of the slave serves Shylock not only as juridical justification but as a point of reference for two of the relations that occasioned his bond to Antonio: that of purse to person, and that of human to animal.

For Shylock as much as for Antonio, purse and personhood are continuous. The Venetians constantly assert his Jewishness to be inhumanity, and that inhumanity to be that of an animal—most often that of a dog, hanging about at the edge of the human, serving instrumental purposes and begging for scraps. His rejoinder is, "Hath a dog money? Is it possible/ A cur can lend three thousand ducats?" (1.3.121–122). This identification of money as the definitively human feature creates its own problems for Shylock, as in Solanio's report of the "passion so confus'd" in which Shylock conflates "my ducats, and my daughter" (2.8.12–17); Shylock will conversely describe his revenge on Antonio as enacting the viciousness of the subhuman part enjoined upon him: "Thou call'dst me dog before thou hadst a cause,/ But since I am a dog, beware my fangs" (3.3.6–7). But in addressing the court, Shylock returns to the distinction he first formulated between the human and the animal as being that between the buyer and the bought. Here the slave, not the Jew, is the horizon at which the human body is reduced to animality, "like your asses, and your dogs and mules." This horizon is that of an animate instrument, "use[d] in abject and in slavish parts, because you bought them." Shylock speaks of such a reduction as a matter of fact; slavery is apparently institutionalized and routine in Venice, and otherwise unremarked upon. Its rights validate Shylock's as property rights. But Shylock's bond to Antonio is not that of master to slave. Shylock preserves Antonio from the category of human animal. What he has bought, what binds him with Antonio, is the death of a citizen.[61]

Shylock, as a Jew, can never live the life of a citizen; he participates in the life of the city as a resident alien, a "stranger" (3.3.27). Yet, "Since that the trade and profit of the city/ Consisteth of all nations," the participation of strangers in the life of the city is extensive—as long as they have money (3.3.30–31). Shylock is integral to that common wealth, "the trade and profit of the city," and even epitomizes it, despite his exclusion from the rights and duties of the citizenry. The cosmopolitan setting of Venice presents a scenario in which the civic, commercial, and religious registers of "common weal" are more obviously divergent than the midcentury reformers and their followers would allow them to be. Antonio is entitled to participate in all three, but even he, according to Salerio, would be distracted by his commercial interests from attending to his spiritual ones:

> Should I go to church
> And see the holy edifice of stone,
> And not bethink me straight of dangerous rocks [imperiling my shipping]?
> (1.1.29–31)

The institutions of the Venetian common weal diverge from those of the *civitas* in being more open and diffuse, and in being more urgent when push comes to shove. Shylock's suit is able to make the latter bow to the former. The social distinction that constitutes the Venetian oligarchy is itself abjected before the claims of common wealth: the Venetian state is embodied in the court not by its helpless Duke but by its ducats. And Shylock verbally dismembers those already doubled ducats into sixths in the course of disavowing them. In that disavowal, Shylock at once forces the court to affirm the ducats' mastery and proceeds to master them.

Shylock's radical and homicidal version of the commonwealth interest is not able to sustain itself before Portia. He experiences, in Portia's excruciating process of ratiocination, the ability of distinction to finesse the letter of the very law before which it ought (from the letter's perspective) to be prostrate.[62] Instead Shylock is both bankrupted of the ducats that incorporated him in the putative supremacy of the common weal, and forced to participate in the exclusive institutions which he almost made bow to him—defined now not as the civic arena of the court but the Christian arena of the church, through a particularly deft fudge on Portia's part back to the ideal continuity of those venues in orthodox commonwealth discourse. Shylock reads the Christians' disavowals of their ducats as a bluff that he can call by articulating commonwealth; like Morocco, he is very close to not being wrong, but not close enough. His definition of commonwealth as arising in a distinction between a minimal, monetarized humanity and the vendible animal is apt, but monetary disavowal is constitutive of that commonwealth, not a repressive mystification of it. Shylock's identification of money as a decoder of power relations is erroneous. As it is expressed in the silver casket and enacted by the fool Launcelot, money serves the commonwealth as a means not of revelation but of self-deception.

The nakedness of monetarized value is what Shylock aims to expose as self-evident, as lying behind the disavowals through which the Christians pretend to find value as virtue. But such a bare monetarization is fully expressed by Bassanio as he addresses the silver casket as "thou pale and common drudge/ 'Tween man and man," and it is not contrary to but continuous with the articulation of disavowal in "fair Portia's counterfeit," the riddle's answer in the lead casket (3.2.103–104, 115). In the defective reflections of the silver casket, self-evidence appears as a redundant and recursive invalidation, not a de-ciphering object lesson. Arragon seizes on silver to announce his own individuated and extramonetary "merit," and his foolishness is measured by the fact that that's exactly what silver doesn't do. As I've argued, the individuation it yields for

Arragon is that of an autonomy of the bad choice, "I am wrong" (in a test in which any child could be right); it defines that individuating wrongness as the revealed object of introspection, such that the self-discovery of Narcissus's uniqueness is the knowledge that, as the oracle had said, he is the one man in the world who ought not to know himself. According to Bassanio, silver's status as medium is its message; "pale and common," it has no material character of its own to differentiate itself from its monetary function as "drudge between man and man," unlike the allegorical freight that gold bears on its comparable errands as angel or Argo.[63] All it is is what men have in "common."

This commonality, like the silver casket itself, is belittling without being insignificant. It works as a kind of minimality for peer relationships in the play, the monetarized means according to which human individuals are not equal, but adequated, to one another. On the outside the silver casket is a mirror, a version of mimesis as unthought and unperformed, an instantaneous circuit between face, surface, and eye.[64] On the inside it's a fool, less than a man but something more than an animal—as the fool Launcelot demonstrates in his capacity for ratiocination, if not reason, in his comic self-debate about fleeing Shylock's household. Shylock himself, whose fine judgments of "kind," Shell argues, are critical to the play's varying accounts of the relation of ideas of money to those of socialization, considers that "the patch is kind enough": affable enough, but also human enough.[65] As just "kind enough," barely and therefore precisely adequate, Launcelot is also the adequation of man—the measure of all things, but in terms of their lowest common denominator.[66] As Steven R. Mentz points out, Launcelot in his shuttling between Shylock's and Bassanio's households himself acts the part of the "common drudge/ 'Tween man and man." Mentz argues for Launcelot's monetarized instrumentality as being commercially self-conscious—and therein, we might add, unlike the "abject and slavish parts" which Shylock ascribes to slaves, "asses, . . . dogs and mules."[67] Animalistic but not animal in his gluttony and sloth, servile but not enslaved, Launcelot is released by Shylock to Bassanio's household in the hope that the fool will devour all the Christian's means in eating up his pork. But Launcelot does understand himself to be a member of "the commonwealth" (3.5.34; the usage is Jessica's paraphrase of Launcelot). He understands the interest of the commonwealth precisely in terms of the price of pork, an interest with which he can gladly identify, and for the sake of which he demands a sacrifice of interest on the part, naturally, of others, in this case the curbing of Lorenzo's appetite for miscegenation and of Jessica's for salvation.[68] The fact that Launcelot is pleased to take for granted the salvation that he would deny Jessica, and is shortly revealed to have indulged too in "the getting up of the

Negro's belly," makes him the basest member of the commonwealth without excluding him from it (3.5.38–39). He is not a hog only by virtue of his interest in the price of hogs.[69]

In the self-image of the fool, the silver casket offers an account of disavowal as socialization, as the commonality of interest that defines the social totality as "commonwealth." What all the caskets, and the subject positions they articulate, have in common is the desire to see inside and be seen inside, to know oneself by knowing even as we are known, in which self-knowing is not directed at the autonomous self but achieved by fully knowing the other who fully knows me. Such knowing, Paul promises, is the epistemic reward of the kingdom of heaven (1 Cor 13:12). The *desire for* such knowing is what we all exploit in one another and in ourselves in the establishment of the earthly commonwealth, promises *The Merchant of Venice*. Desiring knowledge and disavowing knowledge are aspects of the same circuit: through mystifying money in ourselves for the sake of demystifying ourselves through it, each character offers to one another a pretense of being knowable, a counterfeit of the self-evidence each looks for in everyone else. They agree to fool even as they are fooled, to pretend not to know that they are accepting in others what is counterfeit in themselves.

As Portia points out to Shylock, to ask for what we deserve is, from the perspective of Christian theology, to ask for death. But death is not what Aragon gets to see when he asks to see what he deserves. Rather, he is shown his own portrait as a fool, as being himself the instance of the barely, merely, and precisely human, and by that adequated token a definitive participant in the institutions of humans. His passport through the commonwealth of fools is money, the "common drudge 'tween man and man"—through which we all make fools of ourselves in order to participate in making fools of each other, without for a moment fooling anybody.

# CHAPTER FOUR
# Wit without Money in Donne and Nashe

Beggarly lies no beggarly wit but can invent. . . . But I am of another metal: they shall know that I live as their evil angel, to haunt them world without end, if I have cause.

—Thomas Nashe to his "interpreters," 1592[1]

Angels and devils alike attend the precious metal of an Elizabethan coin, hovering athwart the scope of its materiality. The face of England's finest gold coins formed each into "the figure of an angel/ Stamp'd in gold," and the material goodness of the gold converged in these objects with the immaterial goodness cited by the image of the archangel Michael's triumph over the dragon Satan (*Merchant* 2.7.56–57). Yet coins of gold were likewise preeminent among the means of the devil to seduce men to disregard the good of their souls in attention to material goods. Taunting the small-mindedness of his misinterpreters as an impoverishment of wit, Nashe in the preface to *Pierce Penniless His Supplication to the Devil*— the manifesto of his own spectacular wit, enacted in the voice of a demoniac bankrupt—enacts the convergence among his own wit's "metal," the immaterial malice of his detractors, and the thoroughness of his threatened retribution, as the haunting of an "evil angel." The evil angel is a devil, but one defined by its original fineness and power, made vicious in its fall. It has perversely repudiated its own angelic nature, its supermaterial goodness. Yet even after laying waste to itself, something of that nature remains—albeit within the constraints of oxymoron. Nashe's own wit is not golden, if its "other metal" is that of an evil angel, despite its opposition to the "beggarly wit" of the nemeses whom he professes. Rather, it's what arises in the wasting of angelic goodness for the sake of a demonically vituperative haunting.

The order of being that's left behind in the evacuation of gold is figured as a ghostliness by Marlowe's Barabas as well, as we saw in chapter 1. For Barabas, the deprivation of his gold is a dismemberment; he experiences his lost gold as a "soldier's scar," a ghost limb (2.1.9). It's almost the only moment of his victimization in a play where he is otherwise a masterful agent. But Nashe's posture of "evil angel" is as discursively empowering as it is materially disembodying; it has not only diabolical power but a permanence of its own in the material world and, Nashe threatens, beyond it, into the eternal "world without end." Perversely evacuated of its proper nature, a goodness that coordinates the material and transcendental, the "evil angel" instead manifests an improper and effective—and delightful—discursiveness in the place of its own wasted good. Within the scope of *Pierce Penniless* and along this prefatory horizon, Nashe envisions a paradoxically productive relationship between wit and waste, and sites that relationship on the threshold between money's materiality and its openness to the supernatural.

Waste is the last of the material relations joining bodies to coins that I'd like to consider in this book, and the one that is the most disruptive to the paradigms of the commonwealth discourse that, I've argued, strove to define and circumscribe the coinage of Renaissance England. Waste is a crucially negative term within that discourse; as Richard Helgerson has demonstrated, it serves the generation of Sidney and Greene as a definition of poetic activity, as the self-destructiveness of the prodigal.[2] But the wasting of money acquires a counterintuitive, even paradoxical, affirmation in the hands of the wittiest writers of the 1590s, Thomas Nashe and John Donne.

John Carey argues that Donne's "loved contemplation of coins" traverses his production both chronologically and generically, from early elegies to late sermons: "it suggests that the relationship between bullion and stamp presented itself to his mind as an equivalent to the relationship which preoccupied him above all others—that between body and soul."[3] As modeled by the coin, the relationship of body to soul is not that which we find conventional, of exterior container to interior content. As Carey explains, it is the holistic relationship of matter to the form that suffuses its substance and delivers its potentiality into existence, as defined by Aristotle in *De Anima*. Considering Donne as a metaphysically anxious writer, Ramie Targoff declares that "Donne's expression of his belief in the mutual necessity of body and soul, and his obsessive imagining of their parting, is the most continuous and abiding feature of his collected works."[4]

The soul for Donne is not something whose being refers only to the moment of judgment after death and the opening onto transcendental eternity. It is integral to our bodily existence in the material world. But, as Targoff suggests, Donne is as preoccupied with distinguishing the material from the immaterial in us as he is with understanding the "necessity" of their integrity. Here, too, coins serve as a conceptual model—particularly that coin whose immaterially minded name is most ironic to its use, the golden "angel." David Hawkes finds a bleakly satiric pessimism in Donne's poetical handling of "angels"; he argues that

> Donne conceives of monetary value as inauthentic and illusory. Indeed, it is precisely the loss of authenticity, exemplified by the imposition of exchange value on use value, and by the more general displacement of *phusis* by *nomos*, which provokes the epistemological and emotional crises that play such predominant roles in the intellectual dramas of Donne's verse.[5]

My analysis of the work performed by money in two of Donne's early Elegies, "The Bracelet" and "Loves Progress," will remain within the circuit inscribed by the coin, rather than comparing it, as Hawkes does, to the use value manifested in nonmonetary objects, but like Hawkes I find the two elegies to be interested not in integration but in disintegration. I read each poem in terms of its speaker's erotic engagements with the world of matter, transacted in conceits of coinage. In each, the tropic interaction between attraction and repulsion in the "violent yoking" of desire to the incompletely material coin implicates not only the poetics of literary production but the body of the reader holding the poem's manuscript in the prodigal habitus of waste. The desirous relationship between body and world traced by Donne's coins is one of an endless spending, without hope of either exhaustion or recompense—yet violently fearful of both exhaustion and recompense.

Donne's ironical fascination with the attendance of "angels" in the form stamped upon golden discs has its counterpart in the glee with which Nashe imagines the demoniac possibilities of bankruptcy in his wastrel alter ego, Pierce Penniless. Pierce's evacuation is the condition of his "Supplication to the Devil." Though Pierce entreats the devil to pay him in gold, he submits himself to the devil as the prince of his own monetarized emptiness, as a purse-Pierce (like Antonio's purse-person) lacking a single penny. The reduction of a bodily container to its own emptiness serves Nashe as a means to contemplate its materiality as minimal; a purse deprived of its money exists as a margin of substance, something hollow, flimsy, little, and trivial that is nevertheless not quite nothing. This marginality of matter reduced to the threshold of nonexistence—to being as little as possible—is the condition of Pierce's demoniac persona, and of the "stuff" of Nashe's own insistently material prose style. Its self-consciousness knows itself through Pierce's ebullient and inexhaustible waste. But the wittily trivial materiality of Nashe's masculine speakers is not the only relation of wit to money envisioned in his prose. In *The Unfortunate Traveller*, the frivolous, venal, and "unfortunate" narrator manages to meet and seduce the beautiful and bountiful Diamante, whose generosity with her sexual and monetary favors he characterizes as a wit of gold. This feminine wit is not discursive but material, a lushly improbable fantasy of repletion at the margin of the possible opposite to that inhabited by the speaker.

The materialist provocations of Donne's and Nashe's wastrels are aimed squarely at the orthodoxies of the generation of the commonwealths-men. For both writers, the coin serves not as a locus to ground an ethical and political agenda upon an ontological account of what the material world is like, but as an instance of centrifugal discontinuities and disintegrations. The expulsive, evacuative relation of waste contravenes and disrupts the normative values of productivity and thrift that integrate the diverse strata of commonwealth discourse. But—as the open-ended volubility of these self-depriving speakers makes clear—waste is not disruptive of discourse per se. Rather, it redefines the conditions of discourse, and in particular those of monetary discourse. Displaying a face of Mammon that is not retentive but wasteful of himself, these prodigal writers of the 1590s portray miserliness as the disavowed double of a merely fantastical thrift. In defining the irreducibility of what commonwealth discourse construes as waste, Donne and Nashe demonstrate the inadequacy of that discourse's attempts to circumscribe Mammon. They participate in the rupture of monetary thinking from which the central insight of the mercantilist generation would emerge—that England's common profit depends on releasing its domestic store of precious metals to international trade, rather than on attempting to capture and hoard the global flow of metallic currency. And they participate thereby in the emergence, in the nascent discourse of political economy, of a Mammon who will heed no discipline but his own.

## I. TWELVE RIGHTEOUS ANGELS

The gold coin called the angel had a lot to say to Elizabethans—much that was reassuring, even inspiring, and much that was absurd. It was reassuring in the way that any sizable hunk of gold offers reassurance, in the amount of intrinsic value materialized in its massy circumference (only a bit less than its face value under Elizabeth of ten shillings), but also for reasons specific to this coin type: its embodiment of a standard of material purity known to be both finer and much older than that of the Mint's other gold issues and thus a representative of a good old English rectitude which somehow survived even the period of debasement unscathed, and its richly meaningful national-religious iconography, which had somehow survived the Reformation. These factors of purity, historicity, and iconography converged to invest the angel with a particular character of materialized goodness that bordered on idolatry. As the finest thing in this world, finer than human bodies, the angel was important in magico-medical practices to purify bodies and keep them free of disease, as it was in the alchemical practices that defined the progress of purification as the approach to material perfection.

The absurdity articulated by the angel included that inhering in any flirtation with idolatry, but exceeded that as well. Jokes comparing the errands on which God sends his immaterial angels—intercession, revelation, protection from demonic influence—to the sordidly material businesses of exchange, usury, and bribery in which gold angels might be employed are ubiquitous in early modern English discourse. When it was good, the angel was very very good, elevating humans to its standard of fineness, and when it was bad it lent itself to the basest uses of this world. The name "angel" was equally appropriate to this ironic reading of these coins as degrading and degraded—for was not Lucifer the brightest of the angels before his fall? As the world of good and evil spirits surrounded and permeated the material world, so too did the circulation of coined angels define itself as adjacent to both moralized extremities

Figure 8: Elizabeth angel, face and reverse © Trustees of the British Museum

of human materiality, as either superhumanly pure or demonically vile. As I've suggested in my introduction, money is so everyday an instrument that it's difficult to analyze directly—rather, when Renaissance money appears in analogy or analysis, it's more frequent to use the ordinariness of money to help define some other, more unusual concept. But the angel is an unusual coin, so valuable that many fewer people would have the chance to handle them in exchange as routinely as they were handled in discourse.[6] The angel is a way to talk directly about the extraordinariness of money.

The most charismatic product of the English mint, the angel bore rich symbolic freight. It, and its subsidiary denominations (half-angels, double angels), were made according to a standard known to be purer and older than the series minted in "crown gold"—crowns, nobles, ryals—circulating alongside them. Where crown gold had been subject to debasement in the 1540s and '50s (though never to the same degree as the silver coinage) and was reestablished under Elizabeth at 22 carats fine (91.67%), angel gold hardly deviated from its medieval standard of 23 carats 3 1/2 grains fine (99.48%) under any of the Tudors or early Stuarts.[7] Its type, likewise a survivor of the medieval mint, featured as the obverse an image of the Archangel Michael defeating the dragon Satan, and not a portrait of the monarch (fig. 8). The coin's reverse was a ship, whose mast was a cross bearing the monarch's arms as its sail. As Donald C. Baker argues, the particular status of St. Michael as the patron of Land's End in Cornwall—the first landmark England presents to shipping from the south—identifies the face, like the reverse, with England's maritime prowess, while the iconography of impaling a dragon on a lance from above readily conflated St. Michael with the warrior-saint most often identified as England's military patron, St. George (the only difference being that George usually has a horse, while Michael has wings).[8] The angel was itself a great traveler, the English mint's representative to Continental money markets, where its reliable purity (and, perhaps, its memorable type) kept it in demand as an internationally valid currency, like the Tuscan florin and the Venetian ducat.

The coin that was England's *best* money was also the coin that was *least* money among English coins, the most frequently used for purposes outside the scope of monetary exchange. The angel's material purity, which made it not only precious by tale but valuable for its instantly recognizable reliability as *mensura publica*, was continuous with its extramonetary functions, many of which shared a casual and surprisingly underpoliced border with idolatry.[9] The angel had since its inception under Edward IV been used in the medico-magical ceremony of touching for "the king's evil," scrofula, and many more people seem to have used an angel as a general-purpose luck-token than can have participated in that particular ritual. Baker cites the reverence for the coin's antique purity:

> 'Angel-gold' was a phrase signifying purity whether in metal or a person's intentions. It became, indeed, a 'scientific' term, being the alchemical phrase for gold pure enough for experimentation and 'projection.' The combination of popular religious significance and its alchemical associations led to such 'receipts' as one given for the plague, which was to take a gold angel of Elizabeth, 'of good old philosopher's gold,' and to hold it in one's mouth.[10]

Baker does not cite his source for this last reference, but it is evidently a seventeenth-century text; the quality of antiqueness that reinforces the meaningfulness of the angel's purity is emphasized by insisting on an Elizabeth angel as embodying the "good old" standard, although the fineness of the angel was continuous in all issues until the Restoration. A part of the angel that was subject to some change was the obverse motto; Mary adopted for her angels "A DOMINO FACTVM EST ISTVD ET EST MIRABILE IN OCVLIS NOSTRIS" (this thing was done by the Lord and it is wondrous in our eyes, Ps. 118:23), making the suggestion of Catholic belief patterns in the coin even more explicit. Despite the Protestant-baiting intended by this legend, Elizabeth continued to use the type of Mary's angels, only replacing her sister's name with her own on the face. James eventually truncated the verse at "ISTVD" to eliminate the objectionable "MIRABILE." James likewise disliked the "touching" ceremony, though he continued to subject himself to it.[11] I wonder if the presence of "MIRABILE," as well as the character of antiquity inhering in the type, helped make Elizabeth angels more magically efficacious than those of James, as resisting the latter's doctrinaire insistence that miracles had ceased. The angel was by no means an icon of recusancy, but it offered comforting evidence of continuity with the pre-Reformation, pre-debasement past. Those nostalgic continuities entwined an idea of value as material purity with the idiosyncrasies of individual interactions with the supernatural (as luck, as bodily safeguard, as angel), on the one hand, and with the institution of the monarchy on the other; the angel ostentated all three of these factors as changeless, unaffected by the traumas of the mid-sixteenth century.

The angel was not any more valuable as money than the half-sovereign in crown gold; both were current at ten shillings, and both contained the same amount of gold (as the half-sovereign was somewhat less pure, it was correspondingly a bit heavier). Yet the Mint alternated between producing series in crown gold and in angel gold throughout Elizabeth's reign, for reasons that are "not completely clear" even to experts on the Tudor Mint.[12] The crown series directly represented Elizabeth to the commonwealth as she was now (or as she cared to be), in a portrait, consistent with the series of the silver coinage, while the angel series represented her emblematically, as imbricated in a system of meaning that made the Queen herself a representation of a monarchy that integrated the English present with its illustrious past. The different iconographies of the gold coinage offered either an assertion of presence or an assertion of continuity. In asserting the trifold persistence of material purity, of spirituality as white magic, and of the institution of the monarchy, the value of producing angel gold evidently outweighed the embarrassment of idolatrous associations and matched the rival value of directly representing the Queen's person in crown gold series. This is a value embodied in money, but it's not a value of the money form. To the extent that the particular virtues of the angel took it out of circulation to be cherished for luck or melted for medicine, those virtues are opposed to the exchange value adduced upon the object in the money form, and that opposition is indeed counted upon in the Crown's decision to mint angels as being a money that's something more than money. The nostalgic conjunction of those extramonetary virtues of the angel is what's targeted in texts that insist on the angel as being *really only* money—as embodying the twin pressures of futuristic novelty, corruption and commodification, upon the commonwealth, rather than the reassuring presence of the past. "Novelty is only in request," declares the disguised Duke of *Measure for Measure*, "and, as it is, as dangerous to be ag'd in any kind of course, as it is virtuous to be constant in any undertaking. There is scarce truth enough alive to make societies secure, but security enough to make fellowships accurs'd. Much upon this riddle runs the wisdom of the world. This news is old news, yet it is every day's news" (3.2.222–230). And in response to this new-old news the Duke has minted himself an angel to serve as his deputy, as we have seen in chapter 2.

The Duke voices these remarks after his first interview with the louche scandalmonger Lucio, who seems to exemplify to the Duke the baseness of novelty that demands his monetarized redress: Lucio and Angelo do not themselves interact, yet the power which the coining and recall of Angelo ultimately generate for the Duke is brought to bear most fully upon Lucio in the play's denouement. Lucio's point of view, which reduces the complexities of value to the material satisfactions of sex (and violence, of which he and his fellow soldiers pronounce themselves disappointed in 1.2) through the medium of monetary exchange, is opposite to the correspondingly reductive idealism through which angel-Angelo confronts his own insufficient "mettle";

Lucio is of the really-only-money school with respect not only to coins but all values to be interpreted through them, while Angelo aspires to be the kind of angel that isn't money at all. Lucio's point of view is quite congruent, however, with the aspirations to fashionable libertinism voiced by the sophomoric speakers of Donne's elegies. In the longest of the elegies (and, in some compilations, the first), "The Bracelet," the occasion for the speaker to demonstrate his posture of witty and eroticized knowingness—and the occasion for the poet to critique that posture—is a debate staged among the speaker, his mistress, and a male rival over the proper way of valuing "twelve righteous angels" (9).[13]

The occasion of the elegy is a loss: the speaker has mislaid a "sevenfold chain" of gold given him by his mistress, whom he addresses directly (7). The speaker professes a hardheaded materialism and a knowing sexual satisfaction throughout the poem, both of which ought to distance him from a Petrarchan speaking position and move him into the frame of Ovidian expectations that these Elegies, and much other amatory verse of the period, evoke as an opposite pole to Petrarchan poetics. But his carelessness with this token of value, and the implicit threat that his mistress will now reject him if he does not make restitution, are the twin causes that impel his speech, marking him uncomfortably both as prodigal and as supplicant. The Petrarchan fiction of abjection before the mistress, the situation suggests, may be more apt to the circumstances than the speaker's own pretense of mastery.[14] That pretense is enacted by several negative conditions for grief that open the poem before the speaker gets around to articulating the scenario, "that I thy sevenfold chain have lost," in line 7; he grudgingly admits to "mourn" this loss (7), but prefaces that admission with a series of denials that reject the different ways he is afraid the mistress will expect him to have invested emotion in the object. These instances of *negatio* are presented in rhyming couplets with ostentatiously logical balance, in the form "Not . . . ,/ For . . ." (1–6). They dismiss, as fallacies, one possible argument based on a shared material quality (an "accidental," in scholastic logic), "Not that in colour it was like thy hair,/ For armlets of that thou mayst let me wear" (1–2); a second based on proximity and the history of the object, "Nor that thy hand it oft embraced and kissed,/ For so it had that good, which oft I missed" (3–4); and a third based on prolepsis and popular metaphor, "Nor for that silly old morality,/ That as those links are tied, our love should be" (5–6). Instead, he claims to root his mourning for the lost object exclusively in "the bitter cost" (8). Monetary exchange, he argues, is the only rational way to assess his "mourning" of the loss, for the loss will only be recouped at the sacrifice of the "twelve righteous angels" (9).

All of the speaker's premises for rejecting these putative fallacies are themselves recognizably begging the question, however: if the mistress wanted him to be wearing an "armlet" of her hair she would not have given him the chain; his envy of the chain's having touched her hand more than he has is absurd and in any case inadmissible; and calling a maxim a "silly old morality" in no way disproves it. The speaker's articulation of monetary exchange is itself a fallacious attempt to extricate himself from a circuit of gift exchange. Although he manages not to say as much, he could only have had the mistress's chain to lose if she had given it to him, and his affair will not be on the same ground it was until he restores the bracelet to her to give him again—whence, presumably, his proposition that she give him some of her hair instead and forget about the whole chain business. The poem is in fact not about monetary exchange at all, which is remarkable, considering that coins are all the speaker wants to talk about.

For the twelve angels are not going to be used to *buy* the new chain; instead they are to *be* the new chain, to be "damned, and in the furnace thrown" for the purity of their gold (19), in order to replace the substance of the bracelet and thus to be re-formed as jewelry. The speaker's protest is against this destruction of their money form rather than simply against their being spent, "For form gives being, and their form is gone" (76).[15] As John Carey has demonstrated, the speaker is rehearsing the hylomorphic unity of form with matter that Aristotle asserts in *De anima*, which we've discussed in chapter 1, and evoking the way in which Aristotle uses that unity to define the integrity of soul to the body: the coins' angelic natures are not transcendental but material, dependent on the stamp for their being.[16] But neither would the speaker prefer to spend the angels as the money that they are, realizing the end implicit in that form's being. His fantasy, as he tells the coins in an apostrophe, is that some miser (not, indeed, himself) would cherish them forever:

> Destined you might have been to such an one
> As would have loved and worshipped you alone:
> One which would suffer hunger, nakedness,
> Yea death, ere he would make your number less. (85–88)

The shift from addressing the mistress to addressing the money makes it clear that the speaker compares his own bifurcated loyalties to the single-minded passion, not of an ideal lover, but of the miser, abject before a perfect "number" (twelve) rather than before perfect beauty.[17] The only monetary exchange that the speaker is willing to entertain is

that some loud squeaking crier
Well pleased with one lean threadbare groat, for hire,
May like a devil roar through every street,
And gall the finder's conscience, if they meet. (55–58)

Being exchanged for each other, the groat and the crier commissioned with it demean each other, sharing the attributes "lean" and "threadbare" between them; their interchangeable value is not simply less than the value of the panegyrized angels, but opposite to it, for the crier is to be hired to roar "like a devil." The speaker's intent in that panegyric is instead to find a way to value these gold coins outside the circuit of monetary exchange.

He accomplishes this by attempting to insist on the ways in which minted "angels" embody values that surpass not only the intrinsic value of their unminted gold but their own face value as money. The name of "angel" together with the coins' material purity opens a ready way whereby monetary value can invite a value judgment:

Oh shall twelve righteous angels, which as yet
No leaven of vile solder did admit,
Nor yet by any way have stray'd or gone
From the first state of their creation,
Angels, which heaven commanded to provide
All things to me, and be my faithful guide,
To gain new friends, to appease great enemies,
To comfort my soul, when I lie or rise;
Shall these twelve innocents, by thy severe
Sentence (dread judge) my sins' great burden bear? (9–18)

Monetary value is of course still present at every new turn of this conceit, but the speaker's argument (such as it is) is based in the wittily reiterated transformation of value into virtue. The tutelary agency of God's angels is made material in the efficacy of the coined angels; the help that the coins give the speaker in navigating the venalities of the Elizabethan power structure (i.e., through bribery) is itself how the bounty, "guid[ance]," and "comfort" of "heaven" manifest themselves in the world. He opposes these reasons for the angels' preservation in their purity to the parlous state of other currencies, which would, he claims, be perfectly expendable in this situation:

Were they but crowns of France, I cared not,
For, most of these, their natural country rot
I think possesseth; they come here to us
So lean, so pale, so lame, so ruinous.
And howsoe'er French kings most Christian be,
Their crowns are circumcised most Jewishly.
Or were they Spanish stamps, still travelling,
That are become as Catholic as their king,
Those unlicked bear whelps, unfiled pistolets... (23–31)[18]

Sloppily crafted, grotesquely clipped, much debased, and too generally current ("Catholic"), these foreign coins take on the character of homeless debauchees in an advanced stage of syphilis. Despite the attribution of this base persona to them, however, the mention of the Spanish coins immediately provokes from the speaker a digressive rant against their malignant power:

these [enforce] justice, from her course;...
Visit all countries, and have slily made
Gorgeous France, ruined, ragged, and decayed,
Scotland, which knew no state, proud in one day,
And mangled seventeen-headed Belgia. (36, 39–42)

The personification has unintended consequence: through it, Spanish gold, as the instrument of Spanish policy, becomes the powerful agent of that policy. In John Carey's reading of "The Bracelet," both the act of personifying money and this lack of control over it come to seem almost natural:

> Of course, coins were much more human in Donne's day than they are now. Coins circulating in the capital were, as this poem makes clear, extremely varied in type and nationality, thus mimicking the rich cosmopolitan mix of the city population. But, quite apart from that, Elizabethan and Jacobean coins managed to be individuals, as modern coins do not, because they were produced by a haphazard and inefficient method, as people are.... Fat, thin, lop-sided, or vague-looking coins resulted. They were almost as various in their expressions as people, and their precise physiognomy was as worth studying, if not more so.[19]

Carey's irresistibly charming conceit, which analogizes the historical conditions of production at the early modern mint to the timelessly erratic means of sexual reproduction, is at once helpful and misleading; the real clumsiness of

Donne's smug speakers at the point where rhetorical seduction must become sexual action is certainly a preeminent source of the Elegies' humor, but these poems take little interest in reproduction as the result of sex, and do not (as Shakespeare's sonnets do) themselves equate sexual reproduction with minting.[20] Carey makes the speaker's personification of the angels seem less arbitrary a trope than it is, but he does so because he has recognized the way the poem interacts with, and elaborates, systems that the speaker can only incompletely control, of which this move to personification is the most evident instance. Even as the speaker tries to find a context to defend his angels from either melting or exchange, after all, he does admit that he is not the miser figure who would cherish them until death, and keeps referring to ways he might have spent them better in the future.

His wish, then, is to preserve the angels for some medium term where they might be even more useful, to defer the ends that would compel him to expend his means. In the Simmelian sense that I have explicated in chapter 1, he wants to maintain the potentiality of his liquid wealth, against its particular realization into form (here, a bracelet). He internalizes the maintenance of that potentiality as a reservoir of power within the self. And, in a habit he likewise shares with Simmel, he construes that monetary potentiality in terms of love—although Simmel would not be so crass as to identify it directly with sexual potency, as this speaker does:

> But, shall my harmless angels perish? Shall
> I lose my guard, my ease, my food, my all?
> Much hope, which they should nourish, will be dead.
> Much of my able youth, and lustihead
> Will vanish; if thou love let them alone,
> For thou wilt love me less when they are gone. (49–54)

Here the personified money is assimilated to the speaker's own persona, at the very point where that persona shows itself most fragile. The fetish of their love was, according to her, the bracelet which she gave him: "as those links are tied, our love should be" (6); he declares that this was an error, and that the real fetish of his "lustihead," and of her reciprocal passion for it, is the angels. As she depends on him to be himself, so that she can love him, he depends on the money in order to be himself, and so he keeps it; she loves him because he loves the money. And he loves the money because the money loves him.

The whole ménage of the poem thus depends, according to the speaker, upon the bountifully affectionate generosity extended to him by the angels.

Their monetary value is continuous, he claims, with their tutelary efficacy. He preserves them from exchange; they preserve his body. He dreads the day when he and they will fail to save each other:

> Shall they be damned, and in the furnace thrown,
> And punished for offences not their own?
> They save not me, they do not ease my pains,
> When in that hell they are burnt and tied in chains. (19–22)

In the melting of the angels and their reconstitution, "tied in chains," the speaker evokes the tyrannical condemnation by Nebuchadnezzar of the Jewish officials Shadrach, Meshach, and Abed-nego to be cast, bound, into the "fiery furnace" for maintaining their faith (Daniel 3:8–30). Their "righteous" purity is itself the cause of their punishment, for which they are preferred to the motley rabble of foreign, debased coinage which the speaker offers to substitute for them. But Shadrach, Meshach, and Abed-nego were saved not by a more sinful substitute but by an angel of the Lord, who appeared to the astonished Nebuchadnezzar "like the Son of God" (3:25, KJV).[21] The typological relation between the angel's intervention and the sacrifice of Christ will not save the golden angels themselves, and neither will the sacrifice of those angels redeem the speaker. Rather, the melting of the angels will waste the tutelary and medical powers that they have already had in their present form: "They save not me [any longer], they do not ease my pains."

In the circular relation of "form" and "being" that invests the angels with their efficacy, the work of the angels to preserve the speaker and the efforts of the speaker to preserve the angels are reciprocal. As it becomes clear that the speaker is not persuading his beloved to save the angels, that reciprocity itself disintegrates, and he looks to other powers to intercede where he has failed. The first of these is the "crier" who, "well pleased with one lean threadbare groat, for hire,/ May like a devil roar through every street" (55–57); as the circle of white magic inscribed between the speaker and the angels he's been saving crumbles, he ventures to sacrifice a groat on their behalf, a transaction that would call forth a roaring "devil." The conceit of monetary exchange as black magic emphasizes the argument that saving the angels is not merely thrifty but salvific, and the speaker proceeds to literalize this conceit in the next lines, offering that he "creep to some dread conjurer" to divine the fate of the lost chain (59). The conjurer is more a scoundrel than a terror to the speaker's mind; his "fantastic schemes" exploit the superstitious underworld of "whores, thieves, and murderers," whom "he pass[es] . . . all in sin" (60–64).

Like the tutelary powers attributed to the gold angels in their current form, the status of the conjurer as "the mouth of destiny" is asserted less as anything the speaker chooses to believe than as a way to distract or placate the mistress from insisting that the angels be melted (68). But the tensions among preservation, exchange, and dissolution which the speaker locates in the fate of the angels are real to him, and to his erotic relationship to her.

Once the melting of the coins is at last conceded, a rival and doppelganger to the speaker intrudes into the precariously balanced circle of satisfied desire, which had enfolded himself and his mistress within the tutelary influence of the angels. This is the hypothetical finder of the original bracelet, against whom the poem closes with a lengthy and scabrous execration in the second person.[22] The curse that the speaker pronounces against the "thou" who now has his mistress's gift-token reiterates most of the topoi of the speaker's preceding dispute with the mistress—that the finder be "chained to hellish pains; . . . with foreign gold bribed to betray/ Thy country, and fail both of that and thy pay. . . . Lust-bred diseases rot thee; and dwell with thee/ Itchy desire and no ability" (96–104). The disintegration of the angels has left the speaker without his protection against this mysterious masculine rival, who has found his bracelet but whom he cannot himself find. But a curse can find him; the dissolved supernatural blessings of the angels are reconstituted as the baleful knowingness of the "dread conjurer," the antipathetic trajectory of black magic. "May all the evils that gold ever wrought,/ All mischiefs that all devils ever thought/ . . . Afflict thee" (105–109): the dissolution of the form of the angel has revealed "all devils" in the matter of the gold, but has also bound those devils to the service of the speaker's curse.[23] As the guidance and comfort of the angels were always legible as playful conceits upon the everyday efficacy of coin, so too is the curse presumably inefficacious—the railing of desperation, not the execution of remote and demonic power. But the ritual transposition of blessing into curse is clearly magical in form if not in faith, and it sustains the poem's play with the immaterial values, both positive and negative, that lie on either side of the intrinsic value of the gold angel.

The force of the curse is not magical but rhetorical; it finds, not the finder of the gold chain, but the finder of the poem about the chain—the reader, to whom the poem has made its way through the erratic circuits of manuscript circulation. The emulous rivalry between the man who's lost the mistress's chain and the man who must have found it is inscribed into the speaker's relation to the only masculine "thou" addressed by the poem, who is the finder within the poem's fiction, but cannot but slip into being the male reader at the margin of that fiction. The reader's observant position in relation to the fiction is analogous to that of "heaven" to the speaker's material world, and like "heaven" he is implicated into the sordid business of that material world through the angels—not through their beneficent preservation, but through the curse precipitated in their dissolution. Once the curse is complete, however, the speaker offers in the poem's last lines to redeem the reader-finder from it, on certain conditions:

> But I forgive; repent thee honest man:
> Gold is restorative, restore it then.
> But if from it thou be'st loath to depart,
> Because 'tis cordial, would 'twere at thy heart. (111–114)

The medical properties of gold's purity are momentarily offered as a solution for the impasse between the two rivals. Gold is not only preservative, as in the first eighty lines of the poem, but able now to repair physical and spiritual decay—restorative as medicine and redemptive as repentance. But that renewed potential for blessing is available only if the chain is itself "restored"—which the finder, beyond the speaker's reach, presumably will not do, and which the reader cannot do. It's the reader, then, who bears the force of the renewal of the curse in the impossibility of claiming the blessing: "Because 'tis cordial, would 'twere at thy heart." The pun between "cordial," medically restorative, and its etymological origin at the heart (Latin *cor*) shifts the gold from a therapeutic register to an invasive one: since it's good for your insides, why don't you choke on it? Eastern potentates warring with Rome were said to have punished the conqueror's hunger for gold by so literalizing it, pouring the molten metal down the throats of Roman captives, and the same procedure had been attributed to the Indians of the New World in their resistance to the Spanish.[24] The salvific agency of angels has been continuous with the medical efficacy of gold, as long as they retained their form as money—which of course is not the form in which gold is medically efficacious: prescriptions employing gold required it to be dusted into a solution. The poem's decomposition of the angels is not a grinding up, but a melting inflicted by the mistress upon the angels—and, the speaker feels, upon himself. He displaces that decomposition onto the finder's new relationship to the chain, as the lethal ingestion by the finder of molten gold, its interstitial state between angel and chain; and, unable to press that claim upon the finder's body, he viciously attempts to press it upon the reader. The twelve angels are a lot of money, and his loss of the chain and its molten restitution together represent a significant waste. But, despite the speaker's best efforts, he cannot quite make that waste a matter of life and death.

## II. THE SOUL OF TRADE

Donne enlarges on the contacts and contrarieties of bodies and coins in the second of the Elegies that I will consider, "Loves Progress." This poem quite thoroughly enacts a central premise of my study: that in early modernity, people and money shared certain ontological conditions. Both were by and large material objects, people being composed of muscle, sinew, bone, handsomely formed into the image of their Maker, and money being made of an alloy either of silver or of gold, stamped with the portrait of the sovereign. But materiality alone seemed insufficient as an account of either object's present existence. Where people enjoyed memories integrating their presences into the past, faculties of reason and will by which they directed themselves into the future, and souls that finally would divorce themselves from the body's material decay, gold and silver coins took on a motion through the human world that, though obviously propelled by human social convention, weirdly seemed analogous to the means by which humans understood their own materiality to be animated:

> I, when I value gold, may think upon
> The ductileness, the application,
> The wholesomeness, the ingenuity,
> From rust, from soil, from fire ever free.
> But if I love it, 'tis because 'tis made
> By our new nature, use, the soul of trade,

argues the speaker of "Loves Progress" (11–16). Here the material qualities of the metal, gold, that qualify it to be coinage are first cited as "valuable": its ability readily to be divided or recombined in smaller or larger units and its resistance to decay. The transformation into coinage depends upon those material conditions, but causes the object to transcend them in the social world, "our new nature"; the gold coin is made by us an object for "love," like a person (or at least like a woman, misogynistic as the speaker's analogy to human love is), and made not in fact to *have* a "soul" but somehow to *be* a "soul," that definitive instance of immaterial transcendence.[25]

Donne, if not his speaker, intends that this analogy—of the human fulcrum between materiality and transcendence to that posited in the coin—go only so far.[26] The irony that pervades the Elegies focuses in "Loves Progress" on the topos of inversion: the speaker asserts throughout the poem that the most effective way to love a woman is not from the face down, as the convention of the blason would have it, but up from the feet. The speaker's literally preposterous claim to decide "The right true end of love" (2) only transposes "ends" through a hilariously perverse "progress" of means, in which the character of gold is both departure and destination, simultaneously chthonic and sublime. A world in which social agency makes gold a soul is a world turned as upside down as the speaker's beloved is—a world where "our new nature" inverts the natural order in replacing it. The "violent yoking" of the poem's system of conceits propounds a repellent and dispersive tropic force, barely contained by the speaker's shakily framed wit. Although such a dispersal is "the right true end of love" in the elegy's erotic self-conception—a prodigal and perpetuated ejaculation—it expresses itself in a phobic repulsion toward the matter that is, in the conceit, the female body, but of which the male body is likewise made. In the poem's last lines, the fantasy of endless spending will recur back upon the male body as a nightmare of violent repayment.

The material qualities "thought upon" by the speaker "when I value gold" include those prized in it by medico-magical practitioners, the "wholesomeness" and "ingenuity" (which presumably has the sense of "nobility" here) that the metal might communicate to diseased bodies through the channels of sympathy, and which themselves, through the lexicon of purity, approach the status of moral values. But the listed qualities don't include the quality that most obviously qualifies the gold to become "the soul of trade," its rarity.[27] The "valuing" of gold is opposite to "loving" the stuff; "value" resides in these material characteristics, while "love" lies in the convention that animates the stuff as "the soul of trade," so that the particular material characteristic that might seem to make the materiality of the stuff continuous with that convention—the rarity that produces intrinsic value—is elided in order to assert an absolute and discontinuous opposition of "value" and "love." In "the soul of trade," the transcendental and the conventional are joined by their mutual immateriality, which makes even gold, and even a woman, count as lovable.

This opposition gets transposed in the elegy's second verse paragraph, where the paradoxical and specious "soul of trade" is forsaken by "love." Instead, love, in the person of "our Cupid," is to be found in the grossest and most literally base instances of materiality, remotest from the celestial spheres and closest to "the centric part":

> Search every sphere
> And firmament, our Cupid is not there:
> He's an infernal god and under ground
> With Pluto dwells, where gold and fire abound.

Men to such gods, their sacrificing coals
Did not in altars lay, but pits and holes. (27–32)

The speaker adopts for the moment the authoritative posture of an antiquarian, tracing pagan customs back to primeval cult practices: sacrifices to the gods of the "firmament" were elevated toward them on "altars," while sacrifices to the chthonic gods were lowered into the depths of the earth. Cupid is properly such a chthonic force, according to the fictive expertise put on by the speaker.[28] The speaker is not only enlisting the practice of antiquarianism to the service of a dirty joke, he is making that practice itself into a dirty joke. The antiquarian's digging around in the dirt and detritus of the present for precious evidentia of the past becomes itself an act of sacrifice to the filthy, chthonic Cupid of the poem, a deed of worship and of desire. The search for antiquarian knowledge is a whoremongering, a self-insertion into the place "where gold and fire abound"—"fire" suggesting less the wholesome heat of the womb than the scorching of venereal disease, once placed in conjunction with "gold" as (in this metaphorical register) exchanged for sexual service. This soiled and subterranean Cupid, who refuses to be found in the heavens and insists on keeping company with Pluto in the realms of "gold and fire," sounds less like the iconographically familiar blind and winged child than like the Mammon of Spenser's Book Two. But, as we saw in chapter 1, in *FQ* 2 the vast scope of antiquarian ambition, to use material objects such as coins to gain unmediated access to the past, confronted and ultimately confounded the glib presentism of Mammon's worldly knowingness. Here that ambition is a desire as base as any other desire, whether that for sex or for gold or for the whorishness that conflates the two. Desire per se, as Cupid, is definitively worldly, earthbound, a matter of soil:

Although we see celestial bodies move
Above the earth, the earth we till and love:
So we her airs contemplate, words and heart,
And virtues; but we love the centric part. (33–36)

The knowledge of astronomy is a matter of contemplation rather than of satisfaction, and one of theory rather than, like that of agriculture, of practice. Antiquarianism—the practice of orientation in time, in the history of the world—is more like agriculture than astronomy in this opposition; so too will geography, the practice of spatial orientation across the surface of the earth, prove to be, in the long conceit that makes up the next verse-paragraph of the poem. The association of these earthbound knowledge-practices with a desire that astronomy is unable to feel is made possible by the deft slippage at "her" between the earth and the woman's body. The earth has thought-provoking but insubstantial "airs" enveloping it, which correspond to the "words and heart,/ And virtues" of the woman, but both have a fully material "centric part" to serve as the object of a "love" that is the opposite of "contemplation," and that happens not as thinking but as digging.

Appearing as the conclusion of the poem's second verse-paragraph, the hole-worshipping love of the "centric part" takes the place assigned to the "use"-bound love of "the soul of trade" in the first. Exchange and digging are both material practices, and they are in an obvious way continuous: if it weren't for mining, there would be no gold to exchange, much less to love in exchanging. But, like the obvious but unarticulated continuity between rarity and value in the "soul of trade" conceit, the logical sequence of causes that would join digging to the exchange of gold coins is avoided by the speaker. Here the point of digging is only to get to "the centric part," not to bring anything such as ore back up to the surface. The immateriality ascribed to "use" in defiance of logic is replaced across the second verse-paragraph by a correspondingly illogical aspiration to an utter materiality, a journey to the center of the earth.

The third verse-paragraph instead enacts a nautical expedition across the surface of the woman's body, deferring the excavation promised in ll. 33–36 until the poem can traverse half its world to find "this desired place" (39). The long, Odyssean journey downward from the woman's face is full of snares and delays and ends with "shipwreck" just north of the goal, in the pubic hair (70). The speaker reveals this journey to have been only a hypothetical and fallacious alternative, however, in line 73; to "set out below," he insists, is the better way of travelling to the "right true end of love":

> For as free spheres move faster far than can
> Birds, whom the air resists, so may that man
> Which goes this empty and ethereal way,
> Than if at beauty's elements he stay. (87–90)

The downward trajectory into the materiality of the "centric part" now becomes the departure for an ascent into the previously dismissed regions of astronomy. Free from the distractions of the woman's upper "beauties," which have become material hindrances and traps in the navigation conceit, the undifferentiated trajectory up the thigh acquires a superlunary, immaterial nature. What makes it an "ethereal way" is its being empty of "beauty's elements."

Shankar Raman compares the difference between these two traversals to that between older techniques of coastal navigation according to landmarks and the new methods of crossing the blankness of ocean according to maps and celestial reckonings; he argues that this poem "sees 'woman' and 'colonial discovery' as themselves participating in, and indeed even triggering, a wider uncertainty regarding value and authority" than even that suggested in the initial monetary conceit.[29] Raman assesses that "uncertainty" as arising in the widening gap between the abstract and the concrete into which, per Foucault's *Order of Things*, the pre-Enlightenment episteme would ultimately collapse; thoughtful and wide-ranging as his analysis is, it seems to me to take too much about the concrete and the material for granted in the poem. In particular, Raman's assumption that "the right true end of love" is directly comparable to the goals of early modern mercantile venture in the poem strikes me as misleading. The point of the nautical expedition of ll. 39–72 is simply to arrive at "this desired place," and not to bring anything back in a return voyage as a mercantile mariner would; potential trade goods such as wine ("not faint Canary, but ambrosial," 52) and "chosen pearls" (57) are cited as distractions from the real venue of desire. Even the cartographic traversal of ocean by such an expedition is too materially minded for the taste of this speaker: his corrected journey is one that goes out of this world, leaving behind all "beauty's elements," water and "air" among them.

The "ethereal" movement away from materiality toward the "right true end" is one of refinement:

> Civility we see refined[:] the kiss
> Which at the face began, transplanted is
> Since to the hand, since to the Imperial knee,
> Now at the Papal foot delights to be. (81–84)

The "progress" of the poem's title here anticipates the modern sense of a telic development, as the "refining" of "Civility," while still retaining the usual early modern sense of a spatial trajectory. The improvement ascribed to Civility's transplantation of the kiss remembers the work of "our new nature, use" in making gold lovable, as the "soul of trade"; the sense of sophisticating convention has entirely overtaken the material register of metallurgical purification from which "refined" arises. But the journey of the kiss from face to foot has little to do with "trade," despite the mercantile register that the "progress" has evoked but not affirmed; and it has, very obviously, less to do with heteroerotic love than with homosocial dynamics of political supplication, to which the lover's kiss is rather brutally analogized. In order to succeed in its "right true end," the "progress" must be evacuated of "beauty," of "trade," of knowledge—whether of astronomical aids to navigation, or of geographical landmarks of the earth's surface—evacuated indeed of all material "elements." What is left to be the "right true end"?

> Rich Nature hath in women wisely made
> Two purses, and their mouths aversely laid;
> They then, which to the lower tribute owe,
> That way which that exchequer looks, must go.
> He which doth not, his error is as great,
> As who by clyster gave the stomach meat. (91–96)

Despite the exaltation of "use" and the evacuation of matter across the progress, what's left by the poem's last lines is the wisdom of "Rich Nature" in instantiating the relation of "tribute" between "purses" and gold. Exchange is a conventional relation, according to the speaker, but the exaction of "tribute" by power is a natural one, and the payment of "tribute" to the imperious vaginal "exchequer," so naturalized, proves to be the often-deferred "end" of the progress. The goal asserted by the speaker in his erotic interaction with gold is neither exchange (in the domestic context of convention) nor exploitation (in the chthonic context of mining, or the exotic context of protocolonial venture), but evacuation. Where the colonial matrix for "self-fashioning" is typically directed to self-aggrandizement, here the speaker is dedicated to emptying himself by finding something else to fill up, in the payment of "tribute." As we have seen in earlier chapters, the ethical relation between individual and world mediated by coinage tends to bifurcate itself within the paradigm of exchange between one of instrumentality and one of consumption, between the bodily sites of hand and mouth. In the weird convergence here of the woman's inverted body with coinage, which sometimes is determined by a coin's conventional character and sometimes, contradictorily, by its material nature, the speaker charts a third such relation: that of emptying. He rejects both the interaction of the hand, in touching the various features of the woman's upper body that become perilous snares, and that of the mouth, as merely circumlocutory conversation. The only satisfaction to which he claims to attend is that of the penis, which is indifferent to everything in the world that isn't a vagina, or at least enough like a vagina to deceive a penis (as the foot and, in the last line, the anus might be).[30] And the penis's satisfaction upon arriving there is "tribute": a spending that is also a subjection, expecting nothing compensatory in return.

Even in a poem that revels in its own vileness as much as "Loves Progress" does, the threatened anal intrusion of the last line—"As who by clyster gave the stomach meat"—comes as a shock.[31] It's a move like that ending "The Bracelet," a sudden and apparently unprovoked wish for bodily violation to befall the poem's male addressee, who is more or less the reader; both endings surely evoke the currents of competition and erotic anxiety roiling just below the surface of the homosocial coteries of the Inns of Court among the young men who strove to identify themselves as witty, libertine gallants through productions such as these Elegies. But both also specify that violation as an intrusion of materiality upon the reader that is somehow invited by the reader, as a forcible return of what the poem and reader have colluded to repress. In "The Bracelet" it's the pouring of molten gold down the reader's throat as a "cordial"; in "Loves Progress" it's the stuffing of food up the reader's anus for nourishment. Where "The Bracelet" 's speaker acceded to the disintegration of his angels only to wishfully inflict "the bitter cost" upon the "finder"/reader through a kind of antipathetic magic, the speaker of "Loves Progress" uses the conventionality of coins to articulate an antimaterial erotics of evacuation for his reader only to reassert the materiality of that interaction as a chthonic—and grotesquely intrusive—inversion of consumption. The indifferent solipsism with which the speaker's penis empties out the world in perceiving it, as an evacuated trajectory towards a hole, is as like Spenser's autoerotic Mammon as is this Cupid's association with "gold and fire." But equally Mammon-like is the threatened inversion of nourishment and waste, through which the normative sequence of consumption and evacuation that naturalizes the temporal working out of cause and effect becomes confounded in indigestion and constipation—and in sodomy. The goal of expenditure as "the right true end of love" is itself not only endless—the speaker envisions nothing but paying and paying some more as the indefinite (and spatially remote) "end" of the "progress"—but perilously so. The threat displaced on the reader in the last line is that of *being paid back*.[32] The open-ended inability to spend oneself completely, to disburse the matter of "tribute" entirely into the empty nothing of the bottomless vaginal "purse" and have done, leaves an opening for the forcible return of the material. In that return the normative paradigm of consumption, eating "meat," is made a threat simply by relocating it on the body, from mouth to anus, by way of the woman's vagina. The indefinite wastefulness of the man was made possible by locating an insatiable consumption in the woman; what surfaces in the last lines is the possibility that if the man fails to orient that erotic dislocation of consumption according to the speaker's instructions, he will visit it upon himself.

## III. PLENTY OF NOTHING

The disintegration of the form of "The Bracelet" 's angels reduces them to a molten matter that is demonic, inverting the benignant protection that they had extended to the speaker into a malevolent aggression that he hopes to unleash upon the "finder" of the chain. In "Loves Progress," the hinge between the conventional immateriality attributed to "use" and the utter, chthonic materiality of "the centric part" is a "love" that likewise operates as inversion, turning the Petrarchan convention of the blazon upside down to evacuate it. These two elegies share a meditation on the character of matter—in its opposition to form, on the one hand; in its opposition to void, on the other. They also share with each other and with the rest of Donne's elegies the pretense that they are not meditative, through the blustering voice of a speaker who professes to be a practical man, a man who knows what he wants and how to get it—a man of the world. The hilarious disparity between the direct access to the "right true end of love" professed by the speaker of "Loves Progress" and the circuitous, Odyssean trajectory of his discourse marks him as more wordy than worldly. His knowledge of the world is preeminently that of the sciences of the world that he professes to disdain—geography, astronomy, physics, antiquarian humanism—and the practical technique of seduction he advocates is eminently impractical.[33] Real worldliness is a desideratum that lies somewhere beyond the speaker's knowledge, or athwart it. The more that he demonstrates he knows, the more remote he is from the goal of knowingness that he professes.

The disparity between a worldly, pragmatic knowingness and the discursive accretion and display of knowledge that attempts to manifest it posits the material world as the other side of an impossible negation. To achieve what he considers (however rightly or wrongly) "the right true end of love," the speaker has to drag his discourse around the world backwards and upside down, announcing at each station of the "progress" the irrelevance of everything he actually knows to the goal of knowingness, which is that of a materiality that has been evacuated of matter. The way in which the conditions of matter shape their evacuation are figured as the spending of coin: the vaginal "exchequer" is a bottomless "purse," where "the right true end of love" reveals itself as an ejaculatory expenditure that itself must have no end.

The work of a coin in defining the conditions of its own absence is what I'm characterizing as the interaction of waste, or evacuation, among spending bodies, coins as they are spent, and the spaces from which and into which those coins have been emptied. That work is epitomized neatly in the name of

Thomas Nashe's alter ego, Pierce Penniless—for "Pierce" and "purse" are near-homonyms in Elizabethan diction.[34] The empty purse who is Pierce Penniless names himself as a material negation, a container that has been evacuated of the thing proper to it: what's left behind when the money is gone.[35] Pierce's emptiness of money is the means of his fulsome productiveness, generating a wit altogether voluminous, ingenious, and preposterous; his absurdity is manifest in his choice to solicit literary patronage from the devil, whom Pierce portrays as master both of gold and of vacuity. The chthonic character of money interacts complexly in Nashe's prose with the material conditions of plenitude and of privation, each of which are differently diabolical. Both value and nothingness lie just beyond the scope of Pierce's evacuated materiality. He is where money has been and no longer is, but he isn't where nothing is, either; as "purse," however presently empty, he continues to exist in the terms of the absence he is built around. Rather than the angelic transcendence of materiality toyed with by Donne in his elegies, Pierce's is a materiality irreducible because it is minimal. What he is without money is not nothing; both his wit and his diabolism are something substantial, but something made of as little as possible.

It has become a truism over the last half-century that you can't talk about Nashe without talking about nothing. The locus classicus for what critics have come to call "the Nashe problem" is C. S. Lewis's assessment that,

> Paradoxically, though Nashe's pamphlets are commercial literature, they come very close to being, in another way, 'pure' literature: literature which is, as nearly as possible, without a subject. In a certain sense of the verb 'say,' if asked what Nashe 'says,' we should have to reply, Nothing.[36]

It's easy to note in Lewis's remarks a surprised recognition of Nashe as early modern high-modernist: in the continuity of "pure" and "Nothing" that posits literariness as a difficulty whose self-reflexiveness verges on self-cancellation, and in the opposition of "commercial literature" to "pure literature." What's most interesting to me here is not the chance to historicize Lewis's critique, however, but the ways in which he expresses the limitation of the categories he's here articulating in Nashe: "Paradoxically . . . very close . . . as nearly as possible. . . . in a certain sense." These are not, I think, simply historical qualifiers arising in the encounter between one aesthetic paradigm and the artifact of an earlier aesthetic paradigm, in which the former recognizes the latter as congruent but not identical to itself. I think that these hesitations are directly about Nashe: that Lewis is recognizing that what's at stake in Nashe's prose is not so much "Nothing" as the approach to nothing—the asymptotic relation of prose to nothing as it "come[s] very close," "as nearly as possible."

Especially with the word "commercial" hard by, Lewis's "very close to... 'pure'" implies the outcome of an industrial process of refining—that Nashe's prose might be 99.44% pure nothing, like Ivory's relation to pure soap. Refining, in which a material substance is made more and more fully itself and not something else, offers a complementary formula for aesthetic production to that of *poiesis* or "making," a complementarity very evident once we consider the object of each process to be "Nothing": the poetic maker would be working to make something *from* nothing, while the poetic refiner would be working to make something *into* nothing.[37] Where the process of making is accumulative and positive, that of refining works toward its end through reduction and negation. A poetics refining itself into nothing is making its means, its process, continuous with its end. But such a poetics "com[ing] very close..., as nearly as possible," to nothing is encountering a limit upon its process in the limits of its own possibility. It encounters in itself an ineluctable margin of impurity. In manufacturing silver coins, the Tower mint defined the acceptable margin of impurity at 7.5% dross to 92.5% pure silver: this proportion or ratio is the sterling standard. But in the case of Nashe's prose, the impurity that demands such a marginal tolerance in the approach to nothing is its own somethingness.

For Jonathan Crewe, Lewis's analysis is the point of departure for a deconstruction of the ontological relation of *res* and *verba*. Where the text's "subject," to take Lewis's word, was in normative Renaissance expectations of literary production prior to its elaboration into words by the writer—prior not only in its being conceived of before that elaboration, but in its having an origin outside the moment and site of production and in its being detachable from the particular structure of words built upon it once production was complete—Nashe's writing, Crewe argues, manages to be about itself. On the other hand, Julian Yates has more recently pointed out how indebted Lewis's vocabulary for expressing "Nothing" is to the marketplace of print, and argues that the tension at stake in Nashe is not so much that within the humanist categories of *res* and *verba* as that between established humanist practices of bodily and writerly discipline and the emergent regimes of production in the material conditions of the print shop.[38] Coordinating Yates's emphasis on the mutual incorporation of man and machine in the operation of the printing press with the emphasis that Lewis and Crewe both place on the apparent insubstantiality of Nashe's style leads me to think about prose as a kind of prosthesis—a material implement for mediating between self and world that seems both part and not part of that self, and reciprocally part and not part of that material world. "Nothing can be made out of nothing," Lear tells Cordelia and his fool. Nashe may be continually testing the limits of that proverb, as a deconstructive reading such as Crewe's might suggest, but even to begin such a testing he'd first need to produce a nothing to make something out of. Can anything be made *into* nothing? Nashe, I argue, thinks the answer is "no." Instead, Nashe is interested in how close something can get to being nothing, in how much of its own materiality it may divest itself of in approaching the impossible threshold of the immaterial, and in what the selving limit of the material consists. By citing a "*selving* limit of the material," I want to affirm the self-consciousness of Nashe's prose, and to integrate the prose's knowledge of itself with this idea of the materially minimal and marginal. As Reid Barbour has argued, Nashe produces his prose as a tactile "stuff": a substance characterized not only by the textural consistency of its qualities, but by a materiality that is "not just rhetoric or language," that fills up spaces and produces events.[39] It's this diaphanous tangibility that Lewis identifies as the self-consciousness of a nearly " 'pure' literature," which is for him at once paradoxical and continuous in its relationship to "Nothing." The claim of the prose to substance is that of the irreducible minimum of materiality: the closer the prose gets to being nothing without being able to become nothing, the more ineluctably something it is—albeit not much.

Coined money does double duty in Nashe's discourse of flimsiness and triviality. It articulates the conventional standard of substantiality that is gold, and it articulates the standard of quantitative value through which qualities become remarkable or insignificant. Pierce defines his not-muchness in relation to both these standards: a penny is not much money, quantitatively, and a purse empty even of that penny holds not much of anything, substantially. The productivity of an empty purse for Nashe perhaps recalls that of Catullus's "purse full of cobwebs," out of which the poet produces a sublime perfume (*Carmina* 13), but it is markedly different from the fulcrum between prodigality and productivity crafted by Nashe's immediate predecessors in their relation to the institutionalized discourse of commonwealth. In order to define what's remarkable about Pierce Penniless's already wasted relation to his coins, I'll turn to a comparison that would infuriate Nashe: to the rival pamphlet *Greene's Groats-Worth of Wit, Bought with A Million of Repentance*, and in particular to the work of the titular groat to define this text's conversion of wasteful prodigality to vendible precept.

*Groatsworth* was one of three pamphlets rushed into print upon the death of the most notorious man of letters of his day, Robert Greene, in September of 1592. All three pamphlets purported to be Greene's last publication, embodying to an eager public Greene's deathbed repentance of his prodigality. Of the three it seems the least authorial; its most recent editor has argued that *Groatsworth*'s present form was cobbled together by Henry Chettle, partly out of Greene's uncollected papers and partly through pastiche of the most characteristic topoi of Greene's late manner.[40] The pamphlet has guaranteed its place in literary history by providing the earliest datable reference to Shakespeare's dramatic career; the libel against Shakespeare as "an Upstart Crow, beautified with our feathers" occurs toward the end of the pamphlet, in an open letter to three other writers, who are not named but are readily recognizable as Marlowe, Nashe, and Lodge, and in which Nashe is praised as "the English Juvenal." *Groatsworth* appeared in print simultaneously with the manifesto of Nashe's mature style, *Pierce Penniless*. Apparently at least some readers found the coincidence telling enough to suspect Nashe to be the man behind *Groatsworth*—as having exploited his friend Greene's death in order to forge a pamphlet promoting himself as the heir apparent of Greene's mantle, the new genius of popular print.[41] Nashe explicitly disclaims *Groatsworth* as "a scald trivial lying pamphlet" in the front matter to the second edition of *Pierce* that November, and remarks there that he would have liked to include among the papers his protagonist sends to Hell for the Devil's perusal a letter "to the ghost of Robert Greene, telling him what a coil there is with pamphleting on him after his death" (50, 49).[42]

Despite the scorn Nashe claims to feel for the "trivial" rival pamphlet, *Groatsworth* seemed continuous enough with the goals, the means, the occasion, and the medium of *Pierce* that Nashe felt the need explicitly to differentiate *Pierce* from *Groatsworth* in the second edition. The continuity across the two texts is not only that of emulous self-positioning in the print marketplace; it arises from two continuities asserted within the text of *Groatsworth*, which together impose an authorial control over the heterogeneous materials cobbled together in the pamphlet.[43] The first of these continuities is a prodigal narrative, and the second is the persistence in that narrative of the titular groat. As Richard Helgerson has demonstrated, the parable of the prodigal offers a nearly ubiquitous shaping account of literary production for the generation of Sidney, Lyly, and Greene, in which writerly activity constitutes a perverse squandering of time and talent on the author's part, and the culmination of a writerly career is its own renunciation in a profitable act of repentance—an act indeed so profitable that Greene had reenacted his repentance *of* print *in* print a number of times even before the season of his death.[44] In this conventional account, what the prodigal author is wasting is a kind of material resource, but one that is inverse to the scope of its realization as writing, diminishing as the text is produced. The profusion of text both enacts, and self-critically documents, the wasting of the resource: the prodigal author is reducing himself towards nothing, and producing text as the alienated fragment of his pretextual wholeness, while looking forward to the renunciation, the realienation, of that corrupt fragment in his conversion away from poetics to a new and profitable use. Like all Christians, he has to be born again in order to be what he was born to be. Poetic activity is a kind of "unthriftiness" in this discourse—Astrophil calls it a bankruptcy audit in *Astrophil & Stella* 18—but it's less clear what positive form that resource would take were it husbanded in a practice of thrift. Obviously it would be just as wasted, whatever it is, if it were hoarded or hidden under a bushel, if the prospective writer chose to save his talent by burying it. Rather, the talent should be applied to some civic-minded activity, either the direct counsel and implementation of Crown policy, in the exceptional case of Sidney's "great expectation," or for less grandly born writers the advocacy of sound policy through writing—what Lorna Hutson calls the "profitable discourse" of the Elizabethan era, in which a decorous writerly activity is one that mimes, enacts, and advocates an agenda of right-minded activity that will be to the profit of the commonwealth.[45]

In calling the resource misspent by the writerly prodigal a "talent" I'm enacting the implicit correspondence of this resource to money, which is likewise to be used for "profit" and neither hoarded nor squandered, as Christ's terrifying parable of the talents details (Mat. 25:14–30).[46] That implication is necessarily everywhere in the discourse of prodigal writerliness, but it is rarely made fully explicit—rarely is writerly talent directly articulated as cash. In this way, *Groatsworth*'s reanimation of prodigal clichés seems to me unusual; this text, which ostentates itself as the swan song of Greene, the possibly spurious summation and renunciation of his authorship, invests that authorship in a cash transaction that the discourse being summed up here had up till now largely avoided.[47] The title of the pamphlet announces that its reader is getting just what he paid for. A groat, a coin worth four pence, was presumably the purchase price. It's a transaction that is ostentated as taking place between Robert Greene and the buyer of the text, eliding the mediation of the printer and bookseller as well as that of the textual medium; and it's a symmetrical transaction, fully adequated between the quantum of wit that's a groats-worth and the face value of the silver coin. In this symmetry, the purchase of the pamphlet is opposite to the million-to-one disproportion between the wit Greene has gained and the repentance he has himself paid for it.[48] Greene's relation to his life, his sins, and his God is exorbitant; his relation to his reader is tidily located and circumscribed in the modest circumference and minimal depth of a groat.

In the fiction, however, the groat operates across both these relations. The pamphlet begins as the third-person relation of the life of "Roberto Gorinius," the scholarly son of a rich usurer who offends his father with reproaches. The father takes the opportunity of dying to score off Roberto, disinheriting him in favor of his younger brother:

> all [my wealth], *Lucanio* I bequeath to thee, only I reserve for *Roberto* thy wel red brother an old groat, (being the stocke I first began with) wherewith I wish him to buy a groats-worth of wit: for he in my life hath reproovd my manner of life, and therefore at my death, shall not be contaminated with corrupt gaine. (46)

The groat appears here as the site of exclusion. It's a minimum more insulting than nothing, reserved from the indefinitely enormous sum Roberto would have expected to inherit—a sum so disproportionate to the groat as not to be diminished by its exclusion. And the bequest turns the pamphlet's title from the everyday transaction of book buying into something like the apparently hopeless quest of a fairy tale: the father is not sending Roberto round the corner to buy another admonitory pamphlet, he is taunting Roberto with the riddling impossibility of purchasing "wit" as an unmediated material quantity.[49] Disinherited, Roberto turns to his "wit" for a means to live; first he tries to swindle his brother out of the inheritance by conspiring with a courtesan, but the courtesan betrays him. Then he really descends into the gutter, and starts writing plays for the commercial stage. As a playwright Roberto is, the narrator assures us, a great success—his wit seems productive of groats, rather than vice versa—but his remunerations only fuel his exhaustive debaucheries, until he hits rock bottom:

> For now when the number of [his] deceites caused *Roberto* bee hatefull almost to all men, his immeasurable drinking had made him the perfect Image of the dropsie, and the loathsome scourge of Lust tyrannized in his bones: lying in extreame poverty, and having nothing to pay but chalke, which now his Host accepted not for currant, this miserable man lay comfortlesly languishing, having but one groat left (the just proportion of his Fathers Legacie) which looking on, he cryed: O now it is too late, too late to buy witte with thee: and therefore will I see if I can sell to careless youth what I negligently forgot to buy. (75)

It is at this moment, when the first of the pamphlet's title characters confronts the second, that the narrating voice shatters and the only thinly disguised "Roberto Gorinius" is revealed to be "I," that most glamorous and notorious of prodigal playwrights, Robert Greene. Starting a new paragraph, the narrator announces,

> Heere (Gentlemen) breake I off *Robertoes* speach; whose life in most parts agreeing with mine, found one selfe punishment as I have doone. Heereafter suppose me the saide *Roberto*, and I will goe on with that hee promised: *Greene* will send you now his groats-worth of wit, that never shewed a mites-worth in his life: and though no man now bee by to doo me good: yet ere I die I will by my repentaunce indevour to doo all men good. (75)

The groat serves here to materialize a continuity between an author, a narrator, and a protagonist who had until now ostensibly been disparate. The recurrence of the groat as an object in the story enables Roberto, in recognizing it as "the just proportion of his Father's Legacie," to recognize himself. That self-recognition takes a remarkable narratological form, turning "Roberto" into the "I" who immediately evanesces into "Greene," and it is also a recognition of this self as a narrative form, in that the conversion of the groat into a new kind of "wit," in the form of the homiletic precepts that will make up the rest of the pamphlet's text, is the enactment of the parable of the prodigal, converting the self-destructive, alienated "Roberto" into the repentant and authoritative "I" who is "Greene." Where Roberto's story was a waste, its reformation into Greene's repentance via the groat will be profitable across both sides of the relation instantiated between audience and belated author, who will "sell to careless youth what I negligently forgot to buy." The fulcrum of prodigal identity inheres in the almost-nothingness of the groat, its minimal materiality. For *Groatsworth* this minimum is a turning point: reaching it reverses "Roberto's" trajectory of alienation, turns him into the "I" who is "Greene," and directs him to the exorbitant repleteness of a million-groat repentance. I argue that *Pierce Penniless* entails a corresponding encounter with the minimal by means of money; in Nashe's version, the minimum is not the singularity of one last bit of change but the hollowness of a purse from which even that last bit of change has vanished. Here, the minimal is not the nadir and turning point of a story but the point of departure for the protagonist's self-definition; the minimal is not the hinge between two forms of wit, wasteful playwrighting and positive precept, but the condition of wit's production. Nashe's Pierce is a wastrel, but he's not a prodigal, for he never repents. Rather than attempt to resume a salvific wholeness in conversion, Pierce will attempt in his supplication to the devil to perpetuate and exploit the demonic possibilities of littleness.

For Hutson, the eponymous emptiness of the speaker Pierce Penniless is a function of the hollowness of the "profitable discourse of the Elizabethans," the calcification of the commonwealths-men's midcentury arguments for policy reform into the next generation's political and ideological orthodoxy. Pierce belittles this discourse through the means by which he articulates it—as a hodgepodge of clichés, inserted into the context of a bankrupt's petition for favor to "the high and mighty Prince of Darkness, donzel dell Lucifer" (60), which Pierce entrusts to one of the local demons of London, a Knight of the Post (a professional informer and go-between).[50] But I'd like to suggest that, alongside the hollowness of what Hutson argues is a self-serving discourse of power within the homiletic matters of profit and loss, Pierce's self-given name as empty purse emphasizes a lack of matter (rather than the particular qualities of the matter that comes to be rehearsed) as constitutive of the persona. He is made around what isn't there. The absence of money is the ground of many a poetic complaint, Chaucer's complaint to his purse being a ready example. It's the collapse of complainer and complained, as both Pierce and purse, that's interesting from this perspective.

What's inside an empty purse? The devil's dancing school, suggests Pierce, who makes the idea that the devil should be paying him rent on this proverbial space the initial ground of his supplication, "insomuch as no man here in London can have a dancing school without rent, and his wit and knavery cannot be maintained with nothing" (60). What Pierce has to call his own is only his interiority, a present plenitude of emptiness, the condition as well as the occasion of the Supplication's existence. Pierce produces a pretty impressive amount of supplication out of what he and Lewis call "Nothing," then, even as he produces his persona around and within it. Pierce's nothing is not quite void, however: it is the margin or threshold of materiality, being full of devil. The devil is a spirit, and exists on the edge of privation, but he exists. The demonic marks the threshold of the minimal, what separates the spending of Pierce's last penny from the nothingness that emptiness approaches but cannot achieve.

Pierce's emptiness is the venue of the devil's pastime, he argues, and he should be recompensed for the use of his idle vacancy; he counts his vacuity, and his "wit and knavery," as services inadvertently rendered and asks for his newfound patron's compensation. "Or, if this be not so plausible to your honourable infernalship," he offers an alternative: that, rather than paying anything out to Pierce, the devil call in all the souls owed to him from the sinful residents of London, whose hoarding has been keeping the commonwealth's gold in "long imprisonment." This general release of the prisoner, gold, will let it roam throughout the city "to help his friends that have need of him," Pierce included (60). Citing the variety of souls owed to the devil across London is the occasion for Pierce's personification of the Deadly Sins as a pageant of urban grotesques. He begins not with Pride, as this medieval topos generally had, but with the new preeminence of Avarice. Avarice itself turns out not to be a single person but a household, the barren union of Greediness to Dame Niggardize.

Greediness scours the world outside their house for profit, either raking through "dunghills" with his shoes, "which, being nothing else but a couple of crab shells, were toothed at the toes with two sixpenny nails," or "sieving of muckhills and shop dust, whereof he will bolt a whole cartload to gain a bowed pin" (61–62). While he is getting without, Niggardize is keeping within: she "sat barrelling up the droppings of her nose... and would not adventure to spit without half-a-dozen porringers at her elbow" (62). There is no such thing as waste in this household's materialism; the two are unconscious of squandering time and effort in their obsession with extracting and retaining every possible value in the matter that surrounds them. Neither the trash of others nor their own bodily excrescence is dismissible to them. What we find repulsive they find compulsive. Though nothing is to be wasted in the house, neither is there anything to be consumed, save "one single, single kilderkin of small beer," served out in "little farthing ounce-boxes, whereof one of them filled up with froth, in manner and form of an ale-house, was a meal's allowance for the whole household" (63). Their stinginess is that of a duplicitous tapster: as he cheats his customers, they cheat themselves. The ounce-box of froth is as much as they can bring themselves to commit to their meal; to put it another way, it is the minimum to which they have been able to reduce the household's material expenditure.[51] Their barely substantial meal is conducted under the same conditions as Pierce's own ghostly "dinner with Duke Humphrey"—at the tomb in Paul's where penniless gallants go to pass the dinner hour, and where the demonic Knight of the Post and Pierce first find each other (58–59). Pierce's belly is empty because his purse is empty of gold, while Greediness and Niggardize keep their bellies empty that their coffers may stay full of gold.

The dollop of froth is at once the negation of everything fully substantial about beer and the sheer persistence of its substance in the face of that negation; the froth is not much of anything, yet is not quite nothing. The ironic, slangy reformulation of going hungry into "dinner with Duke Humphrey" preserves the form of dinner as an explicitly ghostly event, an emptying out of the meal's substance that arises in Pierce's own monetarized emptiness. His hunger is a second-order phenomenon: his body's knowledge of its emptiness derives from his identity as penniless purse. This threshold of the minimal, the ultimate and petty resistance of matter to its negation, is where the almost-nothingness of Pierce imagines the devil inside himself giving dancing lessons, and it's where Pierce meets the devil's errand-master in the "waste gallery" of Paul's beside Duke Humphrey's tomb (59). In Pierce's imagination and in his experience, the order of being that is the minimally material—dictated to Greediness by the presence of gold, as much as it is dictated to Pierce by its absence—converges with the order of being that is the demonic.

In refuting the Manichean ascription of evil to matter, Augustine argued that evil has no positive existence.[52] In a world created by an omnipotent, omnipresent, and benignant God, existence is a good, a quality that all creation shares with its creator from whom existence flows and through which all things participate in the divine nature according to their capacities. Humans, whose mental faculties more closely approach God's than do those of the beasts or plants or minerals, may be said to exist more fully thereby, in more closely resembling the total existence of God. Sin is a degradation of one's existence, a perversion or turning away of one's own nature from the wholeness of God to address mere nothingness. Evil is not the opposite of God but the privation of God—the withdrawal of the individual from participation in divine wholeness. For Augustine, perversion is a self-ruination, a process in which even a glutton who is making himself physically more massive through sin is paradoxically reducing himself ontologically, diminishing not only his stock in God's accounts in the world to come but his own existence in the material present. Perversion also disrupts an ideal continuity between mimesis and being. The more we seek to cultivate our resemblance to God, the more we will come to share in his nature; the more we cultivate our own degraded wills, the less we will be ourselves and the more we will be nothing at all, for our existence obtains only within the frame of that resemblance.

Two questions that arise from this continuity of material and spiritual being are of particular interest to Nashe here, in the gleeful perversity of Pierce's exercise of wit. One is that of the possibility or impossibility of void in the natural world; the other is the place of the devil. Epicureans such as Lucretius had argued for an atomistic material philosophy that anticipates our modern one, in which all matter is an interpenetration of solid and void. Renaissance orthodoxy was inclined to the opposite position, inherited from Aristotle and the

Stoics, that the created universe was a plenum of continuous matter in different forms of density and diffusion, but nowhere entirely vacuous.[53] And though the power granted by the devil to his believers in witchcraft was a means of deception, a redirection of faith toward eternal ruination, any *dis*belief in the power of the devil seemed as potentially atheistic as a belief in the possibility of void. Orthodoxy demanded that the power of the devil be understood simultaneously as real, urgent, and omnipresent, *and* as illusory, fraudulent, and insubstantial.[54] As Nashe dilates these problems between *Pierce Penniless* and his next publication, *The Terrors of the Night*, these two questions, of material privation and demonic power, become the same question:

> What do we talk of one devil? There is not a room in any man's house but is pestered and close-packed with a camp-royal of devils. . . . Hereunto the philosopher alluded when he said nature made no voidness in the whole universal; for no place (be it no bigger than a pock-hole in a man's face) but it is close-thronged with them. Infinite millions of them will hang swarming about a worm-eaten nose.
>
> Don Lucifer himself, their grand Capitano, asketh no better throne than a blear eye to set up his state in. Upon a hair they will sit like a nit, and overdredge a bald pate like a white scurf. The wrinkles in old witches' visages they eat out to entrench themselves in. . . . In Westminster Hall a man can scarce breathe from them; for in every corner they hover as thick as motes in the sun.
>
> The Druids that dwelt in the Isle of Man, which are famous for great conjurers, are reported to have been lousy with familiars. Had they but put their finger and their thumb into their neck, they could have plucked out a whole nest of them. . . .
>
> Now for worms: . . . . Is there any reason such small vermin as they are should devour so vast a thing as a ship, or have the teeth to gnaw through iron and wood? No, no, they are spirits, or else it were incredible. . . .
>
> If the bubbles in streams were well searched, I am persuaded they would be found to be little better. Hence it comes that mares, as Columella reporteth, looking at their forms in the water run mad. A flea is but a little beast, yet if she were not possessed by a spirit, she could never leap and skip as so she doth. . . . Not so much as Tewkesbury mustard but hath a spirit in it or else it would never bite so. (212–213)

The place of the devil *is* that of void, or rather that of where void would otherwise be; the apparent lacunae in the order of being are teeming with microscopic devils. Hollows, holes, and bubbles are the sites not of emptiness but of profusion. That profusion is made available by the relative lack of more substantial things in these places, which allows little rooms for an infinitude of tininesses and compressibilities. The marginality of the individual spirits' substance is what allows confined and local sites of lack throughout the everyday world to be supplied with the spirits' pervasive plenitude. The spirits' presence produces from that smallness a disproportion of cause (or agent) to effect: a multitude of them, as worms, consume a great ship; one of them, inhabiting a flea, gives the insect the power to jump distances that are enormous in relation to its little body. In their minimal corporeality, the spirits bear an ironic resemblance to the minimal corpora of the Epicurean atomism rejected by the material philosophy of the plenum. But the influence of their disproportion is also ironized; though the spirits' effects are an order of magnitude greater than their agentive tininess, the order of magnitude traversed by the individual spirit is only that which separates the unknowably microscopic from the trivial and everyday. Faith the size of a mustard seed, Christ tells his disciples, would move mountains (Mat. 17:20); a spirit in the mustard seed makes a spicy garnish for beef or pancakes.[55]

Trivial in themselves, the spirits achieve monstrously large effects through their profusion, acting in concert to destroy a ship or burn a town. The threshold of perception, between the microscopic and the insignificant, occupies the same place as the limit of insubstantiality within the plenum, which is also the site of profusion—the bodily surface of the skin, horrifically suffused with a verminous multitude of demons. The fulcrum between horror and triviality at the vanishing point of matter characterizes the scholarly anxieties of *The Terrors of the Night*, which veers back and forth between analyses of such insubstantial things as dreams as harmlessly epiphenomenal, and visions of the porous body's utter vulnerability to the influences of demonic minima.[56] The same balancing act, displaced into the persona of the preposterous wastrel Pierce Penniless, yields the demoniac hilarity of his "Supplication to the Devil." The supplication offers the exercise of Pierce's ingenuity upon a minimal materiality, articulated out of an interiority that is both explicitly defined and otherwise vacant: the least matter with the most art, in Queen Gertrude's devaluing sense of "art." The self-propulsive, heedless wit that defines "Pierce a-God's name" within and without the pamphlet makes itself from the marginality of the stuff it works upon, as Nashe makes clear in the preface to *Lenten Stuff*:

> Every man can say Bee to a Battledore, and write in praise of virtue and the seven liberal sciences, thresh corn out of the full sheaves and fetch water from

the Thames; but out of dry stubble to make an after-harvest and a plentiful crop without sowing, and wring juice out of a flint, that's Pierce a-God's name, and the right trick of a workman. (376)

"Pierce-a-God's name" is what you make of what's left when the good stuff isn't around. In *Lenten Stuff,* Nashe's spectacular mock-encomium of herring, the absent good stuff is meat; in *Pierce Penniless* that stuff is money.

The voice of Nashe's witty speakers is defined by their productive relation to privation across these texts. But the good stuff is not uniformly absent from Nashe's prose. The scapegrace narrator of *The Unfortunate Traveller,* Jack Wilton, is strangely lucky enough to encounter and assimilate the good stuff, when he seduces the wealthy and gorgeous matron Diamante in a Venetian prison. I will read Jack's persona as continuous with Pierce's for my purpose, in terms of the execution of wit through style upon small matter, so that I can look at the advent of Diamante as the production of an unlooked-for material plenitude within his narrative. Upon arriving in Venice, Jack (disguised as his master, the Earl of Surrey, for no very plausible reason) and Surrey (disguised as Jack) are beguiled into the hospitality of the hypocritically pious courtesan Tabitha. When Tabitha hatches a plan to get their wealth by encouraging "Jack" to murder "Surrey"—"to make me away"—the pair's mutual disguise leads her to make her mutinous overtures to the concealed master and not the man (301). The two Englishmen play along with the plot, turn the tables on their conspiring hosts at the crucial moment, and extort money from Tabitha with threats of turning her over to the law.

> So it fortuned (fie upon that unfortunate word of Fortune) that this whore, this quean, this common of ten thousand, so bribing me not to bewray her, had given me a great deal of counterfeit gold, which she had received of a coiner to make away a little before, amongst the gross sum of my bribery. I, silly milksop, under an angel of light took what she gave me, n'er turned it over, for which (Oh falsehood in fair show) my master and I had like to have been turned over. (303)

"[U]nfortunate" refers this moment of transition to the larger process of Jack's travels: the escaping of one plot to fall directly into another, from frying pan to fire, characterizes Jack's experience of Italy. Here, certainly, all Fortune is unfortunate. To the extent that the "silly" traveler allows himself to be subject to contingency without exercising a suspicious foresight, his luck will necessarily be bad, for all possible outcomes for chance are anticipated by and woven into preexisting, subterranean networks of malice. Tugging on the thread of Tabitha's murderous conspiracy, Jack shakes loose only the means of her involvement in another conspiracy, a coining ring.

Where Tabitha's plan in the murder plot was to get and keep the good money of the English duo while disposing of their persons, her role in the coining plot is the converse: she is an utterer of the counterfeits, the person whose job it is to dispose of them for profit, and who here manages to pay for her life with them at negligible cost. The task at hand is remarkably the same, however—that of disbursal, from "to make me away" to "to make away," with only the objects of person and purse transposed. Jack promptly sends some of his delusive profits to

> a delicate wench named Flavia Aemilia lodging... at a goldsmith's, which I would fain have had to the grand test to try whether she were cunning in alchemy or no. Ay me, she was but a counterfeit slip.... my hostess and she were confederate, who having gotten but one piece of my ill gold in their hands, devised the means to make me immortal. (303)

Flavia's sexual knowingness is compressed into metallurgical expertise in the interaction of Jack's present and hopeful wit (she lodges at the goldsmith's, so I'll put her to the test) with the hindsight which, to the narrated present, appears as foreknowledge: the gold which I sent to buy her favors proving to be counterfeit, she herself proved "a counterfet slip" to me. In Flavia's counterfeit sexuality, a third circuit of conspiracy opens, by which Tabitha claims another opportunity to make the Englishmen away.

Jack appreciates the admirable symmetry through which the counterfeit coins negotiate among the circuits of personal deception, but he does not care to point out his and Surrey's own participation in that larger network.[57] While Surrey's money is legitimate, Jack's own currency in passing for Surrey is counterfeit, and it was their own two-man counterfeiting that precluded the success of Tabitha's murder plot. Good money, personal sincerity, and sexual satisfaction are all deferred one into the other by means of the counterfeit; to the extent that the Englishmen participate in these intricate cycles of deception, they can survive. But of course Jack doesn't want merely to deceive and survive by means of these repetitive deferrals, he wants the ends, the good money and the sexual satisfaction that (in Tabitha's Venice) seem like carrots on a donkey's stick. Surprisingly, he happens to get them.

Jack and Surrey's counterfeiting of each other, which had foiled Tabitha's first scheme, only gets them in further trouble once they land in prison for the counterfeits. Their mutual disguise is exposed by the arrival of well-meaning but hapless fellow-Englishmen, who, in undoing the counterfeit, reverse the leniency their jailor (the mint-master) had been inclined to extend them. But in placing them in "a straiter ward," the no longer deferred reversal of their identities offers a reversal of fortune; they find imprisoned with them the wrongly accused matron Diamante, and "As glad were we almost as if they had given us liberty, that fortune lent us such a sweet pew-fellow" (304, 306). The conspiratorial malignancy of Diamante's prior fortunes is explained at length, so that that happy chance of Jack and Diamante's meeting is itself the outcome of the determinism of the individually bad fortune of each. This meeting is a fantastic resolution to the apparently inevitable downward spiral in which fortune colludes with counterfeiting and conspiracy: at a practical level, it seems preposterous that the "strait[ness]" of the men's new ward would have included female company, or that a "magnifico's wife of good calling" should be imprisoned with men no matter how grave the accusation against her chastity (305); and if the three are imprisoned together, where does Surrey go while Jack and Diamante have sex? And at the interpretive level of desire and deferral that I've been advancing, Diamante's fortuitous integration of personal integrity, sexual availability, and monetary wealth seems as fantastic a resolution to Jack's problems as would be his coming by the philosopher's stone or Fortunatus's purse.[58]

But the episode is in its whole about the failure of bad fortune to ensnare Jack, which is to say that the improbability and the excessiveness of the turn of Jack's fortunes in the person of Diamante is the whole point of it. Jack's improvident failures of foresight make him subject to fortune, which is definitionally bad; if he were any unluckier he'd be dead, many times over.[59] And that means he's really pretty lucky.[60] Diamante's appearance seems like a fairy-tale resolution because it is one. Fairy tales are about luck. The fairy-tale protagonist is the ordinary one who happens to succeed where an indefinite number just like him have failed. His success is built into the plot, but only because the stories of his countless predecessors who haven't succeeded speak for themselves (as the bones already ground by the giant, or here the corpses Tabitha is already accustomed to stashing in the vaults of her cellar).[61] He is the statistically inevitable exception, the one who demonstrates the apparently impossible to be merely improbable—the lucky one. Jack's irreducibility as marginally probable contingency proves, in the register of events, the same thing that Pierce Penniless's irreducible flimsiness demonstrated at the level of substance: that nothing is impossible.[62] Like Pierce's evacuated substance, Jack's happy contingency is a monetary function—here, the validating replacement of the "counterfeit slip[s]" Tabitha and Flavia with the golden-minded Diamante. Probability is implicitly quantitative, a matter not of "yes" and "no" but of "more" and "less"; to make that quantification explicit is almost inevitably to monetarize it, either within the context of the present as *price*—what the market seems likely at the moment to bear—or in the relation of present to future as *odds*, the adequation of present risk to future reward performed alike by provident insurers and by gamblers like Jack.

What's remarkable about Jack's meeting with Diamante is neither that it's fantastical nor that it's lucky; the fantasy is lushly improbable, so its realization as luck is, in a story about an improbably lucky guy, inevitable. What's remarkable is Jack's explanation of how it is possible that this conflation of integrity, availability, and prosperity should exist at all in order to fall into his hands. There is a way, he insists, in which these can all be qualities of the same thing, a thing that may exist in the world, and that way is metallurgically. Diamante is a woman, but her qualities are those of gold:

> If in any thing she were culpable, it was in being too melancholy chaste, and showing her self as covetous of her beauty as her husband was of his bags. . . . It is almost impossible that any woman should be excellently witty, and not make the utmost penny of her beauty. This age and this country may admit of some miraculous exceptions, but former times are my constant informers. Those that have quick motions of wit have quick motions in everything; iron only needs many strokes, only iron minds are not won without a long siege of entreaty. Gold easily bends, the most ingenious minds are easiest moved, *Ingenium nobis molle Thalia dedit* saith Psapho to Phao. Who hath no merciful mild mistress, I will maintain, hath no witty but a clownish, dull, phlegmatic puppy to his mistress.
>
> This magnifico's wife was a good loving soul that had mettall enough in her to make a good wit of, but being never removed from under her mother's and her husband's wing, it was not molded and fashioned as it ought. Causeless distrust is able to drive deceit into a simple woman's head. I durst pawn the credit of a page, which is worth ames ace at all times, that she was immaculate honest till she met with us in prison. (306–307; I've reversed the editor's modernization of "mettall" to "mettle")

Probability, Jack declares, is for once on his side: he will "pawn the credit of a page" on Diamante's prior chastity—which is of course negligible ("amesace"= snake eyes), but it's a bet he'd win by losing, while the odds of her remaining chaste in these circumstances are "almost impossible" (unless of course she were a modern-day Englishwoman, which happily she isn't).[63] His fortune has delivered him from the circuit of deceit, conspiracy, sexual disappointment, and counterfeit money to a new network of meaning, across which "deceit" as practiced on Diamante's husband circulates together with beauty, generosity, fineness of temperament, wit, sexual satisfaction, preciousness, and flexibility. Individual meanings are still elusive in the new circuit, as each term slides into the next—but they can't escape, as the scope of this circuit is defined by the prison. The convergence of Jack and Diamante turns "imprisonment" on its head—not only in the Donnean sense that the room where the lovers are is the venue of freedom, so that the rest of the world is imprisoned outside it, but in the innuendo of "How I dealt with her, guess, dear reader, *subaudi* that I was in prison and she my silly jailor" (308). Jack's wit and Diamante's work in concert in his narration of this passage, though Diamante's "wit" seems not in the first instance to denote verbal proficiency—indeed, the question of what language Jack and Diamante communicate in is never addressed, nor does Jack ever cite Diamante's speech directly. Alan Brissenden has argued that "wit" when applied to women offers a bawdy connotation in early modern English, ranging in reference from a woman's sexual desire, to her resourcefulness in achieving it, to her pudenda themselves.[64] Diamante's readiness of mind is realized not in speech but in her "quick motions in everything," and assimilated, via the lurid example of Sappho and the handy conflation of "ingenious" and "ingenuous," to the bountiful frankness that properly pertains only to the latter word.[65]

Diamante's newly realized wit monetarizes her beauty "to the utmost penny," and thereby puts it into circulation. In this, she rejects the example of her miserly husband and transposes the behaviors both of Tabitha, who pollutes the market with counterfeits, and Flavia, herself a "counterfeit slip," thanks to the two of whom Jack is in prison. Jack's own aggression toward the husband is of a piece with Pierce Penniless's self-professed antagonism to Greediness, while the way in which Diamante releases her beauty to circulation recalls not only the "liberty" Pierce demanded for London's gold but Pierce's own wastedness as a "bag" already exhausted of its "utmost penny." "The utmost penny" here implies a scrape against the limit of Diamante's resources even in their bountiful readiness, drawn out to small silver change.[66] The following gesture to the wondrous chastity of witty Englishwomen—"this age and this country may admit of some miraculous exceptions"—perhaps serves less as a pro forma apology to audience and Queen than it does to expand the margins of possibility past this initial moment of material restriction, so that when we return to Diamante it's not in the counting out of pennies but in the comparison of stubborn iron to ductile, malleable gold. Iron is worth little in relation to gold, but the comparison here makes that value relation depend not on the relative rarity of the two metals but on their pliability: an iron mistress is worthless because she takes so much stroking and yet remains unbent.

In *The Unfortunate Traveller*, a woman's mind proves itself golden by stooping to a show of dross. The shared vehicle of coinage across two apparently opposite formulations of wit, Pierce's and Diamante's, defines wit as a kind of interaction with the material world (and not an interaction limited only to verbal "matter"). Furthermore, in suggesting a congruence with some conventions of the gendering of material substance—those built around the commonplace of form as masculine and purposive, working upon a feminine matter that is passive and inert—it undermines others that posit femininity as lack. It's masculine wit that manifests itself through privation, while this feminine wit manifests itself to Jack as bounty beyond anything the witty prodigal could hope to scrounge for himself.

I don't mean to discount the phallocentrism of the fantasy that Diamante arises to fulfill, however. My aim is not to celebrate but only to analyze the way in which Jack uses money to articulate what he considers to be the materiality of that wish fulfillment. There are a number of ways in which the text suggests a reality for Diamante's character that is autonomous and discrepant from the limits of Jack's fantasy: in her capacity for ingenious and effective action throughout the plot, in Jack's inability to express her "wittiness" discursively, and in Jack's general habit of referring to her as "my courtesan" in preference to her name.[67] Not only is that possessive and pejorative phrase designed to belittle in itself, it allows Jack to cling to his understanding of her bountiful value as possessing all the "golden" qualities that he has cited, so that she exists to compensate for his humiliation at the hands of the "counterfeit slips" Tabatha and Flavia, through the sexuality that Jack characterizes in her as malleable and mintable. Were Jack to acknowledge her as "Diamante," a diamond, he would have to articulate her value as contrarily realizing that jewel's qualities of singularity and integrity—neither of which are subject to his dismal erotic history, much less its compensatory fantasy. Value named and known for itself, this reading would suggest, still lies somewhere beyond Jack's capacity to articulate it in the terms of his self-narration, even though it is present in the person of Diamante as he narrates her. Considering Jack's understanding of her value and of their relationship as limited and self-motivated in this way only exacerbates the disproportion that Jack's own fantasy already manifests between his witty privation and Diamante's witty bounty. It's an asymmetry as vast as the disproportion between "Greene's" groatsworth of wit and his million-to-one repentance. Yet, unlike "Greene," Jack does not have to repent his prodigality to cash in his odds. Rather, he is rewarded for continuing to be himself—for maintaining his self-profession as "the King of Pages," where "pages" refer at once to the most marginal and plentiful members of the royal court and to the paper of the book (253). As "King of Pages," the irrepressible and irreducible Jack persists at the limits of privation and profusion, exemplarily inconsequential, master of the margin that separates and conjoins materiality and text.

AFTERWORD

# Before Economy

Vincent's education, which had been materialistic in tendency, prevented him from believing in the supernatural—which gave the demon an immense advantage.

—André Gide, *The Counterfeiters*[1]

In their manifestations of coined money in the most unlikely places—and their evacuation of that object from likelier places—the texts I've considered in this study subject the discursive role of a coin as the epitome of "common wealth" to a rigorous critique from within that discourse's own terms. For the generation of Thomas Smith and Hugh Latimer, the veterans of debasement, the conjunction of metal and stamp in a single coin served to define the productively reciprocal responsibilities among ethical subjects, and between political subjects and the crown, in terms of the ontological category of material purity guaranteed by the minted image. The conceptual possibilities, and the ideological limitations, implicit in that integration are elaborated complexly and ironically by writers of the 1580s and '90s as they address the character of coinage. Mammon is such an ironic characterization, but so too is Pierce Penniless. His name not only defines him as a monetarized character without money, but as a common-wealth character without wealth: as Lorna Hutson demonstrates, Nashe's alter ego is an ironic reflection of the personification of the commonwealth in the figure of Piers Plowman, just as is Spenser's intertextual Munera.[2]

This book has made an attempt to understand what and how English writers of the late sixteenth century thought about their money, before their successors developed the discipline of political economy as a means of thinking about it exclusively. Looking back upon that development, Adam Smith was the first to define an epistemological break, from which his own discipline of "political economy" would at length emerge, in the disputes among a new generation of writers addressing fiscal policy at the turn of the seventeenth century. He grouped these authorities together as professing a "mercantile" nascency of political economy, though it might not have occurred to the four major figures who have since come to be associated in this periodization—Gerald de Malynes, Thomas Milles, Edward Misselden, and Thomas Mun—that any of their shared assumptions outweighed their hotly contested differences to the point of warranting such a unitary label. Malynes, a Mint official, is often considered the most indebted of the four to traditional, idealized, and state-dependent concepts of metallic pricing in international trade, while the merchant Mun's work, proclaiming the independence of value in trade both from bullion and from the will of princes, broke much of the new ground from which Smith's own work later would grow.[3]

The activity of these writers, at least in its most frenetic phase, is readily attributable to the need for innovative thinking in the face of the desperate international depression of the 1610s and '20s, but their ideas are recognizably developing even before that crisis, spurred first of all by England's chronic leakage of precious metals through its imbalance of trade throughout the sixteenth century. As early as 1602, Malynes had inserted himself into an ongoing discourse of writers decrying the net exportation of bullion—as he did himself, though his analyses of that exportation's causes and proposals for its remedy were both novel—but it was not until the early 1620s that both Misselden and Mun responded to his treatises with counterblows of their own, arguing for policies that would encourage the "balance of trade" to tip in England's favor rather than for ever more punitive legislation intended to seal off England's gold and silver from the international money market.[4] Those prior, sixteenth-century understandings of the nature of money, in relation or reaction to which the various mercantilist positions were articulated, were to Smith a medieval or "popular" (i.e., premodern, unscientific, and, finally, extrahistoric) ground for his account of origins for his own science.[5] His followers have characterized these shadowy figures chivvied away by the dawn of mercantilism as "bullionists."

The actual persistence of conservative or "bullionist" ideas against and even within the rise of mercantilism has since been much debated, as scholars of the seventeenth century continue to revisit Smith's still fertile analysis from the perspectives of historiography, economics, and literary study.[6] But Smith's most basic assertion of an epistemological break has, though richly complicated and sometimes relocated chronologically, never seriously been contested, and the so-called bullionists remain divorced from the genealogy of modernity.[7] The nonauthorities who are dismissed in this way from the history of properly economic monetary thought are, of course, the very same writers whom I have characterized as crafting an authoritative discourse of "common weal" for the second half of the sixteenth century, in response to the traumatic monetary developments—inflation and debasement—of the first.

To invalidate the orthodox authority of the commonwealth discourse demanded not only a new vision and direction for monetary policy but a redefinition of the nature of discursive authority and of its relationship to the public good. As Mary Poovey has demonstrated, Mun in particular succeeds in *England's Treasure by Forraign Trade* in crafting a discursive position (or ethos) that attributes authority to expertise, and expertise in turn to practical experience: the merchant, who works most with money, is the most qualified to discuss it.[8] This mobilization of particular expertise to accredit authority is Mun's most radical intervention in fiscal discourse, and it is not an immediately political one. Rather, it is an epistemological intervention with political consequences, consequences that far outstrip Mun's own goals in reshaping policy. It transforms both the speaker of fiscal discourse and the object of that discourse. Mun's speaker is unconcerned, at least overtly, to manifest the previously normative venues of an omnicapable authority adaptable to any rhetorical occasion—such as individual wisdom, passionate commitment, or that grasp of his audience's preexistent, communal expectations that we know either as "consensus" or "common sense." Rather than appealing to what we all know, or to what we know of him as an ethical individual that might encourage us to trust his judgment on a public question, Mun establishes that he knows something—money—better than his audience does, and asks that we defer our expectations on the topic in order that he may teach us the fruits of his expertise.

The effect is not only to validate a new speaking position for the expert. The effect is also to create a new object of discourse that is the expert's particular expertise, precipitating itself out of the larger discursive rubric of which it had previously been an element: in this case, the differentiation of "money" from "policy," which is the first business of Mun's treatise. The preamble to *England's Treasure by Forraign Trade* addresses itself to Mun's son, who eventually brought the treatise into print in 1664.[9] It defines the present text as being the sequel to "a former Discourse," which had explicated everything about the "Common-wealth" *except* money:

> In a former Discourse I have endeavoured after my manner briefly to teach thee two things: The first is *Piety*, how to fear God aright, according to his Works and Word: The second is *Policy*, how to love and serve thy Country, by

> instructing thee in the duties and proceedings of sundry Vocations, which either *order*, or else *act* the affairs of the Common-wealth; In which as some things doe especially tend to *Preserve*, and others are apt to *Enlarge* the same: So am I now to speak of *Money*, which doth indifferently serve to both those happy ends. (viii)

The relationships articulated here among "piety," "policy," and "money" are complex. On the one hand, "money" is defined as a particular topic within the discourse of "policy." But "policy" is set aside, by being placed in its conventionally moralistic pairing with "piety," both of which we are to understand as having already been discussed in the (otherwise unattested) "former Discourse." "Money" apparently would not fit within that "former Discourse," which seems to be an extratextual venue for everything that we should understand as ethically normative, commonsensical, and unexceptionable about this speaker. All that sort of thing is expressly taken as given by this treatise, and although "money" is here ostentated as the merely redundant instance of that "former Discourse's" principles, the force of the self-positioning of *England's Treasure* is rather to define "money" as the particular remainder inexpressible within those principles, which requires a discourse all to itself.[10] The contrast between the rhetorical self-positioning of this treatise and that of the *Discourse of the Commonweal* seventy years before is telling. Thomas Smith's authoritative speaker was a cleric, whose piety and scholarship gave him a universal authority; his voice is that of the community's best representative, as he speaks from common sense to address the common good. From this perspective, Smith's Doctor is able to articulate the interdependence of the ethical and political crises besetting the public good in terms of the ontological crisis of monetary debasement. The mercantile, expert speaker of *England's Treasure* differentiates money from both piety and policy, as a unique discursive object demanding a specialized "discourse."

The epistemological rupture separating *England's Treasure* from the *Discourse of the Commonweal* distinguishes an emergent speakerly ethos grounded in expertise from the classical ethos that is vested by consensus.[11] From a knowledge that was expressed as representative of what's universally credited, and therefore largely static, it distinguishes a new knowledge that is at once narrowing and expansive: specialized, exclusive, and productively self-generative and self-refining. And in so doing, it distinguishes from the integrative model of domestic polity as a "common wealth" that subsumes the particular objects of faith, justice, and money, a newly limited totality of wealth that we will come to call "the economy."

It is certainly not Mun's intent to discredit "commonwealth" in favor of "economy"; he insists that the policy he advocates in relaxing the restrictions on the export of precious metals will benefit all individual English subjects, as well as England's international position in both peace and war.[12] But in order to articulate his understanding of the national interest as it pertains to his topic, he can only acknowledge the still unquestionable communitarian claims of "piety" and "policy" upon the merchant in the course of declaring them to be beside the immediate point. Mun continues to name the national interest as "the Commonwealth," but he defines that interest as the macroscopic version of a unitary private interest:

> For in this case it cometh to pass in the stock of a Kingdom, as in the estate of a private man; who is supposed to have one thousand pounds yearly revenue and two thousand pounds ready money in his Chest: If such a man through excess shall spend one thousand five hundred pounds *per annum*, all his ready mony will be gone in four years; and in the like time his said money will be doubled if he take a Frugal course to spend but five hundred pounds *per annum*; which rule never faileth likewise in the Commonwealth, but in some cases (of no great moment) which I will hereafter declare.... (5–6)

The working definition of "Commonwealth" hinges on synecdoche here, just as it had for Spenser in crafting the analogy between books Two and Five of *The Faerie Queene*, as we saw in chapter 1. But the microscopic instance serving to define the polis for Spenser was that of the ethical individual; the synecdochic relation of ethics to politics is a truism in the Elizabethan discourse of commonwealth. For Mun, the human-scaled instance through which we may understand the impersonal totality of the commonwealth is not the citizen but the household, "the estate of a private man."[13] The claims of ethos in constituting the polis are deferred outside Mun's treatise, in order to represent the polis instead as an *oikos*. This is not to say that the vocabulary of "excess" and "frugality" does not have the same ethical charge for Mun that it did for the previous generations of moralizers upon thrift; it is simply to explicate how Mun can express *as* thrift a policy, the legalized export of bullion, that those previous generations would have found (and their present representatives, such as Malynes, did find) scandalously wasteful.

In order to repudiate the expectation that the export of precious metals should be illegal—the specific and apparently simple goal of *England's Treasure*—Mun must also, as if in passing, repudiate the formulae of the relationship of value to materiality that grounded what Hutson calls "the profitable discourse of the Elizabethans." And in so doing, he must imagine money as detached from the range of relations among the material, the ethical, and the political that I've examined in this study, in order to construe money as an autonomous object of an autonomous discourse. In this moment Mun imagines that he is thinking about the same political totality, "the Commonwealth," that his predecessors and his rival contemporaries have been thinking about; he simply happens for the moment to be imagining that totality as represented by a householder making fiscal choices rather than by an ethical actor making moral choices. He does not know that he is helping to invent a totality that will come to seem neither imaginary nor momentary, but definitively material and permanent—the totality that will be called economy.

From the point of view of Adam Smith's followers, looking back across the invention of economy, the sixteenth-century identification of "common wealth" with the materiality of gold and silver was "bullionism"—a fixation upon intrinsic value as if it were the only kind of value. I have tried to show how the sixteenth-century analysis of materiality in money is not the same thing as a belief that money is simply material. But such a distinction is not transparent to the retrospective gaze of the political economists across that epistemic rupture, which defined "bullionism" as a risibly crude instance of fetish. The veil across that retro-perspective is an ideological one; it is an acknowledgment of epistemological otherness articulated as the divide between the sophisticated and the primitive, and it's a formulation of otherness that works to disavow something fundamental and pernicious within the system being affirmed—in this case, the place of the fetish in capitalist markets and psyches, as explicated by Marx and Freud.[14] But it also acknowledges the mutuality of incomprehension from either side of this epistemic divide. Though the misinterpretation of precapitalist thought is in some sense fundamental to the integrity of capitalist thinking, it remains true that the tenets of protocapitalist thought, as they emerge from the controversies of the 1620s, had implications unthinkable to the commonwealths-men—"unthinkable" not as too sophisticated to yet be thought, but as scandalous to thought.

By the time Mandeville could write *The Fable of the Bees* in 1714, the productive relation of self-interest to national economy, of "Private Vices" to "Publick Benefits," had become only a moral scandal, no longer an epistemological one. But in the rupture of the early seventeenth century, this entire upending of the commonwealth ethos is not yet articulated as such. The point of contention articulable within those controversies is the material relation of value to metal. For the mercantilists Mun and Misselden, the refusal on the part of the state to license the exportation of bullion into the international market is a retentive fetishism for what can be held and kept, which prevents the recognition of the principle that you need to spend money to make money. From the perspective of the commonwealth-minded statesmen, the idea that the gold and silver that England has struggled to capture and maintain from the world should simply be released is legible as an absurd and self-destructive waste. It is here that the threshold of scandal, between the morally outrageous and epistemically unthinkable, lies at the moment of the mercantilist controversy.

The scandal of waste mobilized by Donne and Nashe within the commonwealth ideology of the 1590s has a radical potential. In making that claim, though, I do not wish simply to align these prodigal wits with the merchants who controverted the restriction of international currency transactions in the following decades, nor with the political economy that would develop from that controversy. Rather, Donne and Nashe seem to me to be participating in the sheer negativity of this emerging epistemic rupture. Richard Halpern has characterized Marx's "primitive accumulation" as a negative movement in history, an aspect of the transition from feudalism to capitalism in which the old structures are demolished without, as yet, the structures of the emergent order being founded; what does get built on that rubble-strewn ground of the feudal in that moment fails itself to escape the status of ruin, and is erased in the monumental foundations of capital. Though it is true that "waste" is what the economic ideas that would come to subsume and replace the ideology of commonwealth would look like from commonwealth's own perspective, I imagine the enactment of waste in Donne and Nashe as participating more in commonwealth's undoing of itself than in its replacement. But in articulating the dichotomy of "ruin" and "monument" among the structures of the past, I am also thinking once more of Spenser, and thinking in particular of the remembrance of Mammon enacted by Talus in the display of Munera's severed limbs. This is a thirdhand diminution of remembrance, for Munera is an epigonic version of Mammon, and the metallic hands and feet are in turn a savage reduction of the bodily incorporation of silver and gold that was Munera before her dismemberment; the display serves not as a memorial, but as a replacement for the "memory" of Pollente and Munera's demolished castle (5.2.28).

The temporalities of Renaissance coins, their complex relations to human history and to causal sequence, coexist uneasily with those of Renaissance memory, to which they are sometimes parallel, sometimes convergent, and often contrary. Materiality, temporality, and value are made to cohere forcibly in the minting strikes of a coin's stamping, and as the coin goes on to circulate among the subjects of the monarch's "stampéd face," their various interactions with it variously implicate their own bodies in that difficult coherence. So too does the medium of the coin's currency work to define both ethical relations—those among the parties to a monetary exchange—and political relations—those that connect the exchangers to the commonwealth and Crown—in terms of itself. In this way, a current coin is not only an object of knowledge but a medium of knowledge, a means of inquiring into problems of ontology, ethics, and politics that are not themselves formulated as exchanges. But to use the coin as a lens on such problems entails construing them in terms of improvident contingency, in terms not just of materiality but of materialism as the antithesis of the ideal, and in terms of force. It is to address the world as Mammon would address it. It's the sense that the monetary object is not epistemologically neutral, and cannot therefore be ethically neutral, that my writers share with the commonwealths-men whose analyses they interrogate, and that distinguishes them from the history of political economy to come—from the thought experiment that construes the polis as an *oikos*, and which we have long since forgotten to be a thought experiment. Pierce Penniless strives to define himself as monetary lack in order to imagine and encompass monetary repletion—to think as Mammon would think. Pierce's supplication is an earnest attempt on his part to give the devil his due. But "I believe [the devil] will cun thee little thanks for it," says the demonic Knight of the Post (118), for Nashe's wild, exuberant irony demonstrates that the devil's due is not quite, but almost, nothing.

* * *

In this book I have been engaging literary representations of money from a perspective that is uneconomic, in two senses: first, in the sense that "economy," as the discursive object of "economics," is a concept historically unavailable to my writers; second, in the sense that the texts I've chosen to work with articulate money in contexts that do not appear, even to our eyes, to be economic ones. An impeccably materialist maneuver to address at least the second uneconomy presented by these materials would be to treat the manifestation of money outside contexts of getting and spending as an ideological *symptom*: one that suggests that structures of exchange implicitly order many more behaviors in early modern English culture than those of getting and spending, and one that betrays an anxiety on the part of the writers that the list of behaviors that are being turned into what we would call economic relations is growing. This would imply an answer to the first uneconomy as well, by positing an inability fully to comprehend these developments within sixteenth-century ideology, which simply lacks the proper explanatory frame which economy will make available for our retrospection.

It is certainly true that such historical transformations were sweeping through English society at the turn of the seventeenth century—the forging of a national market centered in London, the installation of a fashion system for conspicuous consumption, and the commodification of money itself in the development of credit instruments. But it's also true that contemporary writers were perfectly capable of recognizing and articulating these changes as historical and ideological process—consider the many comparisons throughout the city comedy between the rustic, unsophisticated past and the urban, commodified present of their settings, which is marked as early as Robert Wilson's *Three Ladies of London* (1584), "Wherein is notablie declared and set foorth, how by the meanes of lucar [i.e., lucre], love and conscience is so corrupted, that the one is married to dissimulation, the other fraught with all abhomination."[15] That being the case, reading these extra-economic appearances of money as symptoms of something directly incomprehensible and inexpressible seems inadequate. But neither do these instances seem only satiric and negative, positing a simple pretense that these contexts and relations are not those of exchange for the sake of exposing it as an ideological mystification. Such a reading, I've argued—one that insists upon the smug demonstration of exchange value as the truth of any material relation—is to think as Mammon himself would have us think.

I too argue that the scope of money's meaning is made evident by representing money outside the context of exchange. But I maintain that, rather than demystifying those contexts as being only really exchanges, these appearances of money show the early modern coin to manifest a spectrum of meanings to the social and material worlds that are tenuously yoked in its scope. It is these meanings that are truths of the Renaissance coin, and its exchange value is a provisional means by which they are made manifest, not an end in itself. The paradigm of mystification-demystification is interior to exchange value, a game that Mammon plays with himself; it has no relation to the truths of the world through which Mammon happens to circulate, however forcefully Mammon may assert himself to be revealing the truth of the world in manifesting exchange value in its objects.

If modern critics are more apt to heed the Renaissance's Mammon on this score than I think his authors were, that is nevertheless understandable; in his claims to demystification, Mammon seems to be telling us a thing about value that we moderns expect to hear. As denizens of capital, we hear Mammon as if he were speaking our native language, expressing what we experience as real in the present. In the first chapters of *Capital,* Marx analyzes exchange value as a delusion, but one which endows itself with the appearance of reality through its reification in the commodity-fetish—the phenomenon that is characteristic of capital, and through which capital proceeds to realize itself as the ideological-material totality that defines modern experience. The relations of mystification and demystification, secrecy and disclosure, ideology and economy, are overdetermined in capital: each is integral to the other, the circuit *between* them is the closed system of our mode of production.

In insisting on the historical validity of "commonwealth," I'm identifying "economy" itself as a historicized feature of our capitalist mode of production. The postulates of economy—the varying scarcity and desirability of different commodities which at once enforce and devalue the labor required to produce them, and the ruthless competition to consume those commodities—are as integral to capital as is the cyclical extraction of surplus value. From the fully developed perspective of capitalist economy, the values of "commonwealth" are what's delusional—either historical misapprehensions of the truths of economy in the pre-economized past, or escapist, nostalgic-utopian fantasies on the part of capital's critics in the present. But the values of commonwealth *were true*, even axiomatic, to sixteenth-century Englishmen and women.[16] They did not necessarily *work*, in terms of determining and accounting for material conditions; I have traced the ways in which commonwealth's values were failing to work, as occasions for the disruptive appearances of Mammon within the systems of those values. But the relations of all ideologies to material conditions are overdetermined. Even if we were to define the truth of the world merely as its materiality, no ideology can be sufficient to determinately express that truth, as ideology and materiality constantly rewrite each other. The reason that capitalist ideology seems better able to account for the truths of economy is that each depends for its validation upon the other, not that economy has in itself a privileged status in inscribing a transhistorical truth of material relations.

Commonwealth, then, is *what value was like* before the rise of economy. Commonwealth's Mammon represents, on the one hand, the awareness that these present truths of value need not be always and everywhere true, but are instead fragile, requiring a constant defense from the contingent and chthonic forces of history; thus Mammon appears as a demonic invader from the future, a future that looks to our own ideological solipsism very like the present of capital. But this Mammon also represents an occasion to define what is worth preserving in those values, given their susceptibility to ruin in time. This definition works not only in reactive contradistinction to Mammon, but—more importantly, I think—in the way that Mammon's own existence really depends upon the existing structures of commonwealth, no matter how much he himself may aspire to unmake them in order to manifest himself as an autochthonous or overdetermined futurity. It's in this way that Mammon is the vehicle for manifesting an ontological ground for both the ethics and the politics of the commonwealth: he is the means by which social interactions and material ones may be understood as different instances of a continuous system of values, and we can tell this is so by how nakedly he resents performing this task, and instead seeks to redefine the world through which he circulates in terms of his own instrumentality. My writers do not articulate Mammon simply to affirm the ideological coherence of commonwealth. By the 1590s, it's simply too late for that, as commonwealth is visibly reactionary and visibly disintegrating; and affirming ideological coherence is not in any case something poetics is very good at (however hard it may assert itself to be trying). Rather, Mammon's aspirations to an ersatz hegemony work to manifest what might be saved, and what is yet worth saving, among the ruins of commonwealth.

Mammon is prescient: he seems to us to address early modernity with the voice of capital, and it may be that capital has realized his historical character beyond his own wildest dreams. But he cannot prove the economy of capital to be a transhistorical truth, either the truth of materiality or the truth of value (much less that those two truths are identical). Economy was not true of the sixteenth century, even if retrospectively the sixteenth century now seems fully explicable in economic terms, as an economy left defective by its own ignorance of itself. Nor, Marx guides us in hoping, will economy remain true beyond the future horizon of capital's history. Should history transform itself to leave capital behind, there might no longer be a demon who plays hide-and-seek with matter, pretending to hide himself inside things in order that we may find him there, constantly revealing himself as if he were the truth of each thing. Instead of the constant play of ostensible secrecy and delusive disclosure that is the operation of exchange value, we could experience the transparency of value that Marx ascribes to the immediacy of use. I'm not sure what that ultra-economic experience of value would be like, of course. In contemplating the historical boundedness of economy, I have turned to modern analyses of value that present themselves as para-economic: Bataille's assertion of the "general economy" beyond the ideologically determined bounds of what he calls the "restricted economy," which is economy as we know it, and from within which the general economy appears ecstatic, horrific, and feculent; Simmel's formulation of a "philosophy of money" discrete from the discipline of economics, which comes to assert what we might call a desire theory of value, one which seeks to evade the ineluctability of the labor theory of value that Marx finds to be the incompletely mystified ground of capital. Mostly, though, I have relied on the fact that the two generations of brilliant men whose writings I've studied—from Smith, Latimer, and Heywood (not to mention Gresham and Burghley) to Spenser, Marlowe, Shakespeare, and Donne—simply did not require economy in their efforts to account for the mutually determining relations of individuals to the social and material worlds. Mammon may have tried to tell them his delusive secrets, to prophesy economy. But in listening to him they chose to hear other values, other truths.

# Appendix: Tudor Monetary Units

Tudor money was understood in two forms, coinage and money of account. The latter was both immaterial and absolute; coins, conversely, were minted in a bewildering variety of denominations relative to the money of account, and could be revalued in that relation by proclamation of the Crown. Thus the debased issue of the late 1540s was declared in May 1551 to be cried down by 25%, so that a shilling coin was worth only nine pence, and then to 50% that same October. Coins did not show their names, much less express their exchange value; they expected to be recognized by the type before the value in money of account could be adduced. (This poses a difficulty to us, but was straightforward enough to those who handled the various coins on a daily basis; we don't need to read "five cents" before knowing what a nickel is worth.)

The denominations of **account** were:

1 pound = 20 shillings = 240 pence.
1 mark = 13 s. 4 d. = 160 pence.
1 shilling = 12 pence.
1 penny = 4 farthings.

**Gold** coins were minted in two different finenesses, crown gold (22 carat) and angel gold (23 carats 3 1/2 grains), into parallel denominations with different stamps. One or the other would be in favor for production at the Mint at particular times, for reasons not well explained, but both remained in circulation throughout the reign of Elizabeth. In the 1590s, gold coins were valued as follows:

angel: 10 shillings.
ryal or royal: 10 shillings (crown gold).

noble: 6s. 8d. (80 d.; crown gold).
half-angel: 5 shillings.
crown: 5 shillings.
half-crown: 2s. 6d. (30 d.).

No coin worth a complete pound was in circulation, though Elizabeth did mint a very few gold sovereigns, enormous gold disks worth thirty shillings, at the beginning of her reign, apparently as display pieces. Angel denominations had on their face the image of the archangel Michael slaying the dragon Antichrist, not a portrait of the monarch; this was a holdover from the medieval coinage, and even the higher fineness of the gold in these coins seems to have been understood as an archaism, a resolution to hold to old-fashioned standards of purity.

**Silver** coins, the vast bulk of the circulating medium, were sterling under Elizabeth (except for a base coinage for Ireland late in the reign, which was not legal tender in England and Wales, though English troops in Ireland were paid with it). The value relation of gold to silver by mass was understood to be one to twelve, though the relative price of both as commodities varied over time. The following denominations were most often minted under Elizabeth:

(silver) crown: 5 shillings.
(silver) half-crown: 2s. 6d.
shilling.
sixpence.
groat: 4 pence.
penny.
three-farthing.
half-penny.

Since the same amount of labor went into making a coin regardless of its value, the Mint found it unprofitable to produce small change; despite laws mandating that a certain proportion of groats and smaller pieces be minted from every hundredweight of silver, there remained a problematic shortage of small coins, exacerbated by the fact that Elizabeth's refusal to issue a base coinage in even the lowest denominations meant that those coins had to be minuscule, since a ha'penny was not very much silver at all. The shortage was compensated for by the habit of letting debts accumulate until they reached an amount worth resolving, as Craig Muldrew has described in *The Economy of Obligation: The Culture of Credit and Social Relations in Early Modern England*

(New York: St. Martin's, 1998), and also by the issuing of tokens—an informal, purely nominal base currency of local circulation—by businesses such as alehouses, and from time to time even by municipalities distant from the Mint, such as Bristol, though the central government frowned upon this practice.

# NOTES

## INTRODUCTION

1. *The Faerie Queene*, ed. Thomas P. Roche, Jr. (New York: Penguin, 1978): 2.7.8; further citations of this edition will be given parenthetically in the text.
2. For the emergence of the comparison of money to writing, simultaneous to the emergence of money, see Marc Shell, *The Economy of Literature* (Baltimore: Johns Hopkins UP, 1978), which I discuss directly below.
3. As I'll discuss below, the disciplinary history of economics is most often understood to begin in the next fiscal crisis following that of the "price revolution," the trade depression of the early seventeenth century.
4. The seventeenth-century populist poet John Taylor narrates the circulation of a shilling as shuttling eccentrically across normative social boundaries of all kinds in *A Shilling, or, The travailes of twelve-pence* (London, 1621); for an analysis of this text, see Deborah Valenze, *The Social Life of Money in the English Past* (Cambridge: Cambridge UP, 2006): 73–79. As I remark below, this discursive ubiquity actually overrepresents the material availability of silver and gold coinage; scarcity is built into a precious coinage just as a notional ubiquity is.
5. *The Merchant of Venice* 3.2.103–104, in *The Riverside Shakespeare*, ed. G. Blakemore Evans (Boston: Houghton Mifflin, 1974); further citations of Shakespeare will be to this edition, and will be given parenthetically in the text.
6. Contemplating the ways in which the inscribed surface contributed to the meaning of early modern inscriptions, Juliet Fleming describes the English Renaissance as "an intellectual moment... which lacked a systematic bifurcation between real and thought objects, and consequently apprehended matter not as that which is deprived of meaning but as a principle of structure that underpins all meaning" (*Graffiti and the Writing Arts of Early Modern England* [Philadelphia: U of Pennsylvania P, 2001]: 21).
7. I imagine these preeconomic writers as in effect concurring with the premise of Georg Simmel, who explicates the difference between his extra-economic project in *The Philosophy of Money* and a project within the discipline of economics in these terms:

   > Not a single line of these investigations is meant to be a statement about economics. That is to say, the phenomena of valuation and purchase, of

exchange and the means of exchange, of the forms of production and the values of possession, which economics views from *one* standpoint, are here viewed from another.... [A]n exchange can be treated as a psychological fact, or as one that derives from the history of morals or even as an aesthetic fact. Even when it is considered to be an economic fact, it does not reach the end of a cul-de-sac; rather, in this guise it becomes the object of philosophical study, which examines its pre-conditions in non-economic concepts and facts and its consequences for non-economic values and relationships.

(*The Philosophy of Money*, trans. Tom Bottomore and David Frisby [London: Routledge and Kegan Paul, 1990]: 54–55)

8. *OED* "Mammon" 1.
9. The interpretation of the parable depends very much upon whether we are to understand its tropic force as pivoting upon the concept of "mammon," of "faith," or of "friend." If the steward's allegiance to Mammon is itself exemplary, it must be so by means of metaphor: that just as the steward covets and withholds material wealth, so should the faithful seek out and store up the friends whom they can make by deeds of charity and justice (which would be symmetrically converse to the literal behavior of the steward). As David Hawkes has pointed out to me, the force of the metaphor would be to relocate "riches" from the material to the semiotic realm: that is, there is a true and righteous mammon, but one that exists not in the world but as metaphoric discourse. If the parable is to be interpreted according to the explanatory sentence "He that is faithful in that which is least is faithful also in much: and he that is unjust in the least is unjust also in much," however, then the relation at stake would not be the comparison between the steward and the "faithful" with respect to "mammon," but the continuity of faith between "least" and "much"—a relation not of metaphor, but of metonymy. Tyndale worries in *That fayth the mother of all good workes iustifieth us before we ca[n] bringe forth anye good worke* (Antwerp, 1528) that the apparent endorsement of "the wicked Mammon" in this parable "may have enforced to draw the people from the true fayth and from puttinge their trust in the trueth of Goddes promyses and in the merites and deseruinge of his Christe oure lorde" (Fo.i.r). He argues that the justification of the "right believing," and the perdition of the unbelieving, nullify the apparent righteousness or unrighteousness of material phenomena such as works and the means by which they are enacted, rather than the latter standing in a metaphoric, antitypical relation to the former: "For vnto the right belevinge shall all thinges be confortable and vnto consolacyon at that terryble daye [of judgment]. And contrary wyse vnto the vnbelevinge all thynge shalbe vnto desperacyon and confucyon" (Fo.xiiii.r). The "friends" of the parable are for Tyndale the poor to whom the justified man would give his wealth, manifesting and signifying his faith metonymically. Conversely, Lambert Daneau brackets the reference of the parable to salvation (whether through metaphor or

metonymy) in order to construe it literally, as referring directly to earthly sociability. He inscribes the parable into the privileged Renaissance discourse of disinterested friendship:

> As touching that sentence of our Sauiour Christ, *Make you friendes of the vnrighteous Mammon*, it is not to bee otherwise vnderstood, then that we must learne to bestowe our wealth and money better, then the common sorte of men doe: namely vpon the poore and needie, which may comme[n]d vs vnto God by their prayers: and not vpon the rich and wealthie, whom we commonly (notwithstanding) are more readie to pleasure and benefite. To conclude therefore with *Cicero*: Where is this holy *Amitie* & godly *Friendship*, if the partie whom wee professe to loue and choose to our friende, bee not truely, sincerely, vnfainedly, and onely for himselfe and by himselfe, ardently, affectionatly, and hartily loued? (*True and Christian Friendshippe*, tr. 1586: B5v-r).

10. In Matthew (26:7–15) and Mark (14:3–11), Judas's decision to betray Christ follows immediately after the anointing of Christ's feet by a woman "with very precious ointment," to which "the disciples" (Mat.) or "some" of the disciples (Mk.) objected, saying that the ointment should be sold to raise money for the poor (i.e., via the common purse). In John's account of the Last Supper, the other apostles assume that Christ's command to Judas, "That thou doest, do quickly," must refer to some errand of monetary exchange: "For some of them thought, because Judas had the bag, that Jesus had said unto him, Buy those things that we have need of against the feast; or, that he should give something to the poor" (13:27–29, KJV). John's telling of the Last Supper story thus singles out two of the apostles who are understood by the others to enjoy privileged relations to Jesus, to which the rest are not party: the evangelist himself, "the disciple whom Jesus loved," whom Peter enjoins to ask Jesus about the betrayal to come; and Judas, who by virtue (so to speak) of bearing "the bag," has a set of everyday tasks associated with the bag which are not the other apostles' business—and which prevent the other apostles, save perhaps its future narrator John, from understanding the nature of the conversation between Jesus and Judas.
11. Like the Pharisee-enraging parable of the unjust steward, "They could not take hold of his words" is unique to Luke; the accounts of the episode in the synoptic gospels are otherwise nearly identical (cp. Matthew 22:15–22 and Mark 12:13–17).
12. For the complexities which the Renaissance found modeled in Paul as eschatological theologian and temporal citizen, see Julia Reinhard Lupton, *Citizen-Saints: Shakespeare and Political Theology* (Chicago: U of Chicago P, 2005): 21–48.
13. For iconoclasm in the literature of post-Reformation England, see Ernest Gilman, *Iconoclasm and Poetry in the English Reformation: Down went Dagon* (Chicago: U

of Chicago P, 1986), and Kenneth Gross, *Spenserian Poetics: Idolatry, Iconoclasm, and Magic* (Ithaca, N.Y.: Cornell UP, 1986); for the category of idolatry in analysis of monetary practice, see David Hawkes, *Idols of the Marketplace: Idolatry and Commodity Fetishism in English Literature, 1580–1680* (New York: Palgrave, 2001).

14. In Aristotle the relation of matter to form is teleological and thus temporal; see *De Anima* Book 2, chapter 1 (412a ff), and my chapter 1.
15. The parable of the talents appears in Mat. 25:14–30; Christ's affirmation of the widow's donation of her mites as exemplary appears in Luke 21:1–4; the parable of the special value of the lost piece of silver relative to those that had not been lost appears in Luke 15:8–10, where it introduces the larger parable of the prodigal son.
16. Simmel, *Philosophy of Money*, 59–62.
17. Yates, *Error Misuse Failure: Object Lessons from the English Renaissance* (Minneapolis: U of Minnesota P, 2003): xix.
18. For the uniqueness of the pace and scope of the sixteenth-century inflation in the history of British prices, see D. M. Palliser, *The Age of Elizabeth: England under the Later Tudors, 1547–1603, Social and Economic History of England*, vol. 5, 2nd ed. (London: Longman, 1992): 152–186. For its traumatic effects upon the everyday users of English money, see Keith Wrightson, *Earthly Necessities: Economic Lives in Early Modern Britain* (New Haven: Yale UP, 2000): 115-31, and Andrea Finkelstein, *The Grammar of Profit: The Price Revolution in Intellectual Context* (Amsterdam: Brill, 2006). For its pan-European character, see F. P. Braudel and F. Spooner, "Prices in Europe from 1450 to 1750," in *The Cambridge Economic History of Europe*, vol. 4, eds. E. E. Rich and C. H. Wilson (Cambridge: Cambridge UP, 1967): 378–486.
19. I don't mean to imply that medieval money was a simpler kind of object than sixteenth-century money—the two are nearly the same in most respects, in their material composition and production as well as in their iconography—but only to emphasize that the major difference between the two was that sixteenth-century money was subject to sustained inflation in a way that the money of previous generations had not been. For the sophistication and complexity of medieval monetary theories, see Odd Langholm, *Economics in the Medieval Schools : Wealth, Exchange, Value, Money, and Usury According to the Paris Theological Tradition, 1200–1350* (Leiden: E. J. Brill, 1992); for the historical relations between those theories and political and material conditions, see Peter Spufford, *Money and Its Use in Medieval Europe* (Cambridge: Cambridge UP, 1988); for the continuities of thought joining the analyses of Aquinas and Oresme to those of the sixteenth century, see Barry Gordon, *Economic Analysis before Adam Smith: Hesiod to Lessius* (London: Macmillan, 1975).
20. [Sir Thomas Smith, attr.], *A Discourse of the Commonweal of This Realm of England*, ed. Mary Dewar (Charlottesville: UP of Virginia, 1969): 38; further citations of this edition will be given parenthetically in the text.

21. *Respublica: An Interlude for Christmas 1553, Attributed to Nicholas Udall*, ed. W. W. Greg (London: Oxford UP, 1952): 4.4.1076.
22. Writing in 1549, Smith did not appreciate the Europe-wide character of the price revolution; the suggestion that other nations are reaping profits from England's crisis is made several times in the original text. The revised text, published in 1581, incorporates continental perspectives on the inflation, as I discuss below.
23. Cited in R. H. Tawney and Eileen Power, eds., *Tudor Economic Documents: Being Select Documents Illustrating the Economic and Social History of Tudor England*, 3 vols. (London: Longmans, Green and Co., 1924, 1953, and 1963), vol. 2: 179.
24. Harrison, *An Historicall description of the Iland of Britaine, with a briefe rehersall of the nature and qualities of the people of England, and such commodities as are to be found in the same,* in vol. 1 of Holinshed et al., *The First and Second Volumes of Chronicles* ([London], 1586): 218. The "mint price" is the price paid by the mint in coins for an ounce of fine (unalloyed) bullion; the higher that price, the less silver is present in the coins returned to the supplier. (It should be noted that the figures Harrison is using cannot distinguish between inflation in the commodity price of pure silver and debasement of the coinage, but the latter managed to outstrip the former in the period he describes.) I will explain the transactions between the mint and suppliers of silver more fully below.
25. Ibid., 218.
26. Nicholas Mayhew, *Sterling: the History of a Currency* (New York: John Wiley and Sons, 1999): 47; Whitney R. D. Jones, *The Tudor Commonwealth 1529–1559* (London: Athlone, 1970): 135.
27. As J. D. Gould argues, "More or less complete knowledge of the whole truth concerning the coinage could... never be concealed for long... it seems impossible to invoke deception as a satisfactory explanation of the apparent readiness of the supply of silver to respond to the step-by-step increases in mint price which... were promulgated over those years" (*The Great Debasement: Currency and the Economy in Mid-Tudor England* [Oxford: Clarendon, 1970]: 14). Stephen Deng analyzes the debasement as a limit case for the power of the sovereign prerogative in *Coinage and State Formation in Early Modern English Literature* (New York: Palgrave Macmillan, 2011). I regret not being able to engage this excellent book more directly, as it came to me when the present volume was already in proofs.
28. Cited and translated in Thomas Joseph Pettigrew, ed., *Chronicles of the Tombs: A Select Collection of Epitaphs* (London: H. G. Bohn, 1857): 310–311. (I have emended Pettigrew's transcription, which gives *redacta* for the *reducta* attested by other transcribers.) James had Elizabeth's body moved from the vault of Henry VII to this freestanding tomb in 1606, along with Mary Tudor's. Elizabeth never entertained any suggestion that she might debase even her smallest change, despite the practical advantages that such a decision would yield (pennies and three-farthing pieces of sterling silver were so miniscule as to be inconvenient to handle, and difficult to manufacture, so that coins smaller than a groat were in particularly short supply). When faced with such proposals under Charles I, political opposi-

tion still recalled Elizabeth's example, and in at least one case cited an extraordinarily impassioned ancedote about William Cecil's opinions on the topic:

> This made the L. Treasurer Burleigh in 1573. when some Projectors had set on foot a matter of this nature, to tell them that they were worthy to suffer Death for attempting to put so great a Dishonour on the Queen, and Detriment and Discontent upon the People.

(From materials collated in the pamphlet "A Speech Made by Sir Robert Cotton . . . Touching the Alteration of Coin" as emerging from a debate before the Privy Council on September 2, 1626, published 1651; reprinted in *Scarce and Valuable Tracts on Money*, J. R. McCulloch, ed. [London: Political Economy Club,1856]: 121–141, esp. 138. Gould is impressed by Cotton's success in arguing against debasement under the circumstances under which this debate was put forward by the King: "even Charles I, in the extremity of his need for revenue, staged a debate on the merits and demerits of debasement before resorting to that expedient, and the outcome of it was a decision to look elsewhere for satisfaction of his needs" [*The Great Debasement*, 1].)

29. For the historical background, and the minimal effectiveness, of the laws that declared offenses against the coinage to be treason, see chapter 2.
30. C. E. Challis, *The Tudor Coinage* (Manchester: Manchester UP, 1978): 61 (the date is approximate).
31. Philip Grierson, *Numismatics* (Oxford: Oxford UP, 1975): 32. As Grierson notes, the imitation of Roman coinage in modern coinage did have as an intermediary form the larger-format portrait medallion, first developed by Pisanello in 1438 for the visiting Byzantine Emperor John VIII Paleologus and then for a variety of Italian princes and personages (175).
32. I discuss the iconography of the angel in chapter 4. Issues in "new gold" (or "crown gold"), unlike those in angel gold, featured either the face or a full-body portrait of the monarch on the pieces known as the "crown," "noble," and "ryal" (or "royal"); crown gold was slightly less fine than angel gold when first issued, and was subject to some further debasement under Henry, but never to the degree that the silver was. Gold comprised less than 3% of the volume of sixteenth-century mint output by weight (Challis, 232—I have converted his figures from £ value to relative mass by dividing by 11, as an approximate average relation of silver price to gold price over the century), and its use was largely a phenomenon of international mercantile transactions rather than of everyday domestic business; each piece of gold coinage was handled with such precision, always tested and weighed in each exchange, that the minting prince could not effectively manipulate its exchange value, and therefore it offered less opportunity for exploitation in the Debasement (Gould, *The Great Debasement*, 17–18).
33. "The relationship of image and value . . . ," writes Kevin Sharpe, "was a delicate one that worked in both directions: if the royal portrait was what guaranteed the

coin's value or worth, decline in the market value of a coin might well also debase the royal brand and image, the signs of royal authority" (*Selling the Tudor Monarchy: Authority and Image in Sixteenth-Century England* [New Haven: Yale UP, 2009]: 155).

34. *Tudor Economic Documents*, vol. 2: 179; see the editors' footnote on this page for the probable dating of Heywood's epigrams on the coinage, which did not appear in print until 1562, when the coins to which they refer had been recalled. Whitney R. D. Jones locates Heywood's commonwealth ideals as emerging from the circle of More and Elyot (*The Tudor Commonwealth*, 24–26); he was a connection of More's by marriage. Mary Thomas Crane characterizes Heywood's epigrammatic voice as deliberately provocative, repudiating the sententious and learned tone of prior English epigrammatists, from More to Heywood's contemporary Crowley: "Heywood disliked their poetic appropriation of secular moral authority and offered instead a homely, vernacular, secular epigram with a flippant, anti-authoritarian stance"; she has in mind a resistance to poetic rather than political authority, but both dimensions seem present in these pointed lines (Crane, "*Intret Cato*: Authority and the Epigram in Sixteenth-Century England," in *Renaissance Genres: Essays on Theory, History, and Interpretation*, ed. Barbara Kiefer Lewalski [Cambridge, Mass.: Harvard UP, 1986]: 158–188, esp. 183; and see also Tom Betteredge, *Literature and Politics in the English Reformation* [Manchester: Manchester UP, 2004]: 140–149, who links Heywood's populist tone more directly to confessional controversy). James Holstun reads Heywood's allegorical magnum opus, *The Spider and the Flie*, as a manifesto for commonwealth as a "post-feudal but anti-capitalist mode of production," a road not taken by history ("The Spider, the Fly, and the Commonwealth: Merie John Heywood and Agrarian Class Struggle," *ELH* 71.1 [Spring 2004]: 53-88, esp. 56).
35. Here "teston" refers to the shilling, though by Harrison's time and Shakespeare's it denoted the sixpence.
36. The most comprehensive account of the practices involved in the Debasement is Challis, *The Tudor Coinage*, 81–111 and passim. J. D. Gould, *The Great Debasement*, offers a somewhat different (and, to my mind, unnecessarily complex) rationale for the success of the Crown in foisting the policy upon the nation. For the desperate circumstances of the Crown's finances that drove the reiterations of debasement, see Jennifer Loach, *Edward VI* (New Haven: Yale UP, 1999), esp. 108–112.
37. *Tudor Economic Documents*, vol. 2: 179.
38. The play *Respublica*, performed at Mary's accession and generally attributed to Nicholas Udall, refers at greater length to the coinage of bells under Edward (op. cit., 4.4.1075–1084); see also n. 46 below.
39. See Whitney R. D. Jones, *The Tudor Commonwealth*, esp. 13–23, and Thomas Meyer, *Thomas Starkey and the Commonweal: Humanist Politics and Religion in the Age of Henry VIII* (Oxford: Oxford UP, 1989), esp. 139–168, for the situation of this discourse within the context of medieval political theory; for the role of hu-

manist principles and training in shaping it, see Quentin Skinner, *The Foundations of Modern Political Thought* (Cambridge: Cambridge UP, 1998), vol. 1: 213–243.

40. Starkey, *A Dialogue between Reginald Pole and Thomas Lupset*, ed. Kathleen M. Burton (London: Chatto & Windus, 1948): 22.
41. In sixteenth-century usage "common weal" or "commonwealth" not only refers to the native peculiarities of English polity, but also renders the Latin *respublica* when Roman authorities are paraphrased by my writers. The politico-philological difference between Elyot's and Starkey's contemporaneous texts regarding this usage is striking. Starkey uses forms of "common" as frequently as possible in his dialogue, as verb (with the various senses "talk," "impart," or "share"), adjective, and noun; Elyot announces his hostility to the word on the first page of *The Boke named the Gouernour*, insisting that the proper usage should be "publike weal." While rejecting the semantic flexibility and communitarian potential exploited by Starkey in "common," Elyot affirms the propertied resonances of "weal":

    > the worde *Res*, hath divers significations, & dothe nat only bitoken that, that is called a thynge, whiche is distincte from a persone, but also signifieth a state, condition, substance, and profit. In our olde vulgare, profite is called weale: And it is called a welthy contraye, wherin is all thyng that is profitable: And he is a welthy man, that is riche in money and substance. (Elyot, *The Boke named the Gouernour* [London: 1531]: A.v-r).

42. Manley, *Literature and Culture in Early Modern London* (Cambridge: Cambridge UP, 1995): 71, 74.
43. Holstun defines sixteenth-century commonwealth ideology as presenting a "monarcho-populist alliance: a post-feudal but anti-capitalist mode of production that attempted to use the resources of a newly centralized Tudor monarchy to maintain and even extend the relative independence enjoyed by free English small producers during their fifteenth-century golden age" (56).
44. Subtitle of Bernard Mandeville, *The Fable of the Bees* (1714).
45. Jones, *The Tudor Commonwealth*, 32. Josiah was a reforming king of Judah (2 Kings 22–23) who at the age of eighteen purged the kingdom of idolatry and restored the ancient rites of the Temple. Loach, *Edward VI*, challenges the hagiographic account of Edward as a precociously gifted, hyperprotestant disciple of Latimer; she portrays him as very much his father's son, an enthusiast of tournaments and military display. But that idealization, later popularized by Foxe in *Acts and Monuments* (1563), was evidently already in play during the protectorship of Somerset.
46. Jones, *The Tudor Commonwealth*, 23. In the allegorical fiction of Robert Crowley's Edwardian pamphlet *Philargyrie of Great Britayne* (1551), the money-hungry giant Philargyrie presides both over the monastic exploitations of the old Catholic regime and the venal expropriations of the new, ostensibly Protestant

one, via a rotating cast of politicians who serve him; only in the story's denouement is the King articulated as the master who corrects those politicians, and up till the articulation of the goodness of the King, Philargyrie has appeared to be sovereign. A similar bifurcation of implicitly sovereign interest from explicitly sovereign righteousness appears in the interlude *Respublica*, staged at Mary's accession, in which the widow Respublica represents an apparently autonomous commonwealth misled by hypocritical vices: Avarice (who calls himself "Policy"), Insolence ("Authority"), Adulation ("Honesty"), and Oppression ("Reformation"). It is "Reformation" who claims the dubious credit of debasing the coinage, as well as that of suppressing the wealth of the monasteries. The play's denouement, like that of *Philargyrie*, produces the previously absent monarch to be the corrector of "Policy." For a more thorough comparison of these two texts, see Christopher Warley, "Reforming the Reformers: Robert Crowley and Nicholas Udall," in *The Oxford Handbook of Tudor Literature, 1485–1603*, eds. Mike Pincombe and Cathy Shrank (Oxford: Oxford UP, 2009): 273–290.

47. For writers such as Henry William Spiegel (*The Growth of Economic Thought*, 3rd ed. [Durham, N.C.: Duke UP, 1991]: 84), Neal Wood (*Foundations of Political Economy: Some Early Tudor Views on State and Society* [Berkeley: U of California P, 1994]), and Jonathan Gil Harris (*Sick Economies: Drama, Mercantilism and Disease in Shakespeare's England* [Philadelphia: U of Penn. P, 2004]: 37–38), who are inclined to regard the *Discourse* as protomercantilist, it is precisely this sophistication of a national analysis that puts the dialogue ahead of its time. Joan Thirsk and Cathy Shrank both note that Smith's Doctor prefers to prescribe positive incentives rather than punitive ones for individuals to act in the commonwealth interest, as for example to pay landowners not to enclose arable land (and not, as most other midcentury reformers might demand, to punish those who do), so that, as Shrank puts it, "self-seeking is harnessed to benefit the commonweal" (*Writing the Nation in Reformation England 1530–1580* [Oxford: Oxford UP, 2004]: 156; and see Thirsk, *Economic Policy and Projects: the Development of a Consumer Society in Early Modern England* [Oxford: Clarendon, 1978]: 9). Jennifer Richards, however, cautions against perceiving Smith's treatise as anticipating a properly economistic validation of self-interest; she refers his articulation of monetary incentives toward the communal interest instead to Craig Muldrew's portrait of early modern commerce as "sociable" rather than atomizing, as a demonstration of "the quite new perception that commerce might create, and not just endanger, social trust" (*Rhetoric and Courtliness in Early Modern Literature* [Cambridge: Cambridge UP, 2003]: 88). Following Richards, I would define the *Discourse* as at the forefront of its time rather than as ahead of its time.
48. For the evidence for this ascription, and for the public career of Smith, see Mary Dewar's Introduction to her edition of the *Discourse* (ix–xxvi).
49. For Smith's use (here and in many other of his writings) of the dialogue form as epitomizing his "belief in counsel as the proper means of policy-making and political intervention," see Shrank, *Writing the Nation*, 143–181, esp. 157.

50. Marx subjects the absolutist position voiced here by the Knight (which he cites as manifested in Montesquieu and two other French authorities) to withering contempt: "Long before the economists, lawyers made fashonable the idea that money is a mere symbol, and that the value of the precious metals is purely imaginary. This they did in the sycophantic service of the royal power, supporting the right of the latter to debase the coinage, during the whole of the Middle Ages. . . ." (*Capital,* vol. I, tr. Ben Fowkes [New York: Penguin, 1990]: 185 n.11).
51. *Discourse,* 112–113. The Doctor cites an army camp as an appropriate venue for leather money, as the emperor Frederick II so paid his troops at the seige of Faenza, promising to redeem the leather for silver later.
52. As the Doctor enquires,

    > Do you not see that our coin is discredited already, especially amongst strangers which before desired to serve us before all other nations at our needs for the goodness of our coin? And now they let us have nothing from them but only [in exchange] for our commodities[,] as wool, fells, tallow, butter, cheese, tin, and lead. And where beforetime they were wont to bring us for the same either good gold or silver or else as necessary commodities again, now they send us other such trifles . . . as glasses, galley pots, tennis balls, papers, girdles, brooches, owches, buttons, dials, or such like wares that stand them in no charge or use—or else, if it be true that I have heard . . . they send us brass [i.e., foreign-made counterfeits of debased English coin] for our treasures of gold and silver and for our said commodities. (77)

    For the insistent differentiation among "treasure," "commodity," and "trifle" in sixteenth-century analyses of England's international trade, see Jeffrey Knapp, *An Empire Nowhere: England, America, and Literature from* Utopia *to* The Tempest (Berkeley: U of California P, 1992).
53. *Sermons by Hugh Latimer, Sometime Bishop of Worcester* (London: J. M. Dent & Co., [1926]): 81. Latimer had been stripped of his bishopric in the Catholic reaction under Henry VIII (1539) and never regained high office; he appeared before the court on this occasion in the capacity of celebrity preacher, giving six Lenten sermons over the course of March and April. Like Smith and many others of the "commonwealths-men," for whom he served as the most visible leader, Latimer seems to have enjoyed the personal patronage of Somerset, though the Lord Protector's sympathy for their ideals and goals was only rarely translated into consistent and effective policy during his tempest-tossed administration (W. Jones, *The Tudor Commonwealth,* 31–40).
54. Latimer, *Sermons,* 86. Deuteronomy 17 dwells on the elevated civic authority of priests and Levites in legal judgments (8–13; verse 12 reads "And the man that will do presumptuously, and will not hearken unto the priest that standeth to minister there before the LORD thy God, or unto the judge, shall die: and thou shalt put

away the evil from Israel," though even Latimer is not quite bold enough to recite this) before proceeding to circumscribe the authority of the king, with regard both to marriage ("Neither shall he multiply wives to himself," 17) and to the seizure of riches; thus Latimer's choice of text enables him to transform the rather anodyne pretext of what kind of queen the boy-king ought to marry into a far-ranging indictment of domestic policy, delivered from a sacrosanct bully pulpit.

55. Latimer, *Sermons*, 116–117.
56. The principle that "bad money drives out good" was just as familiar to Aristotle, however, and was only given that epigrammatic formulation in the nineteenth century: its identification as "Gresham's Law" recognizes the effectiveness of the financier's efforts on Elizabeth's behalf, not any innovation in theory or policy.
57. Furthermore, with the standard of fineness already diminished by 73% from sterling, by 1551 there was simply little scope for further exploitation left in the circulating medium.
58. I regret that I don't have space here to explicate the ideological status of debasement within the epicycle of the Marian religious reaction. Texts sympathetic to Mary's regime seized the opportunity to identify debasement with reformation, as the allegorical interlude *Respublica* does (see n. 46 above, and Kirk M. Fabel, "Questions of Numismatic and Linguistic Signification in the Reign of Mary Tudor," *SEL* 37.2 [Spring 1997]: 237–255); while the Protestant exile John Ponet sought to defray the force of that charge by asserting that the debasement policy orginated with the ministers of the Henrician Catholic reaction, and was (like all of England's disasters) really Stephen Gardiner's fault (*A Shorte Treatise of Politike Power, and of the true Obedience which subiectes owe to kynges and other ciuile Gouernours, with an Exhortacion to all true naturall Englishe men* [[Strasbourg?], 1556]: Fiii.v).
59. John Craig, *The Mint: A History of the London Mint from A.D. 287 to 1948* (Cambridge: Cambridge UP, 1953): 119.
60. Ibid., 123.
61. This coin represents a further development in the regime's program for the mint in that it is a milled issue; that is, it was struck not by hand but by a machine. Milling was introduced to the Tower Mint in 1560 by a Frenchman, Eloi Mestrell, imported by the Crown to modernize mint operations. At this moment the English coinage was produced by the same methods developed in the ancient Mediterranean, by placing a blank—an unminted silver disc—between two dies (the lower one embedded in an anvil) and striking the top one repeatedly with a hammer. Mestrell came to the Tower from Paris, where hammering by hand had been replaced by the screw press, a machine that converted the torque applied by several strong men hauling its arms in a circle into a single sharp and accurate strike. Mestrell's press offered to reduce the margin of error that often resulted when the dies shifted in the course of multiple hammer blows, which spoiled the coin and sent it back to the smelter; to put out coins more quickly than hammering could do; and to offer a much more precise and detailed type than was

possible to impress upon a coin by hammer blows. Unfortunately for Mestrell, the only efficiency his machine was found to deliver in practice was the last and least important, the increased detail of the type. Milling was deemed a failed experiment, and Mestrell was dismissed in 1572 (he opted to continue practicing his trade freelance, however, and was executed for counterfeiting in 1578); mechanized production did not return to the Tower until the reign of Charles I. See Challis, *The Tudor Coinage*, 19, and Burton Milligan, "Counterfeiters and Coin-Clippers in the Sixteenth and Seventeenth Centuries," *Notes and Queries* 182 (February 1942): 100–105, esp. 102. I will return to the confluence of the minting power and the police apparatus in chapter 2.

My milled sixpence is exemplary rather than typical in the quality of its image, then (as well as in its unclipped state): it represents what the regime most wanted sterling to look like, not what most sterling did look like. The difference between the experimental milled issues and the conventionally hammered coin that made up the rest of the circulating medium was evidently pronounced to Elizabethans. Sir Martin Bowes, undertreasurer of the Tower Mint, took such pride in the milled issue that he "kept £40 in new mill money in his iron chest to be distributed to the poor on the day of his death" (Challis, *The Tudor Coinage*, 17n.52). But the visibility of that difference may have been an object of consternation to those uninvolved with the manufacture of these coins: D. F. Allen and W. R. Dunstan note that a number of Elizabethan milled coins survive with an impression deliberately blunted by hammer blows, as if to impose the appearance of unexceptionality upon them ("Crosses and Crowns: A Study of Coinage in the Elizabethan Dramatists." *British Numismatic Journal* 23 [1938–1940]: 287–300). Allen and Dunstan infer that the fineness of the milled impression might have seemed so suspicious as to have reduced the coins' exchange value relative to ordinary hammered coin, or indeed to have made them uncirculable, as if counterfeit; they cite as corroboration for the possibility of a diminished exchange value the complaint of the gull Slender in *The Merry Wives of Windsor* that Pistol has robbed him of "seven groats in mill-sixpences" (1.1.155). Seven groats are worth twenty-eight pence in the money of account, a number indivisible by six. In this passage, then, are three ambiguous possibilities for the exchange value of these sixpences: 1) that Slender considered them worth only four pence apiece, the same as a groat, and had seven of the coins; 2), conversely, that Slender placed a higher value on them than their face value—seven pence—and had four; or 3) that Slender, who, "though well landed, is an idiot," can't count (4.4.86). What is certain within the passage, though, is the fact that thirty-six years after their manufacture these sixpences are still differentiable *within* the circulating medium. Not only have they endured, but so has their recognizable exceptionality; they are still money, and still at least discursively different from other money of the same face value.

62. Among the silver coinage, the double portrait of Philip and Mary under a single, floating crown was struck only on sixpences and shillings. The smaller groats,

half-groats, and pennies continued (presumably for reasons of scale) to portray the Queen alone, with her hair loose and the crown worn atop it, although the legend on them was reinscribed to include Philip's name.

63. For the sophistication and scope of the broader Elizabethan iconographic regime of which Mint production forms a part, see (inter alia) Roy Strong, *The Cult of Elizabeth: Elizabethan Portraiture and Pageantry* (Berkeley: U of California P, 1977); Louis Montrose, *The Subject of Elizabeth: Authority, Gender, Representation* (Chicago: U of Chicago P, 2006); and Kevin Sharpe, *Selling the Tudor Monarchy: Authority and Image in Sixteenth-Century England* (New Haven: Yale UP, 2009), who discusses Elizabeth's coinage in this context (404–410).
64. Keith Wrightson demonstrates, however, that although prices continued steadily to rise throughout the reign of Elizabeth, they did so at a slower rate than they had during the generation of debasement, and also at a slower rate than that suffered over the same period in neigboring Scotland, where debasement continued unchecked (*Earthly Necessities*, 130). This suggests that the recoinage was relatively effective in controlling inflation in England, even if it was unable to halt it.
65. Dewar considers the revisions to be authorial, and notes that Smith did not die until 1577 (xxv–xxvi).
66. *Discourse*, 145. The ascription of the price revolution to the influx of Spanish treasure, formulated in *La Réponse de Maistre Jean Bodin* (1568) and here making its first appearance in English, became historiographic orthodoxy that did not begin to be challenged (by theories of population growth and industrial innovation) until the twentieth century.
67. See Harris, *Sick Economies*, esp. 29–51, for the nearly simultaneous constitution and failure of the English nation as an integral and self-sufficient entity in discourse of the sixteenth century; he analyzes the troping of the commonwealth as a body politic subject to disease.
68. Hutson, *Thomas Nashe in Context* (Oxford: Clarendon, 1989): 38–54.
69. As Pierre Bourdieu declares, "Only at the end of a slow evolution tending to strip away the specifically symbolic aspect of the acts and relations of production was the economy able to constitute itself *as such*, in the objectivity of a separate universe, governed by its own rules, those of self-interested calculation, competition and exploitation; and also, much later, in 'pure' economic theory which records the social separation and the practical abstraction of which the economic *cosmos* is the product, while tacitly writing it into the principle of its object construction" (*Pascalian Meditations*, tr. Richard Nice [Stanford, Ca.: Stanford UP, 2000]: 19; italics *sic*).
70. The origin of the disciplinary history of political economy in the "mercantilist" writers of the early seventeenth century was defined by Adam Smith (*An Inquiry into the Nature and Causes of the Wealth of Nations*, ed. Edwin Cannan [New York: Modern Library, 1937]: 399–400) and has remained orthodox to accounts of that history such as Spiegel's in *The Growth of Economic Thought*; revisionist accounts, such as Wood's *Foundations of Political Economy*, have sought to revalue

the contributions of the "commonwealth" writers to that origin, but the discursive differences between the generation of Thomas Smith and that of Thomas Mun are more salient to my argument than any conceptual commonalities (for which see also my afterword).

71. Dolan, *Dangerous Familiars: Representations of Domestic Crime in England, 1550–1700* (Ithaca, N.Y.: Cornell UP, 1994); Korda, *Shakespeare's Domestic Economies* (Philadelphia: U of Pennsylvania P, 2002); Orlin, *Private Matters and Public Culture in Post-Reformation England* (Ithaca, N.Y.: Cornell UP, 1994); Wall, *Staging Domesticity: Household Work and English Identity in Early Modern Drama* (Cambridge: Cambridge UP, 2002).
72. For the disciplinary regime to be enacted upon objects in this discourse (of dusting, polishing, and accountability), and for how that work shapes the housewife's subjectivity as if a reflection from those objects, see Korda, *Shakespeare's Domestic Economies*, 76–110.
73. Tusser, *Five hundred pointes of good husbandrie* [1580], ed. W. Payne and Sidney J. Herrtage (London: English Dialect Society, 1878): 177. See Wendy Wall, *Staging Domesticity*, 29–42, for the role of fantasy in shaping the premises and desires of household manuals. The Elizabethans had a great appetite for the how-to and self-help genres of print; Tusser's manual alone went through a dozen editions and expansions, making it "the single most popular book of poetry pubished in sixteenth-century England and one of the fifteen most popular books on any subject in the Elizabethan era" (Wall, 36).
74. Muldrew, *The Economy of Obligation: The Culture of Credit and Social Relations in Early Modern England* (New York: St. Martin's, 1998).
75. Comparing individuals' wealth in coin to their wealth in itemized debts in surviving probate inventories of the period 1538–1660, Eric Ketteredge figures the average ratio of the former to the latter as at minimum 1:9, and lists factors excluded from his analysis that might suggest a ratio of as high as 1:20 (*Trade and Banking in Early Modern England* [Manchester: Manchester University Press, 1988]: 98–99). For the inadequate volume of the currency and the practice of local businesses to issue tokens to compensate for the unavailability of change, see Challis, *The Tudor Coinage*, 205–210.
76. Muldrew takes up this question in his essay " 'Hard Food for Midas': Cash and Its Social Value in Early Modern England," *Past and Present* 170 (2001): 78–120.
77. The source of this argument is Aristotle, *Politics* I.x; medieval thinkers buttressed the philosopher's authority with that of Deuteronomy 23:19–20, which forbids lending at interest within kin relationships. Insofar as Christianity was a universal brotherhood, no Christian ought to take interest on any other brother Christian's debt.
78. Stone, *The Crisis of the Aristocracy, 1558–1641* (Oxford: Oxford UP, 1967). Notable analyses of the cultural transformations entailed in the reform of English usury law include Marc Shell's chapter on *The Merchant of Venice* in *Money, Language, and Thought* (Berkeley: U of California P, 1982): 47–83; Norman Jones,

*God and the Moneylenders: Usury and Law in Early Modern England* (Oxford: Basil Blackwell, 1989); Ceri Sullivan, *The Rhetoric of Credit: Merchants in Early Modern Writing* (Madison, N.J.: Fairleigh Dickinson UP, 2002); David Hawkes, *The Culture of Usury in Early Modern England* (New York: Palgrave Macmillan, 2010); and Natasha Korda, "Dame Usury: Gender, Credit, and (Ac)counting in the Sonnets and *The Merchant of Venice*," *Shakespeare Quarterly* 60.2 (2009): 129–153.

79. For analytic method as the preeminent contribution of the Renaissance to intellectual history, see inter alia Ernst Cassirer, *The Individual and the Cosmos in Renaissance Philosophy*, tr. and introd. Mario Domandi (Philadelphia: U of Pennsylvania P, 1963), and Michel Foucault, *The Order of Things: An Archaeology of the Human Sciences* (New York: Vintage, 1973).
80. This story is told in its relation to the human sciences in Mary Poovey, *A History of the Modern Fact: Problems of Knowledge in the Sciences of Wealth and Society* (Chicago: U of Chicago P, 1998), and in relation to the natural sciences in Steven Shapin, *A Social History of Truth: Civility and Science in Seventeenth-Century England* (Chicago: U of Chicago P, 1994).
81. Some important studies of the disciplining of "poesy" into "English literature," and of the relation of that emergent disciplinarity to that of political economy, include John Guillory's *Cultural Capital: The Problem of Literary Canon Formation* (Chicago: U of Chicago P, 1993); Mary Poovey's *Genres of the Credit Economy: Mediating Value in Eighteenth- and Nineteenth-Century Britain* (Chicago: U of Chicago P, 2008); for the seventeenth century, Blair Hoxby's *Mammon's Music: Literature and Economics in the Age of Milton* (New Haven: Yale UP, 2002), Jonathan Gil Harris's *Sick Economies: Drama, Mercantilism, and Disease in Shakespeare's England* (Philadelphia: U of Pennsylvania P, 2004), Richard Halpern's "The Lyric in the Field of Information: Autopoiesis and History in Donne's *Songs and Sonnets*," *Yale Journal of Criticism* 6.1 (1993): 185–215, and David Hawkes's *Idols of the Marketplace*; for the Restoration and eighteenth century, Richard Kroll's *The Material Word: Literate Culture in the Restoration and Early Eighteenth Century* (Baltimore: Johns Hopkins UP, 1991) and Diedre Shauna Lynch's *The Economy of Character: Novels, Market Culture, and the Business of Inner Meaning* (Chicago: U of Chicago P, 1998); for the nineteenth century, Catherine Gallagher's *The Body Economic: Life, Death, and Sensation in Political Economy and the Victorian Novel* (Chicago: U of Chicago P, 2005), David Kaufmann's *The Business of Common Life: Novels and Classical Economics between Revolution and Reform* (Baltimore: Johns Hopkins UP, 1995), and Elaine Freedgood's *The Ideas in Things: Fugitive Meaning in the Victorian Novel* (Chicago: U of Chicago P, 2006).
82. Sidney, *The Major Works*, ed. Katherine Duncan-Jones (Oxford: Oxford UP, 2002): 216. Sidney's primary examples of the contrary modes of knowledge reconciled and subsumed by poesy are history and philosophy; he cites many other bodies of knowledge that poesy can encompass as well (such as astronomy and agriculture).

83. Burckhardt, *The Civilization of the Renaissance in Italy* (New York: Harper & Bros., 1958): 143; italics *sic.*
84. As Ernst Cassirer puts it, "All the intellectual currents that nourish the Renaissance flow into [the] central problem" of "self-consciousness... they loosen up, so to speak, the earth out of which will come forth the new, specifically modern view of the relationship of 'subject' and 'object' " (*The Individual and the Cosmos,* 123). For the ways in which the intellectual trajectory passing from Burckhardt through Cassirer has defined the disciplinary history of Renaissance studies, see William Kerrigan and Gordon Braden, *The Idea of the Renaissance* (Baltimore: Johns Hopkins UP, 1989). Influential reassessments of this passage of Burckhardt for historicist literary criticism include those by Stephen Greenblatt (*Renaissance Self-Fashioning from More to Shakespeare* [Chicago: U of Chicago P, 1980]: 161–175) and Margreta de Grazia ("The Ideology of Superfluous Things: *King Lear* as Period Piece," in *Subject and Object in Renaissance Culture,* ed. Margreta de Grazia, Maureen Quilligan, and Peter Stallybrass [Cambridge: Cambridge UP, 1996]: 17–42, esp. 17–21).
85. Hugh Grady discusses the origin of this coinage in Lukacs's thought and its utility to the postmodern analysis of early modernity in *Shakespeare's Universal Wolf: Studies in Early Modern Reification* (Oxford: Clarendon, 1996): 34.
86. Halpern, *The Poetics of Primitive Accumulation* (Ithaca, N.Y.: Cornell UP, 1991): 11.
87. De Grazia, "The Ideology of Superfluous Things"; Latour, *We Have Never Been Modern,* tr. Catherine Porter (Cambridge, Mass.: Harvard UP, 1993).
88. Brown, "Thing Theory," in *Things,* ed. Bill Brown (Chicago: U of Chicago P, 2004): 1–21.
89. Appadurai, "Introduction: Commodities and the Politics of Value," in *The Social Life of Things,* ed. Arjun Appadurai (Cambridge: Cambridge UP, 1986): 3–63, esp. 5 (this passage is also enlarged upon by Brown, 6–8); Jones and Stallybrass, *Renaissance Clothing and the Materials of Memory* (Cambridge: Cambridge UP, 2000): 1–14, and "Fetishizing the Glove in Renaissance Europe," in *Things,* ed. Bill Brown (Chicago: U of Chicago P, 2004): 174–192. As William Pietz has demonstrated across three magisterial articles, "fetish" is a Renaissance concept: the word emerged in Portuguese to refer to trade goods apparently valued differently by Africans and Europeans, passed from there into ethnographic discourse, and was redirected to the analysis of the closeted, materialized irrationalities of Western modernity by Marx and Freud ("The Problem of the Fetish, I," *Res* 9 [1985]: 5–17; "The Problem of the Fetish, II," *Res* 13 [1987]: 23–45; "The Problem of the Fetish, IIIa," *Res* 16 [1988]: 105–123). Notable attempts to coordinate the Marxian commodity fetish with the Freudian psychologistic fetish include Jean-Joseph Goux, *Symbolic Economies: After Marx and Freud,* trans. Jennifer Curtiss Gage (Ithaca, N.Y.: Cornell UP, 1990) and Slavoj Žižek, *The Sublime Object of Ideology* (New York: Verso, 1989). For the utility of the category to the analysis of early modern culture, see also (inter alia) James Siemon, "Dreams of

Field: Early Modern (Dis)Positions" in *Historicism, Psychoanalysis, and Early Modern Culture,* eds. Carla Mazzio and Douglas Trevor (New York: Routledge, 2000): 36–58; James Kearney, "The Book and the Fetish: The Materiality of Prospero's Text," *Journal of Medieval and Early Modern Studies* 32.3 (2002): 433–468; Lisa Freinkel, "The Shakespearean Fetish," in *Spiritual Shakespeares,* ed. Ewan Fernie (London: Routledge, 2005): 109–129.

90. Heidegger, *Being and Time,* tr. John Macquarrie and Edward Robinson (San Francisco: Harper, 1962): 95–107, esp. 105.
91. Schwenger, *The Tears of Things: Melancholy and Physical Objects* (Minneapolis: U of Minnesota P, 2006): 21–33. Schwenger's book works extensively with Heidegger's analyses of "equipment" and of "the Thing," and has been an influential guide for me through the Heidegger corpus.
92. A grim but compelling account of the shaping of Renaissance English culture by symbiosis is Ernest B. Gilman, *Plague Writing in Early Modern England* (Chicago: U of Chicago P, 2009).
93. Latour, *Aramis, or the Love of Technology,* tr. Catherine Porter (Cambridge, Mass.: Harvard UP, 1996): 81–82. As Latour's title indicates, the ontological category he is investigating is that of "technology," not that of "thing"—Aramis is frustrated that it never quite achieves the reified status of thing, for its concreteness is always (and to oscillating degrees over its lifetime) compromised between its potentiality and its scanty material manifestations; but "technology" in Latour's usage incorporates the senses of a thing's being made, its modality of making, and its modality of function, all of which are apt to the ways in which I examine coinage in this book, though they might not be apt to a "thing" neither made nor used by humans.
94. This capacity of a coin at once to define a desire in its putative master and to forsake him by satisfying that desire's blinkered terms seems particularly diabolical with respect to Renaissance understandings, in that it resembles the modus operandi of Marlowe's Mephistopheles and Shakespeare's "demi-devil" Iago (*Othello* 5.2.301).
95. Shell, *Money, Language, and Thought,* 1.
96. Shell, *The Economy of Literature,* 93.
97. Shell's own formulations are much more subtle and elusive than this, and they engage the reciprocal way in which materiality conditions even the articulation of "money of the mind," purely formal or notional moneys, such that money remains constitutive of the linguistic materials of thought and defies any final analysis as a mere object within philosophic discourse: "the thinking which fails to account for or even to encounter its own internalization of economic form remains insensitive to a sting that goads thought into becoming philosophy and, perhaps, into surpassing it" (*Money, Language, and Thought,* 155). But attempts by Shell's admirers to develop an imitable practice from his wide-ranging analyses cannot but fall short of the chimerical goal he sets for them, that of surpassing philosophy. What's exportable from Shell's work, as Correll argues, is the attrac-

tive analogy between coins and words in the circulating systems of money and of discourse; his practice in this regard is echoed in Stephen Greenblatt's even more influential *Shakespearean Negotiations* (Berkeley: U of California P, 1989), and it is a direct forebear of works such as Kurt Heinzelman's *The Economics of the Imagination* (Amherst: U of Massachusetts P, 1980); Sandra K. Fischer's preface to *Econolingua: A Glossary of Coins and Economic Language in Renaissance Drama* (Newark: U of Delaware P, 1985), a volume which does for financial metaphors what Eric Partridge did for bawdy ones; and several of the essays collected by Martha Woodmansee and Mark Osteen in *The New Economic Criticism* (New York: Routledge, 1999), to which Correll's critique is a rejoinder. That collection, largely aimed at exporting literary-critical concepts into the discipline of economics, produced several responses directed to reevaluating literary history in turn; those located within the Renaissance include *Material Culture and Cultural Materialisms in the Middle Ages and Renaissance*, ed. Curtis Perry (Turnhout, Belgium: Brepols, 2001), *The Culture of Capital*, ed. Henry S. Turner (New York: Routledge, 2002), and *Money and the Age of Shakespeare: Essays in New Economic Criticism*, ed. Linda Woodbridge (New York: Palgrave Macmillan, 2003). For an analysis of the work of metaphor in the homological systems of both Goux and Shell, and of its relation to historicity, see Judith H. Anderson, *Translating Investments: Metaphor and the Dynamic of Cultural Change in Tudor-Stuart England* (New York: Fordham UP, 2005): 172–174.

98. Shell's influence on the "New Economic Criticism" does not by any means exhaust the ways by which the relationship of (what we'd call) literary forms to (what we'd call) economic ones may be articulated in Renaissance studies. Jean-Christophe Agnew's homology between the institutions of theater and market in *Worlds Apart: The Market and the Theater in Anglo-American Thought, 1550–1750* (Cambridge: Cambridge UP, 1986) has been interrogated and redefined (as a spatial one, as an Althusserian overdetermination, as one generating a protopragmatic philosophy of ephemeral value) by many authors, including Stephen Mullaney (*The Place of the Stage: License, Play, and Power in Renaissance England* [Chicago: U of Chicago P, 1988]), Douglas Bruster (*Drama and the Market in the Age of Shakespeare* [Cambridge: Cambridge UP, 1992]), Lars Engle (*Shakespearean Pragmatism: Market of His Time* [Chicago: U of Chicago P, 1993]), and Theodore Leinwand (*Theatre, Finance, and Society in Early Modern England* [Cambridge: Cambridge UP, 1999]).

The reading of monetary language in early modern texts as a symptom of the emergence in the culture of the institutions of capital as described by Marx has been available to literary critics since L. C. Knights's *Drama and Society in the Age of Jonson* (London: Chatto and Windus, 1937). Influential recent exempla include Robert Weimann's work; many of Peter Stallybrass's essays, and *Renaissance Clothing and the Materials of Memory* (op. cit.), which he coauthored with Ann Rosalind Jones; Catherine Gimelli Martin, "Angels, Alchemists, and Exchange: Commercial Ideology in Court and City Comedy, 1596–1610," in *The Witness of Times: Manifestations of Ideology in Seventeenth-Century England*, ed. Katherine

Z. Keller (Pittsburgh: Duquesne UP, 1993: 121–147); and Valerie Forman, "Marked Angels: Counterfeits, Commodities, and *The Roaring Girl*," *Renaissance Quarterly* 54.4.2 (Winter 2001): 1531–1560.

Georg Simmel's influence has generally exerted itself only indirectly on early modern literary criticism—compared to the other founding documents of sociology (such as Weber's or Marx's historicized schemata), *The Philosophy of Money* is a provocative and almost explicitly presentist muddle, offering little in the way of model system to be uncritically applied by the litterateur and much that seems itself literary and open to his critique (as for example in Curtis Perry's essay "Commerce, Community, and Nostalgia in *The Comedy of Errors*" in *Money and the Age of Shakespeare: Essays in New Economic Criticism,* ed. Linda Woodbridge [New York: Palgrave Macmillan, 2003]: 39–52, which introduces Simmel for the sake of proceeding to reject him as "too easily projected back to early modern England," though without citing any critics who have done so [40]). The current enterprise of "material culture" criticism of early modernity owes a couple of debts to Simmel, however, both as the jumping-off point for Arjun Appadurai's seminal collection *The Social Life of Things* and (I would argue) as a precursor to Michel de Certeau's portrayal of everyday life as the antithesis of systematicity. I will articulate these debts further in chapter 1.

The influence of Craig Muldrew's reconception of the credit economy has also begun to make itself felt: see most prominently Ceri Sullivan, *The Rhetoric of Credit,* and Jennifer Richards, *Rhetoric and Courtliness in Early Modern Literature,* as well as such essays as Nina Levine, "Extending Credit in the Henry IV Plays," *Shakespeare Quarterly* 51:4 (Winter 2000): 403–431, and Teresa Lanpher Nugent, "Usury and Counterfeiting in Wilson's *The Three Ladies of London* and *The Three Lords and Three Ladies of London,* and in Shakespeare's *Measure for Measure,*" in *Money and the Age of Shakespeare: Essays in New Economic Criticism,* ed. Linda Woodbridge (New York: Palgrave Macmillan, 2003): 201–217.

For alternatives to my own anatomy of this economistic strain of recent criticism, see Correll's essay and two other essays in the same volume, by Douglas Bruster (67–78) and David Hawkes (79–96).

99. Correll, "Scene Stealers: Autolycus, *The Winter's Tale,* and Economic Criticism," in *Money and the Age of Shakespeare: Essays in New Economic Criticism,* ed. Linda Woodbridge (New York: Palgrave Macmillan, 2003): 53–66, esp. 61–62.
100. Guillory, "A New Subject for Criticism," in *The Culture of Capital,* ed. Henry S. Turner (New York: Routledge, 2002): 223–230, esp. 226–227.
101. Ibid., 227.
102. Pye, "The Theater, the Market, and the Subject of History," *ELH* 61.3 (Fall 1994): 501–522, esp. 503.
103. Jones and Stallybrass, *Renaissance Clothing and the Materials of Memory,* 8.
104. Sinfield, "*Poetaster,* the Author, and the Perils of Cultural Production," in *Material London ca. 1600,* ed. Lena Cowen Orlin (Philadelphia: U of Penn. P, 2000): 75–90, esp. 75–76; italics *sic.*

105. "Worldly Goods" is Lisa Jardine's ironical title for her monograph on early modern commodity culture (*Worldly Goods: A New History of the Renaissance*, New York: Doubleday, 1996); for "methodological fetishism" see Appadurai, "Introduction," (esp. 5), as discussed above.
106. Grady, *Shakespeare's Universal Wolf*, 24.
107. This phrase is how the narrator of William Gaddis's *The Recognitions* sums up the benchmark work of the capitalist self-help genre, Dale Carnegie's *How to Win Friends and Influence People* (Gaddis, *The Recognitions* [New York: Penguin, 1993]: 499).
108. Turner, "Nashe's Red Herring: Epistemologies of the Commodity in *Lenten Stuffe* (1599)," *ELH* 68.3 (2001): 529–561; Bruster, "The New Materialism in Renaissance Studies," in *Material Cuture and Cultural Materialisms in the Middle Ages and Renaissance*, ed. Curtis Perry (Turnhout, Belgium: Brepols, 2001): 225–238; Harris, "Atomic Shakespeare," *Shakespeare Studies* 30 (2002): 47–51, and *Untimely Matter in the Time of Shakespeare* (Philadelphia: U of Penn. P, 2009); Goldberg, *The Seeds of Things: Theorizing Sexuality and Materiality in Renaissance Representations* (New York: Fordham UP, 2009). Michael Witmore analyzes a related aspect of what he dubs "Shakespearean metaphysics" in arguing that the drama's imbrication of actorly bodies into the fabric of authorial text became for Shakespeare an opportunity to engage the metaphysical question of immanence; he places Shakespeare in dialogue with three philosophers similarly preoccupied by immanence, Whitehead, Bergson, and Spinoza (*Shakespearean Metaphysics* [London: Continuum, 2009]). John Rogers analyzes the convergence of literary writing, vitalist ontology, and radical political theory in what he names "the vitalist moment" of the mid-seventeenth century in *The Matter of Revolution: Science, Poetry, and Politics in the Age of Milton* (Ithaca, N.Y.: Cornell UP, 1996).
109. For Serres, atoms and letters are the same things, so the macroscopic ontologies of things and of texts are continuous: *The Birth of Physics*, tr. Jack Hawkes (Manchester: Clinamen, 2000): 22.
110. In *The Material Word*, Richard Kroll likewise assesses the new Epicurean influence upon seventeenth-century natural philosophy and analytic method as a reaction to the centrality of Aristotelian-Stoic models to the received picture of the natural world. A salutary effect both of this strand of material-culture study and of the new economic criticism has been the reevaluation of Aristotelian influence on the thought of sixteenth-century England, often discounted by prior critics focused on the reformation of the curriculum away from the scholastics and on the esoteric charms of Neo-Platonism: see, for example, Henry S. Turner, "Nashe's Red Herring"; Lorna Hutson, *The Usurer's Daughter: Male Friendship and Fictions of Women in Sixteenth-Century England* (New York: Routledge, 1997); Eric Spencer, "Taking Excess, Exceeding Account: Aristotle Meets *The Merchant of Venice*," in *Money and the Age of Shakespeare: Essays in New Economic Criticism*, ed. Linda Woodbridge (New York: Palgrave Macmillan, 2003):

143–158; Helen Cooney, "Guyon and His Palmer: Spenser's Emblem of Temperance," *Review of English Studies* 51.202 (May 2000): 169–192.

## CHAPTER 1

1. Ann Farmer, "In the Metal Recycling Business, It's Loud, Dirty and Suddenly Lucrative," *The New York Times*, June 27, 2008, national edition: C12.
2. For the primacy of the validation function of the coin in exchange, see Mary Poovey, *Genres of the Credit Economy* (Chicago: U of Chicago P, 2008): 57–85.
3. Marlowe, *The Jew of Malta* 3.3.68; Spenser, *The Faerie Queene* 2.proem.1. Citations of *Jew* are to David Bevington's Revels edition (New York: Manchester UP, 1997); citations of *The Faerie Queene* are to Thomas P. Roche's Penguin edition (New York, 1978). Both will hereafter be cited parenthetically in the text.
4. [Sir Thomas Smith?], *A Discourse of the Commonweal of This Realm of England*, ed. Mary Dewar (Charlottesville: UP of Virginia, 1969): 112–113. The Knight, who brings up historical instances of the coinage of leather several times in the dialogues, is particularly interested in the concept of exchange value as determined by the authority of the minting prince: "Why do kings and princes strike these metals and other with a coin but because they would have that coin, of what value soever it be, to bear the state that the coin pretends; which they did in vain if they could not make the metal that bears that to be neither better nor worse in estimation?" (75).
5. The paradigmatic formulation of substance as the unity of *forma* and *materia* is that of *De Anima*, Book 2, chapter 1 (412a ff; in *Basic Works of Aristotle*, ed. Richard McKeon [New York: Random House, 1941]: 535–560). Aristotle there uses the example of wax shaped into a seal, not of metal stamped into a coin, perhaps to avoid the material conundra I take up below; but the formula was recognizable to Renaissance students of Aristotle in either example, as John Carey has demonstrated ("Donne and Coins," in *English Renaissance Studies Presented to Dame Helen Gardner in honour of her Seventieth Birthday*, ed. John Carey [Oxford: Clarendon Press, 1980]: 151–163, esp. 161–162). For the general currency of Aristotelian hylomorphism as "the primary discursive framework for the production of knowledge concerning natural bodies" in sixteenth-century England, see Henry S. Turner, "Nashe's Red Herring: Epistemologies of the Commodity in *Lenten Stuffe* (1599)," *ELH* 68.3 (2001): 529–561, esp. 539–540. Turner's demonstration in this essay of the continuity of Aristotelian categories in the materialist analyses of Hegel and of Marx has greatly aided me in shaping the premises of this chapter, as has Jonathan Gil Harris's response to Turner, "Shakespeare's Hair: Staging the Object of Material Culture," *Shakespeare Quarterly* 52.3 (2002), pp. 479–491.
6. Shakespeare citations are to *The Riverside Shakespeare*, gen. ed. G. Blakemore Evans (Boston: Houghton Mifflin, 1974). Renaissance orthography did not differentiate "mettle" from "metal."
7. Harrison, *An Historicall description of the Iland of Britaine, with a briefe rehersall of the nature and qualities of the people of England, and such commodities as are to be*

*found in the same*, vol. 1 of Holinshed et al., *The First and Second Volumes of Chronicles* ([London], 1586): 188–189.

8. Korda, *Shakespeare's Domestic Economies* (Philadelphia: U of Penn. P, 2002): 3. "Ordinarie" here defines the nature of the service—i.e., at meals—and not, as the modern sense would suggest, its frequency.
9. Simmel, *The Philosophy of Money*, trans. Tom Bottomore and David Frisby (London: Routledge and Kegan Paul, 1990): 204–227.
10. Ibid., 238–247. The trope of the miser's obsessive interaction with gold achieved much urgency in the waning years of the gold standard, not only in Simmel's philosophical-sociological system but in popular novels and in polemic journalism; a classic literary analysis of turn-of-the-century literature in Simmel's terms is Walter Benn Michaels's reading of *MacTeague* by Frank Norris, "The Gold Standard and the Logic of Naturalism" (in Michaels, *The Gold Standard and The Logic of Naturalism: American Literature at the Turn of the Century* [Berkeley: U. of California P, 1987]: 137–180). Arjun Appadurai's Simmelian theorization of the life of objects in exchange, in his introduction to *The Social Life of Things*, Appadurai, ed. (Cambridge: Cambridge UP, 1986: 3–63), has proven fundamental to the criticsm of material culture.
11. Conversely, many scholastic Aristotelians maintained through the Renaissance (in the face of much controversy) the existence of "substantial forms," forms independent of and prior to the matter they affected, which were understood to be transmissible qualities such as heat (see Turner, "Nashe's Red Herring," 539, 555 n.26).
12. See, for example, Jonathan Gil Harris's and Natasha Korda's edited collection, *Staged Properties in Early Modern Drama* (Cambridge: Cambridge UP, 2002).
13. Schuler, "Alchemy," in *The Spenser Encyclopedia*, gen. ed. A. C. Hamilton (Toronto: U of Toronto, 1990): 12–14, esp. 12 (henceforward *Sp Enc*). Recent exceptions to Schuler's rule include two articles by Anthony Esolen, which assess the influence of Lucretius's material philosophy on Spenser ("Spenserian Chaos: Lucretius in *The Faerie Queene*," *Spenser Studies* 11 [1994]: 31–51; and "Spenser's 'Alma Venus': Energy and Economics in the Bower of Bliss," *English Literary Renaissance* 23.2 [Spring 1993]: 267–286); Jonathan Goldberg's *The Seeds of Things: Theorizing Sexuality and Materiality in Renaissance Representations* (New York: Fordham UP, 2009), which extensively critiques Esolen in presenting Spenser's interest in Lucretius's ultrasexual cosmology; and Christopher Burlinson's *Allegory, Space, and the Material World in the Writings of Edmund Spenser* (Cambridge: Brewer, 2006), which traces a relationship of allegory to materiality in Spenser's poem through its production of space, using the conceptual matrix developed by Henri Lefebvre.
14. See, for example, Margreta DeGrazia, "The Ideology of Superfluous Things: *King Lear* as Period Piece," in DeGrazia et al., eds., *Subject and Object in Renaissance Culture* (Cambridge: Cambridge UP, 1996): 17–42; and Ann Rosalind Jones and Peter Stallybrass, *Renaissance Clothing and the Materials of Memory* (Cambridge: Cambridge UP, 2000).

15. The debate over whether Guyon's faint at the close of the canto represents a failure of some kind on his own part—a prideful willingness to be led unto temptation, to take one formulation—or the general frailty of the fallen condition, against which Guyon has endured as long as he may and from which he like all men can be rescued only by grace, was a critical struggle which was reiterated in new keys throughout the 1960s and '70s; the two sides differed both in their choice among specific theological and ethical referents to the allegory and, more generally, in the degree of generosity they imagined the poet to extend to human faults (see Geoffrey A. Moore, "The Cave of Mammon: Ethics and Metaphysics in Secular and Christian Perspectives," *ELH* 42.2 [Summer 1975], 157–170, esp. 157–158, for an overview). Examples of the former view include A. S. P. Woodhouse, "Nature and Grace in *The Faerie Queene*," *ELH* 16 (1949): 194–228, Maurice Evans, "The Fall of Guyon," *ELH* 28 (1961): 215–224, and Harry Berger, Jr., *The Allegorical Temper: Vision and Reality in Book II of Spenser's* Faerie Queene (New Haven: Yale UP, 1957); critics more sympathetic to Guyon include Paul Alpers (*The Poetry of the Faerie Queene* [Princeton, N.J.: Princeton UP, 1967]) and Anne Lake Prescott ("Mammon" in *Sp Enc*, 451–452).
16. Kermode, *Shakespeare, Spenser, Donne: Renaissance Essays* (London: Routledge and Kegan Paul, 1971): 6. Kermode makes this comment while introducing a brilliantly savage riposte against Paul Alpers, which itself may have dissuaded other critics from presuming to contradict him. Four readers who do emphasize the role of economic and historical concepts in canto 7 are Kurt Heinzelman, who, in *The Economics of the Imagination* (Amherst: U of Massachusetts P, 1980), construes Mammon first in terms of Aristotelian *oikonomia*, and finally in terms of Marc Shell's equivalence of money and poetics as systems of signification (35–69); David Read, who reads all of Book II as a prescription for English empire, in reaction to intemperate Spanish methods of conquest and exploitation in the New World (*Temperate Conquests: Spenser and the Spanish New World* [Detroit: Wayne State UP, 2000]); Maureen Quilligan, who cites Mammon's smelting "feendes" as a point of emerging consciousness of slave labor in the English Renaissance in examining the relations of epic to slavery as a mode of production ("On the Renaissance Epic: Spenser and Slavery," *South Atlantic Quarterly* 100:1 [Winter 2001]: 15–39); and Kasey Evans, who considers the evolution of Renaissance concepts of temperance towards the ideology of mature capitalism ("How Temperance Becomes 'Blood Guiltie' in *The Faerie Queene*," *SEL* 49.1 [Winter 2009]: 35–66).
17. Although the argument that follows will discuss Mammon in terms of futurity, the typicality of his miserly representation marks that representation also as an aspect of Spenser's active medievalism. Spenser draws in particular on the iconography associated with Avarice in the tradition of depicting the Seven Deadly Sins. But two factors distinguish Mammon from the Avarice of the deadly-sins pageant of *FQ* 1.4 (of whom the narrator likewise declares, "in his lap an heape of coine he told," 1.4.27). One is the difference between Avarice's person and his

"coine": Avarice wears a "thred-bare cote," while Mammon's coat, though similarly decayed from self-neglect, is made of "yron" and lined "with gold" (1.4.28, 2.7.4). Avarice "made" "his God" of "his wicked pelfe": Mammon is himself Avarice's man-made God, and his own (1.4.27). The second iconographic difference is that Avarice is accompanied wherever he goes by six other icons, while Mammon is emphatically solitary. He has evil dependents in his household, but does not associate with any peers. He is not one among seven Deadly Sins, but *cupiditas* in its aspect of the singular *radix malorum* of 1 Tim 6:10. Like the heaps of gold at the center of the "Pardoner's Tale," which Chaucer's "riotours" find at the root of a tree, Mammon manifests himself to Guyon in "a gloomy glade/ Couer'd with boughes & shrubs" (2.7.3).

18. Cheney, *Marlowe's Counterfeit Profession: Ovid, Spenser, Counter-Nationhood* (Toronto: U of Toronto P, 1997): 144. Cheney in fact only makes this point about Barabas's corresponding "telling," in *Jew* 1.1; but as Cheney is concerned to demonstrate other continuities between the two texts, I feel licensed in reading this one backward to its appearance in Spenser.
19. Or, as Simmel declares, "The quantity of money is its quality" (*Philosophy of Money*, 259–260).
20. Read, *Temperate Conquests*, 66.
21. The failure of utility and circulation here is also obvious as double entendre: the dirty old man who is money keeps his hands in his lap to fondle himself incessantly, in an autoerotic short circuit parallel to that of Phaedria's solitary amusement in her little boat ("Making sweet solace to her selfe alone," 2.6.3). See below for the ways in which solitude seems to enforce solipsism in Book Two.
22. Other notable intrusions of monetary value into the value systems preferred by *FQ* are the inhospitable miserliness of Malbecco (3.9); the bounty that Turpine promises the two mercenary knights for killing Arthur (6.7); Calidore's attempt to pay Melibee for the shepherd's hospitality (6.9.32–33, the only attempt by a good character to use money—which arises from Calidore's understanding that he has left the chivalric genre in deciding to stay with Melibee and play shepherd, without recognizing that in so doing he is entering another genre, the pastoral, where they don't use money either); and the extortions of Pollente and Munera, which I discuss below.
23. Harry Levin charts the use of the Golden Age trope to define primitivism in the Americas in *The Myth of the Golden Age in the Renaissance* (Bloomington: Indiana UP, 1969): 58–83.
24. I will not develop a full reading of the House of Alma, save as it directly pertains to my analysis of Mammon; it is worth noting here, though, that the management of a household is the only meaning of *oikonomia* developed in the Aristotelian tradition, and that the concept of "political economy," from which our sense of "the economy" as a national phenomenon derives, did not develop until the end of the seventeenth century. The House of Alma, then, is Spenser's definitive statement of a normative "economy," which he presents as a self-sufficient unit

(indeed, as a unit forcefully closed against besiegers) without reference to the market, much less to money. It goes almost without saying that not even the grandest noble estates were independent of the national market in the sixteenth century; as Wendy Wall has argued in her reading of manuals of household economy, such a self-contained domesticity was nearly as nostalgic a vision as Guyon's presentation of the Golden Age (*Staging Domesticity: Household Work and English Identity in Early Modern Drama* [Cambridge: Cambridge UP, 2002]: 29–42).

25. Harrison, *Description,* 217.
26. For the humanist interaction with coined portraits, see Sean Keilen, "Exemplary Metals: Classical Numismatics and the Commerce of Humanism," *Word & Image* 18.3 (July–September 2002): 282–294, and John Cunnally, *Images of the Illustrious: The Numismatic Presence in the Renaissance* (Princeton, N.J.: Princeton UP, 1999). Camden used coin finds as archaeological evidence both in *Britannia* and in correspondence with the geographer Ortelius, and illustrated his magnum opus with engravings of coins from the Cotton collection (F. J. Levy, *Tudor Historical Thought* [San Marino, Ca.: Huntington Library, 1967]: 150–152; Arthur B. Ferguson, *Clio Unbound: Perception of the Social and Cultural Past in Renaissance England* [Durham, N.C.: Duke UP, 1979]: 112).
27. Harrison, *Description,* 218.
28. Summit, "Monuments and Ruins: Spenser and the Problem of the English Library," *ELH* 70.1 (Spring 2003): 1–34, esp. 17–20.
29. Evans demonstrates the increasing iconographic attention to temperance's continuity with temporality in the Renaissance ("How Temperance Becomes 'Blood Guiltie,'" 38–44). Elizabeth Fowler cites the "atemporality" of money, its metallic resistance to either growth or decay in time, as a principal term of medieval monetary analyses (*Literary Character: The Human Figure in Early English Writing* [Ithaca, N.Y.: Cornell UP, 2003]: 78–79).
30. See Leonard Barkan, *The Gods Made Flesh: Metamorphosis and the Pursuit of Paganism* (New Haven: Yale UP, 1986): 233–242, for the Ovidian frame of Spenser's Garden of Adonis, where eternity is flux.
31. Milton notably reenacts that fusion of cause and effect into a single phenomenon by means of allegory, in Sin's self-presentation in *Paradise Lost* (2.746–814). For a densely erudite reading of causality and its discontents in the Renaissance's understanding of "events," see Jacques Lezra, *Unspeakable Subjects: The Genealogy of the Event in Early Modern Europe* (Stanford, Calif.: Stanford UP, 1997).
32. The most comprehensive theorization of this Marxian prehistory of capital into the criticism of early modernity is Richard Halpern, *The Poetics of Primitive Accumulation* (Ithaca, N.Y.: Cornell UP, 1991).
33. Marx, *Capital,* Vol. I, tr. Ben Fowkes (London: Penguin, 1990): 871. I don't mean to suggest that Marx is *unconscious* of this allegorical function in discussing primitive accumulation—he is fully conscious of it. He demonstrates in the final pages of the volume that political economy formulates "prior accumulation" in precapitalist history as an allegory of capitalist values, and proceeds to revalue that

allegory through a scathing account of expropriation in precapitalist English history.

34. Obviously, to Althusser theology is itself an ideological phenomenon and only the Marxist "science of history" approaches the position of transcendence in the world's ideology; as Carl Schmitt (*Political Theology: Four Chapters on the Concept of Sovereignty*, tr. George Schwab [Cambridge, Mass.: MIT Press, 1988]) and Ernst Kantorowicz (*The King's Two Bodies: A Study in Medieval Political Theology* [Princeton, N.J.: Princeton UP, 1957]) have pointed out, however, that relation of transcendent thought to the thought of worldlings is a precondition of social theory rather than its discovery, and for many centuries it was theology that occupied the catbird seat therein, as it does for Spenser. Thus I'm using "ideology" here in ventriloquizing Spenser as a shorthand for "the unredeemed thought of the world's totality," without much anxiety over anachronism, anxious as I am about anachronism elsewhere in this study.
35. Leonard Barkan analyzes the mutual implication in this stanza of body, cosmos, and moral abstraction as "the matter of his huge desire" in *Nature's Work of Art: The Human Body as Image of the World* (New Haven: Yale UP, 1975): 211–212.
36. Thus Summit: "While for Bale and Parker the 'monument of antiquity' was grounded in the antiquity's unquestioned authenticity, Spenser's 'antiquity' represents the limits of knowledge, rather than its basis" ("Monuments and Ruins," 18).
37. In considering the "freedom from want" attributed to "our primitive counterparts" that joins the topoi of the pastoral, the classical golden age, and the Christian Eden, Joanna Picciotto argues that "One of the functions of the pastoral mode is to play with the fiction that envy of such a state is possible. The faith that the world of social inferiors offers access to a more desirable, because simpler, past creates Arcadias but cannot survive outside them, and usually is not entertained very seriously within them.... [T]he consolations of pastoral and the fortunate fall are the same: both represent primitive nature (poverty) under the reassuring sign of its loss"—a sign, I argue, that Mammon here makes glibly explicit (*Labors of Innocence in Early Modern England* [Cambridge, Mass.: Harvard UP, 2010]: 134–5).
38. Geoffrey A. Moore recognizes Guyon's failure to escape Mammon in this debate as the knight's accession to the demon's terms: "Guyon is always able to reject Mammon's offers but never able to see through the false premise that underlies them, namely, that we live in a secular world" ("The Cave of Mammon," 168). Prescott concurs: "[Mammon's] arguments are literal-minded... for cupidity was traditionally thought to include sticking to the letter of the law, ignoring the spirit and charity.... Here is Guyon's subtlest, unspoken temptation—to find the world's terms sufficient, to understand the cosmos without reference to its Creator—and to some extent he yields" ("Mammon," 451). It is surely true that Christian faith is the resolution to the difficulty posed by Mammon; my argu-

ment postpones that solution—as does canto 7 itself (for the angel does not arrive to bring Guyon grace until canto 8)—in order fully to investigate the problem.

39. As David Hawkes suggests, "idle" here refers not only to Mammon's present wasted effort but to his offer of idleness (usury being the "lazy trade," as Bacon put it in "On Usury") and to his idolatry: *Idols of the Marketplace: Idolatry and Commodity Fetishism in English Literature, 1580–1680* (New York: Palgrave, 2001): 23. See Helen Cooney's analysis of "care" in Book Two for the symmetrical relation between Phaedria's idolization of idleness and Mammon's idle idolatry: "Guyon and His Palmer: Spenser's Emblem of Temperance," *Review of English Studies* 51.202 (May 2000): 169–192.
40. The most thoroughgoing comparison of the two passages is Berger's (*The Allegorical Temper*, 72–75).
41. Kermode (*Spenser, Shakespeare, Donne*, 73) and Alpers (*Poetry of The Faerie Queene*, 245–247) outline the classical and modern precedents for the first two interpretations of the Tantalus figure, but neither considers the most lurid and memorable of the sins of the founder of the House of Atreus, cannibalism. Among other sources, Ovid references the butchery of Pelops in *Metamorphoses* VI. 405–411 as a story too well-known to need retelling, and Seneca's Fury makes Tantalus the presiding spirit of a second cannibal banquet in Act I of *Thyestes.* Although Tantalus's butchery of Pelops is ascribed in most sources to his desire to test the knowledge of the gods rather than to his own lust for the flesh of his son (Ovid suggests that only one of the gods actually eats any of Pelops, not Tantalus himself), this oddly abstract goal only compounds the enormity of his crime, which, as the Senecan version draws out, collapses the temporal sequence of generation even as it does the distinction of flesh and food, as the son is ingested through the father's act. (I am indebted to Holly Haynes for this reading of *Thyestes.*) Ceri Sullivan cites the typicality of usury troped as cannibalism in early modern England in *The Rhetoric of Credit: Merchants in Early Modern Writing* (Madison, N.J.: Fairleigh Dickinson UP, 2002): 45–46.
42. Prescott notes that the complete rejection of matter together with Mammon that Guyon here implies is not, in Protestant ethics, a temperate response ("Mammon," 452). In the dyspeptic anality of Mammon's cave, the topos of gold's metallic incorruptibility interacts complexly with the topos of gold as corruption. Each of these topoi is an aspect of medieval thinking about money—the former in the analysis of money's "atemporality," as Fowler explains (n.29 above), the latter in the much-iterated scatology of money. For the shittiness of money's materiality in my sixteenth-century texts, see my discussion of Pilate below and my discussion of monetarized waste in chapter 4.
43. Jonson's Subtle explicates these alchemical theories quite thoroughly in gulling Sir Epicure Mammon (*Alchemist* 2.3.125–210). James Elkins argues that the practices by which painting produces beauty—by fiddling about with putrid, squishy materials until they sublime themselves—are essentially alchemical in

*What Painting Is* (New York: Routledge, 1999), which offers the finest modern account of what it would be to experience the world alchemically.

44. The seventeenth-century monetarist Rice Vaughan cites the identification of money with *materia prima* as a commonplace: "So is money [that] by which all things are made equal in value, and therefore it is not ill compared to the *Materia Prima*, because, though it serves actually no use almost, it serves potentially to all uses" (*A Discourse of Coin and Coinage*, printed 1675 [ms. 1630?], reprinted in J. R. McCulloch, ed., *A Select Collection of Scarce and Valuable Tracts on Money* [London: Political Economy Club, 1856]: 1–120, esp. 10).
45. *Politics* 1.3.22. The Aristotelian formulation was used by theologians to theorize the Deuteronomic injunctions against usury; for explication and examples, see Sullivan, *The Rhetoric of Credit*, 44–52, and Norman Jones, *God and the Money-lenders: Usury and Law in Early Modern England* (Oxford: Basil Blackwell, 1989). The ramifications of this imagined contest between the values of abundance in "real" estate (and the vegetables and animals living on it that do the abounding) and those of monetary interest have been detailed by Marc Shell in his influential analysis of Shylock's exemplum of Jacob and Laban's sheep (*Money, Language and Thought* [Berkeley: U of California P, 1982]: 47–83). The relation of nature and art to each other and to the human body plays out in the comparisons between Alma's House and the Bower of Bliss, in this book, and draws in the House of Busyrane and the Garden of Adonis in the next; the problem reaches beyond the scope of my argument in this chapter. For the place of sexuality in that larger context—a place which, like that of instrumentality, strives to efface itself within the consumption-obsessed and ungenitalled House of Alma—see Jonathan Goldberg, *The Seeds of Things*, 63–121. As Goldberg points out, the anus is the only erogenous zone the House of Alma has, a site whose satisfactions are shared with those of the anal Cave of Mammon—satisfactions which the two knights are particularly delighted by in this form.
46. Hugh MacLean and Anne Lake Prescott gloss the passage in these terms in their edition of *Edmund Spenser's Poetry* (New York: Norton, 1993): 197; they read the reference to Babel as a recognition of the imperfection (and intemperance) inherent in human bodies. Sir Thomas Browne reviews the relevant literature on "*Ægyptian* slime" in *Pseudodoxia Epidemica* VI.viii, "Of the River Nilus" (*The Works of Sir Thomas Browne*, vol. 2, ed. Geoffrey Keynes [Chicago: U of Chicago P, 1964]).
47. For a parallel reading of the House of Alma's embodiment of interiority, see Michael C. Schoenfeldt, *Bodies and Selves in Early Modern England: Physiology and Inwardness in Spenser, Shakespeare, Herbert, and Milton* (Cambridge: Cambridge UP, 1999): 40–73. Schoenfeldt develops the episode's relation to the disciplinary regimes prescribed by contemporary dietary manuals that likewise formulated the body as a fortified dwelling, such as Elyot's *Castel of Helth*.
48. Levy, *Tudor Historical Thought*, 130–133.
49. Indeed, Heinzelman considers the convergence of food and gold to be, at least allegorically, the occasion of language itself, citing both Midas and a parable from

the *Prose Edda* to this effect; he goes on to cite many scenes of resistance to the commodification of food, such as Ruskin's dichotomous condemnation of the nineteenth-century political economy writers: "Their minds are continually set on money-gain, not on mouth-gain" (*The Economics of the Imagination*, 5–7).

50. For the analysis of money as an aspect of "common wealth," see my introduction.
51. The moralized incommensurability of food and gold is dwelt upon with approval by Berger and by Heinzelman in particular. Prescott is unusual in giving Mammon his due: "Guyon . . . never suggests a charitable use of Mammon's gold . . . [he] worries about the source of Mammon's wealth but never addresses the issue of 'right usaunce' or examines its relation to enjoyment, result, fruit. . . . Even his prudent fasting and waking may entail a rejection of matter as such; and he forgets, though Mammon cruelly reminds him, that knights need money" ("Mammon," 452).
52. Baudrillard, *For a Critique of the Political Economy of the Sign*, tr. and introd. Charles Levin (St. Louis: Telos Press, 1981): 80–81. The upper strata of Renaissance society were, as many critics have demonstrated, highly aware of their obligations in consumption. As Baudrillard adds, with reference to contemporary society and with more echoes of Lear: "Conversely, just as survival can fall well below the vital minimum if the production of surplus value requires it, the threshold of *obligatory* consumption can be set well above the strictly necessary—always as a function of the production of surplus value: this is the case in our societies, where no one is free to live on raw roots and fresh water. . . . Is the purchase of an automobile or clothing 'discretionary' when it is the unconscious substitute for an unrealistic desire for certain living accomodation? The vital minimum today, the minimum of imposed consumption, is the standard package. Beneath this level, you are an outcast. Is loss of status—or social non-existence—less upsetting than hunger?" (81).
53. Cheney, *Marlowe's Counterfeit Profession*, 142–148 and 306 n. 32.
54. Editors of *AYLI* (including G. B. Evans in *Riverside*, and Alan Brissenden in his Oxford edition of the play [Oxford: Oxford UP, 1993]) tend to be reluctant to find an allusion to Marlowe's death in the line. But Marlowe is obviously the "dead shepherd" addressed by Phebe in 3.4.81–82, citing the erotic expertise of *Hero and Leander*; Touchstone is in this passage talking about Ovid as the master of erotic poetry, and about Ovid's exile as the instance of the misapprehension of poetics by state power; Marlowe was the translator of Ovid's erotic elegies; Marlowe's translation of the *Amores* itself had very recently been burned in the Bishops' Ban, an analogous misadventure of poetry and power (as James Shapiro explains in *A Year in the Life of William Shakespeare: 1599* [New York: Harper Collins, 2005]: 126, 217–218); Marlowe's death occurred while he was the subject of a public scandal and a high-level state investigation and (as David Riggs has pointed out in "The Killing of Christopher Marlowe," *Stanford Humanities Review* 8.1 [2000]: 239–251) managed to happen close enough to the person of

the Queen that it would be the business of the Queen's Coroner and not any local authority; and the line, straightforward if sly when read through the allusion, is obscure to the point of nonsense if the allusion is disallowed. Although the matter must remain one of probability rather than of certainty, Occam's razor suggests that the burden of proof should lie with the rejection of the allusion, not with its acceptance.

55. Garber, "'Infinite Riches in a Little Room': Closure and Enclosure in Marlowe," in Alvin Kernan, ed., *Two Renaissance Mythmakers: Selected Papers from the English Institute, 1975–76* (Baltimore: Johns Hopkins UP, 1977): 3–21.
56. Thus Cheney: "As A. Bartlett Giamatti notes, 'the small space, or container, rammed with life's plenitude and energy, is the basic image of *The Faerie Queene*.' If Marlowe is feeding his eye on Spenser's treasury, we can watch him enclosing his rival's infinite riches in his own little room" (*Marlowe's Counterfeit Profession*, 148).
57. Every instance of Barabas's use of the word "soul" has such an ironic relation to a Christian context: gold is "my soul's sole hope" (2.1.29) and "strength to my soul, death to my enemy" (2.1.49), while a Christian soul is of course extramaterial and the vessel of eternal life. Rather than continually note that obvious irony, I will analyze Barabas's own materialist understanding of his individuality in what follows, taking his use of "soul" in an approximate correspondence to our "self."
58. Marx, *The Economic and Political Manuscripts of 1844*, ed. Dirk J. Struick, trans. Martin Milligan (New York: International, 1964): 169.
59. Eliot, "Notes on the Blank Verse of Christopher Marlowe," in *The Sacred Wood and Major Early Essays* (Mineola, N.Y.: Dover, 1998): 53.
60. Pollan, *The Omnivore's Dilemma: A Natural History of Four Meals* (New York: Penguin, 2006): 287–303.
61. Schoenfeldt, *Bodies and Selves in Early Modern England*, 40–73.
62. The fact that Book 2 begins with the forces of evil, and not (as Book 1 had) with the good protagonist, defines temperance as a reactive virtue, unlike the active one of holiness. One of Guyon's problems is how consistently the world is able to set the terms through which the knight confronts it.
63. "[H]ands" is the climactic fourth rhyme-word of the 'b' sequence in this first stanza (line 7), and the line it ends is the only one in the stanza that is not end-stopped, so we have a strong signal to pay attention to its further appearances in the book.
64. Of the hot (outward-directed) passions Guyon is more prone to wrath than lust, which is one of the reasons that modern readers tend to find him less sympathetic than Redcrosse; but I would suggest that a certain sublimation between the two is at work in Guyon's appetite for righteous anger on behalf of victimized women, which propels his quest on behalf of the suicide Amavia just as it does his wrong-headed aggression toward Redcrosse.
65. A reading that does construe Guyon as more engaged by Redcrosse's lesson about the use of hands than I am inclined to give him credit for being is John

Wesley, "The Well-Schooled Wrestler: Athletics and Rhetoric in *The Faerie Queene*, Book II," *Review of English Studies* 60 (March 2009): 34–60, esp. 51–52.

66. Amavia died by her own hand, though Guyon is inclined (as she is, in a rather self-servingly pagan accounting of responsibility and causation) to attribute the guilt of that death to Acrasia. The child's playful dabbling in her blood might be an identification of sin with aimlessness (rather than limiting sin to evil intent), a category that becomes urgent once Guyon is separated from the guide of his trajectory, the Palmer, by the idle and playful Phaedria. (The fulcrum between Phaedria's indulgent version of *otium* and Mammon's exorbitant version of *negotium* marks the midpoint of Book 2, as Janet Adelman has pointed out to me; operating across the two episodes are not only questions of oral discipline—Mammon wants you to eat gold, Phaedria won't stop babbling—but a complexly brilliant sequence of puns on "ydle" [idol/idle, as per n. 39 above] and "vayne" [vain/futile/self-indulgent/vacuous; vein, as bodily passage and as stratum of ore], which culminates in Pilate's "labor vayne and ydle industrie"). The stain upon what might otherwise appear to be innocence certainly suggests the orthodoxy of original sin, in which we are all complicit by our fleshly birth in the guilt of our forebears; yet at the point that the fountain has refused to wash the baby's hands the Palmer suggests, "let them still be bloudy, as befell,/ That they his mother's innocence may tell," a strikingly counterintuitive thing for any bloody hand to signify (2.2.10). (See Carol Kaske, "Amavia, Mordant, Ruddymane" in *Sp Enc*, 25–27, and Spenser ed. Hamilton, 171n.)
67. Compare the rejection of Guyon's ham-fisted attempts at flirting by the lady whom Alma reveals to be Guyon's own "*Shamefastnesse*," his froward master passion, in the court of the heart (2.9.41–43).
68. Berger, *The Allegorical Temper*, 26–29. Many readers since Berger have emphasized in one way or another the fallacy of Guyon's pretensions to sufficiency, which seem to map onto temperance's failure (as a pagan virtue) to be aware of the dependence of the virtuous individual upon the intervention of grace; see n. 16 above.
69. The fairy-tale motif that had guided the romance plot of Book 1—the offer of the princess's hand to any stranger knight who can meet her royal father's conditions in the cursed or enchanted castle—is subtly and wittily parodied in Mammon's habitual injection of modern banality into the "famous antique history" of Fairyland: the demon's offer sounds rather like a London burgher using a marriageable daughter to woo a junior partner into the family firm.
70. The interaction among the Pharisees, Pilate, Jesus, and the mob occurs in all four Gospels (Matt. 27:1–26; Mark 15:1–15; Luke 23:1–25; John 18:28–19:22), and all four emphasize different vertices of the conflict. In John's account Pilate is engaged by the interaction of politics and divine mystery in the charges against Jesus, asking him "What is truth?" in their interview (a question Jesus does not answer for him, at least not verbally—18:38–39); John not only attributes the inscription of "The King of the Jews" on the cross to Pilate's

authority, which the synoptic gospels do not, but has Pilate refusing the priests' request to disambiguate the inscription (19:19–22). Only Matthew includes the political theater of the hand-washing, and its symmetrical response from the mob, "His blood be on us and our children" (27:24–25); his account is perhaps the most sympathetic to the Gentile reasonableness of Pilate, in insisting on the blood guilt of the Jews. Only Luke explicitly cites Pilate as delivering a "verdict" against Christ (23:24), and that despite the case's falling under Herod's jurisdiction (likewise only cited in Luke) rather than his own; the other gospels are hazier as to whether Jesus is ever formally convicted, so that while in Luke's account Pilate bears responsibility for authorizing a judicial murder, the others leave him as the more-or-less unwilling accessory to a lynching. Spenser's citation of a Pilate who first performs a "doom" as a "Iudge," and washes his hands after, is thus a syncretic one.

71. Helen Cooney points out that the exegetical tradition had a hard time defining the sin of which Pilate was guilty, guilty though he surely was: "it was variously identified as ambition, avarice, pride, and so on," each of which she considers more or less a shot in the dark ("Guyon and His Palmer: Spenser's Emblem of Temperance," *Review of English Studies* 51.202 [May 2000]: 169–192, esp. 178). She argues for Tantalus and Pilate representing complemetary aspects of a sinful *curiositas* (echoing Berger's and Kermode's assessments of the episode) that ramifies from the extreme of worldly carefulness represented by Mammon, in contradistinction to the carelessness of Phaedria: that Tantalus has pried into, and Pilate has presumed to judge, divine things that are none of their business. Her reading accounts for Pilate's verbal self-description as "the falsest Iudge alas," but not for the hand-washing that serves as the gestural disavowal of judgment. It should be noted that in Guyon's judgment of Tantalus the sinner's self-description is self-serving and what's to be interpreted is the punishment; but Guyon obviously fails to establish any hermeneutic for responding to Pilate.

72. For the opposition of the hierarchy of relative values (in which gold and food occupy contrary summits) within the economy of scarcity to the overwhelming feculence of material plenitude in what he calls the "general [or "unrestricted"] economy," see Georges Bataille, *Visions of Excess: Selected Writings 1927–39*, ed. and introd. Allan Stoekl, tr. Stoekl, Carl R. Lovitt and Donald M. Leslie, Jr. (Minneapolis: U of Minnesota P, 1985): 116–129. I discuss this concept in more depth in chapter 3.

73. For Kasey Evans, Pilate's sin is a failure to pity, one which Guyon replicates in failing to respond to Pilate ("How Temperance Becomes 'Blood Guiltie,'" 59). She argues that the generously empathetic response that Guyon first extends to Amavia is disciplined throughout Book Two into a thrifty meanness that becomes the book's normative version of temperance, and which allows Guyon to ignore the suffering of the abject—such as Mammon's smelting slaves—and thereby to be complicit in that suffering, the guilt of which stains Guyon's own hands. The power to make a virtue out of withholding pity, she suggests, will

make temperance integral to the "spirit of capitalism" (and of colonialism) as it is contested between Marx and Weber (42).

74. "The [two sinners'] situations are related but dissimilar," writes Prescott, "for although each killed a son or Son, Tantalus did so by wicked action and Pilate by equally intemperate inaction" ("Tantalus, Pilate" in *Sp Enc*, 677).
75. See Gail Kern Paster, *Humoring the Body: Emotions and the Shakespearean Stage* (Chicago: U of Chicago P, 2004), esp. 25–76, for the integration of body, affect, and environment (not only qua "situation" but qua "atmosphere," as here) in the early modern materialist theory of the passions.
76. Since the explicit goal of the quest was to capture Acrasia, critics continue to debate whether and in what sense the devastation of the Bower is appropriate, or if Guyon is failing here to salvage something of value. I am taking it for my purposes as a fait accompli.
77. Nohrnberg, *The Analogy of the Faerie Queene* (Princeton, N.J.: Princeton UP, 1976): 352.
78. Talus is capable of speech, but he speaks only once. The moment in which he does talk is also the only moment in which he proves capable of embarrassment (Guyon's "Shamefastnesse"), when he has the awkward task of telling Britomart about Artegall's subjection to Radegund (5.6.9–11).
79. A figure who underlines the mediations among Mammon, Munera, Talus, and Guyon's "disdainfull nicitee" is the indestructible "villain . . . all of golden mould" Disdayne, whom Mammon does not allow Guyon to fight (2.7.40–43, esp. 40).
80. Spenser ed. Hamilton, 517 n.5.2.9.9. See John A. Yunck, *The Lineage of Lady Meed: The Development of Mediaeval Venality Satire* (South Bend, Ind.: U of Notre Dame P, 1963), esp. 306–323, for the broad tradition of the satiric personfication of *munera*, engaged by both Langland and Spenser.
81. Notable studies of Langland's influence on Spenser include Judith H. Anderson, *The Growth of a Personal Voice: Piers Plowman and The Faerie Queene* (New Haven: Yale UP, 1976) and Fowler, *Literary Character*. Christopher Bond finds an important source for Spenser's Mammon episode in Langland's version of the Harrowing of Hell, though he does not address what the intertext has to do with money: "Medieval Harrowings of Hell and Spenser's House of Mammon," *ELR* 37.2 (Spring 2007): 175–192.
82. Norbrook, *Poetry and Politics in the English Renaissance* (Oxford: Oxford UP, 2002): 42.
83. For Crowley's editorial agenda, see John N. King, *English Reformation Literature: the Tudor Origins of the Protestant Tradition* (Princeton, N.J.: Princeton UP, 1982): 319–346.
84. Lorna Hutson, *Thomas Nashe in Context* (Oxford: Clarendon, 1989): 172–173; Lawrence Manley, *Literature and Cuture in Early Modern London* (Cambridge: Cambridge UP, 1995): 98–103; King, *English Reformation Literature*, passim. David Norbrook traces Spenser's engagement with the plowman tradition of radical critique through *The Shepheardes Calendar* (*Poetry and Politics*, 42–55); so

too does Annabel Patterson, who refers that engagement to Artegall's encounter with the "egalitarian giant" later in this canto ("'They Say' or We Say: Popular Protest and Ventriloquism in Early Modern England," in *Historical Criticism and the Challenge of Theory*, ed. Janet Levarie Smarr [Urbana: U of Illinois P, 1993]: 145–166). For the concreteness invested in the name "Piers Plowman" by medieval literary and social history (in contradistinction to the elusive, evanescent quality of his author, Langland), see Anne Middleton, "William Langland's 'Kynde Name': Authorial Signature and Social Identity in Late Fourteenth-Century England," in *Literary Practice and Social Change in Britain, 1380–1530*, ed. Lee Patterson (Berkeley: U of California P, 1990).

85. *The Vision of Piers Plowman*, ed. A. V. C. Schmidt (London: J. M. Dent, 1995): B 4.174. The use of money in *Piers Plowman*'s poetics reaches far beyond the Mede episode: for notable analyses, see Margaret E. Goldsmith, *The Figure of Piers Plowman: The Image on the Coin* (Cambridge: Brewer, 1981), and Joerg O. Fichte, "'For coveitise after cros; [th]e croune stant in golde': Money as Matter and Metaphor in *Piers Plowman*," in *Material Cuture and Cultural Materialisms in the Middle Ages and Renaissance*, ed. Curtis Perry (Turnhout, Belgium: Brepols, 2001): 59–74.
86. Dolven, *Scenes of Instruction in Renaissance Romance* (Chicago: U of Chicago P, 2007): 213–216.
87. Nohrnberg, *Analogy*, 392n; *Piers Plowman* B 3.10. The clerk of *PP* does so "Curteisly," however, unlike Talus (B 3.9).
88. Talus's focus on the golden hands and silver feet as being the meaningful things about Munera's body has allowed readers to consider the violence here to be immaterial—to read Munera as a merely emblematic representation being disassembled by the textual means of irony (as Nohrnberg describes Talus's work here as turning her into "a sardonic Isis . . . , for a well-known allegory from Plutarch's *De Iside* represented justice as being without hands" [*Analogy*, 391–392]), and not a female body who is the victim of grotesque violence.
89. In chivalric terms Artegall is correct not to sully his hands upon opponents who are not themselves knights like him—that is indeed Talus's job as squire; but the thornier problems faced by Justice in this canto are political ones, having to do with vertical social relations, not with the confrontation of peers. The exercise of chivalry seems nearly incompatible with the domestic work of Justice in Book Five: after vanquishing Pollente, Artegall finds out he has run out of people he considers himself allowed to strike with deadly force, and does not meet another until after his nicety in this regard has resulted in his unmanned enslavement to Radegund.
90. Guyon has to remind Artegall that he, Artegall, is "our iudge of equity" in order to dissuade him from killing the mouthy Braggadochio at Florimel's wedding (5.3.37). For the complex and multivalent relations of "justice" to "equity" in English legal theory, see Joel Altman, "Justice and Equity" in *Sp Enc*, 413–415, and Andrew Zurcher's *Spenser's Legal Language* (Cambridge: Brewer, 2007).

Zurcher does not consider Guyon's exhortation to be as ironic as I am inclined to read it; he construes Artegall as representing the case-by-case judgment of the equity courts throughout Book V, in its opposition to the more automatized application of justice demanded within the common law and personified in Talus (123–152). I follow Altman in locating "that part of Iustice, which is Equity" with Isis and Britomart; in this formulation (though not, as Zurcher demonstrates, in all possible formulations) equity is a subset of justice, not an opposite to it. I suggest, therefore, that Talus's ruthless contrareity to equity is that of "might" (as in 5.4.1): both terms are subordinate components of justice, and it's Artegall's job to balance their competing claims to jurisdiction. Analyzing a different axis of jurisdictional conflict, between English common law and Irish Brehon law, Bradin Cormack aligns Artegall and Talus together with the force of the common law in this episode, as working to erase a pernicious local—that is, Irish—"custom": "The absolute lack of accommodation here exemplifies Spenser's use of Artegall/Talus to represent the interdependence of justice and force" (*A Power to Do Justice: Jurisdiction, English Literature, and the Rise of the Common Law, 1509–1625* [Chicago: U of Chicago P, 2007]: 165).

91. *OED* "reparation" 3, 5a.

## CHAPTER 2

1. Although I here intend only the casual sense of "an exception proving the rule" in its relation to "sovereignty," my use of "sovereign" in this chapter is generally indebted to Carl Schmitt's *Political Theology: Four Chapters on the Concept of Sovereignty*, tr. George Schwab (Cambridge, Mass.: MIT Press, 1988) and to Giorgio Agamben's response to Schmitt in *Homo Sacer: Sovereign Power and Bare Life*, tr. Daniel Heller-Roazen (Stanford, Calif.: Stanford UP, 1998). Schmitt declares, "Sovereign is he who decides on the exception" (5)—that is, who is able to suspend the due process of law with respect to either an individual (as an outlaw, or conversely a felon who receives pardon) or an interval of time (as a state of emergency). Agamben finds an intimate correspondence, amounting in some ways to identity, between the life of the sovereign and the "bare life" of the individual stripped of his place under the law. A straightforward reading of these two plays in this paradigm might suggest that in *King John*, no one is able to declare the exception, so that life muddles along without a sovereign's shaping—as when John attempts to outlaw the child Arthur, but Hubert nevertheless finds himself restrained from actually killing him; while in *Measure for Measure*, the Duke confers an apparent sovereignty upon Angelo in order to expose him to the condition of bare life, utterly dependent on the true sovereign to save or spill. Reading the ontology of money into these relationships complicates them but does not efface them; as I've demonstrated in my introduction, the production of money was understood to be central among the attributes of the early modern sovereign.
2. My vocabulary for this normative causality is Aristotelian, picking up from chapter 1's discussion of hylomorphism (the relation of matter to form); I contrast

that understanding of the relation of cause to the physical world to a pseudo-Epicurean account of material deviance. In *King John*, the condition of that deviance in the social world is a perversity to meaning; in *Measure*, the parallel condition is arbitrariness. In opposing "cause" to "matter" I am bridging those two vocabularies in order to establish the Epicurean matter that, in these two plays, seems actively resistant to the application of cause and is epitomized by coined money. For Aristotle, matter itself counts as one of the four causes of individual phenomena; the causes of a wooden stool's existence, for example, are its material cause (wood); its formal cause (what it needs to be like in order to fit the category "stool": its three-leggedness, its presenting a flat surface a foot or so in radius and a couple of feet off the ground); its efficient cause, the agent of change (the carpenter who produced this particular relation of matter to form); and its final cause or telos (sitting) (*Physics* 2.3, restated in *Metaphysics* 5.2, in *Basic Works of Aristotle*, ed. Richard McKeon [New York: Random House, 1941]: 240–242, 752–754). When the causality of a material phenomenon is ascribed to providence, the four causes become less knowable across the sequence as it's presented by Aristotle: if a church steeple comes crashing down in a storm, the material causes are evident (stone and wind), but the formal cause less so (an admonitory example against steeples, or a tribulation sent to test the resolve of the parish to rebuild a better steeple? If an example, one directed against the whole congregation, or against individuals with particular relations to the steeple, such as the priest or the sexton or the squire who paid for a new bell?). The interpretation that would determine a formal cause has to refer itself to the efficient cause and the final cause, both of which are the ultimately inscrutable and extratemporal will of God, as understood in different temporal relations to the material cause. In this way, a providential causality draws the latter three causes together into an epistemological opposition between the divine will and the material cause, the only one fully knowable from within the physical world of matter. (From a metaphysical perspective, of course, God is the cause of matter too.)

3. Walsham, *Providence in Early Modern England* (Oxford: Oxford UP, 1999): 8–64.
4. For the ways in which the challenge posed to "intelligible order in the world" by the apparently contingent "accident" or event helped indeed to define the infinite subtlety attributed by sixteenth-century Protestants, and Hamlet, to "a special providence," see Michael Witmore, *Culture of Accidents: Unexpected Knowledge in Early Modern England* (Stanford, Calif.: Stanford UP, 2001), esp. 43.
5. My understanding of the interaction of theological interpretation with the everyday contestations of material and social life is indebted to Ethan Shagan's *Popular Politics and the English Reformation* (Cambridge: Cambridge UP, 2003), and to his generous conversation.
6. Sectarian conflict prompted the formulation of ways in which a particular sovereign might fail to embody right rulership and require replacement with a godly one. The first writer in English to articulate a rationale for tyrannicide was the Marian exile John Ponet (in *A Shorte Treatise of Politike Power, and of the true*

*Obedience which subiectes owe to kynges and other ciuile Gouernours, with an Exhortacion to all true naturall Englishe men,* [Strasbourg?], 1556). For the theopolitical development of "resistance theory" across Reformation Europe, see Quentin Skinner, *The Foundations of Modern Political Thought* (Cambridge: Cambridge UP, 1998): 2.189–348.

7. Shuger, *Political Theologies in Shakespeare's England: The Sacred and the State in* Measure for Measure (Basingstoke, Hants.: Palgrave, 2001). For the confluence of Protestant accounts of providence with royal claims to absolutism (and with their controversion) in the first decades of the seventeenth century, see Victoria Kahn, *Wayward Contracts: the Crisis of Political Obligation in England, 1640–1674* (Princeton, N.J.: Princeton UP, 2004): 63–78.
8. Lezra, *Unspeakable Subjects: The Genealogy of the Event in Early Modern Europe* (Stanford, Calif.: Stanford UP, 1997). Lezra's account of the progressive validation of "event" as an object of knowledge, starting in the seventeenth century, parallels Mary Poovey's narrative of the emergence of "fact" as an epistemological category in *A History of the Modern Fact: Problems of Knowledge in the Sciences of Wealth and Society* (Chicago: U of Chicago P, 1998). Richard Kroll traces the development of a specifically Epicurean mode of inquiry in Restoration science and epistemology, one which reacts against Aristotelian and neo-Stoic natural philosophy in order to evaluate and incorporate the contingent, in *The Material Word: Literate Culture in the Restoration and Early Eighteenth Century* (Baltimore: Johns Hopkins UP, 1991). In modern historiography, as Srinivas Aravamudan puts it, "[t]he *event* has twin temporal aspects of *eventuality* and *eventfulness,* teleology and ontology" ("The Return of Anachronism," *MLQ* 62:4 [December 2001]: 331–353, esp. 332; italics *sic*); but the ontological aspect of the early modern "event" is not teleology's "twin" but its antithesis.
9. *Epicoene,* in *Ben Jonson's Plays and Masques,* ed. Richard Harp (New York: W. W. Norton, 2001): 111–199: 2.4.66–78.
10. Tiffany, *Toy Medium: Materialism and Modern Lyric* (Berkeley: U of California P, 2000): 174–175.
11. The paradoxical challenge of atomism—to understand something imperceptible to be the foundational truth of the perceptual world—is central to the analyses of Lucretian influence by Duncan F. Kennedy and Jonathan Goldberg as well. In *Rethinking Reality: Lucretius and the Textualization of Nature* (Ann Arbor: U of Michigan P, 2002), Kennedy traces the paradox's role in shaping the ascription of reality to the object of modern science; in *The Seeds of Things: Theorizing Sexuality and Materiality in Renaissance Representations* (New York: Fordham UP, 2009), Goldberg, responding to Lucretius's identification of the microscopic tendency of atoms toward productivity as Venus, argues for the representation in Renaissance texts of a cosmically generative desire that both lies below (as microscopic and fundamental) and far exceeds (as universal and endless) the proscriptive formulae for individuals' desire in the period—and, for that matter, the contemporary formulae for individuals' desire as reproduced by critics.

12. As I note in chapter 1, questions of reproduction seem to me to be deferred (or begged) both in Book Two's foregrounding of consumption and in the book's troubling of consumption through questions of instrumentality. Goldberg argues for a constructive ambiguity in the blankness of the House of Alma's genitalia, and in the comparison of that episode to the chthonic productivity of Mammon's cave; for him Book Two's evasiveness on the question of a desire that would be temperate—that is, appropriately measured to the scope of an individual—is fundamental to establishing in Book Three a universal desire that subtends and far surpasses the scope of participating individuals, as demonstrated in the Garden of Adonis (*The Seeds of Things*, 63–121).
13. Kahn, *Machiavellian Rhetoric: from the Counter-Reformation to Milton* (Princeton, N.J.: Princeton UP, 1994).
14. For the ups and downs of *King John*'s reception, see Eugene M. Waith, "*King John* and the Drama of History," *Shakespeare Quarterly* 29.2 (Spring, 1978): 192–211. Criticisms and performances that privilege characterization and affect over compositional concerns have found the play more valuable than either Augustan or New Critical modes of reading could readily allow; the role of Constance was especially dear to Victorian readers, actresses, and audiences.
15. In applying the verb from the first phrase to the object of the second, the compression also interacts tellingly with the tropes of chiasmus and antimetabole, which Maurice Hunt considers to be shaping forces integrating sentence and plot structures throughout the text: "Antimetabolic *King John*," *Style* 34.3 (Fall 2000): 380–401.
16. For ways in which Renaissance writers might imagine the resistance of matter to teleological narrative as productive, see Jonathan Gil Harris, *Untimely Matter in the Time of Shakespeare* (Philadelphia: U of Penn. P, 2009); citing ideas of Michel Serres, Harris argues for the possibilities of multitemporal objects to enrich meaning while resisting official discourse. (As I argue in chapter 1, the "antique shapes of kings and kesars strange and rare"—ancient coins—may be read as such multitemporal objects, but their peculiar memorial qualities are ignored by Mammon himself, who is not multitemporal but antitemporal).
17. Lamb, *Preserving the Self in the South Seas, 1680–1840* (Chicago: U of Chicago P, 2001): 4.
18. The "weak-king dilemma" is defined thoroughly by Michael Mannheim, *The Weak King Dilemma in the Shakespearean History Play* (Syracuse, N.Y.: Syracuse UP, 1973).
19. Marlowe, *Edward the Second*, ed. Charles R. Forker (Manchester: Manchester UP, 1994): 1.1.1–2.
20. Another point of reference for the encounter of theater (as performance, as writerly genre) with self-defeat in the Shakespeare canon is *Love's Labour's Lost*—a play even more roundly despised over the centuries than *King John*.
21. As E. A. J. Honigmann has most recently argued, although the dating of the four Yorkist histories and of *King John* remains hotly controverted, a great deal of in-

ternal evidence confirms the critical consensus that *King John* was composed after the first tetralogy ("Shakespeare's Self-Repetitions and *King John*," *Shakespeare Survey* 53 [2000]: 175–183). From this chronology has developed a corollary consensus that the play's disappointment of the expectations created by the dramaturgy of its predecessors is the result of irony, not of incompetence (although many of these voices seem to me too readily to equate the replacement of incompetence by irony with one or another kind of secret success on the play's part); notable examples include Eamon Grennan, "Shakespeare's Satirical History: A Reading of *King John*," *Shakespeare Studies* 11 (1978): 21–37; David Kastan, "'To Set a Form upon That Indigest': Shakespeare's Fictions of History," *Comparative Drama* 17 (1983): 1–16; Larry S. Champion, "The 'Un-end' of *King John*: Shakespeare's Demystification of Closure," in *King John: New Perspectives*, ed. Deborah T. Curren-Aquino (Newark: U of Delaware P, 1989): 173–185; and Marsha Robinson, "The Historiographic Methodology of King John," also in *King John: New Perspectives*, 29–40.

22. Howard and Rackin, *Engendering a Nation: A Feminist Account of Shakespeare's English Histories* (London: Routledge, 1997): 119–120.
23. Garber, *Shakespeare's Ghost Writers: Literature as Uncanny Causality* (New York: Methuen, 1987): 28–51.
24. The dating of both plays is inconclusive, but Charles R. Forker supports the argument that *Richard III* follows, and is specifically influenced by, the dramaturgy and language of *The Jew of Malta* ("Marlowe's *Edward II* and Its Shakespearean Relatives: The Emergence of a Genre," in *Shakespeare's English Histories: A Quest for Form and Genre*, ed. John W. Velz [Binghamton, N.Y.: Medieval and Renaissance Texts and Studies, 1996]: 55–90, esp. 61–65).
25. The paradigmatic formulation of substance as the unity of form *(morphe)* and matter *(hyle)* is that of *De Anima*, Book 2, chapter 1 (412a and following). For the general currency of Aristotelian hylomorphism as "the primary discursive framework for the production of knowledge concerning natural bodies" in sixteenth-century England, see Henry S. Turner, "Nashe's Red Herring: Epistemologies of the Commodity in *Lenten Stuffe* (1599)," *ELH* 68.3 (2001): 529–561, esp. 539–540, and Jonathan Gil Harris's response to Turner, "Shakespeare's Hair: Staging the Object of Material Culture," *Shakespeare Quarterly* 52.3 (2002): 479–491, as well as my chapter 1. For an analysis of coinage in that framework, see John Carey, "Donne and Coins," in *English Renaissance Studies Presented to Dame Helen Gardner*, ed. John Carey (Oxford: Clarendon, 1980): 151–163.
26. In studying what he calls "the 'un-end' of *King John*," Larry S. Champion argues that from 4.2 onward "Shakespeare seems consciously and methodically to deconstruct the chronicle play, raising expectations only to leave them unfulfilled" ("The 'Un-End' of *King John*," 181).
27. Citing this passage, Virginia Mason Vaughan argues that the text's battle of ideas is articulated between the terms "majesty" and "commodity," but concedes that "majesty" does not put up much of a fight in *King John* ("Between Tetralogies:

*King John* as Transition," *Shakespeare Quarterly* 35.4 [Winter 1984]: 407–420, esp. 413). Peter Stallybrass notes that 3.1.101 is the first citation for "valueless" in *OED*; he connects the advent of this neologism to an emergent contempt for materiality in early modernity that would serve to enable the oblivion of material value (i.e., of values in excess of or incommensurable with exchange value) in mature capitalism: "The Value of Culture and the Disavowal of Things," in *The Culture of Capital*, ed. Henry S. Turner (New York: Routledge, 2002): 275–292.

28. Howard and Rackin, *Engendering a Nation*, 127.
29. Knapp, *Shakespeare's Tribe: Church, Nation, and Theater in Renaissance England* (Chicago: U of Chicago P, 2002): 95–102.
30. Kehler, "'So Jest with Heaven': Deity in *King John*," in *King John: New Perspectives*, 99–113, esp. 99–100.
31. This is not to say that the corpuscular philosophy is an arbitrary and fictive etiology for the macroscopic freedom of the will, in the way that, for example, the fable of the state of nature serves Hobbes's analysis of the contractual state in the present. As Michel Serres argues, the *clinamen* or minimal deviation seems arbitrary only in a physics whose basic instance is the linear motion of solid bodies; to a physics (like that of the ancient world) that is primarily interested in the motion of liquids, the arising of turbulence in any linear flow would seem not only natural but inevitable (*The Birth of Physics*, tr. Jack Hawkes [Manchester: Clinamen, 2000]: 3–18).
32. *On the Nature of Things*, tr. W. H. D. Rouse, ed. and rev. Martin F. Smith (Cambridge, Mass.: Loeb Classical Library/Harvard UP, 1992): 1.464–482, 2.217–260. In addition to the direct reading of Lucretius, Renaissance literati might encounter Epicurean ontology through the mediation of a variety of canonical sources, including a number of unsympathetic remarks by Cicero and, most extensively, Ovid's engagements of Epicurean cosmogony in *Metamorphoses*. For the relations between Ovid's metaphysical poetics and Lucretius, see K. Sara Myers, *Ovid's Causes: Cosmogony and Ætiology in the* Metamorphoses (Ann Arbor: U of Michigan P, 1994).
33. My analysis here credits Shakespeare with enough of a casual acquaintance with Epicurean ontology to be familiar with the relation it posits between microscopic atom and macroscopic contingency through the category of "event." That he had such an acquaintance in the mid-1590s is, as Jonathan Gil Harris has demonstrated, evident from Mercutio's "Queen Mab" speech in *Romeo and Juliet* 1.4.53–103, in which that fairy's minuscule chariot is drawn by a team of "atomi" (Harris, "Atomic Shakespeare"); the speech engages Epicureanism for the sake of a fascinated, lingering belittling of its ideas corresponding to that which I find at work in the dramaturgy of *King John*. Although previous generations of scholars had tended to assume that sixteenth-century English literary culture operated under a generally willed ignorance of Epicureanism, which would enjoy a revival only under the auspices of the seventeenth century's new science, recent scholarship has demonstrated the extent to which Epicurean ideas were engaged by sixteenth-

century writers and has analyzed the habits of reading, thought, and expression which enabled them to coordinate or countervail the most scandalous aspects of Epicurean thinking with more orthodox ideas. See also Hilary Gatti, *The Renaissance Drama of Knowledge* (New York: Routledge, 1989); Gilberto Sacerdoti, *Nuovo cielo, nuova terra: La rivelazione copernicana di "Antonio e Cleopatra" di Shakespeare* (Bologna: Il Mulino, 1990); Lezra, *Unspeakable Subjects*; Goldberg, *The Seeds of Things*; Harris, *Untimely Matter in the Time of Shakespeare*; Gerard Passannante, "The Art of Reading Earthquakes: On Harvey's Wit, Ramus's Method, and the Renaissance of Lucretius," *Renaissance Quarterly* 61.3 (Fall 2008): 792–832; Ayesha Ramachandran, "Edmund Spenser, Lucretian Neoplatonist: Cosmology in the *Fowre Hymnes*," *Spenser Studies* 24 (2009): 373–412; and Stephen Greenblatt, *The Swerve: How the World Became Modern* (New York: Norton, 2011).

34. Among the diverse Latin periphrases Lucretius uses to denote the atoms of Epicurus (as he never imports the Greek word) is *semina*, "seeds." Jonathan Goldberg argues against a heteronormatively masculine connotation for this usage in reading Lucretius, pointing to several critics who have done so (*The Seeds of Things*, 47–50). In equating the Lucretian swerve with a productive deviance from the marriage bed, the Bastard asserts an aspect of its erotically liberatory quality as defined by Goldberg, though he remains bound by more broadly heteronormative understandings of reproduction; and, as I'll argue, the liberatory subtlety of Lucretius's microscopic materialism is rather brutally foreclosed in the play by its transposition into the gross materialism of monetary advantage.
35. Modern editions give the character the speech-prefix "Bastard" throughout, but the Folio text refers to him as Philip until 1.1.138, his response to Eleanor's offer to deny his Faulconbridge patrimony and become a landless Plantagenet.
36. To differentiate coins of different value but similar size and type (as sixpences from shillings, or, as here, three-farthing pieces from pennies), the Mint placed a rose over the shoulder of the portrait on the less valuable coin.
37. Renaissance bowling balls had a weight, or bias, inserted into one side of the ball to make it roll eccentrically, adding challenge to the game.
38. Daniel Tiffany argues that analogy and metaphor are inevitable aspects of corpuscular physics: the imperceptibility of atoms is only articulable by means of macroscopic phenomena (*Toy Medium*, 174–175). Jonathan Gil Harris argues in corresponding terms that the "atomi" of Mercutio's "Queen Mab" speech (*RJ* 1.4.53–103) assert both the fictivity and the temporal motion inhering in the theorization of the fundamental errancy of corpuscular matter ("Atomic Shakespeare," 47–51).
39. The expectation that the maximization of individual profit would result not only in the immediate disadvantage of those from whom the profit was taken but in the eventual decay of the "common-wealth" as a whole (including the disadvantage of those whose present profiteering was forwarding that decay) was a truism of sixteenth-century political thought that I examine in my introduction.

40. A ready comparison to John's frustrated, reactive redundancies would be the scope for action given to Macbeth, between his complex relation to witchy prophecy, on the one hand, and to the working out of providentialist plotting on the other.
41. Kahn, *Machiavellian Rhetoric*, 85–166.
42. Although Shakespeare is often said never to have written city comedy, many commentators have noted the extent to which the claustrophobic urban environment of *Measure* is London's; the only things that keep it from being London are the presence of an actual nunnery (alongside the brothel) and of mendicant friars, as well as the representation of the sovereign on stage, which would not have been possible for a literally English setting. That the setting is explicitly modern as well as implicitly domestic is evident both in the dominance of the local market by the twin diseases of novelty—commodification and syphilis—and in the marked resemblance that Jonathan Goldberg has demonstrated between the Duke's mode of governing and that of James, as both absolute and discreet, in *James I and the Politics of Literature* (Baltimore: Johns Hopkins UP, 1983): 210–239. When *Measure* was first performed at court (December 26, 1604), James had been ruling for only a year and a half.
43. BM Harl. MS 6848, ff. 185–186, transcribed in Millar Maclure, ed., *Marlowe: The Critical Heritage 1588–1896* (London: Routledge and Kegan Paul, 1979): 36–38. Baines was a professional informer who had, astonishingly, been arrested for counterfeiting together with Marlowe in the Dutch port of Vlissingen (then under English governorship and known in English as Flushing) two years before. This testimonial, however, was produced for a second occasion, the investigation into the Dutch Church Libel of spring 1593, an anonymous, threateningly xenophobic tract that implicated Marlowe in its text and was signed "Tamburlaine." Baines's is the second of two surviving juridical testimonials from that spring about Marlowe's atheistic leanings, the first having been extracted from the playwright's former roommate Thomas Kyd under torture. The Baines text has given rise to much speculation both as to its veracity and as to its relation to the circumstances of Marlowe's violent death, which it preceded by a matter of days—for which see Charles Nicholl, *The Reckoning: The Murder of Christopher Marlowe* (London: Jonathan Cape, 1992) and David Riggs, "The Killing of Christopher Marlowe," *Stanford Humanities Review* 8.1 (2000): 239–251. It is particularly remarkable that the text doesn't cite Marlowe's previous arrest in Flushing; both Baines and Marlowe were remanded directly to Lord Burghley by the governor there, Henry Sidney (the late Sir Philip's brother), so Baines knew that Burghley knew the Flushing story, and since neither Baines nor Marlowe was executed or imprisoned for any length of time upon their return from Flushing, we may infer that Burghley thought the whole incident trivial (Nicholl, 234–239).
44. Goldberg, "Sodomy and Society: The Case of Christopher Marlowe," in *Staging the Renaissance: Interpretations of Elizabethan and Early Jacobean Drama*, eds. David Scott Kastan and Peter Stallybrass (New York: Routledge, 1991): 75–82.

45. Peacham, *Minerva Brittana* (London, 1612): 48; Orgel, "Tobacco and Boys: How Queer Was Marlowe?" *GLQ* 6.4 (2000): 555–576; Fisher, "Queer Money," *ELH* 66.1 (Spring 1999): 1–23.
46. With great and ingenious difficulty is how, as demonstrated in the formulae according to which the Commonwealth Parliament at last charged King Charles with treason.
47. Orgel places the emblem, and a Jacobean revival of *Edward II*, in the context of James's defense of his own minions ("Tobacco and Boys," 575).
48. Poovey, *Genres of the Credit Economy: Mediating Value in Eighteenth- and Nineteenth-century Britain* (Chicago: U of Chicago P, 2008): 57–85.
49. Frankfurt, *On Bullshit* (Princeton, N. J.: Princeton UP, 2005): 47. Paul Strohm has unearthed an extraordinary accusation against the historical Sir John Oldcastle: it alleges that the rebel knight conspired with Lollard priests to mint *fine*, sterling silver counterfeits, intended not for material gain but for a blasphemous attack on the immaterial pretensions of the money form, the royal seal, and, of course, the Eucharist (*England's Empty Throne: Usurpation and the Language of Legitimation, 1399–1422* [New Haven: Yale UP, 1998]: 128–152). As Jesse M. Lander has demonstrated, a rhetoric of coining is one of the ways in which Shakespeare's Falstaff, né Oldcastle, establishes the rivalry between the misrule of his tavern kingdom and the dubious legitimacy of Henry IV's reign ("'Crack'd Crowns' and Counterfeit Sovereigns: The Crisis of Value in *1 Henry IV*," *Shakespeare Studies* 30 [2002]: 137–161). The fact that Shakespeare could not have known of the document in drawing up his portrayal of Oldcastle/Falstaff as a counterfeiter makes the convergence more telling rather than less. For Strohm's own, tantalizingly brief reference to Falstaff in this light, see his *Theory and the Premodern Text* (Minneapolis: U of Minnesota P, 2000): 143–148.
50. The earliest codified precedent for counterfeiting as treason is a law of Constantine, reiterated in the code of Theodosius; but, as Michael Neill argues, this law itself looks far back to "ancient magical beliefs" of the Romans in the identity of person and representation, "reflected in the meanings of *imago* as both 'representation' and 'ghost' or 'spirit'" ("Bastardy, Counterfeiting, and Misogyny in *The Revenger's Tragedy*," *SEL* 36.2 [Spring 1996]: 397–416, esp. 401). David Hawkes cites corroborating instances from the Byzantine iconoclastic struggles (*Idols of the Marketplace: Idolatry and Commodity Fetishism in English Literature, 1580–1680* [New York: Palgrave, 2001]: 65–66). Counterfeiting was only intermittently prosecuted as high treason in England until the statute 25 Edw. III c. 2 (1337), which comprehensively defined the offenses subject to such prosecution. It should be noted that this law was perhaps less concerned to define the official heinousness of assaults upon the royal image than to locate counterfeiting in the direct jurisdiction of the royal courts and out of the manorial ones; see below for the practical difficulties of local counterfeiting prosecutions, which solicited the intervention of central government. Over the following centuries, many other related offenses against the coinage (clipping, culling heavier coins,

the counterfeiting of foreign coin) were added to the litany of treasonable offenses. Upon her accession, Mary Tudor rolled back that list (to which her father in particular had made many unpopular and far-fetched additions) to the definitions of the statute of Edward III, but the counterfeiting of foreign coin current in England was revived as treason the same year, and clipping and other diminution of the coin's metal by 5 Elizabeth c. 11 (1563). See William Blackstone, *Commentaries on the Laws of England*, ed. William Draper Lewis (Philadelphia: R. Welsh & Co., 1902), Book 4, chapter 6, "Of High Treason," for an efficient summary, and J. G. Bellamy, *The Law of Treason in England in the Later Middle Ages* (Cambridge: Cambridge UP, 1970) and *Tudor Law of Treason* (London: Routledge and Kegan Paul, 1979) for a more complete account.

51. Blackstone, *Commentaries*, 4.6.
52. George Chapman, Ben Jonson, and John Marston, *Eastward Ho*, ed. R. W. Van Fossen (Manchester: Manchester UP, 1999): 4.1.256–258.
53. The seventeenth-century monetarist Rice Vaughan construes the effect of clipping on the silver coinage in these terms, as in effect redressing the undervaluation of silver relative to gold in the price set by the sovereign at the Mint, although he nevertheless disapproves of both the clippers' practice and the Mint's in this regard (*A Discourse of Coin and Coinage* [1630–1635?, printed 1675], in *A Select Collection of Scarce and Valuable Tracts on Money*, ed. J. R. McCulloch [London: Political Economy Club, 1856]: 1–120, esp. 42).
54. Blackstone, *Commentaries*, 4.6.
55. Gaskill, *Crime and Mentalities in Early Modern England* (Cambridge: Cambridge UP, 2000): 127–130. His final citation is the most engaging, though it does depart from my period: "Around 1700, the Ordinary of Newgate fought a last-ditch attempt to find scriptural grounds for the illegality of clipping, venturing that the act of 'paring-round' or *circumcision* was practiced only by those who had renounced Christianity" (130). The Ordinary probably did not realize that he was repeating what had been a joke about clipping in John Donne's elegy "The Bracelet": "And howso'er French Kings most Christian be,/ Their Crownes are circumcis'd most Jewishly" (lines 27–28); see my chapter 4 for a discussion of these lines.
56. Gaskill, *Crime and Mentalities*, 176. On p. 174 he notes that between 1660 and 1800 fully 58% of coiners convicted at the Surrey assizes were granted clemency, as compared to less than 24% of murderers, and most of the latter group of reprieveds had been condemned on insufficient evidence: "Perhaps, then, this inconsistency reflects high-level resignation to the failure of ideology."
57. Ibid., 153–154.
58. Ibid., 127–130.
59. Even a state as nakedly interventionist as early modern England has become occluded as an economic actor in our recent criticism. In exalting the entrepreneurial spirit of the theater industry, of mercantilist authors, and of London's luxury producers and consumers as forging a national market, we are prone to see these

small-scale actors instituting a new and mercantile concept of nation distinct from the preexisting institutions of the Crown. Rejecting the anachronistic, totalizing expectations of classical economics, critics such as Lena Cowen Orlin, Wendy Wall, and Natasha Korda have reshaped our understanding of Renaissance markets by tracing the genealogy of "political economy" back to the first book of Aristotle's *Economics*, a treatise on the management of a single household, and have anchored the early modern economic in a domestic origin that emphasizes the local, private, and individuated: see Korda, *Shakespeare's Domestic Economies* (Philadelphia: U of Pennsylvania P, 2002); Orlin, *Private Matters and Public Culture in Post-Reformation England* (Ithaca, N.Y.: Cornell UP, 1994); and Wall, *Staging Domesticity: Household Work and English Identity in Early Modern Drama* (Cambridge: Cambridge UP, 2002). Few, though, have yet presented a complementary reading of the second book of *Economics*, which relates domestic economies to politics by listing different manipulations enforced on the larger market by kings or influential citizens across the Greek world for their personal profit. (Modern critics are perhaps influenced to disregard the second book of *Economics* by the consensus among classicists that the attribution of that book to Aristotle is certainly spurious—a judgment that Renaissance scholars were already coming to suspect was the case, though the two books continued to circulate together.) The result of this imbalance is effectively to skew our present perception of the English body politic in the Renaissance toward that of "a nation of shopkeepers," anticipating Napoleon's accusation that private material interests rather than sovereign ones shaped the policy of the imperial British state. To the extent that this may have been the case, it was not for lack of trying on the part of the sovereign; considering as a pattern such individually notorious interventions upon the market as the usury laws, the sumptuary laws, the Statute of Artificers, the wool staple, and the assortment of "projects" forwarded by the Crown will readily show that royal policy makers shared the assumption of the commonwealths-men that everybody's business was also the Crown's business.

60. [Smith, Sir Thomas, attr.], *A Discourse of the Commonweal of This Realm of England*, ed. Mary Dewar (Charlottesville: UP of Virginia, 1969): 76.
61. For the scholastic background of these formulations, see Henry William Spiegel, *The Growth of Economic Thought*, 3rd ed. (Durham, N.C.: Duke UP, 1991): 70–74.
62. In practice, however, coins were routinely clipped throughout their life in circulation, so the amount of precious metal in each did generally diminish; this would only exacerbate the burden of extrinsic value placed upon the stamp, as I've noted above.
63. [Cotton, Sir Robert], "A Speech... Touching the Alteration of Coin" [1626, printed 1651], in *A Select Collection of Scarce and Valuable Tracts on Money*, ed. J. R. McCulloch (London: Political Economy Club, 1856): 121–141, esp. 128.
64. As I note in my introduction, the reformation of the silver coinage to the sterling standard was inscribed as one of Elizabeth's principal accomplishments on the

tomb James built for her in Westminster Abbey in 1606, and remained a point of reference for debates over monetary policy for much of the next century.

65. Simmel, *The Philosophy of Money*, trans. Tom Bottomore and David Frisby (London: Routledge and Kegan Paul, 1990): 259–260.
66. Ian Whitelaw, *A Measure of All Things: The Story of Man and Measurement* (New York: St. Martin's, 2007): 16, 30.
67. The practical results of debasement of a metallic currency are of course much more complex and unpredictable than this picture would have it—debasement will eventually depress the metal price by enlarging the bullion supply, for one thing, and some commodities will be more volatile in an inflationary situation than others owing to the interdependence of their prices—but it must be remembered that Cotton is here trying to make an abstruse theory as lucid as possible for a nonspecialist audience.
68. Even to cite the full range of *Measure* readings "will last out a night in Russia, when nights are longest there" (2.1.134–135). The principal divide among the critics has separated those who argue that the play endorses and is coterminous with the Duke's homiletic description of the resolution he has staged (however unsatisfying we may feel that resolution to be) from those who assert that the play as a whole ironizes that description, detaching itself from the character. The exemplary analysis in the latter vein, to myself and a generation of critics before me, is Jonathan Dollimore, "Transgression and Surveillance in *Measure for Measure*," in *Political Shakespeare: New Essays in Cultural Materialism*, eds. Jonathan Dollimore and Alan Sinfield (Manchester: Manchester UP, 1985): 72–87. Dollimore's resistant reading has guided subsequent readers to critique the convergence in *Measure* of a variety of early modern social institutions, especially religion, the law, gender roles, and finance. My analyses of the Duke's propagation of authority through displacement and representation are likewise much indebted to Goldberg, *James I*, 210–239. A recent reading that anticipates my own in drawing particular attention to the rhetoric of coined money in the play is Teresa Lanpher Nugent, "Usury and Counterfeiting in Wilson's *The Three Ladies of London* and *The Three Lords and Three Ladies of London*, and in Shakespeare's *Measure for Measure*," in *Money and the Age of Shakespeare: Essays in New Economic Criticism*, ed. Linda Woodbridge (New York: Palgrave Macmillan, 2003): 201–217. Shakespeare's employment of that minting rhetoric has more often been studied with reference to *1 Henry IV*; see in particular Stephen Greenblatt, "Invisible Bullets," in *Shakespearean Negotiations* (Berkeley: U of California P, 1989): 21–65; Sandra K. Fischer, "'He Means to Pay': Value and Metaphor in the Lancastrian Tetralogy," *Shakespeare Quarterly* 40:2 (Summer 1989): 149–164; Nina Levine, "Extending Credit in the Henry IV Plays," *Shakespeare Quarterly* 51:4 (Winter 2000): 403–431; and Lander, "Crack'd Crowns." An influential reading of coining outside the Shakespeare canon is Valerie Forman, "Marked Angels: Counterfeits, Commodities, and *The Roaring Girl*," *Renaissance Quarterly* 54.4.2 (Winter 2001): 1531–1560.

In *Coinage and State Formation in Early Modern English Literature* (New York: Palgrave Macmillan, 2011: 103–134), Stephen Deng offers an analysis of debasement and state power in *Measure* that converges with my own at several points; I regret not being able to engage his excellent book more directly, as it came to me when the present volume was already in proofs.

69. Here I'm stepping back from Nigel Smith's declaration that "*Measure for Measure* is a play about *value*" to focus on means before ends ("The Two Economies of 'Measure for Measure,'" *English: The Journal of the English Association* 36:156 [1987 Autumn]: 197–232, esp. 197; his italics). Smith's argument, that the comparison of the differently imperfect social relationships present on stage adumbrates an ideal society which cannot directly be staged, deftly coordinates the idealistic and resistant strains of *Measure* criticism; it is echoed by the "Marxism before Marx" by which Kiernan Ryan defines the sourness of the play's close as an indirectly utopian gesture ("*Measure for Measure*: Marxism before Marx," in *Marxist Shakespeares*, ed. Jean E. Howard and Scott Cutler Shershow [London: Routledge, 2001]: 227–244).
70. Ex. 21: 22–5; Lev. 24: 19–21; Deut. 19: 16–21. See Marc Shell, *The End of Kinship: 'Measure for Measure,' Incest, and the Ideal of Universal Siblinghood* (Baltimore: Johns Hopkins UP, 1988): 97–136, for an intricate meditation on this concept in *Measure.*
71. The Provost's language and the Duke's insist on deferring the identification of the unveiled prisoner with Claudio, such that even in the moment of unveiling they protract the fiction that the original Claudio is dead and that the present individual represents a third term in the circuit of exchange Claudio-Angelo-Claudio:

> *Provost.* This is another prisoner that I sav'd,
> Who should have died when Claudio lost his head,
> As like almost to Claudio as himself.
> *Duke.* [*to Isabella.*] If he be like your brother, for his sake
> Is he pardon'd (5.1.487–490).

The two-for-one quality of this deferred identity draws the Duke's maneuvers into line with the parable of the talents in Matthew and Luke, in which 100% profit rather than equal exchange is defined as the economy of the elect. For the "spiritual usury" of grace in Protestant theology's struggle with this parable, and its relation to the monetary usury alluded to by Pompey, see Nigel Smith, "The Two Economies of 'Measure'"; Shell, *End of Kinship*; Nugent, "Usury and Counterfeiting"; and Huston Diehl, "'Infinite Space': Representation and Reformation in *Measure for Measure*," *Shakespeare Quarterly* 49.4 (Winter 1998): 393–410; for the imbrication of state and theological apparatuses, see Shuger, *Political Theologies.*

72. For the reflection effect of the Marxian commodity form exerting itself on human subjects, see Richard Halpern's reading of the monetized, mirroring figure of the Jew in modern anti-Semitic discourse and in *The Merchant of Venice* in *Shakespeare*

*among the Moderns* (Ithaca, N.Y.: Cornell UP, 1997): 159–226, which I discuss directly in the next chapter.

73. Like Cotton, the Duke avoids rhyming "measure" and "pleasure," Cotton in the framing of his sentence asymmetrically, the Duke by using "leisure" as the rhyme in his ostentatiously and multiply symmetrical couplet (within the single line 411, of course, he tautologically rhymes "measure" with itself). It is hard to understand what lesson, if any, we are to draw from "Haste still pays haste, and leisure answers leisure" in the context of the plot's difficult timing (5.1.410)—"I shall attend your leisure, but make haste," the disguised Duke has oxymoronically demanded of Mariana and Isabella (4.1.56), while it had been the Duke's own arbitrary "haste" in 1.1 that left "unquestion'd/ Matters of needful value" (1.1.54–55). The word "leisure" is the Duke's own property, as no character in the play speaks it but he (at 1.3.49; 3.1.153; 3.2.247; 4.1.56; and 5.1.410). Nevertheless, the Duke uses "pleasure" in preference to "leisure" on the one occasion when either would have an interchangeable sense (of "convenience"): "You shall anon over-read it at your pleasure," he says in giving the Provost a letter from his ducal self (4.2.197).
74. I'm taking naming in particular as an instance of interpellation—of the mode of address by authority that instantiates the addressee as subject to that authority—via the sovereignty over the animals granted by God to Adam in the act of naming. The monarch's selection of officers is routinely understood as a performative "naming," and his naming of nobles to the peerage is a "creation." "Interpellation" has a more everyday and impersonal context in Althusser's original formulation (*Lenin and Philosophy and Other Essays*, tr. Ben Brewster [New York: Monthly Review, 1971]: 117–121).
75. Advocating a recognition of "the poetics of incomprehensibility," Stephen Orgel challenges the assumption that we ought to be able to fully elucidate the Shakespearean text through interpretation: "What is concealed in the process of interpretation . . . is the effort of will, or even of willfulness, involved. This method of elucidation assumes that behind the obscurity and confusion of the text is a clear meaning, and that the obscurity, moreover, is not part of the meaning" ("The Poetics of Incomprehensibility," *SQ* 42.4 [Winter 1991]: 431–437, esp. 433).
76. Pompey does not care that this has always been the law, from which enforcement has lapsed over the past fourteen (or nineteen) years of the present Duke's rule; he understands it in terms of a constraint upon futurity. As I argue in chapter 1, the economic dystopia that Pompey cites here is the future horizon of commodified "novelty" from which the money form invades the present; the fact that Pompey envisions the suppression of his commodity as producing a comparable desolation of the commonwealth suggests that Vienna is in a double bind, as the place where that dystopically monetized futurity has made itself already present as the means of civil continuance.
77. Claudio and Juliet have deferred their marriage in hopes of "propagation" of her dowry (1.2.150), so their motives are in a way mercenary (or, rather, they would

like to have their cake and eat it too, sinning against scarcity, the precondition of economic choice), but this does not seem to be a factor in Angelo's judgment, as Claudio offers it as an excuse.

78. Dollimore, "Transgression and Surveillance," 85.
79. As I argued in chapter 1, Spenser's Guyon must come very close to becoming like Mammon in demonstrating the point at which Mammon falls short; this flirtation with personifying money's qualities in order to show its material limits, a kind of devil's advocacy, is manifest in all the texts that I consider in this study, and it is here imposed upon Angelo from above.
80. I discuss the punning interaction of gold coin and beneficent immaterial agent in more depth in chapter 4, through the 'twelve righteous angels' of John Donne's "The Bracelet."
81. In focusing as I do on the situation of Angelo, I don't have room to read Isabella's intent here, nor the ways in which she reworks Angelo's vocabulary in her attempt to persuade him. Two important readings of the intersection of gendered and economic roles in the person of Isabella are Korda, *Shakespeare's Domestic Economies*, and Barbara Sebek, "'By Gift of My Chaste Body': Female Chastity and Exchange Value in *Measure for Measure* and *A Woman Killed with Kindness*," *Journal x: A Journal in Culture and Criticism* 5.1–2 (2000 Autumn–2001 Spring): 51–85.
82. I emphasize this legal problematic in order to qualify Nugent's argument that "The Duke's disguise suggests that the culture of trust necessary for a credit economy must be founded paradoxically upon counterfeiting; however, such counterfeiting is permissible when (and only when) it is performed by the Duke" ("Usury and Counterfeiting," 212). Her point effectively elucidates the points of contact among the play's official discourses of counterfeiting, usury, and disguise, but I am here pushing against it to argue that the paradox itself is imposed, like the different discourses that intersect in it, by the sovereign Duke, not one "necessary" to "culture."
83. *Prince*, chapter vii; Holland, "*Measure for Measure*: The Duke and the Prince," *Comparative Literature* 11.1 (Winter 1959): 16–20. Machiavelli refers specifically to the discovery of the decapitated body as a theatrical "spectacle," *la ferocità del quale spettacolo*, and Holland cites the passage as a source for the Duke's discomfiting enactment of politics as theater. Holland thinks that Shakespeare is most likely to have encountered the story of Messer Ramirro in the 1602 English translation of Gentillet's *Anti-Machiavel*, which cites the episode three times (17). Shakespeare need not have read either treatise directly to have grasped the principle that underlies both Cesare's action and the Duke's; the shock of Machiavelli's text lies in his insistence on naming the unspeakably obvious. But Kahn demonstrates that many more English men of letters were able to paraphrase or plagiarize Machiavelli's texts than were willing openly to cite him; she considers his thinking to be as central to debates within English political discourse in the Renaissance as was the overt repudiation of his ethos (*Machiavellian Rhetoric*, 85–166).

84. The list could go on: I've already mentioned Mistress Overdone, and Escalus enjoys riffing on the absurd historical pomp of Pompey's name as much as Lucio does. The name of the foolish tavern denizen Master Froth is self-explanatory, but Escalus can't resist explaining it to him anyway. "Juliet," Claudio's partner in crime, seems like a self-citation on Shakespeare's part, in the youthful desire that defers the approval of "friends"—which as Claudio sees it is the way of the world, rather than tragically extraordinary as it is in *R&J*.
85. Goldberg, *James I*, 210–239.
86. Critics such as Shell, *End of Kinship*, who are concerned to humanize the Duke do tend to refer to him by this name rather than by the title through which he is exclusively known to his subjects.
87. In this formulation regarding names and titles I am excluding characters addressed only through pronouns, such as the anonymous companions of Lucio in 1.2 ("gentlemen" according to the stage directions and speech prefixes). The "gentle Provost" is, strikingly, recognized by the Duke as too good for his job, and the horizon of the play's ending entails an unnamed promotion for this character that would be the converse of Angelo's initiating deputization.
88. Dominating the city yet unencumbered by either London's buildings or its rights, the Tower was so recognizable as the site of unmediated sovereign power that popular tradition, as voiced by the little Prince of *Richard III*, backdated its foundation to the first imposition of empire upon the island by Julius Caesar (3.1.68–78); it had in fact been built to mark a second one, by William the Conqueror. The security of the Tower was necessary to the Mint both because of the great amounts of precious metal that passed through its furnaces and because the means of production—the dies that stamped the type upon the coins—themselves required jealous supervision. The outer fortifications of the Tower were separated from the City by a broad open field, Tower Hill, which itself was part of the Liberty of the Tower; the laws of the City had no sway in the Liberty, which was subject to the direct jurisdiction of the Crown. Officers of the Tower, including minters to a certain extent, were not subject to the City administration even when within municipal boundaries.
89. For the difference between the extralegal killing of an outlaw and the juridical execution of a criminal, which Barnardine effectively asserts here, see Agamben, *Homo Sacer*. Agamben argues that the former, not the latter, is the crux of sovereignty. Barnardine is by no means an average hoodlum; he is a gentleman, since he is to be beheaded and not hanged, and he has powerful "friends" (presumably relatives, in the common Renaissance usage) who had been able to keep his sentencing ambiguous under the Duke's regime. In this he is implicitly contrasted to Claudio, whose dead father's reputation carries weight with Escalus but has no influence on Angelo; when the Provost tells the disguised Duke that new proof had been discovered to justify Barnardine's execution under Angelo, I am inclined to hear an excuse for the Duke's not having already executed him.

90. Lezra puts the pirate's head at the center of his argument that *Measure* stages the irreducibility of contingent events to the historicizing narrative of the subject: "the apotropon—Barnardine's sublime refusal and the severed head that takes his place—substitutes a tolerable figure counterphobically for something intolerable, in this case the impossibility or limit of substitution itself" (*Unspeakable Subjects*, 261); "the story discriminating Ragozine's death from his decapitation . . . is not *human* history but an effect of the erasure, the oblivion of its eventful contingency" (294, his emphasis).
91. The large gold coin named "sovereign," a series in crown gold featuring the monarch enthroned on its face, was invented under Henry VII, but hardly ever minted under Elizabeth or in the first years of James's reign (C. E. Challis, *The Tudor Coinage* [Manchester: Manchester UP, 1978]: 229); I don't think Shakespeare ever mentions it, and "sovereign" certainly does not appear directly in *Measure's* vocabulary in either sense.
92. It's hardly possible to imagine *Measure for Measure* as itself intending to resist or demystify what Shuger calls "sacral kingship"; as Shuger demonstrates, the sacrality of the monarch was taken for granted across the theologico-political spectrum in 1604 (*Political Theologies*, 56)—and even if the King's Men could conceive or endorse a resistant position toward that ideologeme, they would hardly have articulated such a stand in the context of the King's Christmas revels, which they opened that year with a performance of *Measure*. If the Duke's actions (and inactions) in *Measure* seem to us hard to swallow, that is because they are strong medicine for the Viennese body politic. Yet the unsparing attention to such a diseased political body, on the one hand, and the silences hedging the ambiguous divinity of the Duke, on the other, do distinguish *Measure* both from the comparatively escapist comic delights of a *Twelfth Night* and from the playful, elaborately articulated idolatries that had been directed at Elizabeth in comparable contexts (for example, the prologue to Dekker's *Old Fortunatus*). As a materialist reading, my analysis has focused more on the compromised means by which the Duke's sacrality interacts with the material corruption of Vienna—finding the minting power to be a defining instance of those means—than on the Duke's ends, which Shuger seems right to argue cannot but be unexceptionable to their audience (1–6), however opaque they may be to his subjects. "The political theme dominates from the outset, its importance signalled by the opening line of the Duke's first speech: 'Of government the properties to unfold,'" Shuger points out in introducing her argument about "what the play makes clear, explicit, and overt" (1, 6); I'm interested in the circumstance that, however patently thematic this line may be, it is spoken only after a hierarchical relation is established between "Escalus" and "My lord," and in the fact that the speech that follows this line makes it clear that "Of government the properties to unfold" is what the Duke will proceed not to do—that those "properties" are first gestured toward and then left unarticulated.

## CHAPTER 3

1. As Freud's editors note, the "metapsychological development" of the concept of disavowal [*Verleugnung*] separates Freud's classic postwar work on the fetish from his earlier analyses ("Fetishism," in *The Standard Edition of the Complete Psychological Works of Sigmund Freud,* vol. 21 [London: Hogarth, 1955]: 149–158, esp. 150; further citations of this essay will be given parenthetically in the text). Those earlier analyses, Lisa Freinkel argues, align the fetish with conventional theories of idolatry, while the emergence of disavowal transposes them; she traces a corresponding transposition of idolatrous terms in Shakespeare's sonnets ("The Shakespearean Fetish," in *Spiritual Shakespeares,* ed. Ewan Fernie [New York: Routledge, 2005]: 109–129).

   "Disavowal" has a sense continuous with that of "disowning," and I am of course indebted here to Stanley Cavell's powerful analyses of skepticism in Shakespeare in *Disowning Knowledge in Six Plays of Shakespeare* (Cambridge: Cambridge UP, 1987) as well. In *The Claim of Reason,* Cavell reads Shylock's "Hath not a Jew eyes?" speech as a rejoinder to Antonio's skepticism of his humanity; Anita Gilman Sherman has recently enlarged upon that analysis to posit Shylock not only as the object of Antonio's skepticism but "as a skeptical subject" (Sherman, "Disowning Knowledge of Jessica, or Shylock's Skepticism," *SEL* 44.2 [2004]: 277–295, esp. 278).
2. For the place of "fetish" as a tool for the analysis of the "material culture" of the Renaissance, see my introduction.
3. Peter Stallybrass articulates such a sense for "disavowal" in his essay "The Value of Culture and the Disavowal of Things" (in *The Culture of Capital,* ed. Henry S. Turner [New York: Routledge, 2002]: 275–292); he argues there that the emergent category of "culture" in early modernity propounds abstract and absolute categories that come to redefine "value" away from premodern concepts of value as a material phenomenon, so that the devaluation of materiality amounts to a disavowal of matter's own ineluctability by modern capitalist ideology. In defining the work of disavowal as taking place both within and across the personae of the play, I follow the coordination of individual and collective instances for psychoanalytic categories offered by Wendy Wall: "Psychoanalytic categories can pose problems for historicists, since they are predicated on nineteenth-century bourgeois family structures, or since they depend on a conception of persons as having interior truths that can be abstracted from social conditions. Yet I work with the assumption that fantasies can be read as cutting through and across persons rather than being tethered to the epiphanies of a volitional self: that is, I find it possible to identify *cultural* fantasies" (*Staging Domesticity: Household Work and English Identity in Early Modern Drama* [Cambridge: Cambridge UP, 2002]: 11).
4. The oddness of Antonio's sadness is the initiating condition of the play, and Salerio characterizes its exceptionality as a wandering of the mind from the everyday habits of Venetian bodies (blowing on soup, watching an hourglass, and going to church) along chains of association to far-flung perils to shipping. Of course, con-

templating such remote perils to shipping is part of Antonio's everyday business, and Salerio is wrong about its relation to melancholy; but the condition he diagnoses, the self-estrangement of being in two places at once, is one that will characterize the doublethink workings of the play as much as the conditions of individual characters, and the exceptionality of that state seems as marked in its working out here as it seems generally implicit in Antonio's profession as merchant.

5. Paster, *Humoring the Body: Emotions and the Shakespearean Stage* (Chicago: U of Chicago P, 2004).
6. Shylock does not want particular information from Antonio, so what he has in mind does not directly correspond to juridical torture, and I am analogizing it here instead to the production of medical knowledge; but the sense in which the desire to expose the heart is mysterious in Shylock, reciprocal to the provoking mystery of Antonio, suggests that his desire participates in the "epistemic crux" that Elizabeth Hanson finds implicated in the torture of Elizabethan recusants, in which " 'troth,' [the subject's] bond to the community of the realm," was in the moment of torture "obscured... as a mode of knowing, marking its transformation, on the one hand, into the imperative to discover the facts of treason, and, on the other, into the truth of the inviolable soul," a subjective truth that Catholic polemicists against torture insisted was not utterable under any circumstances, much less these (*Discovering the Subject in Renaissance England* [Cambridge: Cambridge UP, 1998]: 25). Hanson introduces her topic by citing Hamlet's baffling of Rosencrantz and Guildenstern's attempt to "pluck out the heart of my mystery," and comes to relate Bacon's model of knowledge production in plumbing the mysteries of nature to his endorsement of the legality of torture.
7. It is worth noting that Antonio's shortness of cash allows him to impose his "credit" between Bassanio and the money, exploiting the continuity of ethos and solvency that Craig Muldrew has described in *The Economy of Obligation* (New York: St. Martins, 1998), so that Bassanio has to ask the Rialto to articulate its esteem of Antonio's purse-person before getting his money, and has to hear even Shylock describe Antonio as "a good man."
8. Reading the play's versions of sociality through Derrida's *Politics of Friendship*, Henry S. Turner defines the apparently manifold problems of *Merchant* as manifestations of a single "problem of the more-than-one"—the social individual as being greater than single, but less than two: "The Problem of the More-Than-One: Friendship, Calculation, and Political Association in *The Merchant of Venice*," *Shakespeare Quarterly* 57.4 (January 2006): 413–442.
9. Girard, " 'To Entrap the Wisest': Sacrificial Ambivalence in *The Merchant of Venice* and *Richard III*" [1980], reprinted in *Shakespeare: an Anthology of Criticism and Theory, 1945–2000*, ed. Russ MacDonald (Oxford: Blackwell, 2004): 353–364, esp. 356.
10. Auden, *The Dyer's Hand* (New York: Random House, 1962): 231.
11. Lars Engle reads Antonio's "I know not why I am so sad" as straightforwardly disingenuous, in its context of the conversation with Salerio and Solanio:

"Antonio's reluctance to be sounded by them gives no more reliable clue to his state of mind than Hamlet's answers to the not-dissimilar queries of Rosencrantz and Guildenstern," implicitly comparing the Venetian market's desire to see inside Antonio's accounts to Claudius's desire to decipher Hamlet's intentions ("'Thrift is Blessing': Exchange and Explanation in *The Merchant of Venice*," *SQ* 37:1 [Spring 1986]: 20–37, esp. 21). Engle's analysis of Antonio's professional need to mislead the Rialto as to the state of his finances, which are gradually revealed to be rather more parlous than his initial claims indicate, is persuasive, and it underlines the utility of mystery to the ethos he establishes; but it seems to me likewise to affirm Antonio's desire that the money he is at risk of losing not be about the money, as the instantiation of his mystery. Just because the mystery is disingenuous—is generated in the disavowal of what anyone paying sufficient attention can tell to be the facts of the case—does not make it invalid; the distinction is between our coming to feel, like the trivial gossipmongers Salerio and Solanio, that we have some good ideas as to why Antonio *should be* sad, and Antonio's feeling that he doesn't know why he *is* sad.

12. The mysteries of the faith are enumerated most rigorously by Anglican churchgoers in the Athanasian Creed or *Quicunque vult*, which the Book of Common Prayer requires "be sung or said at Morning Prayer, instead of the Apostle's Creed," on major feast days celebrating those mysteries (including Christmas, Easter, and Trinity Sunday) (*The Book of Common Prayer* [1662], introd. Diarmaid MacCulloch [London: Everyman, 1999]: 92–94).
13. "There can, I think, be little doubt that (although perhaps not always in exactly the same way) issues of sexual difference, the relationship between friendship and love, the nature of heterosexual love and same-sex relations which exercise modern students, were issues which already exercised Shakespeare's original audience and would have caused unease," writes Christopher Hardman, articulating both the play's positioning of its dilemmas as transhistorically permanent topoi for pedagogical discussion and—if we take as symptomatic the series of hedges beginning the sentence, as seeking to protect him from that claim even as he introduces it—his own "unease" at giving voice to that positioning ("'Trouble being gone, comfort should remain': Tranquility and Discomfort in 'The Merchant of Venice,'" *Yearbook of English Studies* 23 [Early Shakespeare special number, 1993]: 189–205, esp. 191).
14. For what clothes are capable of literally embodying in Renaissance England, see Ann Rosalind Jones and Peter Stallybrass, *Renaissance Clothing and the Materials of Memory* (Cambridge: Cambridge UP, 2000).
15. "This *analogy* is the very site of the theologico-political, the hyphen or translation between the theological and the political," argues Derrida about the play's "translation" of justice into mercy, in the course of his explication of how using the verb "*relève*" in translating "when mercy seasons justice" into French would work, in preference to the cognate "*saisonne*": "*when mercy elevates and interiorizes, thereby preserving and negating, justice (or the law)*," following a sense he has already devel-

oped for *relève* as translating Hegel's *Aufhebung* ("What Is a 'Relevant' Translation?," tr. Lawrence Venuti, *Critical Inquiry* 27.2 [Winter 2001]: 174–200, esp. 197, 195; italics *sic*).

16. Since "economy" is Bataille's theoretical vocabulary, I will not attempt to historicize the term here as I do elsewhere in this study. This analysis is staked out in Bataille's early reading of Mauss (*Visions of Excess: Selected Writings 1927–39*, ed. and introd. Allan Stoekl, tr. Stoekl, Carl R. Lovitt and Donald M. Leslie, Jr. [Minneapolis: U of Minnesota P, 1985]: 116–129), though "restricted" and "general" are the vocabulary of his later opus *The Accursed Share*. The sense of "general" to denote the economy of plenitude shares the etymology of our word "generous," but, as *Merchant* suggests, the two are not quite the same (and both have an ambiguous relation to the cognate "gentle" in the play as well). My guide through the Bataille corpus has been Scott Cutler Shershow, *The Work and the Gift* (Chicago: U of Chicago P, 2005). Shershow puts Bataille at the center of a wide-ranging conversation among Mauss and subsequent analysts of the gift (Derrida, Nancy, Hyde...), and both radical and neoconservative accounts of the value of labor (Marx, Goux, Gilder...), to examine the interrelation of these two poles for the interpretation of human productiveness, especially in the case of aesthetic production. In a recent essay, likewise responding to Shershow, Barbara Correll demonstrates the utility of the concept of general economy to the analysis of Shakespeare's sonnets and Donne's elegies, to which she refers the plot of *Merchant* as "a dramatic analogue" ("Terms of 'Indearment': Lyric and General Economy in Shakespeare and Donne," *ELH* 75.2 [Summer 2008]: 241–262, esp. 261 n.50).
17. I've chosen "nice" and "nasty" to articulate the different values of restricted and general economies in order both to recall the "disdainfull nicitee" of the fastidious fountain of *FQ* 2.2 (for which see my chapter 1) and to suggest that this differential value judgment arises from within the relative pettiness of the restricted economy's ideology; judgment itself has no place in the general economy. The protagonist of Kingsley Amis's *Lucky Jim* notoriously uses these adjectives to rationalize his choice between a promising erotic relationship and the perverse one he's presently in: "There was no end to the ways in which nice things are nicer than nasty ones" ([London: Penguin, 1993]: 140; see David Lodge's introduction to this edition for the critical dismay that's been occasioned by this sexist reification).
18. For example, *Visions of Excess*, 85–86. The scatology of money itself was a popular topic of medieval monastic writing, and I detail how Marlowe controverts it with Spenser in my first chapter.
19. Shell, "Portia's Portrait: Representation as Exchange," *Common Knowledge* 7.1 (Spring 1998): 94–144, esp. 105.
20. Harry Berger's apt portmanteau for the pettiness of the generosity which Portia extends to Shylock and to Antonio is "mercifixion," a grace exacting sacrifice: she giveth by taking away ("Marriage and Mercifixion in *The Merchant of Venice*: The Casket Scene Revisited," *SQ* 32.2 [Summer 1981]: 155–162).

21. As Lynn Enterline sees it, Portia's restitution of Antonio's wealth "directs attention away from the seemingly unanswerable question of personal suffering and toward the vagaries of the marketplace. Although the explanation first offered for Antonio's sorrow [by Salerio] is rejected, the comedy nonetheless concludes by giving him back the very thing it had jokingly pointed to as the cause of his sorrow: his merchandise" (*The Tears of Narcissus: Melancholia and Masculinity in Early Modern Writing* [Stanford, Calif.: Stanford UP, 1995]: 229).
22. For the strict impossibility of a gift that expects no reciprocation, see Shershow's study and the range of critics whom he cites there (especially Derrida's *Given Time*). Lowell Gallagher engages this problematic in *Merchant* via modern philosophical responses to St. Paul, in relation to the free gift of grace and the performance of kenosis (i.e., self-emptying), in his essay "Waiting for Gobbo":

    > [Levinas's and Badiou's] respective meditations on eschatology and universalism fruitfully expose a common intuition—which the Gobbos share—of the profound connection between the gift's impossibility and the possibility of a radical ethics: an ethics not content with dutiful observance of given norms but mindful, instead, of the "no thing" that subsists in social relations and challenges all settled forms of knowledge and behavior.

    ("Waiting for Gobbo," in *Spiritual Shakespeares*, ed. Ewan Fernie [New York: Routledge, 2005]: 73–93, esp. 79)
23. Bady, "The Sum of Something: Arithmetic in *The Merchant of Venice*," *SQ* 36.1 (Spring 1985): 10–30, esp. 22–25. F1 and following emended Q1–3's "sum of something" to "sum of nothing," and many modern editors prefer the Folio reading; but Bady's case for retaining the pun seems to me persuasive.
24. Berger, "Marriage and Mercifixion," and Shell, "Portia's Portrait," note this contradiction; Berger considers it an attempt on Portia's part to get Bassanio to dissociate her human qualities from those of her inheritance.
25. Here I'm citing Sidney's idiot-child test of representation, a variant on the innocent-eye test topos of classical art history: "What child is there, that, coming to a play, and seeing *Thebes* written in great letters on an old door, doth believe that it is Thebes?" (*The Defence of Poesy*, in *The Major Works*, ed. Katherine Duncan-Jones [Oxford: Oxford UP, 2002]: 212–250, esp. 235). I contravene here an established strain of *Merchant* scholarship that asserts the riddle to celebrate intuition over logic in the service of valuing romance over calculation, a position staked out notably by C. L. Barber: that what Bassanio executes in his choice is a leap of faith (*Shakespeare's Festive Comedy: A Study of Dramatic Form and its Relation to Social Custom* [Princeton, N.J.: Princeton UP, 1959]: 174–177). It's my argument that the more ostentatious examples of calculation in this text are so willfully mystifying in their meaningless complexity (notably Portia's "sum of something" speech and Shylock's parody of it in his "were every ducat" speech)

as to make the quite simple and straightforward calculus of the riddle *look like* romance; the play's actual romantic is Morocco, and his leap of faith from matter to value is an obviously idolatrous one. Richard Horwich's reading of the relation of riddle to dilemma anticipates my own, and takes a position between Barber's and that which I'm adopting, though he seems to me to diffuse the sense of "riddle" in his argument in doing so ("Riddle and Dilemma in *The Merchant of Venice*," *SEL* 17.2 [Spring 1977]: 191–200); I am indebted to his shrewd and provocative lectures on this play as well as to his essay.

26. An archetypal analysis like Freud's in "The Theme of the Three Caskets" would point out that the failure of two competitors before the success of the third is a necessary aspect of this fairy-tale motif (in *Writings on Art and Literature* [Stanford, Calif.: Stanford UP, 1997]: 109–121); failure is the only reason for Morocco and Arragon to be in this story at all. But the two princes aren't portrayed as failing out of simple necessity (however right Nerissa may be in declaring that "hanging and wiving goes by destiny," 2.9.83): rather, each talks himself into failing. Morocco manages to cancel himself, and Arragon to make a fool of himself, through elaborate rhetorical ratiocinations.
27. For the location of self-evidence in objecthood, see also Julian Yates's analysis of the "object lesson" of early modern pedagogy (*Error Misuse Failure: Object Lessons from the English Renaissance* [Minneapolis: U of Minnesota P, 2003]: xi–xx).
28. See Marc Shell's chapter "The Wether and the Ewe" for the complex relation of propagation and money to Biblical referents through the citation of sheep in *Merchant* (*Money, Language, and Thought* [Berkeley: U of California P, 1982]: 47–83).
29. What begins by citing Troilus becomes, once Cressida is named, a list only of women whose unnamed, exogamous lovers are absent (recalling the *Heroides*)—the conversation clearly is about Jessica, and about her relationships to her paternity and posterity (for which see Janet Adelman, *Blood Relations: Christian and Jew in* The Merchant of Venice [Chicago: U of Chicago P, 2008]: 66–98). The progression toward extinction in both of those directions is vividly marked: the paternity of Troilus and especially of Cressida is significant to their story both allegorically and to the shape of its plot (in that Cressida is the daughter of Calchas, whose knowledge of the future prompts his treason, and in that the lovers are separated by Calchas's desire to be reunited with his daughter in the Greek camp), but in the Pyramus and Thisby story, the lovers' death actually reshapes the initial blocking condition of the parents' enmity (they are transformed into allies by their now mutual childlessness), while Dido's suicide is, she claims at the end of *Aeneid* IV, determined by the negative condition of not being pregnant (had she a little Aeneas to look forward to, she would be willing to live). The barbarian witch Medea, whose crimes are the bride-price Jason paid in winning the golden fleece, is cited here as she prepares to revivify Jason's father, a process she will claim to reenact in tricking the daughters of Pelias, Jason's enemy, into murdering their father; she will at last murder her and Jason's own children to

spite her husband (*Metamorphoses* VII). The attention to transuming distance and to the prolongation of erotic danger, as long as "nobody comes," also recalls Salerio's prematurely ejaculatory vision of a faraway shipwreck, "scatter[ing] all her spices on the stream," from the very beginning of the play (1.1.33).

30. Bassanio's ekphrasis of Portia's portrait does not address any details of her body below the lips, so presumably only her face and hair are represented in it.
31. Morocco puts the case for silver better than Arragon himself does: "And yet to be afeard of my deserving/ Were but a weak disabling of myself" (2.7.29–30). It's also true that "Arragon" is a near-anagram of "arrogant," as "Caliban" famously is of "cannibal," and that the prideful obsession with *limpieza de sangre* was as stock a trope for comic Spaniards on the stage as was the fashion-chasing of the Englishman.
32. *Metamorphoses* III: 339–510—though part of the joke is that masturbation is *only* allegorically present: were Narcissus to touch himself, rather than fail to touch his reflection, this would be a very different story. In his compulsive fondling of the coinage that is his own substance, Spenser's Mammon is, like the casket's prophecy of the Arragon of the future, a dirty old man playing with himself (for which see my chapter 1).
33. Eric Partridge cites *R&J* 2.4.91–93, "for this drivelling love is like a great natural that runs lolling up and down to hide his bauble in a hole," in *Shakespeare's Bawdy* (New York: Dutton, 1960): 70.
34. Sinfield, "How to Read *The Merchant of Venice* without Being Heterosexist," in *Alternative Shakespeares 2*, ed. Terence Hawkes (London and New York: Routledge, 1996): 122–139.
35. Adelman, *Blood Relations*, 133. In borrowing Adelman's point about the mechanism of disavowal in the play I am displacing it from the object to which she argues it is directed, which is the play's "own fear and guilt about Christianity's relation to the Jews" (ibid.). I am reluctant to totalize an identification between Shylock and the money form, as Halpern does; although the play's Christian characters may treat the two as if they were similar objects, Adelman's reading suggests that the play is not able entirely to forget that Shylock is a person and that a coin is a thing. In both my argument and Adelman's, what's being disavowed is neither a person nor a thing per se but a "relation"—the way in which an apparently unitary and objective identity draws together disparate realities.
36. To our eyes, lead and silver are also similarly gray in color, but the suitors tend to address the silver as white and the lead as black (the exception being Bassanio's citing both silver and lead as "pale" [3.2.103, 106]). The ascription of whiteness to silver is conventional in Renaissance English, as in the phrase "white money" for silver coins.
37. Halpern, *Shakespeare among the Moderns* (Ithaca, N.Y.: Cornell UP, 1997): 189–190.
38. ibid., 190, alluding to a joke of Marx's in *Capital*, Vol. I (p. 144, in my edition [tr. Ben Fowkes, London: Penguin, 1990]).

39. Compare again Portia's ostentation of self-evidence to her oddly bewildered new fiancé, "You see me, Lord Bassanio, where I stand/ Such as I am" (3.2.149–150).
40. Poovey, *Genres of the Credit Economy: Mediating Value in Eighteenth- and Nineteenth-century Britain* (Chicago: U of Chicago P, 2008): 57–85.
41. Such another man might be not only Bassanio ("thy paleness moves me more than eloquence" [3.2.106], a line whose comparison of visual and verbal evidences is pointed up by Theobald's impulse to emend "paleness" to "plainness," and so make it an intrarhetorical comparison between the Attic and Asiatic styles of oratory [cited in the matrix for the line in *A New Variorum Edition of Shakespeare*, ed. H. H. Furness (Philadelphia: J. B. Lippincott, 1871–); henceforward *Var*]) but also Freud: in "The Theme of the Three Caskets," he argues that dumbness is one of the traits that integrate the third casket with the feminized allure of death, and compares the casket-trial here to Paris's judgment in favor of a mute Aphrodite in Offenbach's *Belle Hélène* (113).
42. In the *Rhetoric*, Aristotle defines rhetorical reasoning as generated in probability (while logic deduces new certainties on the basis of established ones), and probability as generated in consensus, the common sense shared by (enough of) the constituents of the polis. It thus resembles the adequating production of prices, which is why Bacon calls the treatment of commonplaces as if they were truths an "idol of the marketplace" (Bacon, *The New Organon*, in *Francis Bacon: A Selection of His Works*, ed. Sidney Warhaft [New York: Macmillan, 1982]: 337; and see David Hawkes, *Idols of the Marketplace: Idolatry and Commodity Fetishism in English Literature, 1580–1680* [New York: Palgrave, 2001], esp. 33–36, and Joel Altman, *The Improbability of Othello: Rhetorical Anthropology and Shakespearean Selfhood* [Chicago: U of Chicago P, 2010]). Asking whether "lead contains *her*" seems like Morocco's obvious error, idolatrously mistaking the representation (the portrait) for the thing represented (Portia). But if it is a mistake, it is such an easy one to make that not only do Morocco and Arragon make it, to whom "portrait" and "Portia" are near-homonyms, but so too does Portia, despite calling herself "I" and "me": though in speaking to Morocco she calls the content sought within the caskets "my form," she directs Arragon to "that wherein *I* am contained," and likewise tells Bassanio, "*I* am lock'd in one of them;/ If you do love me, you will find *me* out" (2.7.61; 2.9.5; 3.2.40–41).
43. Girard, *A Theater of Envy: William Shakespeare* (Oxford: Oxford UP, 1991). Victoria Kahn cites Hobbes as associating mimetic desire with the genre of romance, and in particular with the indecorous importation of romance aesthetics and narratives to remote contexts (*Wayward Contracts: The Crisis of Political Obligation in England, 1640–1674* [Princeton, N.J.: Princeton UP, 2004]: 140–154); Morocco presents just such an exotic (and swiftly repudiated) importation of romance values in this play.
44. As Jesse M. Lander demonstrates, Falstaff is the Lancastrian cycle's resident expert on counterfeiting: "'Crack'd Crowns' and Counterfeit Sovereigns: The Crisis of Value in *1 Henry IV*," *Shakespeare Studies* 30 (2002): 137–161.

45. See chapter 4, and figure 4.1, for the iconography of the coined angel.
46. I assume it's a coincidence that "Falconbridge, the young baron of England" shares the surname of *King John*'s Bastard: the name seems generic, chosen for its ring of Anglo-Saxon, masculine prowess suggestive of chivalric romance (compare the historical Sir John Hawkwood, whose exploits as a mercenary captain in Italy are commemorated by Uccello's equestrian portrait in the Florentine Duomo).
47. For analyses of the emblem format, see E. H. Gombrich, *Symbolic Images: Studies in the Art of the Renaissance* (London: Phaidon, 1972), and Michael Bath, *Speaking Pictures: English Emblem Books and Renaissance Culture* (New York: Longman, 1994).
48. In modern usage, "counterfeit" is legal vocabulary referring immediately to the crime of producing false money, and its use outside that reference is metaphorical, comparing whatever activity we denote by it both to the context of currency and to a behavior that is criminal. (Thus the precision of Gide's title *Les Faux-monnayeurs* is accurately rendered in modern English as *The Counterfeiters.*) Neither the sense of currency nor the sense of criminality was inherent in early modern usages of "counterfeit," which had the more general senses of "imitate," "falsify," and "pretend" as primary (*OED* a. and n. A–C); conversely, the crime we know as "counterfeiting" was often called "coining" in the law-books and the courts. The transgressive register inherent in the word's etymology (*contre-fait*, "made against") is certainly exploited with great frequency by early modern writers, but often with the expectation that it would be heard ironically rather than immediately; when Timon tells the Painter, "Thou draw'st a counterfeit/ Best in all Athens; thou'rt indeed the best,/ Thou counterfeit'st most lively," Timon requires that the Painter hear the technical sense in which Timon is paying the painter a compliment on his craft, as "counterfeiting" (*OED*, v. 8–9), while asking the audience (who know, as the Painter does not, that Timon is on to him) to hear him calling the Painter crafty in his flattering lies (*Timon* 5.1.77–79, and see Shell, "Portia's Portrait," 96). On stage, the transgressive craft to which this register of "counterfeit" necessarily refers is *acting*: "Now counterfeit to swoon" (*AYLI* 3.5.17). Even in playtexts preoccupied with money and with duplicity, the register of falsifying money need not be audible in verbal and adjectival usages of "counterfeit." Timon's diatribe against the duplicity of all money renders trivial the validity or invalidity of individual coins in that technical sense, such that the beatings he hands out to Poet and Painter alike at the end of this scene under the name of "gold" are not counterfeits but, to Timon's mind, true money, what money really is.
49. Frankfurt, *On Bullshit* (Princeton, N.J.: Princeton UP, 2005): 47.
50. See Leonard Barkan, "The Heritage of Zeuxis: Painting, Rhetoric, and History," in *Antiquity and Its Interpreters*, ed. Alina Payne, Ann Kuttner, and Rebekah Smick (Cambridge: Cambridge University Press, 2000): 99–109.
51. Halpern, *Shakespeare among the Moderns*, 200.

52. Preeminent among Bataille's monsters of unrestricted excess is the abominable, celestial "fecal eye of the sun" (*Visions of Excess*, 17–19 and 79–90, esp. 85).
53. The lining of coffins in lead is for Morocco the definition of opacity—the thing that makes it impossible to see the difference between a living and a dead body—which eliminates lead, to his mind, from the competition: "it were too gross [too obtrusive in its materiality]/ To rib her cerecloth in the obscure grave." As gold, the envelopment of Portia's body should not embody but obviate the invisible difference between life and death, imbuing that body with the permanent presence of "this mortal breathing saint" enjoyed by a reliquary. It's a happy coincidence that this opacity persists in the protection of our bodies from the dangerously penetrating vision of the dentist's X-ray by a lead apron—though doubtless a gold one would work just as well.
54. For the topos of the fractious sister arts, see, inter alia, G. E. Lessing, *Laocoön: An Essay on the Limits of Painting and Poetry*, tr. E. A. McCormick (Baltimore: Johns Hopkins UP, 1984); W. J. T. Mitchell, *Iconology: Image, Text, Ideology* (Chicago: U of Chicago P, 1986); Clark Hulse, *The Rule of Art: Literature and Painting in the Renaissance* (Chicago: U of Chicago P, 1990); and Leonard Barkan, "Making Pictures Speak: Renaissance Art, Elizabethan Literature, Modern Scholarship," *Renaissance Quarterly* 48.2 (Summer 1995): 326–351.
55. "It is the first time that ever I heard breaking of ribs was sport for ladies," Touchstone comments on a similar courtly blunder (*AYLI* 1.2.138–139).
56. In his reading of Bourdieu, Shershow finds that "The point of misrecognition, of absent knowledge, is also the very point at which a market [i.e., restricted] economy can be wrested... into some paradoxical resemblance of the gift [i.e., general] economy" (*The Work and the Gift*, 105).
57. Hamlet's remarks on the social bifurcation of taste produced by the Pyrrhus speech as being "caviary to the general" (2.2.437), and his subsequent charge to the players, express the continuity of social and aesthetic distinction within the art of the theater; Pierre Bourdieu theorizes that continuity in *Distinction: A Social Critique of the Judgement of Taste*, tr. Richard Nice (Cambridge, Mass.: Harvard University Press, 2000). Robert Darcy argues that the codes of distinction indirectly articulated in the riddle test are those of nation, rather than (as I am here arguing) of class; he cites the resistance of the play's fathers to exogamy as a potentially incestuous response to the pressures toward distribution of international commerce ("Freeing Daughters on Open Markets: The Incest Clause in *The Merchant of Venice*," in *Money and the Age of Shakespeare: Essays in New Economic Criticism*, ed. Linda Woodbridge [New York: Palgrave Macmillan, 2003]: 189–200).
58. Portia's servant, who is presumably accustomed to the sight of luxury, raves over the spectacular entrance Bassanio has crafted for his entourage—"Yet have I not seen/ So likely an embassador of love"—and speculates, as Bassanio has presumably intended, as to what "costly summer" will manifest itself in Bassanio's own arrival, to which this anticipatory messenger is only "a day in April" (2.9.91–94).

59. Tracing out a logic of mirroring from Arragon's interaction with the silver casket that would identify Shylock with the Marxian money form's reflection of one commodity's value through another, Halpern argues that criticism of *Merchant* necessarily bifurcates between aesthetic and resistantly ironic readings (from which latter point of view, one might add, the aesthetic ones are instead anaesthetizing), because both modes of reading seem fully present, and irreconcilable, in the play. The former is epitomized for him by Lorenzo's speech on harmony and the latter by Shylock's literalist, protocritical deafness to spirit: "Literalist, ironist, and materialist, Shylock both preempts and allegorizes any theoretical reading of *Merchant*, including my own" (*Shakespeare among the Moderns*, 213). Halpern's assertion that all criticism can hope to do is to make itself a more or less degraded reflection of the play has prompted my own attention to the modality of recursiveness in *Merchant*, which, I am arguing, is better understood as desiringly imitative than as automatically reflective. The play's coinage is not merely mirroring, as Halpern reads it, but mimetic; even when Bassanio succeeds in disavowing its substance as gold and silver, it persists as being made of pictures. In this way the play seems to claim as its own a Pauline aesthetic of defective reflection, as I suggest in this chapter's conclusion.
60. See Furness's matrix in *Var* to this chilling quip of Portia's for the extent of the dismay it has elicited over its reception history.
61. Shylock is unaware of the Christologically radical connotations of his speech here—not to mention of the way in which they have been, perhaps ironically, realized in Bassanio, who has been "dear bought" (as Portia says) in order to be married to the heir.
62. "Sovereign is he who decides on the exception," Carl Schmitt tells us (*Political Theology: Four Chapters on the Concept of Sovereignty*, tr. George Schwab [Cambridge, Mass.: MIT Press, 1988]: 5): the Duke of *Merchant* explicitly has no capacity to make an exception of either Antonio or Shylock. Instead, he has to get someone else to claim that Antonio and Shylock (whose suit is, as I've argued, manifestly exceptional, and only disingenuously adopts a routine-izing form that gains it entry into the court) can be incorporated into the law, and thereby to make an example of Shylock. (See Giorgio Agamben, *Homo Sacer: Sovereign Power and Bare Life*, tr. Daniel Heller-Roazen [Stanford, Calif.: Stanford UP, 1998], for the inverse identity of exception and example.) From the Duke's point of view, this someone else could be anybody with a claim to participate in the state apparatus, as long as it isn't the Duke himself—anybody but the Duke can trump up some ground to get Antonio off the hook, while for the Duke to do it would be for the Duke to claim a sovereign power, a disastrous coup d'état. In this juridico-political reading, the ruling of Portia would demonstrate not the magical problem-solving power of her bounty but the fact that literally anyone who is not the Duke, even a precocious transvestite, can solve the problem to the satisfaction of the Venetian state.

63. Thomas Tusser's ubiquitous household manual, *Five hundred pointes of husbandrie*, cites small change as a "drudge" or menial servant, performing errands with which the householder or housewife can't be bothered: "What husband prouideth with monie his drudge,/ the huswife must looke to, which waie it doth trudge"; "If pennie for all thing be suffred to trudge,/ trust long, not to pennie, to haue him thy drudge" (*Five hundred pointes of good husbandrie* [1580], ed. W. Payne and Sidney J. Herrtage [London: English Dialect Society, 1878]: 65, 177). I discuss the latter passage in my introduction.
64. For the recent arrival of silver-glass mirror technology in England as short-circuiting the Pauline hermeneutic of seeing "through a glass darkly," materialized in the distortions of the older polished-steel mirrors, see Rayna Kalas, *Frame, Glass, Verse: The Technology of Poetic Invention in the English Renaissance* (Ithaca, N.Y.: Cornell UP, 2007), esp. 106–132.
65. Shell, *Money, Language, and Thought*, 50–55; *Merchant* 2.5.46.
66. The quantity "enough," so readily eclipsed in *Merchant* in the other characters' anti-monetary eagerness to "exceed account" or be "less than nothing," will be the inescapable quandary of *Lear*; my "adequated man" has in mind Lear's erroneous evaluation of Poor Tom as "unaccomodated man."
67. Mentz, "The Fiend Gives Friendly Counsel: Launcelot Gobbo and Polyglot Economics in *The Merchant of Venice*," in *Money and the Age of Shakespeare: Essays in New Economic Criticism*, ed. Linda Woodbridge (New York: Palgrave Macmillan, 2003): 177–188, esp. 181–182.
68. For the definition of commonwealth as a restraint of individual self-interests (and, in its demotic usage, the restraint of everybody else's self-interests in preference to one's own), see my introduction.
69. Whereas a slave can (unlike a hog) know his own price, and can find it interesting, but still can't have an interest *in* it (in the sense of an investment) like that of his master. In defining the minimum standard for membership in the commonwealth as an investment in pork-belly futures, Launcelot is proclaiming himself to be not only more than a slave but more than a Jew, however minimally he is a man; see Adelman, *Blood Relations*, 38–65, for an analysis of the character's liminal religious situation. Despite Launcelot's enthusiasm for hogs' meat (one which rivals that of Sancho Panza, who uses it to denote his security as an Old Christian in a converso-filled Spain), several critics have taken Shylock's reference to him as "that fool of Hagar's offspring" (2.5.44) to indicate that he is Muslim, as a descendant of Ishmael. Given Shylock's interest in genealogy, that reading can't be easily dismissed, though it seems odd for Shakespeare to be making such a point of Jewish dietary restrictions as a mark of incompatible sociability and to ignore Muslim ones, unless we are to imagine Launcelot as, like Jessica, newly converted in his transfer of households. I do wonder if Hagar's status as bondwoman, or the Lord's prophecy that Ishmael would be "a wild ass of a man" (Gen. 16: 12), might be a more pertinent point of reference, as citing either Launcelot's servitude or the approach to animalism in his folly.

## CHAPTER 4

1. From "A private Epistle of the Author to the Printer," prefacing the second edition of *Pierce Penniless* (Nashe, *The Unfortunate Traveller and Other Works*, ed. J. B. Steane [London: Penguin, 1972]: 51; all citations of Nashe's texts are to this edition unless otherwise noted). As I note below, Nashe apparently did not intend *PP* to have any prefatory material at all; this "epistle" is defensive not only against the hostile interpreters of the first edition but against the printer's addition of an expository title and preface to it on his own initiative. I borrow the title of my chapter from John Fletcher's comedy *Wit without Money* (c.1614).
2. Helgerson, *The Elizabethan Prodigals* (Berkeley: U of California P, 1976).
3. Carey, "Donne and Coins," in *English Renaissance Studies Presented to Dame Helen Gardner*, ed. John Carey (Oxford: Clarendon, 1980): 151–163, esp. 151, 161.
4. Targoff, *John Donne: Body and Soul* (Chicago: U of Chicago P, 2008): 5.
5. Hawkes, *Idols of the Marketplace: Idolatry and Commodity Fetishism in English Literature, 1580–1680* (New York: Palgrave, 2001): 144.
6. As I note in the introduction, the bulk of the circulating medium was silver, and gold tended to circulate within specialized mercantile contexts (C. E. Challis, *The Tudor Coinage* [Manchester: Manchester UP, 1978]: 292); a large proportion of the gold in circulation was crown gold (after a long period of producing angels, the Mint in 1593 had started issuing crown denominations instead).
7. Challis, *The Tudor Coinage*, 165–172.
8. Baker, "The 'Angel' of English Renaissance Literature," *Studies in the Renaissance* 6 (1959): 85–93, esp. 87.
9. For the practices of "white magic" in Renaissance England, see Keith Thomas, *Religion and the Decline of Magic* (London: Weidenfeld and Nicholson, 1971).
10. Baker, "The 'Angel' of English Renaissance Literature," 91.
11. Ibid., 88. Stephen Deng evaluates James' relation to the touching ceremony, and to the angel that was its medium, in "Healing Angels and 'Golden Blood': Money and Mystical Kingship in *Macbeth*," in *Macbeth: New Critical Essays*, ed. Nick Moschovakis (New York: Routledge, 2008): 163–181.
12. Challis, *The Tudor Coinage*, 228–229. Both series were minted at the beginning of Elizabeth's reign, but crown gold eclipsed angel gold for a decade thereafter, during the ascendancy of goldsmith Thomas Stanley as the Mint's undertreasurer. Stanley was executed in 1571, and the new regime at the Mint included a return to angel gold, which prevailed until 1593, when crown gold again eclipsed the finer issues. Tempting though it is to ascribe this historical alternation to the iconographic difference I'm interested in here, the swings in production seem too definitive and too widely spaced to be prompted only by the desire to fine-tune the Queen's minted image. Left to its own devices, the Mint would presumably have preferred to produce crown gold, as it required somewhat less rigorous smelting. Challis points to two counterpoising values for the production of angel gold: one, the need for angels in the touching ritual, which grew more and more popular until, at the eve of the Civil War, Charles was issuing 5,500 tickets to the

yearly ceremony; and two, the Continental appetite for angels, which Challis suggests might have been the target of the angel production of the 1570s and '80s, the period of Elizabeth's most interventionist foreign policy, which she conducted as best she might through angels in preference to troops (ibid., 229).

13. Donne citations are to *The Complete English Poems*, ed. A. J. Smith (London: Penguin, 1986), and will be given parenthetically (by line) in the text.
14. It's the articulation of internal tensions such as this that prompt Heather Dubrow to characterize Donne as a "resident alien" among the laurel groves of Petrarchan discourse (*Echoes of Desire: English Petrarchism and Its Counterdiscourses* (Ithaca, N.Y.: Cornell UP, 1995): 203–248). This situational irony between amatory posturing and the possibilities of lack or of failure is frequent in the Elegies (see Arthur Marotti, *John Donne, Coterie Poet* [Madison: U of Wisconsin P, 1986]: 52); compare particularly "Natures lay idiot," "The Comparison," and "To His Mistress Going to Bed," and the belligerent speaker's actual impotence before the mistress's father in "The Perfume."
15. For Barbara Correll, the threat of degeneration against the angels works not so much through their dissolution from form qua being, but through their treatment as a commodity (gold about to become jewelry) rather than as "angel," in which their monetary character would be pure and abstract to the point of being metaphysical: "the righteous angels are also fallen angels: their essential and earthbound status is unveiled when they are condemned by their material metamorphosis to become the object of the lovers' exchange: the bracelet" ("Chiasmus and *Commodificatio*: Crossing Tropes and Conditions in Donne's Elegy 11, 'The Bracelet,'" *Exemplaria* 11.1 [1999]: 141–165, esp. 158). She reads the chiasmus between erotic and fiscal values within these objects as exemplifying the metaphoric identity asserted by Jean-Joseph Goux between the Lacanian phallus and the Marxian money form. Correll's reading of "the demystifying material debasement of coins to goods" relies on the equation of melting ("metamorphosis") to exchange, which I don't read as being quite the case in the poem, concerned as it is to decouple the molten materiality of the coins from exchange (158), but I am otherwise much indebted to her probing and witty analysis.
16. Carey, "Donne and Coins," 161–162.
17. The perfection of twelve was generally insisted upon in Renaissance numerology: it encompasses factorially all the different virtues of one, two, three, and four, and Christ was understood to have recognized and demonstrated that perfection in choosing twelve as the number of his apostles (often referred to collectively as "the twelve" in the Gospels). At a more practical level, the ready divisibility of twelve into so many different fractions explains the survival of base twelve in reckoning monetary units (the shilling and the mark) long after the adoption of decimal notation.
18. Donne puns on traditional titles of the Kings of France ("Most Christian") and of Spain ("Most Catholic"). Coburn Freer suggests that the association of clipping with circumcision refers as much to associations of Jews with fiscal criminality as

it does to deformed penises ("John Donne and Elizabethan Economic Theory," *Criticism* 38.4 [Fall 1996]: 497–520, esp. 506). Freer demonstrates that Donne's position as secretary to the Privy Councilor Sir Thomas Egerton would have put him in contact with the most high-level and cutting-edge discussions of monetary policy, in relation both to the domestic market and to international exchange.

19. Carey, "Donne and Coins," 152–153. The "physiognomy" of gold coins was "worth studying" in the most direct sense of "worth," because foreign gold circulated in England according to its intrinsic value more generally than its stamp: thus it was important to assess each coin for its precise gold content according to purity and mass. "Fat" (overweight) English coins, conversely, were worth more in gold than their more slender fellows of the same stamp, and therefore were routinely culled from circulation and exported abroad.
20. "A Valediction: Of Weeping" does touch upon this meaning: "For thy face coins [my tears], and thy stamp they bear,/ And by this mintage they are something worth,/ For thus they be/ Pregnant of thee;/ Fruits of much grief they are, emblems of more..." (3–7), but I am not inclined to read the mintage trope as sustained alongside the pregnancy trope in the swift movement of this conceit, nor either one as metaphor for the other (both, instead, are successive metaphors for the mistress's reflection in each tear). The reference to the bestiary topos of "unlicked bear-whelps" (in which bear offspring are said to be born shapeless and immediately licked into cub form by the dam) in "The Bracelet" is directed less at any question of human reproduction than at introducing the problems of matter and form that will become important later in the poem. The bear-whelp recurs as a phobic metaphor for cunnilingus (and not reproduction) in "Loves Progress": see note 30 below. For readings of the monetarization of lyric production in Shakespeare's sonnets, see Thomas M. Greene, "Pitiful Thrivers: Failed Husbandry in the Sonnets," in *Shakespeare and the Question of Theory*, eds. Patricia Parker and Geoffrey Hartman (New York: Methuen, 1985): 230–244; Neal Dolan, "Shylock in Love: Economic Metaphors in Shakespeare's Sonnets," *Raritan* 22.2 (Fall 2002): 26–51; and Barbara Correll, "Terms of 'Indearment': Lyric and General Economy in Shakespeare and Donne," *ELH* 75.2 (Summer 2008): 241–262.
21. KJV massages the Hebrew toward a Christological interpretation (via the Aramaic version); NRSV renders the passage as "the fourth has the appearance of a god."
22. The poem is continuous in its direct address, but the addressee shifts twice: from the mistress to the angels at line 83, and from the angels to the finder at line 91.
23. The binding of devils in conjuration was typically imagined to depend on the defilement of some very good material thing (a consecrated Host, or the body of an innocent), to compound the verbal profanation of the name of God.
24. In surveying the Elegies as a group, Arthur Marotti argues that the speaker of this one moves in its close to a self-rebuking sincerity: "'heart' (114), the last word of

this love elegy, dramatically reasserts the love that was disingenuously denied at the poem's outset" (*John Donne: Coterie Poet*, 62). This seems to me unreasonably generous; the speaker's relationship to the mistress has been so entirely eclipsed by the homosocial aggression of the speaker's "hate" for the finder (91) over the poem's last twenty-four lines that the passionate wishfulness of "would it were at thy heart" has to refer to a violence directed at the finder's body, before it could say much about the possibility of "love" toward the mistress.

25. The speaker might exculpate himself from the blasphemous overtones of this phrase by claiming that he is using "soul" in the technical sense of Aristotle's *De Anima* (usually translated as "Of the Soul"), where it refers to the property of living matter that might be more specifically translated as "animating principle," and not to the Christian expectation that that principle will continue to exist after the death of the matter it animated (cp Carey, "Donne and Coins," 161–163). Certainly this sense is at play here at the point that the way in which market exchange gives gold the semblance of animate life (i.e., motion) is articulated; so too is the misogynist debate topos of whether women had souls in the Christian sense (or rational souls in the Aristotelian sense) at all. But the comparisons that follow between the material "centric part" defined by the speaker as the "right true end of love" and the virtuous and immaterial qualities associated with the wrong end of love make it clear that "soul" has its normatively Christian sense of transcendent immortality.

26. Richard Halpern argues that

> for Donne, resemblance is a way of negating causality, metaphor a way of fending off metonymy or continuity. Dr. Johnson's famous description of the metaphysical conceit as "the most heterogeneous ideas . . . yoked by violence together" captures the precise dynamic of Donne's metaphors, in which the conjunction of vehicle and tenor serves to drive the two apart, generating the semantic equivalent of a repulsive force. The Donnean conceit is a structure of absolute difference or separation generated paradoxically through the medium of resemblance. ("The Lyric in the Field of Information: Autopoiesis and History in Donne's *Songs and Sonnets*," *Yale Journal of Criticism* 6.1 [1993]: 185–215, esp. 201.)

Identity, in this reading, would not be Wallace Stevens's "vanishing point of resemblance" but the *antithesis* of metaphoric resemblance: metaphor is a trope not of convergence but of strife (*The Necessary Angel* [New York: Knopf, 1951]: 72). Halpern argues that the posture of lyric autonomy emerges in Donne and his generation as a reaction that at once opposes and confirms the ramifying differentiation of social structures in the moment of primitive accumulation. Donne's intent in deploying his "violently yoked" conceits is thus to display the trope of metaphor as generated in a real and radical unlikeness of poetry from the other social formations (the law, the court, the church, the shop, etc.) to which it has the power to compare itself. Halpern grounds this thesis in the socio-biological theories of Niklas Luhmann, who contends that all such knowledge structures can only be self-referential, and can recognize outside information only insofar as its external pressures deform the structure's internal systems or inhibit its expansion. Luhmann's assertion of knowledges that are intransmissible beyond the circumstances that have produced them, and that serve principally to affirm and extend the systems within which they are generated, recalls for me the peculiarly blinkered notion of his own universality that Mammon enjoys in chapter 1, as well as Christopher Pye's rejoinder that the apparent authority of economy to criticism rests in economy's dissembling of its own "status as a system" ("The Theater, the Market, and the Subject of History," *ELH* 61.3 (Fall 1994): 501–522, esp. 503). In Halpern's reading, the impossibility of objective knowledge (in this sense, that of a knowledge that might be understood as discrete from the circumstances of its production and therefore portable to different systemic settings, in the way that a physical object can be passed from hand to hand) is an intradiscursive phenomenon; but, if anything, the problematics of system are only compounded by addressing them to the extradiscursive consideration of materiality.

27. Shankar Raman cites the late medieval monetary analyst Nicolas Oresme and several of his modern interpreters to explicate, very effectively, the discrepancy between the material rarity that generates intrinsic value and the convention that generates extrinsic value, but he does not note that the speaker doesn't actually articulate rarity or preciousness as a cause of "value" in these lines ("Can't Buy Me Love: Money, Gender, and Colonialism in Donne's Erotic Verse," *Criticism* 43.2 [Spring 2002]: 135–168, esp. 137–138).
28. The rhetorical topos of debating alternative origins for gods, whether in the form of etiology or of genealogy, goes back to Hesiod; a comparably parodic origin for Love is detailed in both versions of Sidney's *Arcadia.*
29. Raman, "Can't Buy Me Love," 148.
30. "Some symmetry the foot hath with that part/ Which thou dost seek, and is thy map for that[,]/ Lovely enough to stop, but not stay at" (74–76): a foot-job will stimulate the penis but will not distract it from its vaginal goal. The perils of the speaker's interacting with the woman by hand or mouth, conversely, lie not only in the speaker's penile impatience with foreplay, but in the risk that she could be satisfied without penetration ever taking place: that hand or mouth might be co-opted as means to *her* "end," leaving him, so to speak, adrift—whence his particular horror of cunnilingus ("love's a bear-whelp born, if we o'er lick [i.e., 'over-lick']/ Our love, and force it strange new shapes to take,/ We err, and of a lump a monster make," 3–6) and of the clitoris lurking in the pubic hair ("Yet ere thou be where thou wouldst be embayed,/ Thou shalt upon another forest set,/ Where many shipwreck, and no further get," 68–70).
31. The aggressive intrusion materializing the reader's body is what seems unlooked-for here, not the anal eroticism; the Mammon-like dirtiness of this poem's Cupid suggests that anal and vaginal satisfactions are continuous. The debate staged

here among contrary approaches to such pleasure limits itself to intrafeminine trajectories, but it recalls the classical topos of the debate between a girl-lover and a boy-lover as to which is the superior object of desire. In the iteration of the topos by the pseudo-Lucianic author of the *Erotes*, the two opponents are able to find common ground in appreciating the back of a statue of Aphrodite, whose lovely buttocks, uninflected by the differentiating sex characteristics on the front of the statue (the hair, breasts, etc., that Donne's speaker likewise counsels his reader to disregard), appeal to each alike (Leonard Barkan, "Praxiteles' *Aphrodite* and the Love of Art," in *The Forms of Renaissance Thought*, ed. Barkan, Braden Cormack, and Sean Keilen [New York: Palgrave, 2009]: 15–45, esp. 38–39).

32. For the ambivalence between repayment and retribution in the cycle of exchange, which the notion of gift strives (impossibly) to escape, see Jacques Derrida, *Given Time: I. Counterfeit Money*, trans. Peggy Kamuf (Chicago: U of Chicago P, 1992).
33. In that the technique strives to obviate not only foreplay, not only social and conversational interaction, but even the evaluation of a potential lover's particular attractions, what the speaker seems finally to be advocating to the reader in paying "tribute" to the vaginal "exchequer" is that he simply hire the first prostitute he happens upon.
34. Niel K. Snortum, "The Title of Nash's *Pierce Penniless*," *MLN* 72.3 (March 1957): 170–173.
35. Lowell Gallagher has demonstrated that the paradoxical relation between emptiness and fullness is crucial to St. Paul's understanding of Christ's incarnation, which in Philippians 2 he articulates as the kenosis or emptying out of Christ's own divine nature to take on human abjection:

   > For Paul, kenosis, the gesture of self-emptying, describes the ultimate theological gift: the descent of God into human form. It also constitutes a radically selfless new ethics. The depiction of Christ's person as exalted in self-emptying discloses an altered concept of personhood, where personhood refers not to a historically determinate set of properties, but instead to an ongoing process of separation from familiar contours of identity, and consequent exposure to further, unexpected vistas of responsiveness and responsibility. ("Waiting for Gobbo," in *Spiritual Shakespeares*, ed. Ewan Fernie [New York: Routledge, 2005]: 73–93, esp. 82)

   I don't want to claim a Christological significance for Pierce Penniless (nor even a radical sense of responsibility), but Gallagher's case for a Pauline analysis of identity as an emptying out suggests how Pierce's vacuousness may be understood as the condition of his self-authorization.
36. Lewis, *English Literature in the Sixteenth Century Excluding Drama* (Oxford: Oxford UP, 1954): 416.
37. I'm thinking here too of the conventional opposition within the visual arts of painting as additive (the application of matter to a blank surface) and sculpture in

wood or stone as subtractive (the production of an elephant from marble as getting rid of everything that isn't the elephant).

38. Crewe, *Unredeemed Rhetoric: Thomas Nashe and the Scandal of Authorship* (Baltimore: Johns Hopkins UP, 1982): 1 and passim; Yates, *Error Misuse Failure: Object Lessons from the English Renaissance* (Minneapolis: U of Minnesota P, 2003): 101–137, esp. 103. The topos of "nothing" has been engaged continuously in Nashe criticism post-Lewis. For James Nielson (*Unread Herrings: Thomas Nashe and the Prosaics of the Real* [New York: Peter Lang, 1993], Nashe's writing ostentates its nothingness for the sake of a kind of self-effacement, in order to be about "the real" (by which Neilson seems principally to mean the material, everyday, and self-evident, though Neilson animates Lacanian categories in his analysis as well). Neilson's own prose enacts what he considers to be Nashe's peculiar variety of opaque mimesis, aiming to recreate for us the repulsiveness that earlier generations felt in Nashe by imitating Nashe's style within a genre—literary criticism—that is still expected to maintain a purposive distinction between *res*, the literary text, and the *verba* of monograph, no matter how excited we are to observe that distinction breaking down within the text. For Lorna Hutson (*Thomas Nashe in Context* [Oxford: Clarendon, 1989]), the quality of nothing is ironic: what the prose "says" is the ironic relation of about-itselfness to commerce. This irony works to demonstrate the vapidity and the bad faith of the sixteenth century's conventional "profitable discourse" of productiveness and thrift, and rises to offer a new model of recyclical production. For Charles Nicholl (*A Cup of News: The Life of Thomas Nashe* [London: Routledge and Kegan Paul, 1984]), the nothingness of the prose is that of "Newes": it's about its own topicality, novelty, and freshness. *Pierce*, for example, coordinates its hoary topoi of the Seven Deadly Sins with a faddish posture of diabolism and a sophisticated engagement of the arguments around the emergence of the public theater, all of which place the pamphlet in the orbit of the great succès de scandale of the early 1590s, *Doctor Faustus*.

39. Barbour, *Deciphering Elizabethan Fiction* (Newark: U of Delaware P, 1993): 64–126, esp. 71.

40. Introduction by D. Allen Carroll to his edition of *Groatsworth* (*Greene's Groatsworth of Wit, Bought with a Million of Repentance,* attrib. to Robert Greene and Henry Chettle, ed. D. Allen Carroll [Binghamton, N.Y.: Medieval and Renaissance Texts and Studies, 1994]: 1–31); I will cite this edition parenthetically in the text. Alexandra Halasz and Steve Mentz have both referred the possibility of forgery to the pamphlet's self-conscious creation of a marketable persona for print, as detached from the circumstances of whose hand inscribed the text for the printer. Mentz cites the pamphlet as "a practical form of literary criticism, a pioneering investigation into what we now call the 'author function,'" but one that, in epitomizing in the variety of its materials the great range of Greene's production across his career, seems motivated by "proliferation rather than thrift" (Mentz, "Forming Greene: Theorizing the Early Modern Author in the *Groats-*

*worth of Wit,"* in Kirk Melnikoff and Edward Gieskes, eds., *Writing Robert Greene* [Burlington, Vt.: Ashgate, 2008]: 115–132, esp. 116, 129; and see Halasz, *The Marketplace of Print: Pamphlets and the Public Sphere in Early Modern England* [Cambridge: Cambridge UP, 1997]: 38–39).

41. *Pierce* was registered with the Stationers on August 8, *Groatsworth* on September 20; Greene had died on September 18. Given the exceptional haste with which *Groatsworth* was rushed into print after Greene's death, and the more typical interval between the registration of a title with the Stationers and its printing and sale, it seems likely that *Groatsworth* could have hit the bookstalls even more closely on the heels of the first edition of *Pierce* than the six-week registration interval would indicate, or might indeed have preceded *Pierce* into print.
42. The front matter to the second edition of *Pierce* is 'A private Epistle of the Author to the Printer,' devoted both to disclaiming the front matter of the first edition as an interpolation by the printer—Nashe had intended that the book simply begin without any prefatory material for dedication or interpretation, but the printer, failing to understand the intent of that counterintuitive omission, supplied some on his own initiative—and to disclaiming *Groatsworth* (49–51). Both elements seem in this way continuous, as together making up what Nashe considers the misleading apparatus of interpretation within which *Pierce* was wrongly enfolded in its first entrance to the print market, which has both vitiated the force of *Pierce*'s strangeness to normative publishing formulae and made the text as susceptible as *Groatsworth* to the taste for libelous scandal. Carroll thinks it likely that Shakespeare was threatening to sue everyone who might be connected to *Groatsworth's* publication; Chettle's subsequent publication under his own name, *Kind-Hearts Dreame* (1592), includes an evasive account of Chettle's role in preparing *Groatsworth* for the press, an exoneration of Nashe from any association with its publication, and an elaborate and courteous apology to Shakespeare for "Greene's" jaundiced account of his career. (The apology to Shakespeare is balanced in *Kind-Heart* by remarks even more hostile to Marlowe than those published in *Groatsworth.*)
43. The generic variety of *Groatsworth's* episodes and interpolations range from the sexual double-crossing of Italianate *novelle,* to a beast fable, to versified complaint, to homiletic compilations of proverb. For Carroll, "Introduction," this diffuseness points to the work of another hand in collating disparate fragments among Greene's papers after his death; Mentz, "Forming Greene," argues that it's the mark of a deliberate retrospection, and he includes a chart indexing the divisions of the text to the different phases of Greene's career (124–125).
44. Helgerson, *The Elizabethan Prodigals,* passim.
45. Hutson, *Thomas Nashe in Context,* 38–54.
46. Mat. 25:14–30; the interpretation of the monetary talent of the parable as an individual's particular, God-given abilities and resources was standardized by the sixteenth century, and this interpretive sense for "talent" was beginning to be articulated without direct reference to the literal sense—in other words, without making explicit its status as interpretation (*OED,* 2nd ed., s.v. "talent," 5–6).

47. Astrophil calls himself a "bankrout . . . of all those *goods* which heaven to me hath lent" (18:3–4, my emphasis); he is of course too much the aristocrat to think of the presence or absence of coin as determinative of his assets. Helgerson argues that what his prodigals understand themselves to be wasting is not money but time, both in the sense of the relation of present to future that is the potential of their gifts and opportunities, and in that of the time and effort devoted to cultivating their gifts in the past:

"[P]ecuniary imprudence is only a part, and not often an essential part, of their vision of prodigality. Whetstone gives the name 'The Garden of Unthriftiness' to a section of his book that has nothing to do with money, to a collection of 'wanton' sonnets. He is unthrifty in the pursuit of beauty and in the celebration of love; he wastes not money, but time, wit, and learning, goods that should be spent in some way 'beneficial unto the commonweal' and 'profitable to himself.'

"This ideal of thrift, which recurs in the mercantile metaphors of Elizabethan love poetry, the audits and accounts which always prove the lover a bankrupt, the 'expense of spirit in a waste of shame,' is very much the product of an educational system so intent on using every hour and so convinced that it knew how to use the hours profitably" (*The Elizabethan Prodigals*, 27).

48. The gnomic chiasmus of the transaction has a proximate source in Lyly's *Euphues*. "It hath been an old said saw, and not of less truth than antiquity, that wit is the better if it be the dearer bought," remarks the narrator in introducing his protagonist (*Euphues: The Anatomy of Wit and Euphues and His England*, ed. Leah Scragg [Manchester: Manchester UP, 2003]: 33). Tilley confirms the proverbiality of that formula, but it's Lyly who goes on to develop it into the terms by which *Groatsworth* will define its titular transaction: "Seeing thou wilt not buy counsel at the first hand good cheap, thou shalt buy repentance at the second hand at such an unreasonable rate that thou will curse thy hard pennyworth, and ban thy hard heart" (42).
49. For Halasz, the bequest identifies the purchase of the pamphlet by the reader with the will of the usurious father: *Groatsworth* "locates its value in the marketplace and identifies it with the practice of usury," even as it strives "to deny the mediation of the marketplace" (*The Marketplace of Print*, 35–36).
50. Hutson, *Thomas Nashe in Context*, 172–196.
51. The house also has an oven "about the compass of a parenthesis in proclamation print" which produces "diminutive dishes," but the food therein—which Pierce invites the reader to imagine, rather than detailing it himself—seems no more substantial than the beverage he does specify (60). Nashe is obviously not invoking here the "vital anthropological minimum" whose fictivity is demonstrated by Baudrillard (for which see my chapter 1): "froth" is not literally enough to sustain any human body's need for liquids, and Greediness and Niggardize are not particularly human. The exercise of hyperbole is built into this emblematically allegorical topos, and here it is displayed as the hyperbolically minimal. What they are coming up against in the froth, I argue, is the irreducibility of a minimal but universal materiality, not the specific material demands of particular bodies.

52. *Confessions* 6; *City of God* 11.22, 11.27–28.

53. This inclination was prompted partly by the expectation that God's creation ex nihilo should reflect His own repleteness and leave the condition of nothing entirely behind, and partly by the general association of atomism with atheism in the reception of Lucretius. When Enobarbus says that in the otherwise deserted town of Cydnus "th' air, . . . but for vacancy,/ Had gone to gaze on Cleopatra too,/ And made a gap in nature," he is citing the commonplace impossibility of vacuum, and offering the unfulfillable desire of the air to violate the order of the plenum in order to see Cleopatra as the climax of the paradoxes of *physis* out of which her barge is built (*A&C* 2.2.216–218).

54. See the (hostile) reception of Scot's *Discoverie of Witchcraft* for the sense that such debunking texts undermined the solidity of positive belief in portraying witchcraft as a hoax.

55. Meeting the spirit Mustardseed, Bottom comments courteously on the fame of his pedigree: "That same cowardly, giant-like ox-beef hath devour'd many a gentleman of your house. I promise you your kindred hath made my eyes water ere now" (*Dream* 3.1.192–195). The relation of mustard to pancake becomes that of honor to truth in Touchstone's first foolery in *AYLI* 1.2.60–80.

56. For the relation of dreams to the stuff of prose in *Terrors*, see Barbour, *Deciphering Elizabethan Fiction*, 72–81.

57. Hutson demonstrates the reflexive continuity between Tabitha's techniques of manipulation and Jack's own (*Thomas Nashe in Context*, 227–228).

58. As Yates writes of Jack's later escape from the clutches of yet another Italian courtesan, Juliana, "Hey presto! Diamante ex machina—and Jack is saved the labor of an ending" (*Error Misuse Failure*, 136).

59. Stephen Hilliard draws larger patterns of Jack's relations to fortune, arguing that Jack is generally able to rely on his luck in the scrapes and gambles of his career before entering Italy, but there becomes more and more subjected to a providential badness of fortune—as when he walks away from the expatriate English earl's good advice to flee the country and falls immediately into Zadoch's cellar (*The Singularity of Thomas Nashe* [Lincoln: U of Nebraska P, 1986]: 148–168). I agree that Jack's swings of fortune become more extreme the longer he stays among the horrors of Italy—and that the good fortune which, in Venice, not only compensates for the initial bad fortune of imprisonment but yields fantastic satisfactions therefrom is less and less able to make up for the horrors into which Jack is placed by bad fortune. Nevertheless I'm not sure that the means by which Jack's skin is always eventually saved are adequate to any normative idea of providence. For the resistances of material contingency to the ideologeme of providence, see my chapter 2.

60. Mentz argues that "the nihilistic uncertainty of Tabitha's house" does not, as some critics have argued, epitomize a general unbelief in interpretation on Nashe's part; he offers as its antithesis the positive version of "artistic dishonesty" manifested in the Roman banqueting house (*Romance for Sale in Early*

*Modern England: The Rise of Prose Fiction* [Burlington, Vt.: Ashgate, 2006]: 199). He points to the emergence of Diamante as a point of transformation for *The Unfortunate Traveller* as a whole, as giving Jack's previously desultory travels the new generic impetus of Hellenistic romance, and to Diamante's resourceful agency as inhabiting the type of the romance heroine, while the sexuality and deceitfulness through which she exercises that agency contravene the type.

61. Yates argues that Jack's travels are propelled by the need to survive by means of becoming an exception: "to exist as an anonymous court functionary raises the specter of imminent dissolution, of dying in the stead of another, a named superior" (*Error Misuse Failure,* 122).
62. For the problematic relations of probabilistic reasoning to the categories of possibility and certainty at the end of the sixteenth century, see Joel Altman, *The Improbability of Othello: Rhetorical Anthropology and Shakespearean Selfhood* (Chicago: U of Chicago P, 2010).
63. Joan Pong Linton argues that this passage (as well as some lines preceding it that I haven't cited here) emphatically defines Diamante's personal integrity, and that the contradiction it seems to articulate within that integrity between sexuality and chastity is to be understood as "transgress[ing] the gender binary underwriting conventional femininity"—that is, as exterior to her "sovereign self," society's fracture rather than hers ("Counterfeiting Sovereignty, Mocking Mastery: Trickster Poetics and the Critique of Romance in Nashe's *The Unfortunate Traveller,*" in *Early Modern Prose Fiction: The Cultural Politics of Reading,* ed. Naomi Conn Liebler [New York: Routledge, 2007]: 130–147, esp. 144).
64. Brissenden ed., *As You Like It* (Oxford: Oxford UP, 1993): 36, 229–231.
65. A not uncommon etymological lapse (*OED,* 2nd ed., s.v. "ingenious," II.4–6), but one that Nashe would have known better than to commit ignorantly: he addresses Southampton as "ingenuous" in the epistle to the first edition of *UT* (251). The citation in the voice of Sappho is from Ovid's *Heroides* (XV.84).
66. I don't have space here to go into the two interesting passages in which Nashe compares the coining of words to the exchanging of small change for large, foreign gold coins; one occurs in the defensive epistle to the second edition of *Christs Teares* (in *Works of Thomas Nashe,* ed. R. B. McKerrow, 3 vols. [London: A.H. Bullen, 1904]: 2.184) and the other in *Have with You to Saffron Walden* (ibid., 3.52).
67. For Diamante's autonomous efficacy, see both Mentz, *Romance for Sale,* and Linton, "Counterfeiting Sovereignty."

## AFTERWORD

1. André Gide, *The Counterfeiters* (*Les Faux-monnayeurs*), tr. Dorothy Bussy (New York: Modern Library, 1955): 150.
2. Hutson, *Thomas Nashe in Context* (Oxford: Clarendon, 1989): 172–173.
3. Adam Smith, *An Inquiry into the Nature and Causes of the Wealth of Nations,* ed. Edwin Cannan (New York: Modern Library, 1937): 398–402. Smith character-

izes these voices for change as "merchants" rather than as themselves authors, in keeping with his general characterization of the market's self-realization as the triumph of practice over the self-defeating strictures of theory (400); Mun is the only one he cites directly.

4. The principal texts (all printed in London) are Malynes, *A Treatise of the Canker of England's Common-Wealth* (1602), *Lex Mercatoria* (1622), *The Maintenance of Free Trade* (1622), and *The Center of the Circle of Commerce* (1623); Misselden, *The Circle of Commerce, or the Ballance of Trade* (1623); and Mun, *England's Treasure by Forraign Trade* (1623?). Mary Poovey locates these debates near the origin point of her *History of the Modern Fact* (Chicago: U of Chicago P, 1998: 66–91). Blair Hoxby analyzes their impact upon the literary production of the seventeenth century in *Mammon's Music: Literature and Economics in the Age of Milton* (New Haven: Yale UP, 2002). Jonathan Gil Harris compares them to dramatic texts of the sixteenth century in *Sick Economies: Drama, Mercantilism, and Disease in Shakespeare's England* (Philadelphia: U of Pennsylvania P, 2004). Judith H. Anderson considers the metaphoricity of Malynes's writing, both in the treatise form and in his allegorical *St. George for England* (1601), in *Translating Investments: Metaphor and the Dynamic of Cultural Change in Tudor-Stuart England* (New York: Fordham UP, 2005).
5. Smith, *Wealth of Nations*, 399–400.
6. Important analyses of this transition in monetary theory, and in economic history, include M. Beer, *Early British Economics* (London: Allen and Unwin, 1938); R. H. Tawney, *Religion and the Rise of Capitalism* (London: Penguin, 1938); Lawrence Stone, *The Crisis of the Aristocracy, 1558–1641* (Oxford: Oxford UP, 1967); Joan Thirsk, *Economic Policy and Projects: The Development of a Consumer Society in Early Modern England* (Oxford: Clarendon, 1978); Joyce Oldham Appleby, *Economic Thought and Ideology in Seventeenth-Century England* (Princeton, N.J.: Princeton UP, 1978); and Craig Muldrew, *The Economy of Obligation: The Culture of Credit and Social Relations in Early Modern England* (New York: St. Martin's, 1998).
7. The goal even of revisionist historians of sixteenth-century monetary thought such as Neal Wood has often been to integrate sixteenth-century writers into the history of political economy (effectively moving what Wood's monograph calls the "Foundations of Political Economy" from the generation of Misselden and Mun to that of Thomas Smith and Robert Crowley), not to evaluate the possibility of finding meaning in their discrepancy (*Foundations of Political Economy: Some Early Tudor Views on State and Society* [Berkeley: U of California P, 1994]). The disciplinary history of economics tends otherwise to disregard a period apparently unattached to its own development; while literary critics, however much attentive to early modern fiscal matters, likewise are more attracted to narratives that can claim to adumbrate modern formations than to the dead wood of "bullionism." Richard Halpern's *The Poetics of Primitive Accumulation* (Ithaca, N.Y.: Cornell UP, 1991), perhaps the most comprehensive materialist criticism of the

English sixteenth century, does not address Tudor monetary theory at all; it has no place in even the complexly counterproductive genealogy of capital that he locates in contemporary literary texts.

8. Poovey, *A History of the Modern Fact*, 79–85.
9. Mun, *England's Treasure by Forraign Trade: Or, The Ballance of Our Forraign Trade Is the Rule of Our Treasure* (Fairfield, N.J.: Augustus M. Kelley, 1986); citations to this edition will be given parenthetically in the text.
10. The first chapter of *England's Treasure* continues to address the son, establishing the speaker's authority as an experienced merchant by giving advice to a novice merchant. Once the equation of authority to mercantile experience is established, the address of the son disappears from the text, and Mun begins to unfold his argument against the restraint of export of gold and silver through the concept of the balance of trade.
11. For the decaying authority of the ethos of communal consensus and probabilistic expectation inherited from classical and medieval rhetoric at the turn of the seventeenth century, see Joel B. Altman, *The Improbability of Othello: Rhetorical Anthropology and Shakespearean Selfhood* (Chicago: U of Chicago P, 2010).
12. The ethical positions that Mun asserts are by no means controversial, much less scandalous. Like every previous English writer on international trade, he preaches self-restraint for individual consumers, thinking it vital that "we would soberly refrain from excessive consumption of forraign wares in our diet and rayment" (7; for the long-standing anxiety over English appetites for foreign "trifles," see Jeffrey Knapp, *An Empire Nowhere: England, America, and Literature from* Utopia *to* The Tempest [Berkeley: U of California P, 1992]; for Mun's chosen term of "consumption" as denoting at once a buying practice and a wasting disease, see Harris, *Sick Economies*, 163–185). Mun scrupulously differentiates the profits of individual merchants from the totality of the common weal, arguing not only that individual merchants can profit from the suffering of the public interest but that the common weal can sometimes be a gainer when individuals' profits are restricted:

   > We find that twenty five in the hundred less in the price of [wool and cloth] and some other Wares, to the loss of private mens revenues, may raise above fifty upon the hundred in the quantity vented to the benefit of the publique (8).

   The fiscal insight here is the role that price plays in soliciting demand: a relatively small price reduction can capture a greater share of the market for the product, or expand that market, so that the diminished profit on individual transactions is more than compensated for by the volume of transactions. This is not a concept that, as economics, would require the articulation of an adversarial relationship between the public and the private. Rather, that antagonism is an inheritance from the commonwealth ethic, which expected that the public interest would regularly demand the restraint of private interests. For Mun, the point at which public and private interests diverge is the moment where a higher price begins to suppress the volume of sales; this marks the price as the short-sighted exploitation of the market by an individual to the detriment of the public good and ultimately his own—a formulation which we have seen to be characteristic of sixteenth-century commonwealth discourse. Mun consistently identifies the public interest with the volume of goods vended internationally, not the revenues therefrom, whenever he identifies the two as divergent—this represents one of many potentially contradictory fractures within Mun's own comprehensive ideal, that of "the balance of trade."

13. Here Mun's thought is closer to that of Aristotle, who formulates the polis as constituted of householders in *Politics* book I, than it is to the Platonic train of thought which expected that a ruler must be a good man in order to rule well—i.e., that good politics arises in the education in ethics of the individuals who participate in governance. I do not, of course, mean to suggest that nobody before Mun posited a synecdoche between the household and the *state*. As for example in Katherina's final speech in *Shrew* (5.2.136–189), the assertion of a husband's mastery of a household is routinely analogized to that of a king over a country, as mutually reinforcing instances of patriarchal order between micro- and macrocosm. The difference between Mun's analogy and Katherina's is that Mun's analogy is between the household and the *commonwealth*, and that the analogized term is not power but thrift. For the emergence of that metaphoric analogy in the early seventeenth century, and the relations between Mun's treatise and Aristotle in Mun's reformulation of ethics into economy, see Stephen Deng, "Global Œconomy: Ben Jonson's *The Staple of News* and the Ethics of Mercantilism," in *Global Traffic: Discourses and Practices of Trade in English Literature from 1550 to 1700*, ed. Barbara Sebek and Stephen Deng (New York: Palgrave Macmillan, 2008): 245–264.
14. See Jean-Joseph Goux, *Symbolic Economies: After Marx and Freud*, trans. Jennifer Curtiss Gage (Ithaca, N.Y.: Cornell UP, 1990), for the relation of the coin to what he argues are the homological structures of market and psyche.
15. Wilson, *The Three Ladies of London* (London, 1584), title page.
16. While for Halpern the English sixteenth century is an era of "primitive accumulation," an interregnum between the collapse of feudalism and the rise of capitalism, James Holstun presents sixteenth-century commonwealth as itself a mode of production, a postfeudal "monarcho-populist" alternative to capital that he offers as a road not taken by history: "The Spider, the Fly, and the Commonwealth: Merie John Heywood and Agrarian Class Struggle," *ELH* 71.1 (Spring 2004): 53–88.

# WORKS CITED


Adelman, Janet. *Blood Relations: Christian and Jew in* The Merchant of Venice. Chicago: U of Chicago P, 2008.

Agamben, Giorgio. *Homo Sacer: Sovereign Power and Bare Life.* Tr. Daniel Heller-Roazen. Stanford, Calif.: Stanford UP, 1998.

Agnew, Jean-Christophe. *Worlds Apart: the Market and the Theater in Anglo-American Thought, 1550–1750.* Cambridge: Cambridge UP, 1986.

Allen, D. F., and W. R. Dunstan. "Crosses and Crowns: A Study of Coinage in the Elizabethan Dramatists." *British Numismatic Journal* 23 (1938–40): 287–300.

Alpers, Paul J. *The Poetry of the Faerie Queene.* Princeton, N.J.: Princeton UP, 1967.

Althusser, Louis. *For Marx.* Tr. Ben Brewster. New York: Pantheon, 1969.

———. *Lenin and Philosophy and Other Essays.* Tr. Ben Brewster. New York: Monthly Review, 1971.

Altman, Joel B. *The Improbability of Othello: Rhetorical Anthropology and Shakespearean Selfhood.* Chicago: U of Chicago P, 2010.

———. "Justice and Equity." In *The Spenser Encyclopedia.* Ed. A. C. Hamilton. Toronto: U of Toronto P, 1990: 413–415.

Amis, Kingsley. *Lucky Jim.* Ed. David Lodge. London: Penguin, 1993.

Anderson, Judith H. *The Growth of a Personal Voice: Piers Plowman and The Faerie Queene.* New Haven: Yale UP, 1976.

———. *Translating Investments: Metaphor and the Dynamic of Cultural Change in Tudor-Stuart England.* New York: Fordham UP, 2005.

Appadurai, Arjun. "Introduction: Commodities and the Politics of Value." In *The Social Life of Things.* Ed. Arjun Appadurai. Cambridge: Cambridge UP, 1986: 3–63.

Appleby, Joyce Oldham. *Economic Thought and Ideology in Seventeenth-Century England.* Princeton, N.J.: Princeton UP, 1978.

Aravamudan, Srinivas. "The Return of Anachronism." *MLQ* 62:4 (December 2001): 331–353.

Aristotle. *Basic Works.* Ed. Richard McKeon. New York: Random House, 1941.

———. *Politics and Economics.* Tr. Edward Walford. London: George Bell and Sons, 1876.

Aubrey, John. *Brief Lives.* Ed. Oliver Lawson Dick. London: Secker and Warburg, 1950.

Auden, W. H. *The Dyer's Hand.* New York: Random House, 1962 (reprinted 1989).

Bacon, Francis. *The New Organon.* In *Francis Bacon: A Selection of His Works.* Ed. Sidney Warhaft. New York: Macmillan, 1982.

Bady, David. "The Sum of Something: Arithmetic in *The Merchant of Venice.*" *SQ* 36.1 (Spring 1985): 10–30.

Baker, Donald C. "The 'Angel' of English Renaissance Literature." *Studies in the Renaissance* 6 (1959): 85–93.

Barber, C. L. *Shakespeare's Festive Comedy: A Study of Dramatic Form and its Relation to Social Custom.* Princeton, N.J.: Princeton UP, 1959.

Barbour, Reid. *Deciphering Elizabethan Fiction.* Newark: U of Delaware P, 1993.

Barkan, Leonard. *The Gods Made Flesh: Metamorphosis and the Pursuit of Paganism.* New Haven: Yale UP, 1986.

———. "The Heritage of Zeuxis: Painting, Rhetoric, and History." In *Antiquity and Its Interpreters.* Ed. Alina Payne, Ann Kuttner, and Rebekah Smick. Cambridge: Cambridge University Press, 2000. 99–109.

———. "Making Pictures Speak: Renaissance Art, Elizabethan Literature, Modern Scholarship." *Renaissance Quarterly* 48.2 (Summer 1995): 326–351.

———. *Nature's Work of Art: The Human Body as Image of the World.* New Haven: Yale UP, 1975.

———. "Praxiteles' *Aphrodite* and the Love of Art." In *The Forms of Renaissance Thought,* ed. Barkan, Braden Cormack, and Sean Keilen. New York: Palgrave, 2009: 15–45.

Bataille, Georges. *Visions of Excess: Selected Writings 1927–39.* Ed. and introd. Allan Stoekl. Tr. Stoekl, Carl R. Lovitt and Donald M. Leslie, Jr. Minneapolis: U of Minnesota P, 1985.

Bath, Michael. *Speaking Pictures: English Emblem Books and Renaissance Culture.* New York: Longman, 1994.

Baudrillard, Jean. *For a Critique of the Political Economy of the Sign.* 1972. Tr. and introd. Charles Levin. St. Louis: Telos, 1981.

Beer, M. *Early British Economics.* London: Allen and Unwin, 1938.

Bellamy, J. G. *The Law of Treason in England in the Later Middle Ages.* Cambridge: Cambridge UP, 1970.

———. *Tudor Law of Treason.* London: Routledge and Kegan Paul, 1979.

Berger, Harry, Jr. *The Allegorical Temper: Vision and Reality in Book II of Spenser's* Faerie Queene. New Haven: Yale UP, 1957.

———. "Marriage and Mercifixion in *The Merchant of Venice*: The Casket Scene Revisited." *SQ* 32.2 (Summer 1981): 155–162.

Betteredge, Tom. *Literature and Politics in the English Reformation.* Manchester: Manchester UP, 2004.

Blackstone, William. *Commentaries on the Laws of England.* Ed. William Draper Lewis. Philadelphia: R. Welsh & Co., 1902.

Boehrer, Bruce. "Shylock and the Rise of the Household Pet: Thinking Social Exclusion in *The Merchant of Venice.*" *SQ* 50.2 (Summer 1999): 152–170.

Boethius [Anicius Manlius Severinus Boethius]. *The Consolation of Philosophy*. Tr. Richard Green. New York: Macmillan, 1962.

Bond, Christopher. "Medieval Harrowings of Hell and Spenser's House of Mammon." *ELR* 37.2 (Spring 2007): 175–192.

*The Book of Common Prayer.* Introd. Diarmaid MacCulloch. [1662.] London: Everyman, 1999.

Bourdieu, Pierre. *Distinction: A Social Critique of the Judgement of Taste*. Tr. Richard Nice. Cambridge, Mass.: Harvard University Press, 2000.

———. *Pascalian Meditations*. Tr. Richard Nice. Stanford, Calif.: Stanford UP, 2000.

Braudel, F. P., and F. Spooner. "Prices in Europe from 1450 to 1750." In *The Cambridge Economic History of Europe*, vol. 4. Eds. E. E. Rich and C. H. Wilson. Cambridge: Cambridge UP, 1967: 378–486.

Brown, Bill. "Thing Theory." In *Things*. Ed. Bill Brown. Chicago: U of Chicago P, 2004: 1–21.

Browne, Thomas. *Pseudodoxia Epidemica*. In *The Works of Sir Thomas Browne*. vol. 2. Ed. Geoffrey Keynes. Chicago: U of Chicago P, 1964.

Bruster, Douglas. *Drama and the Market in the Age of Shakespeare*. Cambridge: Cambridge UP, 1992.

———. "The New Materialism in Renaissance Studies." In *Material Cuture and Cultural Materialisms in the Middle Ages and Renaissance*, ed. Curtis Perry. Turnhout, Belgium: Brepols, 2001: 225–238.

———. "On a Certain Tendency in Economic Criticism of Shakespeare." In *Money and the Age of Shakespeare: Essays in New Economic Criticism*. Ed. Linda Woodbridge. New York: Palgrave Macmillan, 2003: 67–78.

Burckhardt, Jacob. *The Civilization of the Renaissance in Italy*. New York: Harper & Bros., 1958.

Burlinson, Christopher. *Allegory, Space and the Material World in the Writings of Edmund Spenser*. Cambridge: Brewer, 2006.

Carey, John. "Donne and Coins." In *English Renaissance Studies Presented to Dame Helen Gardner*. Ed. John Carey. Oxford: Clarendon, 1980: 151–163.

Cassirer, Ernst. *The Individual and the Cosmos in Renaissance Philosophy*. [1927.] Tr. and introd. Mario Domandi. Philadelphia: U of Pennsylvania P, 1963.

Cavell, Stanley. *Disowning Knowledge in Six Plays of Shakespeare*. Cambridge: Cambridge UP, 1987.

Challis, C. E. *The Tudor Coinage*. Manchester: Manchester UP, 1978.

Champion, Larry S. "The 'Un-end' of *King John*: Shakespeare's Demystification of Closure." In *King John: New Perspectives*. Ed. Deborah T. Curren-Aquino. Newark: U of Delaware P, 1989: 173–185.

Chapman, George, Ben Jonson, and John Marston. *Eastward Ho*. Ed. R. W. Van Fossen. Manchester: Manchester UP, 1999.

Cheney, Patrick. *Marlowe's Counterfeit Profession: Ovid, Spenser, Counter-Nationhood*. Toronto: U of Toronto P, 1997.

Chettle, Henry. *Kind-Harts Dreame*. London, 1592.

Cohen, Walter. "The Undiscovered Country: Shakespeare's Mercantile Geography." In *Marxist Shakespeares*. Eds. Jean Howard and Scott Cutler Shershow. London: Routledge, 2001: 128–158.

Cooney, Helen. "Guyon and His Palmer: Spenser's Emblem of Temperance." *Review of English Studies* 51.202 (May 2000): 169–192.

Cormack, Bradin. *A Power to Do Justice: Jurisdiction, English Literature, and the Rise of the Common Law, 1509–1625*. Chicago: U of Chicago P, 2007.

Correll, Barbara. "Chiasmus and *Commodificatio*: Crossing Tropes and Conditions in Donne's Elegy 11, 'The Bracelet.'" *Exemplaria* 11.1 (1999): 141–165.

———. "Scene Stealers: Autolycus, *The Winter's Tale*, and Economic Criticism." In *Money and the Age of Shakespeare: Essays in New Economic Criticism*. Ed. Linda Woodbridge. New York: Palgrave Macmillan, 2003: 53–66.

———. "Terms of 'Indearment': Lyric and General Economy in Shakespeare and Donne." *ELH* 75.2 (Summer 2008): 241–262.

[Cotton, Sir Robert]. "A Speech… Touching the Alteration of Coin." 1626, printed 1651. In *A Select Collection of Scarce and Valuable Tracts on Money*. Ed. J. R. McCulloch. London: Political Economy Club, 1856: 121–141.

Craig, John. *The Mint: A History of the London Mint from A. D. 287 to 1948*. Cambridge: Cambridge UP, 1953.

Crane, Mary Thomas. "*Intret Cato*: Authority and the Epigram in Sixteenth-Century England." In *Renaissance Genres: Essays on Theory, History, and Interpretation*, ed. Barbara Kiefer Lewalski. Cambridge, Mass.: Harvard UP, 1986: 158–188.

Crewe, Jonathan. *Unredeemed Rhetoric: Thomas Nashe and the Scandal of Authorship*. Baltimore: Johns Hopkins UP, 1982.

Crowley, Robert. *Philargyrie of Great Britayne*. London, 1551.

Cunnally, John. *Images of the Illustrious: The Numismatic Presence in the Renaissance*. Princeton, N.J.: Princeton UP, 1999.

Daneau, Lambert. *True and Christian Friendship*. London, 1586.

Darcy, Robert. "Freeing Daughters on Open Markets: The Incest Clause in *The Merchant of Venice*." In *Money and the Age of Shakespeare: Essays in New Economic Criticism*. Ed. Linda Woodbridge. New York: Palgrave Macmillan, 2003: 189–200.

de Certeau, Michel. *The Practice of Everyday Life*. Tr. Steven Rendall. Berkeley: U of California P, 1984.

de Grazia, Margreta. "The Ideology of Superfluous Things: *King Lear* as Period Piece." In *Subject and Object in Renaissance Culture*. Ed. Margreta de Grazia, Maureen Quilligan, and Peter Stallybrass. Cambridge: Cambridge UP, 1996: 17–42.

Deng, Stephen. *Coinage and State Formation in Early Modern English Literature*. New York: Palgrave Macmillan, 2011.

———. "Global Œconomy: Ben Jonson's *The Staple of News* and the Ethics of Mercantilism." In *Global Traffic: Discourses and Practices of Trade in English Literature from 1550 to 1700*. Ed. Barbara Sebek and Stephen Deng. New York: Palgrave Macmillan, 2008: 245–64.

———. "Healing Angels and 'Golden Blood': Money and Mystical Kingship in *Macbeth*." In *Macbeth: New Critical Essays*. Ed. Nick Moschovakis. New York: Routledge, 2008: 163-81.

Derrida, Jacques. *Given Time: I. Counterfeit Money*. Trans. Peggy Kamuf. Chicago: U of Chicago P, 1992.

———. "What Is a 'Relevant' Translation?" Tr. Lawrence Venuti. *Critical Inquiry* 27.2 (Winter 2001): 174–200.

Diehl, Huston. "'Infinite Space': Representation and Reformation in *Measure for Measure*." *Shakespeare Quarterly* 49.4 (1998 Winter): 393–410.

Dolan, Frances. *Dangerous Familiars: Representations of Domestic Crime in England, 1550–1700*. Ithaca, N.Y.: Cornell UP, 1994.

Dolan, Neal. "Shylock in Love: Economic Metaphors in Shakespeare's Sonnets." *Raritan* 22.2 (Fall 2002): 26–51.

Dollimore, Jonathan. "Transgression and Surveillance in *Measure for Measure*." *Political Shakespeare: New Essays in Cultural Materialism*. Eds. Jonathan Dollimore and Alan Sinfield. Manchester: Manchester UP, 1985: 72–87.

Dolven, Jeff. *Scenes of Instruction in Renaissance Romance*. Chicago: U of Chicago P, 2007.

Donne, John. *The Complete English Poems*. Ed. A. J. Smith. London: Penguin, 1986.

Dubrow, Heather. *Echoes of Desire: English Petrarchism and Its Counterdiscourses*. Ithaca, N.Y.: Cornell UP, 1995.

Eliot, T. S. "Notes on the Blank Verse of Christopher Marlowe." *The Sacred Wood and Major Early Essays*. Mineola, N.Y.: Dover, 1998.

Elkins, James. *What Painting Is*. New York: Routledge, 1999.

Elyot, Thomas. *The Booke called the Gouernour*. London, 1531.

Engle, Lars. *Shakespearean Pragmatism: Market of His Time*. Chicago: U of Chicago P, 1993.

———. "'Thrift is Blessing': Exchange and Explanation in *The Merchant of Venice*." *SQ* 37:1 (Spring 1986): 20–37.

Enterline, Lynn. *The Tears of Narcissus: Melancholia and Masculinity in Early Modern Writing*. Stanford, Calif.: Stanford UP, 1995.

Esolen, Anthony. "Spenserian Chaos: Lucretius in *The Faerie Queene*." *Spenser Studies* 11 (1994): 31–51.

———. "Spenser's 'Alma Venus': Energy and Economics in the Bower of Bliss." *English Literary Renaissance* 23.2 (Spring 1993): 267–286.

Evans, Kasey. "How Temperance Becomes 'Blood Guiltie' in *The Faerie Queene*." *SEL* 49.1 (Winter 2009): 35–66.

Evans, Maurice. "The Fall of Guyon." *ELH* 28 (1961): 215–224.

Farmer, Ann. "In the Metal Recycling Business, It's Loud, Dirty and Suddenly Lucrative." *The New York Times*. June 27, 2008. National edition: C12.

Ferguson, Arthur B. *Clio Unbound: Perception of the Social and Cultural Past in Renaissance England*. Durham, N.C.: Duke UP, 1979.

Fichte, Joerg O. "'For coueitise after cros; [th]e croune stant in golde': Money as Matter and Metaphor in *Piers Plowman*." *Material Culture and Cultural*

*Materialisms in the Middle Ages and Renaissance*, ed. Curtis Perry. Turnhout, Belgium: Brepols, 2001: 59–74.

Fischer, Sandra K. *Econolingua: a Glossary of Coins and Economic Language in Renaissance Drama*. Newark: U of Delaware P, 1985.

———. "'He Means to Pay': Value and Metaphor in the Lancastrian Tetralogy." *Shakespeare Quarterly* 40:2 (Summer 1989): 149–164.

Fisher, Will. "Queer Money." *ELH* 66.1 (Spring 1999): 1–23.

Fleming, Juliet. *Graffiti and the Writing Arts of Early Modern England*. Philadelphia: U of Pennsylvania P, 2001.

Forker, Charles R. "Marlowe's *Edward II* and Its Shakespearean Relatives: The Emergence of a Genre." In *Shakespeare's English Histories: A Quest for Form and Genre*. Ed. John W. Velz. Binghamton, N.Y.: Medieval and Renaissance Texts and Studies, 1996: 55–90.

Forman, Valerie. "Marked Angels: Counterfeits, Commodities, and *The Roaring Girl*." *Renaissance Quarterly* 54.4.2 (Winter 2001): 1531–1560.

Foucault, Michel. *The Order of Things: An Archaeology of the Human Sciences*. New York: Vintage, 1973.

Fowler, Elizabeth. *Literary Character: The Human Figure in Early English Writing*. Ithaca, N.Y.: Cornell UP, 2003.

Frankfurt, Harry G. *On Bullshit*. Princeton, N.J.: Princeton UP, 2005.

Freedgood, Elaine. *The Ideas in Things: Fugitive Meaning in the Victorian Novel*. Chicago: U of Chicago P, 2006.

Freer, Coburn. "John Donne and Elizabethan Economic Theory." *Criticism* 38.4 (Fall 1996): 497–520.

Freinkel, Lisa. "The Shakespearean Fetish." *Spiritual Shakespeares*. Ed. Ewan Fernie. London and New York: Routledge, 2005. 109–129.

Freud, Sigmund. "Fetishism." In *The Standard Edition of the Complete Psychological Works of Sigmund Freud*, vol. 21. London: Hogarth, 1955: 149–158.

———. "The Theme of the Three Caskets." *Writings on Art and Literature*. Stanford, Calif.: Stanford UP, 1997. 109–121.

Furness, H. H., ed. *A New Variorum Edition of Shakespeare: The Merchant of Venice*. [1888.] New York: Dover, 1964.

Gaddis, William. *The Recognitions*. New York: Penguin, 1993.

Gallagher, Catherine. *The Body Economic: Life, Death, and Sensation in Political Economy and the Victorian Novel*. Chicago: U of Chicago P, 2005.

Gallagher, Lowell. "Waiting for Gobbo." In *Spiritual Shakespeares*. Ed. Ewan Fernie. New York: Routledge, 2005: 73–93.

Garber, Marjorie. "'Infinite Riches in a Little Room': Closure and Enclosure in Marlowe." *Two Renaissance Mythmakers: Selected Papers from the English Institute, 1975–76*. Ed. Alvin Kernan. Baltimore: Johns Hopkins UP, 1977: 3–21.

———. *Shakespeare's Ghost Writers: Literature as Uncanny Causality*. New York: Methuen, 1987.

Gaskill, Malcolm. *Crime and Mentalities in Early Modern England*. Cambridge: Cambridge UP, 2000.

Gatti, Hilary. *The Renaissance Drama of Knowledge*. New York: Routledge, 1989.

Giamatti, A. Bartlett. *Play of Double Senses: Spenser's "Faerie Queene."* Englewood Cliffs, N.J.: Prentice, 1975.

Gide, André. *The Counterfeiters*. Trans. Dorothy Bussy. New York: Modern Library, 1955.

Gilman, Ernest B. *Iconoclasm and Poetry in the English Reformation: Down Went Dagon*. Chicago: U of Chicago P, 1986.

———. *Plague Writing in Early Modern England*. Chicago: U of Chicago P, 2009.

Girard, René. *A Theater of Envy: William Shakespeare*. Oxford: Oxford UP, 1991.

———. "'To Entrap the Wisest': Sacrificial Ambivalence in *The Merchant of Venice* and *Richard III*." [1980.] Reprinted in *Shakespeare: An Anthology of Criticism and Theory, 1945–2000*, ed. Russ MacDonald. Oxford: Blackwell, 2004: 353–364.

Goldberg, Jonathan. *James I and the Politics of Literature*. Baltimore: Johns Hopkins UP, 1983.

———. *The Seeds of Things: Theorizing Sexuality and Materiality in Renaissance Representations*. New York: Fordham UP, 2009.

———. "Sodomy and Society: The Case of Christopher Marlowe." In *Staging the Renaissance: Interpretations of Elizabethan and Early Jacobean Drama*. Eds. David Scott Kastan and Peter Stallybrass. New York: Routledge, 1991: 75–82.

Goldsmith, Margaret E. *The Figure of Piers Plowman: The Image on the Coin*. Cambridge: Brewer, 1981.

Gombrich, E. H. *Symbolic Images: Studies in the Art of the Renaissance*. London: Phaidon, 1972.

Gordon, Barry. *Economic Analysis before Adam Smith: Hesiod to Lessius*. London: Macmillan, 1975.

Gould, J. D. *The Great Debasement: Currency and the Economy in Mid-Tudor England*. Oxford: Clarendon, 1970.

Goux, Jean-Joseph. *Symbolic Economies: After Marx and Freud*. Trans. Jennifer Curtiss Gage. Ithaca, N.Y.: Cornell UP, 1990.

Grady, Hugh. *Shakespeare's Universal Wolf: Studies in Early Modern Reification*. Oxford: Clarendon, 1996.

Grennan, Eamon. "Shakespeare's Satirical History: A Reading of *King John*." *Shakespeare Studies* 11 (1978): 21–37.

Greenblatt, Stephen. *Renaissance Self-Fashioning from More to Shakespeare*. Chicago: U of Chicago P, 1980.

———. *Shakespearean Negotiations*. Berkeley: U of California P, 1989.

———. *The Swerve: How the World Became Modern*. New York: Norton, 2011.

Greene, Thomas M. "Pitiful Thrivers: Failed Husbandry in the Sonnets." In *Shakespeare and the Question of Theory*. Eds. Patricia Parker and Geoffrey Hartman. New York: Methuen, 1985: 230–244.

*Greene's Groatsworth of Wit, Bought with a Million of Repentance*. Attrib. to Robert Greene and Henry Chettle. Ed. D. Allen Carroll. Binghamton, N.Y.: Medieval and Renaissance Texts and Studies, 1994.

Greteman, Blaine. "Perplex't Paths: Youth and Authority in Milton's *Mask.*" *Renaissance Quarterly* 62.2 (Summer 2009): 410–443.

Grierson, Philip. *Numismatics.* Oxford: Oxford UP, 1975.

Gross, Kenneth. *Spenserian Poetics: Idolatry, Iconoclasm, and Magic.* Ithaca, N.Y.: Cornell UP, 1986.

Guillory, John. *Cultural Capital: The Problem of Literary Canon Formation.* Chicago: U of Chicago P, 1993.

———. "A New Subject for Criticism." In *The Culture of Capital.* Ed. Henry S. Turner. New York: Routledge, 2002: 223–230.

———. *Poetic Authority: Spenser, Milton, and Literary History.* New York: Columbia UP, 1983.

Hakluyt, Richard. *Voyages and Discoveries: the Principal Navigations, Voyages, Traffiques, and Discoveries of the English Nation.* Ed. and abridged Jack Beeching. London: Penguin, 1972.

Halasz, Alexandra. *The Marketplace of Print: Pamphlets and the Public Sphere in Early Modern England.* Cambridge: Cambridge UP, 1997.

Halpern, Richard. "The Lyric in the Field of Information: Autopoiesis and History in Donne's *Songs and Sonnets.*" *Yale Journal of Criticism* 6.1 (1993): 185–215.

———. *The Poetics of Primitive Accumulation.* Ithaca, N.Y.: Cornell UP, 1991.

———. *Shakespeare among the Moderns.* Ithaca, N.Y.: Cornell UP, 1997.

Hammill, Graham. "Time in Marlowe." *ELH* 75.2 (Summer 2008): 291–314.

Hanson, Elizabeth. *Discovering the Subject in Renaissance England.* Cambridge: Cambridge UP, 1998.

Hardman, Christopher. "'Trouble being gone, comfort should remain': Tranquility and Discomfort in 'The Merchant of Venice.'" *Yearbook of English Studies* 23 (1993): 189–205.

Harris, Jonathan Gil. "Atomic Shakespeare." *Shakespeare Studies* 30 (2002): 47–51.

———. "Shakespeare's Hair: Staging the Object of Material Culture." *Shakespeare Quarterly* 52.3 (2002): 479–491.

———. *Sick Economies: Drama, Mercantilism, and Disease in Shakespeare's England.* Philadelphia: U of Pennsylvania P, 2004.

———. *Untimely Matter in the Time of Shakespeare.* Philadelphia: U of Pennsylvania P, 2009.

———, and Natasha Korda, eds. *Staged Properties in Early Modern Drama.* Cambridge: Cambridge UP, 2002.

Harrison, Charles Trawick. "The Ancient Atomists and English Literature of the Seventeenth Century." *Harvard Studies in Classical Philology* 45 (1934): 1–79.

Harrison, William. *An Historicall description of the Iland of Britaine, with a briefe rehersall of the nature and qualities of the people of England, and such commodities as are to be found in the same.* Vol. 1 of Raphael Holinshed et al., *The First and Second Volumes of Chronicles.* [London], 1586: 1–250.

Hawkes, David. "Exchange Value and Empiricism in the Poetry of George Herbert." In *Money and the Age of Shakespeare: Essays in New Economic Criticism*. Ed. Linda Woodbridge. New York: Palgrave Macmillan, 2003: 79–96.

———. *Idols of the Marketplace: Idolatry and Commodity Fetishism in English Literature, 1580–1680*. New York: Palgrave, 2001.

———. "Sodomy, Usury, and the Narrative of Shakespeare's Sonnets." *Renaissance Studies* 14.3 (2000): 344–361.

Heidegger, Martin. *Being and Time*. [1926] Tr. John Macquarrie and Edward Robinson. San Francisco: Harper, 1962.

Heinzelman, Kurt. *The Economics of the Imagination*. Amherst: U of Massachusetts P, 1980.

Helgerson, Richard. *The Elizabethan Prodigals*. Berkeley: U of California P, 1976.

Hilliard, Stephen S. *The Singularity of Thomas Nashe*. Lincoln: U of Nebraska P, 1986.

Holland, Norman N. "*Measure for Measure*: The Duke and the Prince." *Comparative Literature* 11.1 (Winter 1959): 16–20.

Holstun, James. "The Spider, the Fly, and the Commonwealth: Merie John Heywood and Agrarian Class Struggle." *ELH* 71.1 (Spring 2004): 53–88.

Honigmann, E. A. J. "Shakespeare's Self-Repetitions and King John." *Shakespeare Survey* 53 (2000): 175–183.

Horwich, Richard. "Riddle and Dilemma in *The Merchant of Venice*." *Studies in English Literature 1500–1900* 17.2 (Spring 1977): 191–200.

Hoxby, Blair. *Mammon's Music: Literature and Economics in the Age of Milton*. New Haven: Yale UP, 2002.

Howard, Jean E., and Phyllis Rackin. *Engendering a Nation: A Feminist Account of Shakespeare's English Histories*. London: Routledge, 1997.

Hulse, Clark. *The Rule of Art: Literature and Painting in the Renaissance*. Chicago: U of Chicago P, 1990.

Hunt, Maurice. "Antimetabolic King John." *Style* 34.3 (Fall 2000): 380–401.

Hutson, Lorna. *Thomas Nashe in Context*. Oxford: Clarendon, 1989.

———. *The Usurer's Daughter: Male Friendship and Fictions of Women in Sixteenth-Century England*. New York: Routledge, 1997.

Jardine, Lisa. *Worldly Goods: A New History of the Renaissance*. New York: Doubleday, 1996.

Jones, Ann Rosalind, and Peter Stallybrass. "Fetishizing the Glove in Renaissance Europe." In *Things*. Ed. Bill Brown. Chicago: U of Chicago P, 2004: 174–192.

———. *Renaissance Clothing and the Materials of Memory*. Cambridge: Cambridge UP, 2000.

Jones, Norman. *God and the Moneylenders: Usury and Law in Early Modern England*. Oxford: Basil Blackwell, 1989.

Jones, Whitney R. D. *The Tudor Commonwealth 1529–1559*. London: Athlone, 1970.

Jonson, Ben. *The Alchemist*. Ed. Elizabeth Cook. New York: Norton, 1991.

———. *Epicoene*. In *Ben Jonson's Plays and Masques*. Ed. Richard Harp. New York: W. W. Norton, 2001: 111–199.

Kahn, Victoria. *Machiavellian Rhetoric: from the Counter-Reformation to Milton*. Princeton, N.J. : Princeton UP, 1994.

———. *Wayward Contracts: the Crisis of Political Obligation in England, 1640–1674*. Princeton, N.J. : Princeton UP, 2004.

Kalas, Rayna. *Frame, Glass, Verse: The Technology of Poetic Invention in the English Renaissance*. Ithaca, N.Y.: Cornell UP, 2007.

Kantorowicz, Ernst H. *The King's Two Bodies: A Study in Medieval Political Theology*. Princeton, N.J.: Princeton UP, 1957.

Kaske, Carol. "Amavia, Mordant, Ruddymane." In *The Spenser Encyclopedia*. Ed. A. C. Hamilton. Toronto: U of Toronto P, 1990: 25–27.

Kastan, David Scott. "'To Set a Form upon That Indigest': Shakespeare's Fictions of History." *Comparative Drama* 17 (1983): 1–16.

Kaufmann, David. *The Business of Common Life: Novels and Classical Economics between Revolution and Reform*. Baltimore: Johns Hopkins UP, 1995.

Kearney, James. "The Book and the Fetish: The Materiality of Prospero's Text." *Journal of Medieval and Early Modern Studies* 32.3 (2002): 433–468.

Kehler, Dorothea. "'So Jest with Heaven': Deity in *King John*." In *King John: New Perspectives*. Ed. Deborah T. Curren-Aquino. Newark: U. of Delaware P., 1989: 99–113.

Keilen, Sean. "Exemplary Metals: Classical Numismatics and the Commerce of Humanism." *Word & Image* 18.3 (July–September 2002): 282–294.

Kennedy, Duncan F. *Rethinking Reality: Lucretius and the Textualization of Nature*. Ann Arbor: U of Michigan P, 2002.

Kermode, Frank. *Shakespeare, Spenser, Donne: Renaissance Essays*. London: Routledge and Kegan Paul, 1971.

Kerrigan, William, and Gordon Braden. *The Idea of the Renaissance*. Baltimore: Johns Hopkins UP, 1989.

Ketteredge, Eric. *Trade and Banking in Early Modern England*. Manchester: Manchester UP, 1988.

King, John N. *English Reformation Literature: The Tudor Origins of the Protestant Tradition*. Princeton: Princeton UP, 1982.

Knapp, Jeffrey. *An Empire Nowhere: England, America, and Literature from Utopia to The Tempest*. Berkeley: U of California P, 1992.

———. *Shakespeare's Tribe: Church, Nation, and Theater in Renaissance England*. Chicago: U. of Chicago P., 2002.

Knights, L. C. *Drama and Society in the Age of Jonson*. London: Chatto and Windus, 1937.

Korda, Natasha. "Dame Usury: Gender, Credit, and (Ac)counting in the Sonnets and *The Merchant of Venice*." *Shakespeare Quarterly* 60.2 (2009): 129–153.

———. *Shakespeare's Domestic Economies*. Philadelphia: U of Pennsylvania P, 2002.

Kroll, Richard. *The Material Word: Literate Culture in the Restoration and Early Eighteenth Century*. Baltimore: Johns Hopkins UP, 1991.

Lamb, Jonathan. *Preserving the Self in the South Seas, 1680–1840*. Chicago: U of Chicago P, 2001.

Lander, Jesse M. "'Crack'd Crowns' and Counterfeit Sovereigns: The Crisis of Value in *1 Henry IV*." *Shakespeare Studies* 30 (2002): 137–161.

Langholm, Odd. *Economics in the Medieval Schools: Wealth, Exchange, Value, Money, and Usury According to the Paris Theological Tradition, 1200–1350*. Leiden: E. J. Brill, 1992.

Langland, William. *The Vision of Piers Plowman*. Ed. A. V. C. Schmidt. London: J. M. Dent, 1995.

Latimer, Hugh. *Sermons by Hugh Latimer, Sometime Bishop of Worcester*. London: J. M. Dent & Co., [1926].

Latour, Bruno. *Aramis, or the Love of Technology*. Tr. Catherine Porter. Cambridge, Mass.: Harvard UP, 1996.

———. *We Have Never Been Modern*. Tr. Catherine Porter. Cambridge, Mass.: Harvard UP, 1993.

Leinwand, Theodore B. *Theatre, Finance, and Society in Early Modern England*. Cambridge: Cambridge UP, 1999.

Lessing, G. E. *Laocoön: An Essay on the Limits of Painting and Poetry*. Tr. E. A. McCormick. Baltimore: Johns Hopkins UP, 1984.

Levin, Harry. *The Myth of the Golden Age in the Renaissance*. Bloomington: Indiana UP, 1969.

Levine, Nina. "Extending Credit in the Henry IV Plays." *Shakespeare Quarterly* 51:4 (Winter 2000): 403–431.

Levy, F. J. *Tudor Historical Thought*. San Marino, Calif.: Huntington Library, 1967.

Lewis, C. S. *English Literature in the Sixteenth Century Excluding Drama*. Oxford: Oxford UP, 1954.

Lezra, Jacques. *Unspeakable Subjects: The Genealogy of the Event in Early Modern Europe*. Stanford, Calif.: Stanford UP, 1997.

Linton, Joan Pong. "Counterfeiting Sovereignty, Mocking Mastery: Trickster Poetics and the Critique of Romance in Nashe's *Unfortunate Traveler*." In *Early Modern Prose Fiction: The Cultural Politics of Reading*. Ed. Naomi Conn Liebler. New York: Routledge, 2007.

Loach, Jennifer. *Edward VI*. New Haven: Yale UP, 1999.

Lucretius [Titus Lucretius Carus]. *On the Nature of Things*. Tr. W. H. D. Rouse. Ed. and rev. Martin F. Smith. Cambridge, Mass.: Loeb Classical Library/Harvard UP, 1992.

Lupton, Julia Reinhard. *Citizen-Saints: Shakespeare and Political Theology*. Chicago: U of Chicago P, 2005.

Lyly, John. *Euphues: The Anatomy of Wit and Euphues and His England*. Ed. Leah Scragg. Manchester: Manchester UP, 2003.

Lynch, Diedre Shauna. *The Economy of Character: Novels, Market Culture, and the Business of Inner Meaning*. Chicago: U of Chicago P, 1998.

Machiavelli, Niccoló. *The Prince*. Trans. Russell Price. Ed. Quentin Skinner. Cambridge: Cambridge UP, 1988.

Maclure, Millar, ed. *Marlowe: The Critical Heritage 1588–1896*. London: Routledge and Kegan Paul, 1979.

Mandeville, Bernard. *The Fable of the Bees and Other Writings.* Ed. E. J. Hundert. Indianapolis: Hackett, 1997.

Manley, Lawrence. *Literature and Culture in Early Modern London.* Cambridge: Cambridge UP, 1995.

Mannheim, Michael. *The Weak King Dilemma in the Shakespearean History Play.* Syracuse, N.Y.: Syracuse UP, 1973.

Marlowe, Christopher. *Edward the Second.* Ed. Charles R. Forker. Manchester: Manchester UP, 1994.

———. *The Jew of Malta.* Ed. David Bevington. New York: Manchester UP, 1997.

Marotti, Arthur. *John Donne, Coterie Poet.* Madison: U of Wisconsin P, 1986.

Martin, Catherine Gimelli. "Angels, Alchemists, and Exchange: Commercial Ideology in Court and City Comedy, 1596–1610." In *The Witness of Times: Manifestations of Ideology in Seventeenth-Century England.* Ed. Katherine Z. Keller. Pittsburgh: Duquesne UP, 1993: 121–147.

Marx, Karl. *Capital.* Vol. I. Tr. Ben Fowkes. New York: Penguin, 1976, reprinted 1990.

———. *The Economic and Political Manuscripts of 1844.* Ed. Dirk J. Struick. Tr. Martin Milligan. New York: International, 1964.

Mauss, Marcel. *The Gift: The Form and Reason for Exchange in Archaic Societies.* Tr. W. D. Halls. New York: Norton, 1990.

Mayhew, Nicholas. *Sterling: The History of a Currency.* New York: John Wiley and Sons, 1999.

McCulloch, J. R., ed. *Scarce and Valuable Tracts on Money.* London: Political Economy Club, 1856.

Mentz, Steven R. "The Fiend Gives Friendly Counsel: Launcelot Gobbo and Polyglot Economics in *The Merchant of Venice.*" In *Money and the Age of Shakespeare: Essays in New Economic Criticism.* Ed. Linda Woodbridge. New York: Palgrave Macmillan, 2003: 177–188.

———. "Forming Greene: Theorizing the Early Modern Author in the *Groatsworth of Wit.*" In *Writing Robert Greene.* Eds. Kirk Melnikoff and Edward Gieskes. Burlington, Vt.: Ashgate, 2008: 115–132.

———. *Romance for Sale in Early Modern England: The Rise of Prose Fiction.* Burlington, Vt.: Ashgate, 2006.

Meyer, Thomas F. *Thomas Starkey and the Commonweal: Humanist Politics and Religion in the Age of Henry VIII.* Oxford: Oxford UP, 1989.

Michaels, Walter Benn. *The Gold Standard and the Logic of Naturalism.* Berkeley: U of California P, 1987.

Middleton, Anne. "William Langland's 'Kynde Name': Authorial Signature and Social Identity in Late Fourteenth-Century England." In *Literary Practice and Social Change in Britain, 1380–1530.* Ed. Lee Patterson. Berkeley: U of California P, 1990.

Milligan, Burton. "Counterfeiters and Coin-clippers in the Sixteenth and Seventeenth Centuries." *Notes and Queries* 182 (February 1942): 100–105.

Mitchell, W. J. T. *Iconology: Image, Text, Ideology*. Chicago: U of Chicago P, 1986.
———. *Picture Theory: Essays on Verbal and Visual Representation*. Chicago: U of Chicago P, 1994.
Montrose, Louis. *The Subject of Elizabeth: Authority, Gender, Representation*. Chicago: U of Chicago P, 2006.
Moore, Geoffrey A. "The Cave of Mammon: Ethics and Metaphysics in Secular and Christian Perspectives." *ELH* 42.2 (Summer 1975): 157–170.
Muldrew, Craig. *The Economy of Obligation: The Culture of Credit and Social Relations in Early Modern England*. New York: St. Martin's, 1998.
———. "'Hard Food for Midas': Cash and Its Social Value in Early Modern England." *Past and Present* 170 (2001): 78–120.
Mullaney, Steven. *The Place of the Stage: License, Play, and Power in Renaissance England*. Chicago: U of Chicago P, 1988.
Mun, Thomas. *England's Treasure by Forraign Trade. Or, The Ballance of Our Forraign Trade Is the Rule of Our Treasure*. Fairfield, N.J.: Augustus M. Kelley, 1986.
Myers, K. Sara. *Ovid's Causes: Cosmogony and Ætiology in the* Metamorphoses. Ann Arbor: U of Michigan P, 1994.
Nashe, Thomas. *The Unfortunate Traveller and Other Works*. Ed. J. B. Steane. London: Penguin, 1972.
———. *Works of Thomas Nashe*. Ed. R. B. McKerrow. 3 vols. London: A.H. Bullen, 1904.
Neill, Michael. "Bastardy, Counterfeiting, and Misogyny in The Revenger's Tragedy." *SEL* 36.2 (Spring 1996): 397–416.
Nicholl, Charles. *A Cup of News: The Life of Thomas Nashe*. London: Routledge and Kegan Paul, 1984.
———. *The Reckoning: The Murder of Christopher Marlowe*. London: Jonathan Cape, 1992.
Nielson, James. *Unread Herrings: Thomas Nashe and the Prosaics of the Real*. New York: Peter Lang, 1993.
Nohrnberg, James. *The Analogy of* The Faerie Queene. Princeton: Princeton UP, 1976.
Norbrook, David. *Poetry and Politics in the English Renaissance*. Oxford: Oxford UP, 2002.
Nugent, Teresa Lanpher. "Usury and Counterfeiting in Wilson's *The Three Ladies of London* and *The Three Lords and Three Ladies of London*, and in Shakespeare's *Measure for Measure*." In *Money and the Age of Shakespeare: Essays in New Economic Criticism*. Ed. Linda Woodbridge. New York: Palgrave Macmillan, 2003: 201–217.
Orgel, Stephen. *Impersonations: The Performance of Gender in Shakespeare's England*. Cambridge: Cambridge UP, 1996.
———. "The Poetics of Incomprehensibility." *SQ* 42.4 (Winter 1991): 431–437.
———. "Tobacco and Boys: How Queer Was Marlowe?" *GLQ* 6.4 (2000): 555–576.
Orlin, Lena Cowen. *Private Matters and Public Culture in Post-Reformation England*. Ithaca, N.Y.: Cornell UP, 1994.
———, ed. *Material London ca. 1600*. Philadelphia: U of Pennsylvania P, 2000.

Palliser, D. M. *The Age of Elizabeth: England under the Later Tudors, 1547–1603. Social and Economic History of England,* vol. 5. London: Longman, 1983.

Passannante, Gerard. "The Art of Reading Earthquakes: On Harvey's Wit, Ramus's Method, and the Renaissance of Lucretius." *Renaissance Quarterly* 61.3 (Fall 2008): 792–832.

Paster, Gail Kern. *Humoring the Body: Emotions and the Shakespearean Stage.* Chicago: U of Chicago P, 2004.

Patterson, Annabel M. *Censorship and Interpretation: The Conditions of Writing and Reading in Early Modern England.* Madison: U of Wisconsin P., 1984.

Peacham, Henry. *Minerva Brittana.* London, 1612.

Perry, Curtis. "Commerce, Community, and Nostalgia in *The Comedy of Errors.*" In *Money and the Age of Shakespeare: Essays in New Economic Criticism.* Ed. Linda Woodbridge. New York: Palgrave Macmillan, 2003: 39–52.

———, ed. *Material Culture and Cultural Materialisms in the Middle Ages and Renaissance.* Turnhout, Belgium: Brepols, 2001.

Petrarch [Francesco Petrarca]. *Letters.* Trans. A. S. Bernardo. 3 vols. Baltimore: Johns Hopkins UP, 1985.

Pettigrew, Thomas Joseph, ed. *Chronicles of the Tombs: a Select Collection of Epitaphs.* London: H. G. Bohn, 1857.

Picciotto, Joanna. *Labors of Innocence in Early Modern England.* Cambridge, Mass.: Harvard UP, 2010.

Pietz, William. "The Problem of the Fetish, I." *Res* 9 (1985): 5–17.

———. "The Problem of the Fetish, II." *Res* 13 (1987): 23–45.

———. "The Problem of the Fetish, IIIa." *Res* 16 (1988): 105–123.

Pollan, Michael. *The Botany of Desire: A Plant's-Eye View of the World.* New York: Random House, 2001.

———. *The Omnivore's Dilemma: A Natural History of Four Meals.* New York: Penguin, 2006.

Ponet, John. *A Shorte Treatise of Politike Power, and of the true Obedience which subiectes owe to kynges and other ciuile Gouernours, with an Exhortacion to all true naturall Englishe men.* [Strasbourg?], 1556.

Poovey, Mary. *Genres of the Credit Economy: Mediating Value in Eighteenth- and Nineteenth-Century Britain.* Chicago: U of Chicago P, 2008.

———. *A History of the Modern Fact: Problems of Knowledge in the Sciences of Wealth and Society.* Chicago: U of Chicago P, 1998.

Prescott, Anne Lake. "Mammon." In *The Spenser Encyclopedia.* Ed. A. C. Hamilton. Toronto: U of Toronto P, 1990: 451–452.

———. "Tantalus, Pilate." In *The Spenser Encyclopedia.* Ed. A. C. Hamilton. Toronto: U of Toronto P, 1990: 676–677.

Pye, Christopher. "The Theater, the Market, and the Subject of History." *ELH* 61.3 (Fall 1994): 501–522.

Quilligan, Maureen. "On the Renaissance Epic: Spenser and Slavery." *South Atlantic Quarterly* 100:1 (Winter 2001): 15–39.

Ramachandran, Ayesha. "Edmund Spenser, Lucretian Neoplatonist: Cosmology in the Fowre Hymnes." *Spenser Studies* 24 (2009): 373–412.

Raman, Shankar. "Can't Buy Me Love: Money, Gender, and Colonialism in Donne's Erotic Verse." *Criticism* 43.2 (Spring 2002): 135–168.

Read, David. *Temperate Conquests: Spenser and the Spanish New World*. Detroit: Wayne State UP, 2000.

Richards, Jennifer. *Rhetoric and Courtliness in Early Modern Literature*. Cambridge: Cambridge UP, 2003.

Riggs, David. "The Killing of Christopher Marlowe." *Stanford Humanities Review* 8.1 (2000): 239–251.

Robinson, Marsha. "The Historiographic Methodology of *King John*." In *King John: New Perspectives*. Ed. Deborah T. Curren-Aquino. Newark: U of Delaware P, 1989: 29–40.

Ryan, Kiernan. "*Measure for Measure*: Marxism before Marx." In *Marxist Shakespeares*. Ed. Jean E. Howard and Scott Cutler Shershow. London: Routledge, 2001: 227–244.

Sacerdoti, Gilberto. *Nuovo cielo, nuova terra: La rivelazione copernicana di "Antonio e Cleopatra" di Shakespeare*. Bologna: Il Mulino, 1990.

Schmitt, Carl. *Political Theology: Four Chapters on the Concept of Sovereignty*. Tr. George Schwab. Cambridge, Mass.: MIT Press, 1988.

Schoenfeldt, Michael C. *Bodies and Selves in Early Modern England: Physiology and Inwardness in Spenser, Shakespeare, Herbert, and Milton*. Cambridge: Cambridge UP, 1999.

Schuler, Robert M. "Alchemy." In *The Spenser Encyclopedia*. Ed. A. C. Hamilton. Toronto: U of Toronto P, 1990: 12–14.

Schwenger, Peter. *The Tears of Things: Melancholy and Physical Objects*. Minneapolis: U of Minnesota P, 2006.

Sebek, Barbara. "'By Gift of My Chaste Body': Female Chastity and Exchange Value in *Measure for Measure* and *A Woman Killed with Kindness*." *Journal x: A Journal in Culture and Criticism* 5.1–2 (2000 Autumn–2001 Spring): 51–85.

Serres, Michel. *The Birth of Physics*. Tr. Jack Hawkes. Manchester: Clinamen, 2000.

Shagan, Ethan. *Popular Politics and the English Reformation*. Cambridge: Cambridge UP, 2003.

Shakespeare, William. *As You Like It*. Ed. Alan Brissenden. Oxford: Oxford UP, 1993.

———. *A New Variorum Edition*. Ed. H. H. Furness. Philadelphia: J. B. Lippincott, 1871–.

———. *The Riverside Shakespeare*. Gen. ed. G. Blakemore Evans. Boston: Houghton Mifflin, 1974.

Sharpe, Kevin. *Selling the Tudor Monarchy: Authority and Image in Sixteenth-Century England*. New Haven: Yale UP, 2009.

Shapin, Steven. *A Social History of Truth: Civility and Science in Seventeenth-Century England*. Chicago: U of Chicago P, 1994.

Shapiro, James. *A Year in the Life of William Shakespeare: 1599*. New York: HarperCollins, 2005.

Shell, Marc. *The Economy of Literature*. Baltimore: Johns Hopkins UP, 1978.

———. *The End of Kinship: 'Measure for Measure,' Incest, and the Ideal of Universal Siblinghood*. Baltimore: Johns Hopkins UP, 1988.

———. *Money, Language, and Thought*. Berkeley: U of California P, 1982.

———. "Portia's Portrait: Representation as Exchange." *Common Knowledge* 7.1 (Spring 1998): 94–144.

Sherman, Anita Gilman. "Disowning Knowledge of Jessica, or Shylock's Skepticism." *SEL* 44.2 (2004): 277–295.

Shershow, Scott Cutler. *The Work and the Gift*. Chicago: U of Chicago P, 2005.

Shrank, Cathy. *Writing the Nation in Reformation England 1530–1580*. Oxford: Oxford UP, 2004.

Shuger, Debora Kuller. *Political Theologies in Shakespeare's England: The Sacred and the State in* Measure for Measure. Basingstoke, U.K.: Palgrave, 2001.

Sidney, Philip. *The Major Works*. Ed. Katherine Duncan-Jones. Oxford: Oxford UP, 2002.

Siemon, James. "Dreams of Field: Early Modern (Dis)Positions." In *Historicism, Psychoanalysis, and Early Modern Culture*. Eds. Carla Mazzio and Douglas Trevor. New York: Routledge, 2000: 36–58.

Simmel, Georg. *The Philosophy of Money*. Trans. Tom Bottomore and David Frisby. London: Routledge and Kegan Paul, 1990.

Sinfield, Alan. "How to Read *The Merchant of Venice* without Being Heterosexist." In *Alternative Shakespeares 2*. Ed. Terence Hawkes. London and New York: Routledge, 1996. 122–139.

———. "*Poetaster*, the Author, and the Perils of Cultural Production." In *Material London ca. 1600*. Ed. Lena Cowen Orlin. Philadelphia: U of Pennsylvania P, 2000: 75–90.

Skinner, Quentin. *The Foundations of Modern Political Thought*. 2 vols. Cambridge: Cambridge UP, 1998.

Smith, Adam. *An Inquiry into the Nature and Causes of the Wealth of Nations*. Ed. Edwin Cannan. New York: Modern Library, 1937.

Smith, Nigel. "The Two Economies of 'Measure for Measure.'" *English: The Journal of the English Association* 36:156 (Autumn 1987): 197–232.

[Smith, Thomas, attr.] *A Discourse of the Commonweal of This Realm of England*. Ed. Mary Dewar. Charlottesville: UP of Virginia, 1969.

Snortum, Niel K. "The Title of Nash's *Pierce Penniless*," *MLN* 72.3 (March 1957): 170–173.

Spencer, Eric. "Taking Excess, Exceeding Account: Aristotle Meets *The Merchant of Venice*." In *Money and the Age of Shakespeare: Essays in New Economic Criticism*. Ed. Linda Woodbridge. New York: Palgrave Macmillan, 2003: 143–158.

Spenser, Edmund. *Edmund Spenser's Poetry*. 3rd ed. Ed. Hugh Maclean and Anne Lake Prescott. New York: Norton, 1993.

———. *The Faerie Queene*. Ed. Thomas P. Roche, Jr. New York: Penguin, 1978.

———. *The Faerie Queene*. Ed. A. C. Hamilton. New York: Longman, 2006.

Spiegel, Henry William. *The Growth of Economic Thought*. 3rd ed. Durham, N.C.: Duke UP, 1991.

Spufford, Peter. *Money and Its Use in Medieval Europe*. Cambridge: Cambridge UP, 1988.

Stallybrass, Peter. "The Value of Culture and the Disavowal of Things." In *The Culture of Capital*. Ed. Henry S. Turner. New York: Routledge, 2002: 275–292.

Starkey, Thomas. *A Dialogue between Reginald Pole and Thomas Lupset*. Ed. Kathleen M. Burton. London: Chatto & Windus, 1948.

Stone, Lawrence. *The Crisis of the Aristocracy, 1558–1641*. Oxford: Oxford UP, 1967.

Strohm, Paul. *England's Empty Throne: Usurpation and the Language of Legitimation, 1399–1422*. New Haven: Yale UP, 1998.

———. *Theory and the Premodern Text*. Minneapolis: U of Minnesota P, 2000.

Strong, Roy. *The Cult of Elizabeth: Elizabethan Portraiture and Pageantry*. Berkeley: U of California P, 1977.

Sullivan, Ceri. *The Rhetoric of Credit: Merchants in Early Modern Writing*. Madison, N.J.: Fairleigh Dickinson UP, 2002.

Summit, Jennifer. "Monuments and Ruins: Spenser and the Problem of the English Library." *ELH* 70.1 (2003): 1–34.

Targoff, Ramie. *John Donne: Body and Soul*. Chicago: U of Chicago P, 2008.

Tawney, R. H. *Religion and the Rise of Capitalism*. London: Penguin, 1938.

Tawney, R. H, and Eileen Power, eds. *Tudor Economic Documents: Being Select Documents Illustrating the Economic and Social History of Tudor England*. 3 vols. London: Longmans, Green and Co., 1924, 1953, and 1963.

Taylor, John. *A Shilling, or, The travailes of twelve-pence*. London, 1621.

Thirsk, Joan. *Economic Policy and Projects: The Development of a Consumer Society in Early Modern England*. Oxford: Clarendon, 1978.

Thomas, Keith. *Religion and the Decline of Magic*. London: Weidenfeld and Nicholson, 1971.

Tiffany, Daniel. *Toy Medium: Materialism and Modern Lyric*. Berkeley: U of California P, 2000.

Turner, Henry S. *The English Renaissance Stage: Geometry, Poetics, and the Practical Spatial Arts 1580–1630*. New York: Oxford UP, 2006.

———. "Nashe's Red Herring: Epistemologies of the Commodity in *Lenten Stuffe* (1599)." *ELH* 68.3 (2001): 529–561.

———. "The Problem of the More-Than-One: Friendship, Calculation, and Political Association in *The Merchant of Venice*." *SQ* 57.4 (January 2006): 413–442.

———, ed. *The Culture of Capital*. New York: Routledge, 2002.

Tusser, Thomas. *Five hundred pointes of good husbandrie*. [1580.] Ed. W. Payne and Sidney J. Herrtage. London: English Dialect Society, 1878.

Tyndale, William. *That fayth the mother of all good workes iustifieth us before we ca[n] bringe forth anye good work*. . . . 1528.

[Udall, Nicholas, attrib.] *Respublica: An Interlude for Christmas 1553, Attributed to Nicholas Udall*. Ed. W. W. Greg. London: Oxford UP, 1952.

Valenze, Deborah. *The Social Life of Money in the English Past*. Cambridge: Cambridge UP, 2006.

Vaughan, Virginia Mason. "Between Tetralogies: *King John* as Transition." *Shakespeare Quarterly* 35.4 (Winter 1984): 407–420.

Vaughan, Rice. *A Discourse of Coin and Coinage*. 1630–35?, printed 1675. In *A Select Collection of Scarce and Valuable Tracts on Money*. Ed. J. R. McCulloch. London: Political Economy Club, 1856: 1–120.

Waith, Eugene M. "King John and the Drama of History." *Shakespeare Quarterly* 29.2 (Spring 1978): 192–211.

Warley, Christopher. "Reforming the Reformers: Robert Crowley and Nicholas Udall." In *The Oxford Handbook of Tudor Literature, 1485–1603*. Eds. Mike Pincombe and Cathy Shrank. Oxford: Oxford UP, 2009: 273–290.

Watson, Robert. "The State of Life and the Power of Death: *Measure for Measure*." In *Shakespearean Power and Punishment*. Ed. Gillian Murray Kendall. Madison, N.J.: Fairleigh Dickinson UP, 1998: 130–156.

Wall, Wendy. *Staging Domesticity: Household Work and English Identity in Early Modern Drama*. Cambridge: Cambridge UP, 2002.

Walsham, Alexandra. *Providence in Early Modern England*. Oxford: Oxford UP, 1999.

Wesley, John. "The Well-Schooled Wrestler: Athletics and Rhetoric in *The Faerie Queene*, Book II." *Review of English Studies* 60 (March 2009): 34–60.

Whitelaw, Ian. *A Measure of All Things: The Story of Man and Measurement*. New York: St. Martin's, 2007.

Wood, Neal. *Foundations of Political Economy: Some Early Tudor Views on State and Society*. Berkeley: U of California P, 1994.

Woodbridge, Linda, ed. *Money and the Age of Shakespeare: Essays in New Economic Criticism*. New York: Palgrave Macmillan, 2003.

Woodhouse, A. S. P. "Nature and Grace in *The Faerie Queene*," *ELH* 16 (1949): 194–228.

Woodmansee, Martha, and Mark Osteen, eds. *The New Economic Criticism*. New York: Routledge, 1999.

Wrightson, Keith. *Earthly Necessities: Economic Lives in Early Modern Britain*. New Haven: Yale UP, 2000.

Yates, Julian. *Error Misuse Failure: Object Lessons from the English Renaissance*. Minneapolis: U of Minnesota P, 2003.

Yunck, John A. *The Lineage of Lady Meed: The Development of Mediaeval Venality Satire*. South Bend, Ind.: U of Notre Dame P, 1963.

Žižek, Slavoj. *The Sublime Object of Ideology*. New York: Verso, 1989.

Zurcher, Andrew. *Spenser's Legal Language: Law and Poetry in Early Modern England*. Cambridge: Brewer, 2007.

# INDEX

CPSIA information can be obtained
at www.ICGtesting.com
Printed in the USA
BVOW08s1946170217
476357BV00002B/3/P

9 780190 628222